A Very Dangerous Locality

A Very Dangerous Locality

The landscape of the Suffolk Sandlings in the Second World War

Robert Liddiard and David Sims

UNIVERSITY OF HERTFORDSHIRE PRESS

First published in Great Britain in 2018 by
University of Hertfordshire Press
College Lane
Hatfield
Hertfordshire
AL10 9AB

British Library Cataloguing in Publication Data
A catalogue record for this book is available from the British Library

ISBN 978-1-912260-08-9

Design by Arthouse Publishing Solutions Ltd
Printed in Great Britain by Charlesworth Press

Contents

Figures

Tables

Abbreviations

HE	Historic England
IWM	Imperial War Museum
NMR	National Monuments Record
SRO	Suffolk Record Office
TNA	The National Archives

Acknowledgements

This book has been a long time in the making and many people have had a hand in bringing it to completion. What is presented here represents the principal academic output of two major research projects of which the authors were a part: the 'Walberswick' project (2012), funded by the University of East Anglia, and the 'World War Two Heritage', funded by the European Union Inter-Region IV (Two Seas) programme (2012–15). Robert Liddiard was the academic lead for UEA on both these projects and David Sims was employed as a researcher. The work undertaken on these projects (and much thereafter) involved considerable archival research and so we would like to thank the staff at the National Archives, Kew, the Imperial War Museum, Bovington Tank Museum, Orford Museum and the Suffolk Record Offices at Ipswich and Lowestoft, as well as the numerous individuals who made their private archives available for use. The fieldwork component of this study has been equally involved and we would also like to thank the agencies and private individuals who have allowed access to the monuments in their care or use of their existing data, especially Mel Kemp, Aaron Howe and David Thurlow from the RSPB, Angus Wainwright and Grant Lohoar from the National Trust, Adam Burrows from Natural England, James Rolfe from Suffolk Archaeological Service, as well as the staff at Historic England, Swindon and at Suffolk Wildlife Trust. We would also like to thank Wayne Cocroft, Sarah Poppy and Roger Thomas at Historic England for advice and comments on various aspects of the work presented here. This book could not have been completed without the support of the School of History at the University of East Anglia. We would like to thank John Charmley, Cathie Carmichael and Katy Cubitt in particular, but also colleagues who have helped along the way, especially Stephen Church, Jon Gregory, Ben Jones, Camilla Schofield and Tom Williamson.

Chapter 1

A regional landscape at war

This book is the result of many years of work on the landscape history of the Second World War along a narrow strip of coastline on the east of England stretching from Lowestoft to Landguard Point near Felixstowe. This area is known as the Suffolk Sandlings and it saw extensive use by the British army during the conflict, principally in the construction of anti-invasion defences and the establishment of large training grounds. This short period in the area's history has left a considerable legacy, one in many ways out of all proportion to the time actually spent at war. The physical remains of the conflict are numerous and the events that saw their construction are now part of not just the region's history and collective memory but increasingly its heritage and folklore. But the landscape of the Sandlings is, of course, far from unique in being heavily militarised during the mid-twentieth century and this, together with the fact that the Second World War is the most written-about conflict in human history, as well as the most globalised, means that the reader might with some justification ask why a book such as this is needed, especially one that focuses on this rather remote part of the coastline.

Our response is that this is a particular *kind* of study, one that approaches its subject matter from the viewpoint of the landscape historian. Landscape history can bring a slightly different view to these much-discussed events but what exactly a 'landscape approach' involves deserves a little explanation at the start. At its most basic, landscape history, or landscape archaeology as it is often known, is the study of the interplay between human affairs and the natural environment. Its chief focus is the analysis of upstanding structures and monuments and their spatial patterning on the ground – both as it exists now and in the past – and the relationship of these structures to physical geography and topography. Patterns of monuments can represent powerful categories of evidence in their own right that can variously confirm, amplify or shed completely new light on historical processes and narratives. Secondly, as a discipline landscape history is also heavily concerned with 'antecedent structures', a short-hand for saying that in any given period human activity in the present is shaped by what has been inherited from the past. This most obviously includes patterns of settlement, land use and social organisation, but also extends to more experiential aspects such as perceptions of landscape, which are often formed and maintained over centuries and usually themselves intimately connected to distinctive environments. In turn, this concern with the natural environment and land use over long periods of time also serves to make landscape history deeply sympathetic to notions of regionalism and regional identity. Landscape studies tend to stress the almost autonomous long-term development of regional societies, which also tend to be influenced by topography, environment and land use. In such an approach national and international events are not unimportant, but their significance is usually discussed in terms of how they were mediated, directly and indirectly, by the regional context. Finally, as a subject landscape history is also slightly unusual in that its methodology is inherently inter-disciplinary and characterised by an eclectic use of source material that includes the documentary material familiar to mainstream historians, but also archaeological evidence of all kinds, cartographic material, geographical datasets and, in this case, oral history. Since the development of the subject in the 1950s the vast majority of works that have taken this 'landscape approach' to their material have been concerned with pre-modern societies and as a result our understanding of subjects as diverse as Iron Age hillforts, medieval settlements and field systems and ancient woodland have been transformed. But a new generation of scholars are increasingly attempting to apply its methods to monuments and landscapes of the more recent past, but studies taking an explicit 'landscape approach' to the conflicts of the twentieth century are, as yet, conspicuous by their absence and it is here that this book hopes to make a contribution.

In accordance with the principles explained above, the study presented here is chiefly concerned with how topography, geography and land use affected the actions of military men in one regional landscape during the Second World War. At first glance this might seem slightly odd or perhaps unnecessary; a statement to the effect that military planning is often linked to landscape is so obvious that it barely needs spelling out. Soldiers at all levels of command are taught to 'read the ground' in order to gain tactical benefit and place their opponents at a disadvantage, and the importance of terrain in 'shaping the battlefield' is one of the longest standing principles in the history of warfare.[1] But, in academic writing the role of environment and topography in military works is often assumed, sometimes rather glibly, rather than actually analysed, as if it is so immediately intelligible that it does not require attention. In fact, the relationship between terrain and military landscapes is often far more subtle and complex than it initially might appear and repays close attention in its own right.[2] At the national level, field marshals and generals may have had requirements for defence works or for training, but these schemes were actually worked out on the ground by those lower down the chain of command. It was less senior and middle-ranking officers that had to transform plans into reality and here choices were informed by military doctrine, the availability of manpower and equipment and various practical issues, such as the ranges of particular weapons. But while it might seem a banal point

---

1   Sun Tzu, *The Art of War*, Chapter 10, in T.R. Phillips (ed.) *Roots of Strategy* (Harrisburg, 1985).

2   P. Doyle and M.R. Bennett (eds), *Fields of Battle. Terrain in Military History* (London, 2002).

to make, the schemes that resulted from military decisions did not take place in an undifferentiated environment and this, in our view, deserves greater attention. Because whatever defence scheme or training exercise was ordered, human agency was framed by, or was mediated through, the physical landscape. At its most straightforward, topography and geography provided opportunities and imposed constraints, and so often structured what could be undertaken and where. But in addition, the physical landscape of the wartime Sandlings was not a blank canvas upon which the military could undertake whatever they wished wherever they liked; rather, its management over centuries had resulted in particular patterns of land use that were, like topography, an active force in structuring military activity on the ground. Even at a time of national emergency, the military landscape was shaped by the inherited patterns of settlement, land use and farming and also by the requirements of the civilian population. As will be seen, at times the needs of the military overrode these other interests; in other cases they were structured by them; while in yet others they were, perhaps surprisingly, subordinated. The Second World War was also not the first time that the Sandlings had experienced militarisation and this longer view is crucial to understanding the perception of the wartime landscape by those who, to use the modern academic phrase, 'inhabited' it.

Crucially for this study, the exploration of many of these issues is best achieved not by the use of documents alone but alongside the study of the physical remains of the conflict. Here landscape history is well placed because, as has been mentioned above, the subject is, by its very nature, inter-disciplinary. But there is a common perception, even among some academics, that the Second World War is so well documented that its archaeology cannot add anything to our understanding. This is in fact a fallacy and the case for the value of 'conflict' archaeology of the twentieth century and the archaeological study of the more recent past generally has been well made by a number of scholars.[3] In this specific case, the structuring role of topography in the siting of built structures is precisely the kind of issue that does not easily find its way into the historical record, but is well illustrated by archaeological evidence. Given that so much of the study that follows uses material evidence, albeit chiefly from the point of view of what the distribution of wartime remains can tell us, and because it is by no means the first to consider the archaeological evidence for the Second World War, it is worth spending a little time exploring how the study of this aspect of the conflict has developed historiographically.

Conflict landscapes

While the Second World War has a huge documented history, the archaeological approach to the study of the conflict in Britain is a relatively new field of research and

---

3   J. Schofield, *Combat Archaeology* (London, 2005); R. Harrison and J. Schofield, *After Modernity: Archaeological Approaches to the Contemporary Past* (Oxford, 2010).

put onto its modern footing in the 1990s as part of an upsurge of interest in the material legacy of twentieth-century conflict on the part of academics and national heritage bodies.[4] Up until this point wartime structures were chiefly of interest to independent researchers, the most significant of whom was Henry Wills, who pioneered the study of pillboxes and established a tradition of independent study that has flourished ever since.[5] The 50th anniversary of the conflict was the catalyst for renewed interest and occasioned a number of landmark projects undertaken under the auspices of what was then English Heritage and the Council for British Archaeology and which have served to define the subject as it exists today.[6] One of the most important was the Defence of Britain Project (1995–2002), a nationwide survey which aimed to establish the extent and nature of twentieth-century military remains in the United Kingdom. Owing to the sheer numbers of sites that proved still to be in existence, the focus of the project shifted towards Britain's Second World War anti-invasion defences and over seven years thousands of structures were recorded (chiefly by volunteers) and the results made available to researchers via the Archaeological Data Service. As work drew to a close, a further survey by William Foot, the 'Defence Areas Project' (2002–04), identified over 60 places where anti-invasion defences survived to such an extent that they were representative of wider arrangements. The chief outcome of this research was a substantial report, much of which was published in 2006 as *Beaches, Fields, Streets, and Hills: The Anti-Invasion Landscapes of England, 1940*, which, while making use of documentary sources, chiefly took an archaeological approach to the material to reveal both the extent of surviving structures at a local level and also their often very regional character. Foot's work represents the most detailed assessment of the physical legacy of anti-invasion landscapes to date and is very much the starting point for the archaeological component of the present study; our debt to this work and to the Defence of Britain project in what follows here will be obvious.

Concurrent with this work on archaeological remains, what was then English Heritage also sponsored as part of the Monuments Protection Programme a major investigation of the documentary records of twentieth-century conflict held at The National Archives, Kew, with an emphasis on those records relating to the Second World War.[7] This work was undertaken by Colin Dobinson and had the primary aim of quantifying the number and nature of military sites recorded in documents, the likelihood of their archaeological survival and the general historical background and

---

4   J. Carmen, *Archaeologies of Conflict* (London, 2013), pp. 5–9.

5   H. Wills, *Pillboxes: A Study of UK Defences* (Trowbridge, 1985).

6   W. Foot, *Beaches, Fields, Streets, and Hills: The Anti-Invasion Landscapes of England, 1940* (York, 2006), pp. 5–6.

7   C. Dobinson, J. Lake and J. Schofield, 'Monuments of War: Defining England's Twentieth-Century Defence Heritage', *Antiquity*, 71 (1997), pp. 288–99; C.S. Dobinson, 'Twentieth-Century Fortifications in England: the MPP Approach', in J. Scofield (ed.), *Monuments of War. The Evaluation, Recording and Management of Twentieth-Century Military Sites* (English Heritage, 1998), pp. 2–5.

circumstances that had led to their construction. One of the most significant points to emerge from this work was an awareness of the sheer quantity of documentary material available for study, which gave the lie to the assumption made by Wills that the building of structures such as pillboxes was a purely archaeological phenomenon. As a result, detailed overview studies of major aspects of Britain's wartime remains and the strategies that underpinned their construction and use were produced in a level of detail hitherto unknown. While some of this research has been published in a series of dedicated volumes, a quantity of material exists in the form of unpublished reports and, again, our debt to this pioneering work will be obvious in what follows.[8]

In addition to the research undertaken by Dobinson, Foot and others within national heritage bodies, a considerable body of work has been conducted by independent scholars, many of whom are connected either directly or indirectly with the Defence of Britain project or involved with specialist organisations such as the Fortress Study Group. The most prolific has been Mike Osborne, whose steady stream of publications represents an important toolkit for the classification of structures. The publication in 2004 of his *Defending Britain* marked an important milestone in the development of the secondary literature, as, for the first time, a 'scholarly but accessible' book on twentieth-century fortifications appeared that not only catered for a wider audience but also did so from a strong empirical background.[9] The appearance of such works is a sign that the subject has attained academic maturity rapidly, something which is a testament to a successful marriage between volunteers, professionals and national heritage organisations. The result is that a number of significant studies of Britain's wartime archaeology are now in print.[10] This coming of age is perhaps best seen in the publication of a research agenda for twentieth-century military remains published in 2004 by the Council for British Archaeology, which represents a growing consensus about how the subject might move forward and, at a wider intellectual level, in 2005 by the inaugural edition of the *Journal of*

---

8   The unpublished CBA reports by Dobinson consulted here are: *Twentieth-Century Fortifications in England, Vol. 2 Anti-Invasion Defences of World War II* (York, 1996); *Twentieth-Century Fortifications in England, Vol. 4 Operation Diver* (York, 1996); *Twentieth-Century Fortifications in England, Vol. 5 Operation Overlord* (York, 1996); *Twentieth-Century Fortifications in England, Vols 6.1–2 Coast Artillery: England's Fixed Defences Against the Warship* (York, 2000); *Twentieth-Century Fortifications in England. Supplementary Study. Experimental and Training Sites: An Annotated Handlist* (York, 2000) and published volumes *Fields of Deceptions: Bombing Decoys of World War Two* (London, 2000); *AA Command: Britain's Anti-Aircraft Defences of the Second World War* (London, 2001); *Building Radar: Forging Britain's Early-Warning Chain, 1935–1945* (2010).

9   M. Osborne, *Defending Britain: Twentieth-Century Military Structures in the Landscape* (Stroud, 2004).

10   B. Lowry (ed.), *20th Century Defences in Britain: An Introductory Guide* (York, 1996); C. Alexander, *Ironside's Line* (Storrington, 1998); B. Lowry, *British Home Defences 1940–45* (Oxford, 2003); M. Wilks, *The Defence of Worcestershire and the Southern Approaches to Birmingham in World War II* (Logaston, 2007); B. Lowry, *Pillboxes and Tank Traps* (Oxford, 2014); see also the county *Twentieth-Century Defences in Britain* series of volumes, of which the most relevant here is M. Osborne and A. Graham-Kerr, *Twentieth-Century Defences in Britain: Suffolk* (Market Deeping, 2008).

Conflict Archaeology, which is dedicated solely to study of the materiality of conflict.[11] Following this lead, it is in a number of specific areas that this book hopes to make a wider contribution to the subject.

Rationale

While the importance of the Second World War as an archaeological horizon is now no longer in doubt, gaps in our understanding still remain. Analyses of its physical legacy are at times somewhat diffuse: excellent national overview studies of monument types exist, as do a mass of local studies, but there is comparatively little 'middle ground': methodologically and theoretically informed discussions dealing with empirical data but which also address the intellectual concerns of a wider constituency of researchers.

In part, this is because until recently much of the ground-breaking research that has framed our understanding has focused on the extreme ends of the chain of command. In the case of anti-invasion defences, given the mass of documentary material available for study, Dobinson's pioneering work chiefly concerned itself with the higher-level activities of Commands, Corps and Divisions in order to provide an overall explanatory framework. By contrast, Foot's national survey of archaeological remains adopted a local case-study approach in order to give a sense of how defences physically differed on the ground. A conclusion common to both, however, was the need for *regional* studies in order to show how national schemes of defences actually manifested themselves and to give wider historical context to local archaeological sites.[12] That structures such as pillboxes often reflect very local circumstances is now well known, but the broader issue of a lack of detailed interpretation has recently been highlighted by Barclay in his study of anti-invasion defences in Scotland: relatively little work has been done to contextualise local defence works, historical accounts are often general in their commentaries and there is an underlying assumption that defences were a 'mass' of structures that were a response to a singular threat. Similar remarks could be applied to elsewhere in the United Kingdom: as Osborne has commented 'too often, local Second World War histories seem to consist of vague and non-specific anecdotes strung together by often inappropriate references to the salient events and the mythology of the war'.[13] Osborne's and Barclay's work, by contrast, stresses the importance of the chronological development of anti-invasion works as well as their strong provincial identity.[14] Similar comments could be made about

---

11   J. Schofield, *Modern Military Matters. Studying and Managing the Twentieth-Century Defence Heritage in Britain: A Discussion Document* (York, 2004); T. Pollard and I. Banks, 'Why a Journal of Conflict Archaeology and Why Now?', *Journal of Conflict Archaeology*, 1 (2005), pp. iii–vi.

12   Dobinson, *Anti-Invasion*, p. 11. Much of the work presented here would be classed as Dobinson's 'tactical' and 'micro' levels, which in 1996 were noted as a 'pressing need'. Foot, *Beaches*, pp. 625–32.

13   M. Osborne, 'Review of J. Wells, *The Anti-Invasion Defences at Bognor Regis in World War Two*' *Casemate* 109 (2017), pp. 44-5.

14   G. Barclay, *If Hitler Comes. Preparing For Invasion: Scotland 1940* (Edinburgh, 2013).

the state of research in others areas of military activity, such as training; the larger picture is relatively clear and numerous structures on the ground are known to exist, but there is a need for an overview at a regional level. In addition, the way in which the study of wartime archaeology has developed tends to compartmentalise aspects of military activity and their associated monuments: anti-invasion defences are usually treated separately from training infrastructure and also from air defences and so on. While there are, again, entirely cogent reasons for this, such an approach inevitably inhibits the study of interrelationships between monuments and means that the overall chronological development of wartime landscapes is sometimes opaque.

Introducing the Sandlings

The decision here to undertake a 'biography' of the Sandlings, rather than concentrate on one form of monument or one period of the conflict, was therefore taken not just because the regional case study is a well-trodden investigative route for landscape historians, but also because it addresses a number of current research agendas. It is also ideal here as it focuses attention on the 'middle ground' between the well-documented policies of the high command and otherwise uncontextualised local remains. It also permits the discussion of a range of wartime monuments and their inter-relationships, while at the same time setting these against a longer time frame and wider geographic and environmental context.

The Suffolk Sandlings has been chosen for close attention, rather than elsewhere, for a number of reasons. The region was one of two areas of the United Kingdom where the coastline was felt to be particularly vulnerable to invasion (the other being that of Kent and Sussex) and this was reflected in a sustained building programme of defence works. Investigation of the Sandlings' anti-invasion defences is facilitated by the fact that from 1940 until 1942 the area from Lowestoft to Landguard Point was designated as a *Sector*: a specific stretch of coastline that was occupied by a single infantry division (approximately 15,000 men). This study does not concentrate solely on one formation or on one period of construction, but on the series of divisions that rotated through the Sector from 1939 until coastal defence officially ceased in 1942, which enables analysis of the anti-invasion landscape over time. To date, no study of a Sector exists, yet it occupies the place in the chain of command where the higher-level national schemes were made to work in a regional context.[15] The anti-invasion landscape of the Sandlings is discussed in two chapters: Chapter 2 deals with the Phoney War and the invasion crisis of 1940, while Chapter 3 discusses how the framework inherited from that period was altered and adapted in the two years that followed.

While the anti-invasion defences were never put to the test, it would be erroneous to think that the Sandlings spent the war entirely at peace. Its position facing the North

---

15   On a broader strategic level, this 'middle ground' is discussed in P. Kennedy, *Engineers of Victory: The Problem Solvers Who Turned the Tide of the Second World War* (London, 2013).

Sea and close proximity to the occupied Low Countries meant that it had an important role in the defence of Britain's airspace. The Suffolk coastline was part of the national chain of RAF radar stations and that at Bawdsey Manor was the first such station to become operational. While the absence of large population centres meant that the region never experienced the heavy bombing raids on cities elsewhere, it was a regular target for air attacks and its two chief ports, Lowestoft and Felixstowe, were designated 'Gun Defended Areas' and given defences by Anti-Aircraft Command. In 1944 a brief but intense period of military activity was associated with Operation 'Diver', the defence against the flying bomb, which led to a rapid refortification of the coastline in response to a new aerial threat. The defence of airspace is discussed in Chapter 4.

In addition to anti-invasion defences, three nationally important army training areas – Dunwich, Southwold and Orford – lay in the coastal hinterland. As is discussed in Chapter 5, training had been an important military activity in the Sandlings since the start of the conflict; its intensification from the middle of the war in preparation for the D-Day landings is discussed separately in Chapter 6. Here the region played a unique role in that it was the setting for one of the first exercises to inform the planning of Operation Overlord – Exercise Kruschen – in 1943, while the Battle Training Area at Orford was one of the main training grounds for 79th Armoured Division, Britain's specialist armoured formation that was specifically tasked with breaching the Atlantic Wall defences of occupied Europe.

Chapters 2–6 relate the nature of the Sandlings' physical defences and training infrastructure, but of course military archaeology is not just the passive by-product of strategy and tactics. For the majority of servicemen, the war was not one in which they were party to the bigger picture, and their lives were governed by mundane routines that took place within prescribed bounds. The 'experience' of war from the point of view of the men in the ranks, the material conditions of service and how wartime works were perceived are discussed in Chapter 7. But at the same time, the Sandlings was never exclusively a military landscape and the fortification of the region took place alongside an attendant civilian population. Military works were disruptive and occasioned numerous changes to the lives of non-combatants. The civilian perception of the wartime landscape is discussed in Chapter 8, which examines how, at a local level, relationships were negotiated.

An additional reason for singling out the Sandlings for attention is that a distinctive pattern of post-war land use saw extensive areas given over to conservation bodies, with the result that the survival and condition of wartime monuments in the area is in places exceptionally good. The study of the archaeological remains not only informs much of the discussion throughout this book but is the focus of Chapter 9, which discusses the removal or survival of military structures and their rise to the status of archaeology, as well as how these monuments are increasingly becoming embedded in local folklore. Overall, this book is perhaps best thought of as comprising three parts. The first deals with the range of defensive works in the region and is largely an exercise in historical geography, or what is often termed 'historical archaeology'. The second takes a broadly similar approach, but is concerned with army training. The third part concerns perception and lived experience from the point of view of soldier and civilian. But what unites these themes is the constant backdrop of the physical environment.

Sources

But before the subject matter is addressed in detail, some discussion of the evidence upon which this particular study is based needs to be outlined. In very general terms, post-war land use across much of the Sandlings has tended to preserve military structures of all kinds. This includes the familiar concrete structures such as pillboxes, gun emplacements and coastal battery positions, but also many earthworks: trench systems built both as defensive positions and for training; gun sites; and anti-tank and anti-landing ditches. The survival of these remains, which are often more ephemeral, is important not least because they often give archaeological context to concrete structures that normally appear as isolated monuments. In the course of the fieldwork undertaken for this study hundreds of above-ground monuments have been recorded, many for the first time, chiefly by GPS, but in the case of more important or larger sites by theodolite. Field survey data can be compared against documentary lists of defence works in order to test the latter's accuracy (simply because something appears in a document, that does not always mean that it existed on the ground) and give a clearer sense of military works as actually built. The evidence of physical structures is also valuable in that it often sheds light on aspects of military use of the landscape that did not enter the historical record, either because they did not warrant recording or because they were conducted under conditions of secrecy and thus are poorly documented. The field survey work undertaken for this study has been augmented by the use of data from aerial photographs recorded as part of the wider English Heritage National Mapping Programme (NMP), which logged wartime sites, among others, in detail and subsequently entered the results on the Suffolk Historic Environment Record.[16] Literally hundreds of archaeological sites have been identified and while this work has proceeded concurrently with the field and archival work undertaken by the present authors, considerable use has been made of the data, especially for mapping defence works. But as the NMP survey took place within defined areas – in places,

16   C. Hegarty and S. Newsome, *The Archaeology of the Suffolk Coast and Inter-Tidal Zone. A Report for the National Mapping Programme* (2912) (Suffolk County Council, English Heritage, 2005); E. Ford, S. Horlock and S. Tremlett, *National Mapping Programme Project for Lothingland, Greater Lowestoft and North Suffolk Coasts and Heaths*, National Heritage Protection Project Commissions Programme Project No. 6642 (Norfolk Museums Service, English Heritage, 2015); for a discussion of the results see C. Hegarty and S. Newsome, *Suffolk's Defended Shore, Coastal Fortifications from the Air* (Swindon, 2007); S. Newsome, 'The Coastal Landscape of Suffolk During the Second World War', *Landscapes*, 4 (2003), pp. 42–59.

only a narrow strip along the coast rather than inland – this evidence does not exist for the whole Sandlings and so has been supplemented by photographic material held by Historic England. But in using this material to write a historical narrative, rather than describing what remains or classifying what exists on the ground, this book hopefully takes the subject further.

As the historical records of the Second World War exist in such abundance and detail an exclusively archaeological study would represent something of an own goal and so here the documentary record is used extensively to shed light on various aspects of the materiality of the conflict. The chief documentary source is the unit war diary, which comprised a daily record of events compiled by the headquarters of military formations and units down to battalion or equivalent level. This study has made use of the war diaries of all principal military units in the Sandlings from 1939 to 1945 from battalion level upwards, together with associated War Office material contained in Registered Files: over 500 separate files in total.[17]

The compilation of war diaries was a requirement of the War Office and one of the great strengths of this evidence lies in the fact that they are contemporary accounts of events and so free from hindsight. Given that wartime events often moved very fast and were subject to revision and reinterpretation even during the conflict itself, this is significant. While a war diary was a secret document with an official reporting form and a set of prescriptive instructions as to what should be included, the contents are far from uniform.[18] At their least informative, daily entries amount to one or two lines or simply record mundane administrative arrangements such as the posting of officers in and out of the unit concerned. In other cases diaries are much fuller documents and in cases where the author took to their task with enthusiasm it became a vehicle for expressing their own thoughts and for passing comment on wider issues. In addition to a daily record of events, war diaries also contain – albeit again far from consistently – copies of other documents, such as defence plans, locations of units, operational orders and training instructions. In a small number of cases there are also maps of dispositions, fire plans and arcs of fire of individual weapons, and maps drawn up for training exercises. For landscape historians who are used to dealing with incomplete datasets or mapping distributions of monuments for which the original population is unknown, such material is something of a bonanza, as it provides huge quantities of spatial data, much of which is given exact military grid references and so can be mapped with ease. The use of such sources for the purposes of *landscape* history,

---

17   For discussion, see Dobinson, *Anti-Invasion*, pp. 4–8; the exception are the diaries of the Czech Brigade in Sub-Sectors 1 and 2 in 1942–3 and which are not deposited in The National Archives.

18   For official guidance on war dairies, War Office, *Field Service Regulations, volume 1: Organisation & Administration* (1930, reprinted 1939), Section 174. Close study of the documents themselves shows that, in some cases, entries were made day to day, while in others entries were written up on a weekly or monthly basis from a quantity of notes or reports that are now lost. In a small number of cases, diaries were being written up months after the events they describe.

rather than just social or military history, has barely started and this book hopes to show both the detail that exists in war diaries and also their potential for use as part of wider surveys.

But, for all their undoubted value, the information in war diaries must be used with caution. As an official record they are not necessarily an unprejudiced view of events, as they reflect the *moeurs* of the organisation that created them – hierarchical, authoritarian, male – and the attitudes of the officer class to which the individual diarist belonged. The views of the private soldier are therefore largely irrelevant and so can be glimpsed only obliquely.[19] In addition, while the authors of war diaries were anonymous, the officer responsible was usually the battalion adjutant or intelligence officer, meaning that the view of the diary is that of the headquarters company, which might not be quite the same as that of the rifle company, battery or squadron in which the majority of the fighting men of a unit served. Moreover, war diaries represent only the official version of events from a unit in the field, a copy of which was sent to the War Office and eventually came to be deposited at the National Archives. The mass of day-to-day paperwork, which could potentially yield up much greater information, does not appear to have survived for any of the units researched here; searches in relevant military museum archives suggest that these records have long since been destroyed and anecdotal evidence attests to military papers at former headquarters sites being burnt as waste in the decades after the war.[20]

A number of other sources have also informed this study. Considerable quantities of photographic and film footage of the British Home Army exists at the Imperial War Museum and provides valuable visual evidence of defence works and training exercises; in a large number of cases, it has been possible to identify otherwise unnamed locations on the ground. More miscellaneous evidence in the form of newspapers, literary compositions, works of art and relevant documents in Suffolk's County Record Offices and in the archive of the Mass Observation Survey has also been employed to get a sense of the civilian perception of the wartime landscape. In places use has been made of oral history, from both civilians and former servicemen, the records of which are chiefly deposited at the Imperial War Museum and in the Suffolk Record Offices. A small number of interviews were also conducted by the authors. Where it exists, oral history is unparalleled at giving a vivid picture of events as viewed from the perspective of participants. But, as with any other source, oral history is far from problem-free. Recollections can fade over time or be influenced and clouded by post-war reinterpretations; and, by its very nature, this type of history is highly personalised

---

19   For an illuminating account of how an incident of a private soldier heckling Montgomery in Sicily in 1943 was subsequently recorded in the unit war diary with a positive edge see F. Mowat, *And No Birds Sang* (Vancouver, 2012), 80.

20   During the research for this study numerous accounts have been related of stores of military papers at former headquarters sites destroyed in the decades after the conflict.

and often anecdotal.[21] The activities of the army during the period from Dunkirk to D-Day have not tended to attract as much attention as campaigns aboard and so there is a tendency, starting in official unit histories published after 1945 and often repeated in oral history interviews for decades afterwards, for time at home to be glossed over in favour of recounting the later events of battle.[22]

All these classes of evidence represent large and powerful datasets in their own right. But it is their use in *combination* here to investigate one regional landscape for the whole war that hopefully makes this book distinctive. Parts of this book could be characterised variously as history, military history, archaeology, historical geography or cultural studies. Nevertheless, this study is a slave to none of these genres and instead the discussion that follows attempts to bring a holistic approach to the subject matter. The point to emphasise is that landscape history is a different form of historical enquiry and here it is the grouping of archaeological evidence and oral history alongside the historical record that is used to nuance our understanding of events. The resulting narrative is very much 'bottom up', rather than 'top down' and one in which the chronology of events is regional, albeit one influenced by national and international affairs. The conflict in the Sandlings was not that of Kent, Devon or the Midlands and so what follows is not a book dominated by the defence of heavy industrial sites, factories, internal Stop Lines or airfields; rather, it is chiefly concerned with coastlines, air defences and training, because these defined the wartime experience here. This is not in any way to claim that this book blazes a completely new trail, because it does not; rather, it is to say that in taking a 'landscape approach' it is possible to write a different kind of historical narrative about this conflict with the vast quantities of information that it has left to us.

The Suffolk coast: soils, geology and the topographic context

At the intellectual core of this book is the idea that the Second World War military structures of the Sandlings, both as they existed in the past and as archaeology today, cannot be fully understood without a clear sense of the region's landscape and its historic development, sometimes at a very detailed level. For this reason, some time needs to be spent explaining the character of the study area in terms of both its natural environment, soils and geology and also its pattern of historical development (Figure 1.1).

The Suffolk Sandlings is the name given to the strip of sandy land between the North Sea and the large clay plateau that occupies the centre of the county. The exact boundaries lack precise definition, but 'Sandlings' is used here in its widest geographical sense to describe the coastline from Lowestoft to Landguard Point. This is a distinctive and, in many ways, unique landscape: one of muted, shallow valleys

---

21   P. Thompson, *Voice of the Past: Oral History*, 3rd edition (Oxford, 2000).

22   Anon., *The Story of 79th Armoured Division* (Hamburg, 1945); H.G. Martin, *The History of the Fifteenth Scottish Division 1939–1945* (Edinburgh and London, 1948).

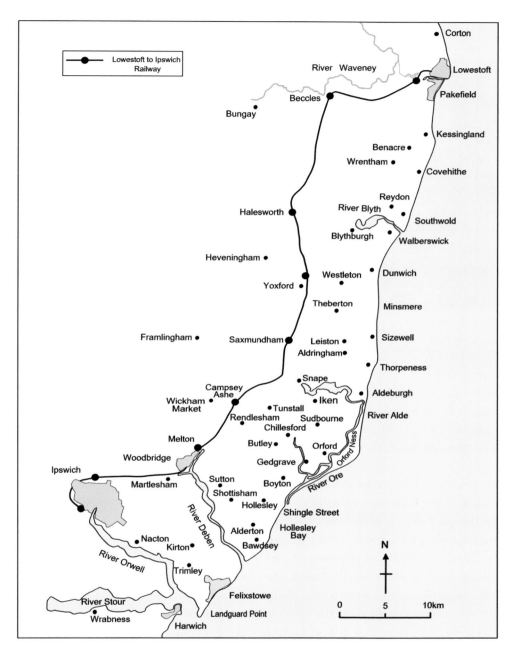

Figure 1.1. Map of the Sandlings, showing principal areas mentioned in the text. The boundary of the study area is marked by the line of the Lowestoft–Ipswich railway.

Figure 1.2. The landscape of the Sandlings, looking north over Sizewell power station (built post-war). Minsmere Nature Reserve is in the centre, with Dunwich Heath to the north. It is the configuration of coast, wetland and heath that gives the Sandlings its character. (Mike Page)

and estuaries, with a coastline of low sandy cliffs and long beaches and a hinterland characterised by large expanses of wetland and heath (Figure 1.2). The solid geology of this region is principally crag, a complex series of sequential layers of gravels, clays and sands laid down in the late Pliocene and early Pleistocene periods. These soft rocks are prone to erosion, which helps give rise to a characteristic coastline of gentle curves and long beaches. The geology of the Sandlings is not uniform, however. Around Dunwich a specific formation of gravels and sands known geologically as the Westleton Beds was deposited on the edge of the sea after the formation of the crag, while at the southern tip of the area covered in this book the geology is dominated by London Clay.[23] Of greater relevance to the long-term landscape history and character of the region are the substantial layers of glacial sand and gravel (on average ten metres thick) that overlie the solid geology and which were left by watercourses running out of the ice sheet that originally covered the upland centre of the county. It is the dominance of these well-drained, acidic soils that gives the region its historic name, first documented in the early seventeenth century: the 'Sandlands'.[24] The width of this sandy belt varies, however, being narrow in the north around Lowestoft, typically between three and five kilometres wide in the area between Kessingland

23   J. Wymer, 'Surface Geology', in D. Dymond and E. Martin (eds), *An Historical Atlas of Suffolk* (Ipswich, 1999), pp. 18–19.

24   T. Williamson, *Sandlands* (Macclesfield, 2005), 1.

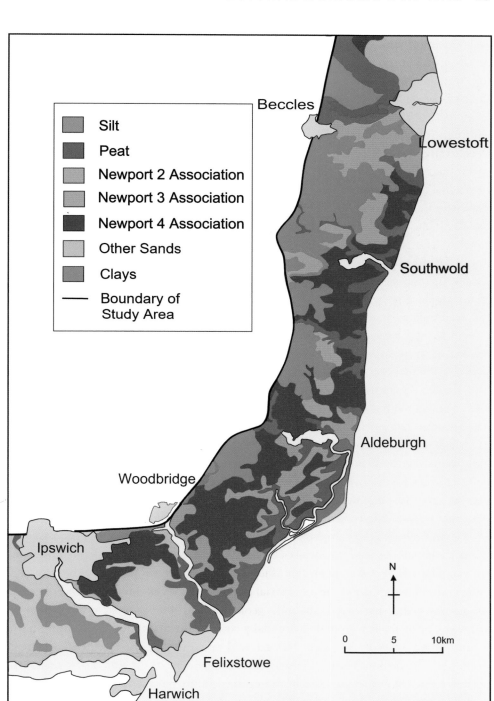

Figure 1.3. Soil map of the Sandlings. (After the Soil Survey of England and Wales)

and Aldeburgh and reaching its maximum width of over ten kilometres in the area between Aldeburgh and Woodbridge. The most infertile of these sands are those of the strongly acidic Newport 4 Association, which often lie in deep deposits and exist in large concentrations to the north of Southwold and Dunwich and to the east of Woodbridge. Elsewhere, chiefly in areas of slightly lower relief, soil types tend to fall within the Newport 2 and 3 Associations, which, while still acidic, are more amenable to cultivation (Figure 1.3).[25]

Topographically, the most significant landscape features of the region are the rivers that flow eastwards towards the sea and their attendant shallow valleys: the Waveney, the Hundred River, the Blyth, the Minsmere, the Alde (which becomes the Ore), the Butley, the Deben and the Orwell, together with additional minor streams. The geography of their outfalls is, however, subtly different between the northern and southern Sandlings. North of the Alde, most low ground (often below sea level) comprises the estuaries of rivers and smaller watercourses whose entrances to the sea have been blocked by longshore drift. As their water seeps slowly through the accumulated material, pools of fresh water tend to form inland, as at Oulton, Covehithe and Benacre Broads and Thorpeness Mere. Here, and also in the lower reaches of rivers such as the Minsmere and the Dunwich Rivers that make their way slowly to the sea, peaty deposits tend to form in their waterlogged and poorly draining hinterlands. By contrast, south of the Alde river valleys (such as those of the Alde, Deben and Butley) are characterised by clay and silty alluvial deposits formed in the lee of much larger spits.

Much of the essential character of the Sandlings landscape derives from the long-term farming practices of both the alluvial soils and peat making up the low-lying areas of the valleys and the acid, sandy soils found on the intervening higher ground (Figures 1.4 and 1.5).[26] In the river valleys significant areas were historically managed as wetland. Those areas formed of peaty deposits were chiefly fen, which, while sometimes possible to graze, were chiefly used for the production of reeds and rough fodder crops and sometimes dug for fuel. In salt marshes characterised by alluvial deposits, however, from the Middle Ages a piecemeal process of reclamation took place in which areas were cut off from the sea by embankments and drained; fresh water was taken off by sluices that closed at high tide to prevent the ingress of salt water. Such areas, with their rich soils, were good grazing grounds. This long-term history of reclamation was also characterised by episodic periods of abandonment during economic downturns. The agricultural recession of the 1930s was one such period, especially for fenland areas, and resulted in the partial inundation of wetland environments around Walberswick and along the Butley and the Alde. Nevertheless,

---

25   C. Hodge, R. Burton, W. Corbett, R. Evans and R.S. Searle, *Soils and Their Use in Eastern England* (Harpenden, 1984), pp. 277–8.

26   For what follows see the more detailed treatment in Williamson, *Sandlands*, pp. 2–9.

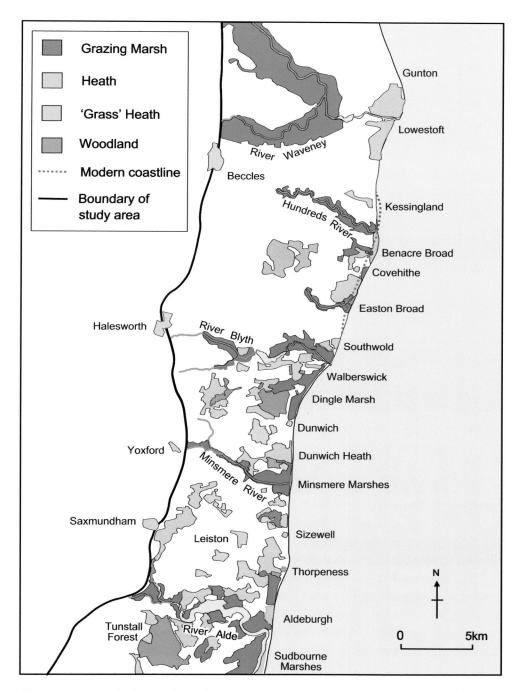

Figure 1.4. Inter-war land use in the northern Sandlings. Here the topography structured a landscape of wetland along valley bottoms, with heath and forestry on the intervening interfluves. (After Land Utilisation Survey)

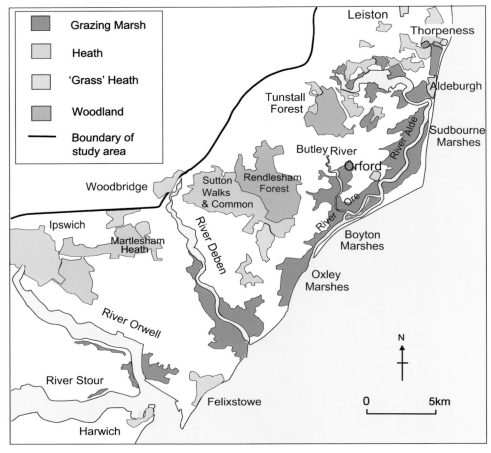

Figure 1.5. Inter-war land use in the southern Sandlings. Here the sandy belt of the region is at its widest, reflected in the large expanses of heath and forestry plantations. The extensive wetlands are a legacy of tidal salt marshes gradually reclaimed from the sea. (After Land Utilisation Survey)

the extent of permanent pasture on the coast and in riverine esturies on the eve of the war was in places extensive, particularly around Orford (Figure 1.6).[27]

On the relatively high, flat interfluves, by contrast, and especially those on the poorest, most acidic sands, much of the landscape was characterised by heath, of which in 1941 there was some 6000 hectares (15,000 acres) (Figure 1.7).[28] Large areas of common or 'sheepwalks' as they were known were a prominent feature of the medieval and early modern landscape and, while progressive enclosure from the eighteenth century gradually reduced their extent, the Land Utilisation Survey showed in 1935 that extensive heaths existed right across the Sandlings, but especially to the

---

27   R.W. Butcher, *The Land of Britain. The Report of the Land Utilisation Survey of Britain. Parts 72–73 Suffolk (East and West)* (London, 1941), p. 328; Williamson, *Sandlands*, p. 48.

28   Butcher, *Suffolk*, Appendix II.

Figure 1.6. Wetland at Minsmere, now part of the RSPB nature reserve. The ruined medieval chapel visible on the left was converted into a pillbox in 1940.

Figure 1.7. Typical Sandlings heath at Dunwich. During the war, such environments were ideal military training grounds.

east of a line between Woodbridge and Iken, to the north of Aldeburgh and between Westleton and Southwold. In the inter-war period these areas had undergone changes as a result of planting by the Forestry Commission from the 1920s onwards. Just before the outbreak of war a little under 2000 hectares (5000 acres) had been planted, chiefly around Rendlesham and Tunstall and to a lesser extent at Dunwich.[29]

But this is not to give the impression that the landscape of the Sandlings was made up of either wetland or heath. In places, arable cultivation was widespread, especially in those areas characterised by the less acidic Newport 2 soils. It was only on the most intractable soils or wetlands that the planting of crops tended to be resisted. South of Lowestoft and where the sandy strip was at its narrowest and interspersed with clay, the landscape comprised small, anciently enclosed fields bounded by well-established hedgerows and here, on the eve of the war, there was considerable arable.[30]

In addition to soils, topography and land use, the distinctive character of the Sandlings comes from the presence of the coastline that defines its eastern boundary. This is characterised by low cliffs separated by long runs of open beach chiefly made up of shingle, but in a few cases sand. Geologically, the majority of the region's cliffs, which are rarely over 20 metres high, are comprised of soft sand and are found chiefly at Kessingland, immediately north of Southwold, Dunwich, Sizewell and Bawdsey. Over generations erosion has served to even out the landform, leaving a familiar East Anglian pattern of long beaches and an absence of prominent headlands or rocky outcrops.

The natural geography has also tended to structure the pattern of settlement. The more significant villages and towns, such as Southwold and Aldeburgh, tend to lie on the coast, in close proximity to the river mouths and along valley sides. Away from here, on the intervening interfluves, settlement was constrained by availability of water.[31] As a result, the region's chief road (the modern A12) is a little way inland and runs north–south, with more minor roads running west to east to connect up with seaside resorts. The same is true of the pre-war rail network, which comprised a north–south line running from Lowestoft to Ipswich, with separate branch lines running east to Southwold, Aldeburgh and Felixstowe. Historically, the population density of the region has been relatively low; outside of the ports of Lowestoft and Felixstowe there are few towns of any note and those that do exist, such as Leiston and Saxmundham, are relatively small.

It is important at this early stage to draw out some of these sub-regional contrasts, as they were subsequently important to the pattern of military land use, especially in the siting of defence works. In broad terms, prior to the outbreak of war, the area to the north of the Blyth was characterised more by arable and the landscape was made up of smaller fields with irregular pockets of woodland, while to the south the landscape

---

29   *Ibid.*, 332; Williamson, *Sandlands*, pp. 111–12.

30   Butcher, *Suffolk*, pp. 320–26.

31   T. Williamson, *Sutton Hoo and its Landscape. The Context of Monuments* (Macclesfield, 2008), pp. 68–70.

retained larger areas of heath, marshland and forestry plantations. But together it was, and still is, the combination of coastline, heath and wetland that gave the Sandlings its unique character.

A defended coastline

As an economic resource, the North Sea made for a prosperous fishing industry from the Middle Ages onwards and towns such as Lowestoft and Southwold thrived on the back of the prodigious quantities of herring that came from it. The existence of estuaries and relatively sheltered anchorages at numerous points along the coastline, and the long beaches where it was possible for small craft to make landfall relatively easily, made for extensive maritime links across the North Sea rim, but particularly with the Low Countries, Scandinavia and, to a lesser extent, the Baltic. The Sandlings' place in a wider 'North Sea World' brought considerable prosperity to the coastline, most readily seen today in the architecture of its parish churches, such as at Blythburgh, Southwold and Walberswick, whose fine perpendicular towers attest to the viability of trading connections throughout the Middle Ages. For complex reasons, this medieval prosperity declined in later centuries and the coast was instead valued by artists drawn to the seascapes and by holidaymakers attracted to its beaches. From the late nineteenth century places such as Lowestoft, Southwold, Aldeburgh and Felixstowe began to develop as holiday destinations. During the inter-war period the greater use of motor cars promoted the development of dedicated holiday camps with chalet accommodation, such as that at Pakefield, to the south of Lowestoft, and also more exclusive resorts, such as that developed by the Ogilvie family at Thorpeness. But other parts escaped some of the commercialisation that took place at this time, in part because of difficulty of access; in 1935 it was remarked that the county 'contains some of the quietest rural country to be found anywhere and a coast which, owing to its unusual formation cannot be opened up from North to South by a single road'.[32]

While the sea provided opportunities for economic and cultural exchange it also represented a highway for invaders and this, too, left its mark on the region's landscape. For most of the post-medieval period the direction of threat was from the Low Countries and fortification building was chiefly intended to defend against the Dutch Republic and, to a lesser extent, France; the most northerly of Britain's chain of Martello Towers was at Aldeburgh. Fortifications tended to be built in, or close to, ports in order to cover those locations where an invasion fleet could disembark troops in safety, as at Lowestoft Roads, Sole Bay, Hollesley Bay and, most significantly, Harwich Haven – the only deep water anchorage between the Thames and the Humber. Here Landguard Point, on the Suffolk side, received its first fort in the 1530s and this building was successively rebuilt in subsequent centuries and became East Anglia's only

---

32 *East Suffolk Regional Planning Scheme* (1935), quoted in S. Wade-Martins and T. Williamson, *The Countryside of East Anglia: Changing Landscapes, 1870–1950* (Woodbridge, 2008), p. 113.

fortification of true national importance.[33] The strategic importance of the Sandlings increased with the emergent threat from Germany in the late nineteenth century and, in the lead-up to the First World War, consideration was given to the possibility of an invasion of Great Britain by Germany via the North Sea.[34] In keeping with the British policy of concentrating fixed defences at major ports, Landguard underwent a major programme of works, with state-of-the-art batteries constructed outside the Victorian fort.[35] The vulnerability of the east coast was highlighted during the First World War when Lowestoft and Great Yarmouth were shelled by ships from the German High Seas Fleet and this conflict also marked a turning point, in that it was in this period that the East Anglian beaches, rather than just ports and anchorages, were provisioned with field defences and manned by regular soldiers as part of an organised scheme for home defence. It was also at this time that Britain came under attack from the air: Zeppelin airships often made landfall over the East Anglian coast and the region experienced its first ever air raids. Although the archaeological remains of coastal and air defences from this period are slight, the scene was set for what was to happen some 20 years later.[36]

Despite the fact that the Fall of France during the Second World War opened up the long-standing invasion routes to England from the French coast, the idea that a major landing might take place on the east coast consistently exercised the mind of British planners throughout 1940 and beyond.[37] This idea was not altogether wide of the mark, as initial German contingency plans for an invasion of Britain imagined just such a scenario. In November 1940 German naval commanders envisaged an invasion force sailing from the Baltic and North Sea ports and landing between the Thames and the Tyne, while the army staff preferred the embarkation of troops from ports in the Low Countries and landings in East Anglia. An airborne attack would take place on Lowestoft and Yarmouth, followed by infantry divisional landings on these and adjacent beaches, with elements of another division landing around Dunwich and Hollesley Bay. These elements would link up before reinforcements would arrive and drive on London.[38] That Operation Sealion subsequently envisaged an amphibious operation against the south-east coast of Kent and Sussex is immaterial here because, as Dobinson has stressed, the *perceived* nature of the threat, rather than the threat that

33   P. Kent, *Fortifications of East Anglia* (Lavenham, 1988), chapter 9.

34   A. Saunders, *Fortress Britain* (Liphook, 1989), p. 192.

35   M. Brown, N. Barrett and P. Patterson, *Landguard Fort Report No. 3: Right Battery, Felixstowe, Suffolk* (English Heritage, Archaeological Investigation Report Series AI/34/2004); P. Patterson, A. Williams and L. Barker, *Landguard Fort Report No. 4: Darrell's Battery, Felixstowe, Suffolk* (English Heritage, Archaeological Investigation Report Series AI/8/2005).

36   C. Appleby, W. Cocroft and J. Schofield (eds), *The Home Front in Britain, 1914–1918. An Archaeological Handbook* (York, 2015), pp. 45–9, 131–5.

37   P. Fleming, *Invasion 1940* (London, 1957), pp. 167–71.

38   Alexander, *Ironside's Line*, 11.

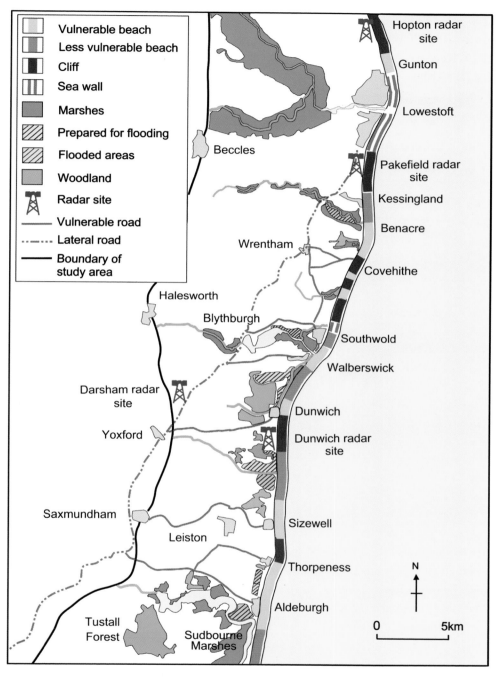

Figure 1.8. Tactical appreciation of the northern Sandlings as mapped from wartime reports. Those areas seen as most vulnerable were those with good landing beaches and roads inland. Intervening low-lying areas were less vulnerable, as they tended to comprise wetland or could be flooded. Such considerations were important in structuring the wartime anti-invasion defences.

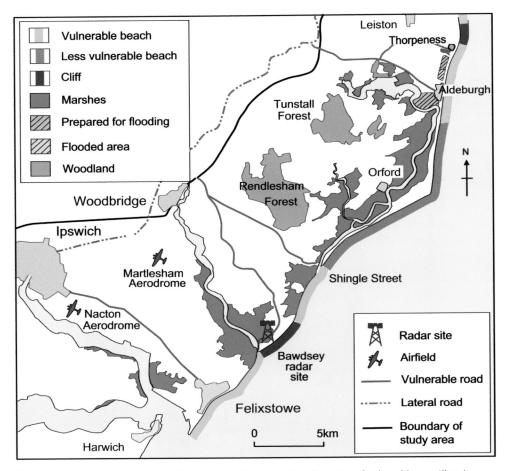

Figure 1.9. Military appreciation of the southern Sandlings, showing areas of vulnerable coastline. In contrast with the northern Sandlings, the south of the region contained a greater number of military installations that required defence.

actually existed, was crucial. British planners consistently over-estimated German capabilities and so, up to the middle of the war, the Sandlings was seen as a coastline that could be subject to a major attack as a diversion for a main effort against the south coast or as one part of a 'pincer' movement intended to capture London.[39] Even after it was clear that the Wehrmacht was mired in Russia, the idea that some desperate gamble might be made against the east coast persisted. It was not until 1942, when British commanders estimated that at least one month's notice could be guaranteed before an invasion attempt, that the perception of the east coast's vulnerability diminished. Alongside the threat of invasion was the possibility of a raid directed

---

39   TNA WO 277/37 (Defence Plans for the United Kingdom, 1939–45), Cabinet Historical Section (1948), 31, 41, 60, 64–5, sketch 13.

against a port, radar site or other target, for either military or propaganda purposes. Here, British expertise in such operations undoubtedly contributed to a sense that they might themselves be subject to a similar enterprise.

The landscape approach: geography, topography and military planning

These broad environmental, geographical and military contexts are crucial to understanding military use of the Sandlings during the Second World War. In a significant way, the region's topography formed the basis of how it was used by the military, something best grasped through an analysis of the tactical appreciations drawn up at various stages during the conflict (Figures 1.8 and 1.9).[40] A constant theme was the distinction between the low-lying river valleys and the intervening higher ground. One typical military appreciation of the area between the Blyth and the Alde undertaken in 1942 drew attention to:

> Certain well-defined spurs [Aldeburgh, Thorpness (sic), Sizewell, Dunwich and Walberswick] along which run the main approaches inland and are divided from one another by marshy areas [and cliffs] where the streams run into the sea. This formation will necessitate the capture of the spurs by an invader before ingress inland on a large scale can be made. It therefore lends itself to defence by strong locations on the spurs, the intervening marshes being made as impassable as possible.[41]

As will be seen, such observations had a direct effect on the distribution of wartime works (Figure 1.10). The series of rivers cutting across the Sandlings were important structuring agents for other reasons: they broke a long coastline up into discrete blocks and also provided flank protection, and so tended to mark unit or formation boundaries. The course of rivers prevented an enemy force that had landed at multiple points along the coast from linking up as they moved inland, and as natural anti-tank obstacles they channelled invaders into particular places. Areas of low-lying marsh and fen were natural obstacles in themselves and could be improved by cutting channels or by inundation. Furthermore, in those places where wetlands were in close proximity to the actual shoreline there was less of a need to place troops on the ground; here, rather, static obstacles could deter a landing and troops themselves could be placed at more vulnerable locations elsewhere. The presence of cliffs, similarly, meant that manning levels need not be as high as elsewhere. By contrast, those beaches that were suitable for a landing were usually also seaside resorts and so had roads leading inland. Here the defending troops were very close to the sea or often right on the beach itself.

From north to south, the beaches most vulnerable were those with long runs of sand and shingle upon which vehicles could land: Gunton Denes at Lowestoft,

---

40   TNA WO 199/85 (HQ Home Forces), Beach Defence Reconnaissance, 3.6.40.
41   TNA WO 166/329 (War Diary, XI Corps), Defence Scheme, Landing Places.

Figure 1.10. The view from Dunwich, one of the 'spurs' that underpinned the defence of the area during the Second World War. The view is to the south and shows another spur – Sizewell – separated from Dunwich by the Minsmere levels. In 1940 the fear was that a German armoured column would use such higher ground to move inland after a beach landing before driving on London via the modern A12.

Benacre and Kessingland, Covehithe and Eastern Broad, Southwold and Walberswick, Dunwich, Sizewell, Aldeburgh, Shingle Street and Felixstowe. Not all were felt to be equally vulnerable, however, and those places where larger ships could anchor ashore or where there were roads leading immediately from the beach itself, as at Sizewell and Aldeburgh, were singled out as priorities for defence. Those beaches deemed less vulnerable were those that fronted immediately onto cliffs or those places where extensive areas of wetland existed in close proximity to the shoreline, as at Corton, Pakefield, between Walberswick and Dunwich, Minsmere and Bawdsey. While it would be perfectly possible to effect a landing at such places, little would be gained by so doing. At Orford Ness the presence of the river Ore immediately inland ruled it out as a landing place, as any invading force would immediately find itself marooned, while, in other cases, man-made obstacles existed, such as the extensive sea walls at Lowestoft and Pakefield.

Immediately back from the coastline, the hinterland presented a similarly mixed picture. The places where roads from the beaches met the A12 were significant junctions and usually marked by large villages and towns that formed potential bottlenecks and so could be defended, such as Wrentham, Blythburgh, Saxmundham and Leiston. But while the series of east–west roads were the lines of enemy approach, they were also the routes by which reserves could be brought up to meet any invader. And here, too, topography and land use complicated the picture. The existence of bodies of water such as Oulton, Benacre and Easton Broads and Thorpeness Mere and areas of extensive wetland in places such as Minsmere and from Orford to Felixstowe acted both as physical obstacles to movement and also deterrents to parachute troops. Forestry plantations, especially those around Dunwich and Tunstall, served a similar role. By contrast, especially in the central and southern Sandlings, the larger expanses of heath represented more of a danger, as these were ideal environments for the landing of troops by glider or parachute and the muted terrain of the region more generally meant it was a good operating environment for armoured vehicles. Those places of chief concern were those where good beaches, access inland and favourable hinterland existed in combination. This described much of the area from Lowestoft to Felixstowe, but especially the area from Aldeburgh to Dunwich, which in the summer of 1940 the national beach reconnaissance of the UK coastline noted as 'a very dangerous locality'.[42]

The Sandlings also contained a small number of military assets that marked themselves out as targets and so required defence. The most obvious were the port facilities at Lowestoft and Felixstowe. After the outbreak of war Lowestoft rapidly developed into the base for the ships that escorted the inshore convoy system, and some five Royal Navy shore establishments came to be based in the town.[43] Harwich haven remained an important anchorage throughout the war and in the hinterlands of both ports heavy anti-aircraft artillery defences came to be concentrated. A number of radar stations also lay within the Sandlings. Bawdsey Manor, the first operational radar station in the country, lay in the south at the mouth of the river Deben, while Dunwich and Hopton stations lay on the coastline further north and Darsham a little inland, with later sites established at Thorpeness and a second site at Dunwich. Coastal sites were placed on cliffs in order to facilitate use of their embryonic equipment and their defence remained an important aspect of military use throughout the war. In addition, a number of airfields lay within or on the bounds of the Sandlings. Pre-war airfields existed at Nacton (Ipswich) and Martlesham, and an airstrip also existed as part of a government experimental facility at Orford. The latter was rapidly immobilised in 1940, but the presence of the other two had an important effect on the deployment of troops on the ground, as it was thought probable that their early capture would be a part of any major German operation directed against this part of the coast. Finally, during the war itself airfields were constructed at Butley (Bentwaters) (1942), Leiston (1942) and Woodbridge (1943). The detailed history of these airfields is outside the scope of this study, but they are discussed in terms of how their presence affected the deployment of the regular army.

---

42   TNA WO 199/85 (HQ, Home Forces), Beach Defence Reconnaissance, 3.6.40.

43   F. Jenkins, *Port War: Lowestoft at War* (Lowestoft, 1984); J.P. Foynes, *The Battle of the East Coast, 1939–1945* (privately published, 1994).

Military organisation

As this book is chiefly concerned with the landscape it does not attempt to catalogue in encyclopaedic detail which unit held which part of the coastline at any given time in the war. Nor does it list in minute detail the litany of changes to unit boundaries that were a regular feature of military occupation of the coastal zone, or the technical specifications of weaponry. But, even with this book's broad remit, for reasons of space there is much about the wartime landscape that cannot be discussed here. This book is not concerned with the Auxiliary Units, whose activities were completely separate to those of the regular army and civil defence is discussed only when relevant to the broader defence schemes and in relation to civilian attitudes to the conflict. But a small number of technical issues do require some discussion at an early stage. For the purposes of organisation, the army divided the United Kingdom into four (later five) Commands, of which the Sandlings formed part of Eastern Command. The next level down the chain of command was Corps and then Division. The Suffolk coastline was held for most of the war by an infantry division of c.15,000 men, the core strength of which were its three brigades, each made up of three infantry battalions. Each battalion was in theory c.800 men strong and divided into four rifle companies, each of about 120 men, and a larger headquarters company. Companies were sub-divided into platoons, which in rifle companies were made up of three sections of ten men and a platoon headquarters. In addition to the infantry, the division was made up of two other fighting arms: the artillery, which comprised a number of regiments sub-divided into batteries and in turn troops of four guns each; and engineers, normally three field companies, which were larger than their infantry counterparts, one of which was attached to each infantry brigade. To these fighting units were added a series of ancillary support units that, while critical to the division's effectiveness, are not of chief concern here.[44]

The formations that rotated through the Sandlings on coastal defence duty were, in turn, 54th Division (October 1939–April 1940), 55th Division (April–November 1940), 42nd Division (November 1940–February 1941), 15th Division (February–November 1941) and then 54th Division again (November 1941–43). The exact length of coastline held by each formation was subject to minor changes throughout the war but for the majority of the conflict the Divisional *Sector* stretched from Lowestoft to Felixstowe. This was sub-divided into *Sub-Sectors* that were normally held by the division's constituent brigades.[45] For much of the war the coastline was divided into four Sub-Sectors. Each Sub-Sector comprised a number of *Areas*

---

44 For longer discussions, G. Forty, *Handbook of the British Army* (Stroud, 1998); Barclay, *If Hitler Comes*, pp. 23–8; D. French, *Raising Churchill's Army* (Oxford, 2000), pp. 190–91.

45 Sub-Sectors also existed for inland defence and for the placing of reserves, but are not considered here. From late 1940 the divisional strength in the Sector was increased with an additional independent infantry brigade.

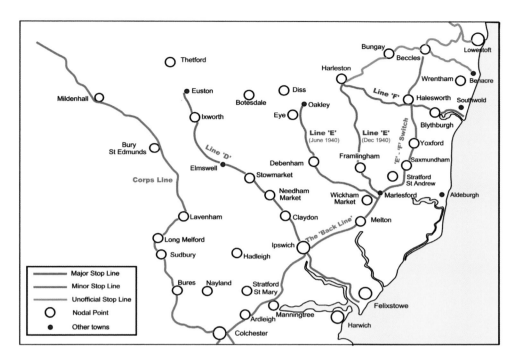

Figure 1.11. The wartime Sandlings in a regional context. While not directly discussed in this book, the landscape of the Sandlings needs to be set against Suffolk's Stop Lines and Nodal Points that formed the backbone of interior defence in 1940–42.

(normally three) for each brigade's infantry battalions, which were themselves sub-divided and descended through the military hierarchy via *Sub-Area*, *Locality* and *Post* for Company, Platoon and Section respectively. The coastal defences were integrated with interior defences that largely fall outside of this study but, in brief, comprised a series of anti-tank Stop Lines that crossed the region and a series of Nodal Points scattered across the countryside (Figure 1.11). These elements of the anti-invasion landscape were established in 1940 and subsequently reorganised the following year, with most Stop Lines abandoned and interior defence based mainly upon the series of Nodal Points. When 54th Division was effectively disbanded in the summer of 1943 coastal defence ceased and the Sandlings became the principal training area for 49th (Infantry) Division and 79th Armoured Division. At this point the Sector and Sub-Sector system effectively became redundant and military activity focused exclusively on the large training areas of Orford, Dunwich and Southwold and their immediate hinterlands.[46] Air defence lay with Anti-Aircraft Command, whose formations tended to extend over much wider territories, with the Sandlings covered

---

46   For detailed breakdowns of orders of battle for these formations, see H.F. Joslen, *Orders of Battle of the Second World War* (London, 1960).

initially by 6th AA Division and from 1942 by 5th AA Group, with their constituent regiments manning anti-aircraft guns and searchlights that were also subdivided into batteries and troops.

This discussion has attempted to set the scene for an account of one military landscape during the Second World War. As we hope to show, by bringing together a range of sources under the umbrella of a 'landscape approach' we can shed valuable light on the processes by which it was created, used and abandoned.

Chapter 2

Crisis on the coastline, 1939–40

This and the next chapter examine the origin and development of the anti-invasion defences in the Sandlings. On one level what follows is a chronological narrative, but this is necessary in order to explain the complexity of how the coastline was fortified at this time and why. But it is also a narrative that is, quite deliberately, closely allied to the study of topography. In taking this approach, it hopes to dismiss the idea that the building of coastal defences during the conflict was straightforward or that its material remains are always easily interpreted. While there is nothing in what follows that takes issue with Dobinson's statement that nationally coastal defences were 'established in 1940, extended in 1941, adapted in 1942, maintained in 1943 and – in part – dismantled from mid 1944', the following discussion relates how this broad chronology played out at a regional level.[1] It also shows, through an analysis of both the archaeological and the historical sources – under the umbrella of a 'landscape approach' – why some parts of the Sandlings were defended for nearly four years and others only for a matter of months.

The Phoney War

On the outbreak of war in September 1939 the defence of Suffolk was the responsibility of the 4th, 5th and 6th (Territorial) battalions of the Suffolk Regiment, whose chief task was guarding vulnerable points such as radar stations, docks, aerodromes and bridges. The coastline was mainly the concern of the 4th battalion with elements of the 5th, but their ability to repel any external threat was negligible; a single company of the 4th Battalion at Leiston defended the beaches between Southwold and Aldeburgh with some three civilian buses providing transport.[2] While the likelihood of an invasion was deemed remote, particularly during the autumn and winter, when weather conditions precluded beach landings, the eventuality was considered and contingency measures explored. The first systematic national anti-invasion scheme was laid down in November 1939 by Commander in Chief Home Forces General Kirke in the 'J.C. Plan' – the name derived from the codewords 'Julius' and 'Caesar', which signified invasion

---

1   Dobinson, *Anti-Invasion*, p. 3.

2   TNA WO 166/4707 (War Diary, 4th Suffolk Regiment), 5.9.39; TNA WO 166/4709 (War Diary, 6th Suffolk Regiment); W.N. Nicholson, *The Suffolk Regiment, 1928–1946* (reprinted from the *East Anglian Magazine*, 1960), pp. 191–3; G. Dewing, *Aldeburgh, 1939–45* (Aldeburgh, 1995).

contemplated and invasion imminent respectively.[3] A significant German incursion, it was believed, would be an attempt to land a division of troops via a port that had already been captured by troops landed by air. On the east coast the most likely targets were thought to be the Humber estuary and Harwich, although Lowestoft was considered a secondary possibility.[4] The J.C. Plan led to a series of changes in the order of battle in East Anglia and troop levels in Suffolk were increased. Coastal batteries at Harwich and Landguard were upgraded and two obsolete 12-pounder field guns were established in sandbagged emplacements at Lowestoft.[5] The battalions of the Suffolk regiment were assigned to the newly created 18th Division and moved north, with another division, the 54th, taking over responsibility for coastal defence from Foulness Point in Essex to Pakefield, just south of Lowestoft.[6] Two of its three infantry brigades were assigned for coastal defence between Pakefield and Aldeburgh (Sub-Sector A) and from Aldeburgh to Harwich (Sub-Sector B), with the third in Essex. The two brigades in Suffolk arranged their constituent battalions in a 'two up-one back' formation: two battalions forward on the coast itself and one in reserve, with an additional battery of anti-tank guns and a cavalry regiment providing a mobile reserve from the division. The primary task of the infantry was the containment of any airborne attack until those kept back could be brought into the area to defeat the invaders.[7]

Despite this build-up in manpower, there was an acceptance that, in the unlikely event that it occurred, any major German operation against the Suffolk coast could at best only be slowed down. Operating Instructions admitted as much, those for 163 Brigade between Pakefield to Aldeburgh stating that

> It is obvious, that, with the means available at our disposal, the Brigade cannot prevent a landing *in force* … we can and must … inflict as heavy casualties as possible on the enemy and disorganise him during the actual landing. Our second and more important task is to prevent him exploiting an initial landing success by blocking all main approaches until such time as T[roo]ps from the mobile Division can arrive in the area and effectively deal with the enemy.[8]

Such a strategy was the only viable option given the low numbers of troops concerned: the 2nd/4th Essex Regiment, for example, with a strength of approximately 450–500 men, was responsible for defending the 22 kilometres between Walberswick and

---

3   TNA WO 277/37 (Defence Plans for the United Kingdom, 1939–45), Cabinet Historical Section (1948), pp. 25–6.

4   TNA WO 166/1 (War Diary, GHQ Home Forces), Proceedings of GHQ Conference, 30.10.39.

5   R. Jarvis, *Fortress Lowestoft* (Lowestoft, 2002), p. 30; Patterson *et al.*, *Landguard Fort Report No. 4*, pp. 9–10.

6   TNA WO 166/673 (War Diary, 54th Division, GS), October 1939–April 1940, *passim.*

7   TNA WO 166/1036 (War Diary, 163rd Infantry Brigade), Movement Order No. 1, 31.10.39.

8   *Ibid.*, Operation Instruction No. 1, 18.11.39.

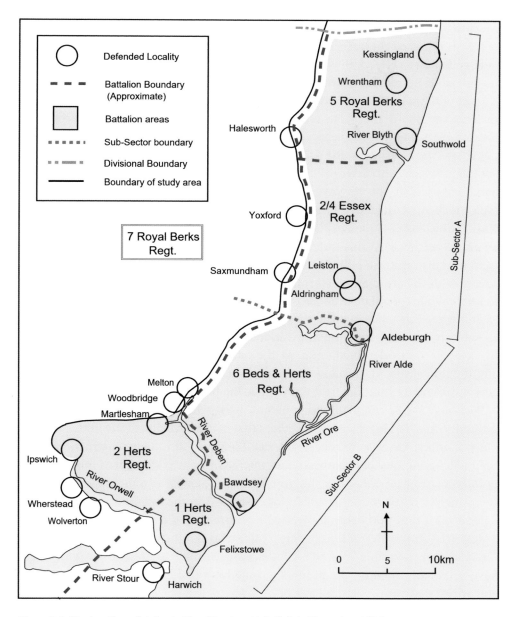

Figure 2.1. The location of defended localities in mid-Suffolk in November 1939.

Aldeburgh and ten kilometres back from the beaches.[9] On the ground, a thin screen of troops occupied the coastline itself, with orders to withdraw if they were attacked in large numbers. Inland, those areas thought attractive for airborne landings and the roads leading in from the beaches were to be defended by troops in prepared positions. As part of the scheme roads were to be kept open so that the divisional reserve could rush to any points that were under threat or where German troops, particularly paratroops, had been able to concentrate (Figure 2.1).[10]

It was as a result of the J.C. Plan that the initial infantry defences in the Sandlings were constructed, with the digging of defensive posts first recorded in a battalion war diary on 16 November 1939.[11] The defences put in place at this time took the form of 'defended localities', which comprised small numbers of trenches and sandbagged positions in places that were felt particularly important to resisting an enemy advance. At this early stage of the war wherever possible these localities were to utilise existing pillboxes from the First World War and were to be sited to accord with the principle of 'all round defence': that is, the position as a whole was to be able to fire in all directions. These infantry posts, together with key sites such as Dunwich radar station, were also provided with what little field artillery existed as support.[12] Inland from these positions defensive lines that could be manned by reserves were identified, such as the Saxmundham–Halesworth railway line and the line of the A12 around Campsea Ashe, along with other significant places where the enemy could be held up, such as the bridge crossing of the river Deben at Melton.[13] While the plan was coherent, what was actually put in place on the ground comprised insubstantial defences that could have done little in the event of a major attack. One junior officer described how at this time his instructions were to hold a beach until outnumbered and then withdraw to a prepared inland strong point consisting of 'a hole in the ground with a couple of sandbags'.[14] Although the principle of 'all round defence' was enshrined in the operational orders, most defended localities probably comprised no more than a few rifle pits excavated in a single day and with wide arcs of fire.[15] It is also significant, perhaps, that during the field survey for this volume no archaeological trace of these infantry defences have been confirmed on the ground – something that suggests insubstantial and ephemeral structures.

---

9   TNA WO 166/4271 (War Diary, 2nd/4th Essex Regiment); T.A. Martin, *The Essex Regiment, 1929–50* (London, 1952), p. 349.

10 TNA WO 166/673 (War Diary, 54th Division, GS), 54 Division Home Defence Scheme, December 1939.

11 TNO WO 166/4271 (War Diary, 2nd/4th Essex Regiment), 16.11.39.

12 TNA WO 277/37 (Defence Plans for the United Kingdom, 1939–45), p. 138.

13 TNA WO166/4339 (War Diary, 1st Hertfordshire Regiment), Appendix J, Appreciations, 7.11.39.

14 Dewing, *Aldeburgh*, p. 8.

15 The positions constructed on 16 November 1939 might have been completed the following day, when they were subject to inspection; thereafter no mention is made of works continuing.

The attitude of senior officers to the J.C. Plan was disparaging. The commander of the neighbouring 18th Division commented that it was 'impracticable' owing to a lack of resources and questioned whether it was even worth the effort to create fieldwork defences.[16] The brigadier of 162 Brigade was more colourful when he expressed that view that a landing by sea on his front between Aldebugh and Harwich would be attempted only 'as a desperate remedy or by a lunatic'.[17] Some in the ranks clearly agreed, especially those near Leiston, who abandoned their posts over Christmas 1939 in favour of a nearby public house, so giving burglars the opportunity to steal a regimental cash box. The prevailing mood across East Anglia at this time is summed up in the history of the Essex Regiment, which quickly passes over the 2nd/4th battalion's time on the coast by noting only that it was a 'curious period of lull and unreality' with many hours spent on guard duty and training.[18]

The invasion of Denmark and Norway on 9 April, however, concentrated the minds of the Chiefs of Staff regarding German capabilities and how any attack on Great Britain might be conducted. The scale and nature of the German operations allowed planners to make a more informed assessment of the nature of the threat, but in the immediate term invasion was still thought unlikely, particularly as the ports and airfields in the Netherlands that would be needed to mount an airborne attack on Britain were not in enemy hands.[19] The changing situation in Europe coincided with administrative changes in the military organisation of the Sandlings. On 18 April 54th Division were withdrawn for overseas training and replaced by 55th Division, a new embodied Territorial formation that would bear the brunt of the invasion crisis that would erupt three weeks later.[20] The arrangement of their constituent brigades and battalions on the ground broadly followed that of 54th Division and in the case of the 2nd/4th South Lancashire Regiment a map of dispositions between Pakefield and Dunwich dated 30 April shows the battalion defence scheme.[21] The battalion was strung out over a wide front in platoon localities, chiefly covering roads leading in from the coast. Further inland, emergency concentration areas existed to which troops could retreat in the event of being overwhelmed. These areas were to be taken up only on receipt of specific orders, however; when invasion was considered imminent the forward companies were to patrol their respective fronts to avoid the possibility of an unobserved landing (Figure 2.2). So at the end of the Phoney War, while the numbers of troops defending the coast had increased, the system of defence was very much based upon the principles that been established the previous November.

16   TNA WO 166/464 (War Diary, 18th Division, GS), Letter to Headquarters, Eastern Command, 6.11.39.

17   TNA WO 166/4339 (War Diary, 1st Hertfordshire Regiment), Appendix J, Appreciations, 7.11.39.

18   Martin, *Essex*, p. 349; D.Y. May and K. May, *From Flint Knappers to Atom Splitters. A History of Leiston cum Sizewell* (Leiston, 2001), p. 214.

19   Dobinson, *Anti-Invasion*, pp. 14–15.

20   TNA WO 166/1 (War Diary, GHQ Home Forces), J.C. Plan H.Q. Reserves, 29.3.40.

21   TNA WO 166/4680 (War Diary, 2nd/4th South Lancashire Regiment) Appendix A, 30.4.40.

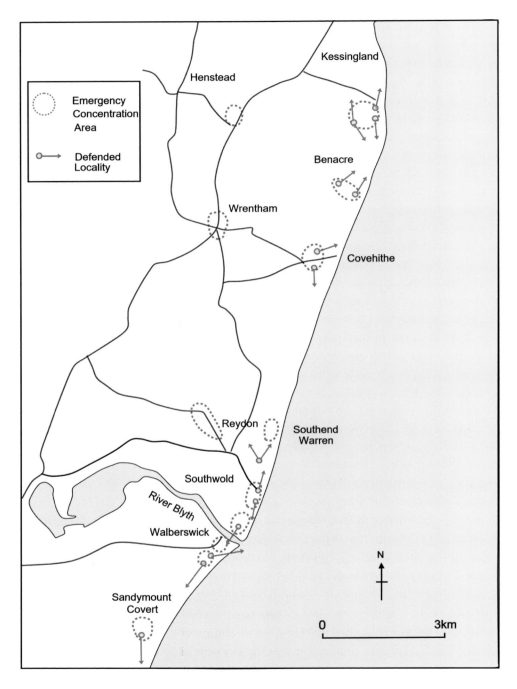

Figure 2.2. Map of dispositions of the 2nd/4th South Lancashire Regiment immediately before the invasion crisis of May 1940.

While it is often passed over, this early period of the conflict is important in that it marked the beginning of the meaningful 'militarisation' of the Sandlings. It was at this time that the first detailed tactical considerations on how the coastline could be defended were drawn up and troops deployed accordingly. Efforts were also made to rehearse a number of possible eventualities, such as in February 1940, when the cliffs at Dunwich were scaled in order to test the defences of the radar station, which demonstrated not only that this method of attack was feasible but that the radar mast within 13 metres of the cliff edge was vulnerable to such an operation.[22] This early period is also important for other reasons. It would be misleading to characterise this time as one of rigid stasis or simply as a prelude to what was to come later; rather, there was more flux than might at first be imagined. Early in 1940, for example, detached companies from the 2nd/4th Essex rejoined the battalion, which in turn led to a reordering of positions in order to provide more effective all-round defence – work that was proceeding as late as March 1940.[23] Perhaps more importantly, the situation before May 1940 points up the dramatic changes later in the year, when the character of coastal defences changed completely. By April of that year, however ineffectually manned and under-resourced it may have been, a scheme of defended localities with artillery support, inland defensive lines and mobile reserves all existed, at least in outline plan, for the purposes of coastal defence. As will be seen in the following chapter, this had more in common with schemes put in place from 1941 and 1942 than with those that immediately followed in 1940. Some of the thinking that lay behind the J.C. Plan also had a much longer-term resonance – the emphasis on the defeat of paratroopers was something that would characterise defensive planning almost until the end of the conflict.

Invasion crisis: the origins of the coastal crust and the geography of defence

The unexpected attack by Germany on the Low Countries and France on 10 May changed the international situation out of all recognition and provoked an immediate reaction on the Suffolk coast. The Codeword 'Julius' was issued and a degree of panic subsequently ensued: troops hurriedly took up war positions; civilian buses, still carrying passengers, were requisitioned for military use, and ploughs and farm carts were suddenly pressed into use as improvised roadblocks.[24] With German intentions unclear and the east coast looking a likely target for an incursion, by the end of the month orders simply assumed that invasion was imminent.[25]

The placing of units onto a war footing was ostensibly only a matter of putting existing defence schemes into operation. But in the chaotic early stages of the invasion

---

22   TNA WO 166/4271 (War Diary, 2nd/4th Essex Regiment), 3.2.40.
23   *Ibid.*, 1.3.40.
24   TNA WO 166/4434 (War Diary, 2nd Liverpool Scottish), 10–11.5.40.
25   *Ibid.*, 30.5.40.

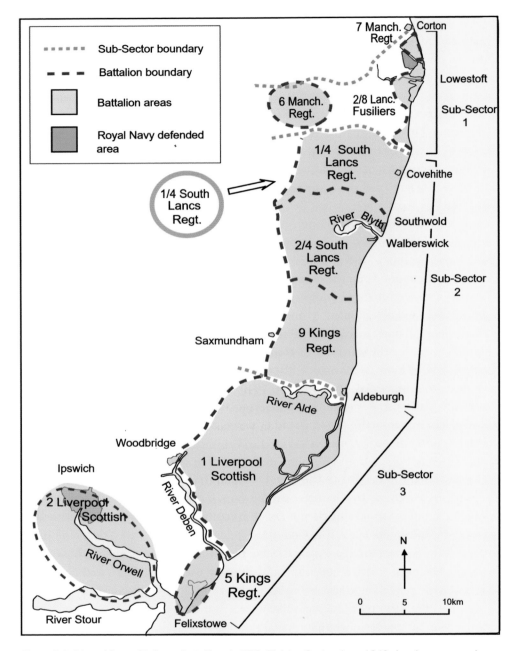

Figure 2.3. Dispositions of infantry battalions in 55th Division Sector, June 1940 showing move up by the 1st/4th South Lancashire Regiment.

crisis this evidently did not occur everywhere, with the result that the disposition of troops was haphazard, and this was compounded by a series of administrative changes. In May the Sector boundary was shortened to the south as the Essex section was given up, while in early June the northern boundary was extended to include Lowestoft. Sub-Sectors A and B were redesignated Sub-Sector 1 (Lowestoft), Sub-Sector 2 (Pakefield to Aldeburgh) and Sub-Sector 3 (Orford to Felixstowe), each held by one of 55th Division's infantry brigades.[26]

Right from the start, a tension existed between an aspiration to defend as much coastline as possible and the need to concentrate scarce resources in those places that were felt to be particularly vulnerable to attack. This ambiguity lay at the heart of the 55th Divisional instruction issued right at the start of the invasion crisis on 10 May stating that, on the one hand, Sub-Sector [Brigade] commanders were to adopt the positions in their existing defence schemes, while, on the other, units were to be concentrated wherever those same Sub-Sector commanders thought necessary.[27] In Sub-Sectors 1 and 3 the infantry brigades in question arranged their three constituent battalions in a 'two up, one back' formation.[28] In Sub-Sector 1 two battalions held the coastline at Lowestoft, with a reserve at Beccles, while in Sub-Sector 3 one battalion held Felixstowe, the second the coastline from Bawdsey to Orford, with the third inland in reserve and guarding the airfields at Ipswich and Martlesham (Figure 2.3).[29] In Sub-Sector 2, however, a different deployment occurred and the form of defence envisaged prior to 10 May was abandoned in favour of an alternative arrangement. Here, too, a 'two up, one back' deployment initially took place, but, rather than taking up the positions in their defence scheme drawn up some ten days earlier, a decision was taken to concentrate the two forward battalions at Southwold (2nd/4th South Lancashire Regiment) and Aldeburgh (9th Kings Regiment). There is no suggestion that this was in any way part of prior planning; rather, the decision seems to have been arrived at on 10 or 11 May.[30] The positions put in place as a result of this new deployment differed markedly to those intended previously. Instead of being strung out along the whole coastline with designated areas to which to retreat if overrun, the two forward battalions were now defending Southwold and Aldeburgh and constructing defences that were to be permanently manned

---

26 TNA WO 166/688 (War Diary, 55th Division, GS), 24.5.40, 1.6.40, renumbering of Sub-Sectors took place 10.6.40.

27 *Ibid.*, Operational Order No. 5, 10.5.40.

28 In the case of Sub-Sector 1, when 199 Brigade joined 55th Division's order of battle it adopted the 'two up, one back' formation of the previous units. TNA WO 166/1052 (War Diary, 199th Infantry Brigade), 23–30.6.40.

29 TNA WO 166/688 (War Diary, 55th Division, GS), Home Defence, 24.4.40.

30 TNA WO 166/1037 (War Diary, 164th Infantry Brigade) Operational Order No. 1, 11.5.40; TNA WO 166/4680 (War Diary, 2nd/4th South Lancashire Regiment), Battalion Conference, 11.5.40; R. Liddiard and D. Sims, 'A Piece of Coastal Crust: The Origins of a Second World War Defence Landscape at Walberswick, Suffolk', *History*, 97 (2012), pp. 402–30.

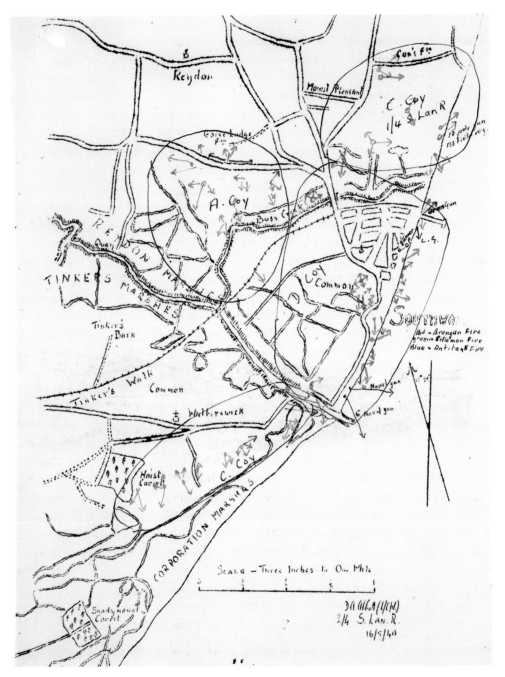

Figure 2.4. Distribution of infantry positions of the 2nd/4th South Lancashire Regiment at Southwold and Walberswick shown on a hand-drawn map appended to battalion war diary for August 1940. The company areas are shown within large circles, with arrows marking directions of fire from infantry section posts (red = Bren gun fire; green = riflemen fire; blue = Boys anti-tank rifle fire). This was quite different to the scheme envisaged before the invasion crisis, see Figure 2.3. (TNA WO166/4680)

(Figure 2.4).[31] A by-product of this move was that, while it had always been recognised that the whole coastline could not be adequately held with the number of troops available, the situation was now exacerbated. Concentrating at Southwold and Aldeburgh meant that beaches at Covehithe and Kessingland were now left entirely undefended.[32] The resulting gap in the line between Sub-Sectors 1 and 2 created in the first two days of the invasion crisis seems to have become apparent only with hindsight and necessitated a further change ten days later, when, on 20 May, the reserve battalion at Wrentham (1st/4th South Lancashire Regiment) was pushed up to the north of Southwold to create a 'three up' arrangement.[33] When this move had been completed the majority of fighting troops in Sub-Sector 2 were now directly on the coast, meaning that, apart from what could be provided from the division, there was now no inland reserve to counter any breakthrough from the beaches. But in all cases the troops concerned immediately set about adopting war positions and digging defensive trenches.

The differing arrangements in Sub-Sector 2 were a response to the twin demands of needing to adequately defend the most vulnerable beaches (in this case at Southwold and Aldeburgh) while at the same time maintaining a presence along the whole brigade front. While this problem was common across the Sector, here it was more acute because the Sub-Sector front was longer and contained proportionally more vulnerable areas of coastline. In Sub-Sector 1 on average there were 102 men per kilometre, not including additional manpower available from the Royal Navy at Lowestoft. In Sub-Sector 3 the unsuitability of Orford Ness for a landing meant that the length of coastline requiring defence was shorter and so here manning was on average 105 men per kilometre. By contrast, in Sub-Sector 2, with two battalions 'up' the manning level averaged 51 men per kilometre and even after moving to a 'three up' formation it was still comparatively short, at 90 men per kilometre.[34] But what cannot be emphasised enough here is that, however they were configured, 55th Division were almost impossibly stretched. In battle, depending on the terrain and the strength of the enemy, a British infantry division could reasonably expect to occupy a front of about 9.5 kilometres (six miles) in defence, less if it was in the attack. But 55th Division occupied a 90-kilometre (56-mile) front. Put another way, in places along the Sandlings coast battalions of 800 men held a front that some 15,000 might be expected to defend in normal circumstances.

This discussion of the events of 10–12 May is important for two reasons. Firstly, the new scheme represented a clear break with that envisaged before; a new arrangement

---

31   The Battalion HQ and 'A' company were at Blythburgh, 'B' and 'D' companies in Southwold and 'C' Company in Walberswick. While it is the case that in their earlier defence scheme there were more localities in the Southwold/Walberswick area, the new arrangement was significantly different.

32   Although unrecorded, it is probable that standing and bicycle patrols were kept along the whole battalion front.

33   TNA WO 166/4679 (War Diary, 1st/4th South Lancashire Regiment), 25–28.5.40.

34   Assuming 820 men per battalion and a brigade strength at 2600.

had been worked out very quickly on the ground. Secondly, given the short time period involved (some 48 hours) there was little opportunity for reconnoitring and detailed planning. In the speedy redeployment that had been forced upon them by circumstance, battalion and probably company commanders had decided where they would place their men. The creation of the anti-invasion landscape of 1940 was therefore not so much an operation directed from above, but one very much initiated from the bottom up.

At this point it is worth returning briefly to the national picture.[35] As a result of the rapid German advance through Europe in May and June and the subsequent withdrawal of the British Expeditionary Force from France, the Chiefs of Staff turned their attention away from evaluating the possibility of invasion to how such an operation might actually be resisted. More detailed arrangements for the defence of ports and their immediate hinterlands were ordered and a national beach reconnaissance of possible landing areas on the south and east coasts was undertaken. On 27 May Kirke was replaced as Commander in Chief Home Forces by General Sir Edmund Ironside, the figure with whom British anti-invasion defences during the crisis of 1940 are most closely associated. The situation he inherited was believed to be precarious: the day after assuming command the Chiefs of Staff advised the War Cabinet that it was highly probable that Germany was preparing a full-scale invasion of Britain.

While acknowledging that a great deal had already been undertaken by Kirke, Ironside set in motion a programme of anti-invasion works that would dwarf what had gone before. A thin 'coastal crust' was to hold up any German beach landing for as long as possible, with potential landing grounds obstructed eight kilometres back from the coast, exits from beaches blocked and vulnerable beaches receiving concrete pillboxes, barbed wire and mines. Once the invaders had broken through and moved inland they would be constantly delayed by fortified Nodal Points at natural bottlenecks on the road network and by a series of anti-tank Stop Lines. With their main intentions revealed, what was left of Britain's mobile reserves would meet the enemy and defeat them decisively in a pitched battle.[36]

The chronological relationship between this national scheme and the situation on the ground in the Sandlings is important. As the detailed reconstruction of the events of May 1940 shows, the underlying skeleton of the 1940 defences and the deployment of troops were laid down *before* Ironside took up his post as Commander in Chief, meaning that those elements most closely associated with his command, such as pillboxes and anti-tank blocks, which are discussed below, were additions to an existing framework. Much has been written about the characteristics of Ironside's

---

35   For what follows see Dobinson, *Anti-Invasion*, pp. 14–53.
36   Dobinson, *Anti-Invasion*, pp. 24–47.

defences and their potential effectiveness.[37] Later in 1940 their 'linear' character, especially the static Stop Lines, drew extensive criticism for being outmoded and Ironside was removed from command. But the criticisms of these defences and their subsequent reorganisation in 1941 need to be set against a clearer understanding of the circumstances of their origin. As will be seen in the following chapter, in the Sandlings much of what was deemed problematic about the 1940 coastal crust stemmed from the initial deployment in May, rather than how they were subsequently developed during Ironside's tenure as Commander in Chief.

It is also worth emphasising that a discussion of how the coastal defences evolved during the invasion summer inevitably imposes a false impression of organisation. The war diaries of 55th Division's units are replete with instances of operational orders being continually modified or changed, false invasion alarms, reports of fifth columnists, routines being subject to revision and equipment shortages. The comment by one officer engaged in the construction of inland defences in the south-west of the county is equally applicable to the situation on the coast: 'Indescribable chaos'.[38] It was in this febrile atmosphere that the fortification of the coastline took place.

Watery landscapes

Alongside the taking up of war positions and the digging of trenches, one of the first measures taken to defend the coastline was to utilise the advantages presented by geography. Almost as soon as the invasion crisis struck, areas of fen and marsh were identified that could be flooded in order to restrict the movement of any attacking force. For centuries in the Sandlings landowners had fought a prolonged battle to drain the coastal marshes and fens and keep the sea at bay, but in 1940 years of work was undone in a matter of days (Figure 2.5).

The natural geography permitted inundation of wetland in Sub-Sector 2 chiefly between Benacre and Aldeburgh and this dovetailed neatly with the military necessity; as has just been seen, this was where troops were most heavily stretched. On 20 May bridges crossing drainage ditches were either removed or blown up by engineers and drainage sluices controlling the marshes at Walberswick were opened, allowing the ingress of sea water.[39] Here the inundation was highly successful and flooded Westwood, Corporation, Reedland and Dingle marshes and resulted in a stretch of water inland from Walberswick beach as far south as Dunwich. Significant flooding also took place to the north of Minsmere 'New Cut' up to Minsmere cliffs, in the area now occupied by the RSPB bird reserve, with the water stretching nearly three kilometres inland (Figure 2.6). As a defensive measure inundation required little

---

37   Osborne, *Defending Britain*, chapter 1; Foot, *Beaches, Fields, Streets, and Hills, passim*; for Suffolk in particular, Hegarty and Newsome, *Suffolk's Defended Shore*, chapter 5; Osborne and Kerr, *Suffolk*, chapter 1.

38   TNA WO 166/3698 (War Diary, 229th Field Company, Royal Engineers), 23.7.40–4.10.40.

39   TNA WO 166/4680 (War Diary, 2nd/4th South Lancashire Regiment), 20.5.40.

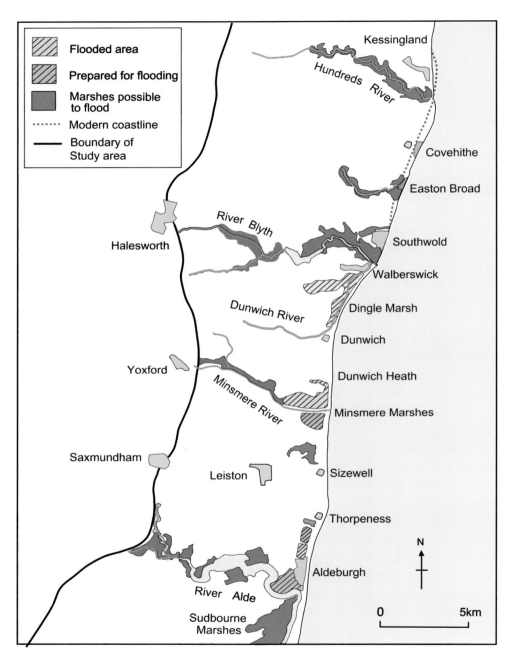

Figure 2.5. Map showing inundations and areas prepared for flooding in Divisional Sector.

Figure 2.6. The coastline between Walberswick and Dunwich in 2011 after inundation by the sea, giving an impression of how the deliberate flooding of marshland during the war altered the landscape. (Mike Page)

effort and could clearly be effective, but even at a time of national crisis a balance had to be struck between the needs of the military and the agricultural value of the marshland grazing that would be destroyed by the salt water. Those places that were flooded in 1940 tended to be those badly draining peat fens that had suffered ever since the agricultural depression of the late nineteenth century and were already in some cases reverting to reed beds. Grazing marshes on former silt-beds were more valuable, however, and so had tended to be upkept even during times of agricultural recession. Large-scale flooding of these areas would have dealt a serious blow to the farming economy and so was resisted. The extensive grazing marshes adjacent to Aldeburgh were a case in point. Here the spur upon which the town was situated could be made into a peninsular by the flooding of Aldeburgh marshes to the south and the low-lying area around North Warren to the north. In the event, however, only a relatively small parcel of the latter was permanently flooded to a depth of half a metre, with the remaining areas to be inundated only upon receipt of 'Action Stations': in effect, when invasion was underway.[40] Similar arrangements to delay flooding were put

---

40   TNA WO 166/4180 (War Diary, 9th Cameronians), Defence Scheme, September 1941.

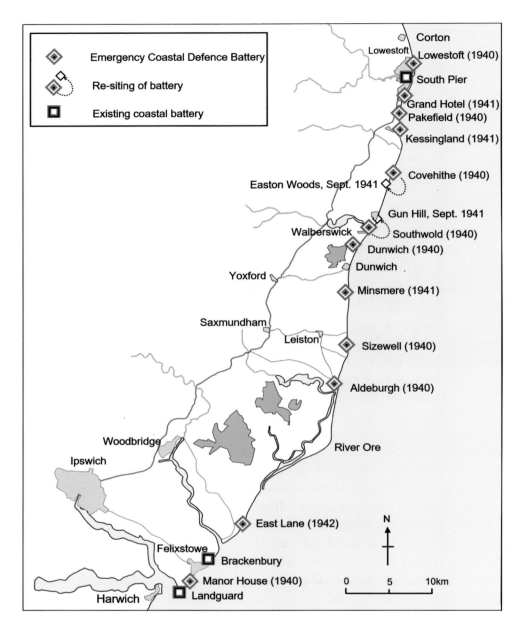

Figure 2.7. Location map of Emergency Coastal Defence Batteries (ECDB), 1940-42.

into place elsewhere: along the lines of the rivers Minsmere, Blyth, Waveney and also probably along the Hundred River at Benacre. The use of wetlands in the anti-invasion landscape therefore reflected the nature of the pre-existing environment as much as military exigency.

In addition to flooding, the earliest stages of the invasion crisis also saw measures to obstruct port facilities and harbours. Sections of the pleasure piers at Felixstowe, Lowestoft and Southwold were blown up in order to prevent their use as landing stages; at Southwold these efforts were extended by the effects of a stray mine.[41] Access to harbours was reduced by a variety of means. At Lowestoft and Harwich Haven booms protected the entrance channels, an arrangement augmented at Lowestoft by the existence of a Royal Navy block ship that could be placed at the harbour mouth to prevent entry by hostile craft.[42] Similar arrangements existed at Walberswick, where two wooden trawlers were sunk at the mouth of the Blyth; these were broken up by the action of the sea after a month, and so were replaced with a net or boom, probably similar to that on the Ore, south-west of Boyton, intended to hinder the movement of small craft and submarines.[43]

But by far the most important measure to defend the seaward approaches to ports and vulnerable beaches was the Emergency Coastal Defence Battery (ECDB) programme, which saw mothballed Royal Navy 6-inch and 4-inch guns from vessels scrapped after the First World War hurriedly removed from storage and placed in pairs along the coastline (Figure 2.7).[44] Emergency batteries of 6-inch guns were ordered for Felixstowe, Aldeburgh, Southwold and Lowestoft on 22 May, followed by sites at Covehithe and Thorpeness on 8 June, with a battery of 4-inch guns at Dunwich later in the year.[45] The speed with which these batteries became operational was a testament both to the logistical skill behind the operation and the perceived vulnerability of the east coast. The Aldeburgh battery was one of the first nationally to be declared ready for action on 6 June, with that at Sizewell following on 18 June and Southwold at about the same time.[46] In the Divisional Sector the ECDBs represented the most significant firepower on the coastline outside the fixed batteries at Felixstowe and Harwich.

The primary purpose of ECDBs was to engage enemy shipping at a range of five kilometres (three miles), especially vessels approaching harbours, but they were also

---

41   TNA WO 166/1038 (War Diary, 165th Infantry Brigade), 13.5.40; 29.5.40; TNA WO 166/1529 (War Diary, 117th Field Regiment, Royal Artillery), 5.6.40.

42   TNA WO 166/4412 (War Diary, 2nd/8th Lancashire Fusiliers), 4.8.40; Hegarty and Newsome, *Suffolk's Defended Shore*, p. 44; boom at Lowestoft illustrated in Jarvis, *Fortress Lowestoft*, p. 26.

43   TNA WO 166/4433 (War Diary, 1st Liverpool Scottish), 4.7.40; TNA WO 166/1038 (War Diary 165th Infantry Brigade), 16.6.40; Foot, *Beaches, Fields, Streets, and Hills*, p. 123.

44   For extended discussion see Dobinson, *Coast Artillery*.

45   Dobinson, *Coast Artillery*, p. 60.

46   TNA WO 166/11 (War Diary, GHQ Home Forces, Coast Artillery); TNA WO 166/1835 (War Diary, 355th Coast Battery).

Figure 2.8. The ECDB at Pakefield in November 1940, showing the gunhouses, ancillary buildings and the holiday camp that served as the domestic site. A long line of anti-tank blocks cutting off the inland approaches can be seen in the background, with shorter lengths on the beach preventing access to the battery site. Aerial photograph from Fort Book. (TNA 192/215)

tasked with firing on smaller boats approaching the coastline. The batteries were sited accordingly: at Lowestoft, the Kent Battery at Gunton was part of the 'examination service' that controlled the entry of vessels into the port, with the southern approaches protected by that at Pakefield; while the northern approaches to Felixstowe were given extra defence by the establishment of a battery at Manor House. Elsewhere, batteries directly covered landing beaches themselves: those at Aldeburgh, Southwold, Sizewell and Covehithe all had fields of fire across those areas of water likely to be traversed by incoming invasion craft.

As Dobinson has made clear, ECDBs were often idiosyncratic in their layout and design, and those in the Sandlings show considerable variation in local arrangements (Figure 2.8). All were, however, 'nucleated' sites, in that their component structures were in close proximity, which served to make batteries discrete elements in the wider anti-invasion landscape (Figure 2.9).[47] In time ECDBs developed into substantial

---

47   Dobinson, *Coast Artillery*, pp. 77–8, 96.

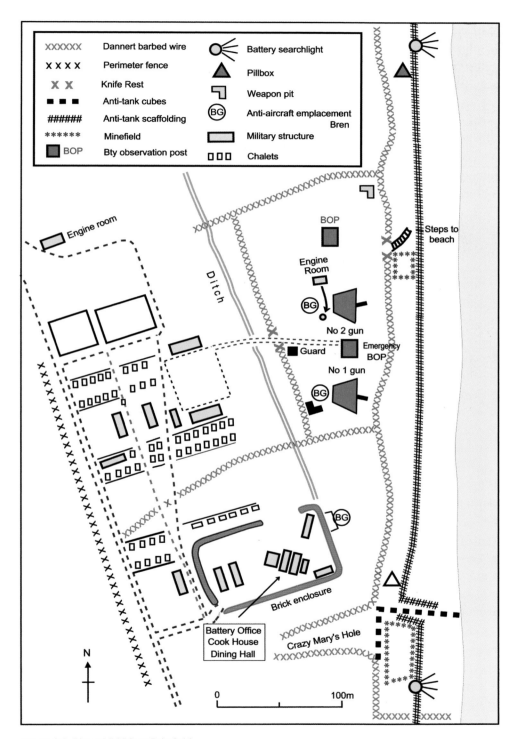

Figure 2.9. Plan of ECDB at Pakefield.

complexes with concrete gun houses, observation posts, searchlights, generators, ammunition stores, personnel accommodation, workshops and structures for battery defence, but during the summer of 1940 facilities were rudimentary and only latterly did they attain a degree of sophistication. At Lowestoft Kent battery the two semi-mobile 6-inch guns were initially mounted in concrete slabs with sandbag emplacements, which were replaced from June with gun houses made of steel frames with corrugated iron walls and roof, which were themselves later replaced by brick and concrete gun houses.[48] Similarly, at Aldeburgh the initial gun houses comprised holdfasts covered by sandbags placed over a steel frame, which were then replaced in concrete the following year.

The standard morphological form for each battery saw the gun houses spaced slightly apart, with their ancillary buildings and observation post immediately adjacent, searchlights dispersed on either side and the domestic structures at the rear of the main site. At the level of the individual battery there were variations in the design of buildings but differences in morphology were usually on account of topography and the nature of the pre-existing site. At Pakefield there were separate structures for gun houses, the engine room and personnel shelters, but all were connected via subterranean passages. In contrast, at Dunwich gun houses were integrated into a single structure and served by a service passage with below-ground magazines. The favoured position for the observation post was between the two guns, either in an improvised building, as at Aldeburgh, where a redundant windmill was originally pressed into use, or more usually in a purpose-built structure, as at Dunwich, where the observation post sat over the main structure housing the guns. In all cases searchlights were placed individually on each side of the battery position, usually some distance away. At Pakefield these were on the beach below the cliff site and at Dunwich the topography of the site demanded that they were well removed from the gun themselves and lay on islands of higher ground amid low-lying marsh; in October, gunners manning the lights could report that 'there is water all round except for a spit about 300 yards wide leading to the mainland'.[49] The battery domestic sites tended to make use of existing facilities wherever possible. At Pakefield the accommodation, office, dining hall and cookhouse were in the holiday camp facilities located immediately to the rear of the battery position, while at Aldeburgh the troops were billeted in neighbouring houses and hotels on the sea front adjacent to the guns. Where local accommodation did not exist hutted camps were usually constructed, but these were more a feature of 1941; at Dunwich as late as October 1940 there was an open cookhouse and the personnel were housed in tents. The infrastructure required for each ECDB was therefore considerable and efforts, not always successful, were made to camouflage the sites. The schemes of 1940 tended to lack the sophistication of those later in the war and chiefly used

---

48   Kent, *Fortifications of East Anglia*, pp. 168, 256.
49   TNA WO 166/1885 (War Diary, 58th Heavy Regiment, Royal Artillery), 30–31.10.40.

Figure 2.10. Detail of the ECDB at Dunwich in 1941, camouflaged as a Dutch barn. The gun barrel is positioned in such a way as to avoid casting a tell-tale shadow and so give away the real purpose of the building. (IWM H11453)

camouflage netting, but that at Dunwich, the final battery position constructed that year, was by far the most elaborate, with the gun houses disguised as a Dutch barn (Figure 2.10).

The coastal crust: obstacles

The ECDBs were primarily intended to prevent the enemy from reaching the shore, but those who did reach the Sandlings' beaches would encounter a range of obstacles intended to impede the movement of men and vehicles. These elements formed part of Ironside's national scheme and were closely related to the infantry defences that were already being built on the ground and which are discussed in detail below. But before the development of the anti-invasion landscape can be discussed as a whole, it is necessary to consider the purpose of each kind of obstacle, as this is crucial to understanding not only their placement in the landscape but also why particular structures were used in combination.

In 1940 the initial line of defence on the shoreline was marked by 'dragon's teeth', a term sometimes used for pyramid-shaped concrete anti-tank blocks, but which in 55th Division referred to steel spikes intended to rip the bottom out of landing barges

Figure 2.11. Dragon's teeth at Dunwich *c.*1948 (By permission of Dunwich Museum)

and small craft as they reached the shore.[50] Each tooth was formed from bent and pointed steel angles or girders set in a concrete slabs sunk into the sand or shingle at 4.5-metre (15-foot) intervals between high and low water mark, pointing seaward. Almost 12,000 spikes were laid on 55th Division's front, of which nearly 7000 were of 'heavy' type and contained apertures through which cable or barbed wire could be strung to provide a continuous barrier (Figure 2.11) and 5000 were of a smaller design, which photographs show were simple spikes that lacked the apertures of their heavier counterparts.[51]

On the beaches themselves one of the most straightforward methods of slowing up an invader was barbed wire, which was laid in prodigious quantities from the very beginning of the invasion crisis.[52] Wire could easily turn an open area into an altogether more daunting prospect to negotiate and had the advantage that it could be laid by infantrymen rather than by specialist engineers only. From May there are references to 'Dannert Wire', the name given to the rolls of high-quality wire – also known as 'concertina' owing to its circular shape when uncoiled – being erected along

50   TNA WO 166/1529 (War Diary, 117th Field Regiment, Royal Artillery), 5.6.40 refers to anti-tank blocks as dragon's teeth. For clear references to steel rails see TNA WO 166/494 (War Diary, 42nd Division, GS), 42 Div Defence Scheme, Section 1, November 1940; TNA WO 166/957 (War Diary, 49th Infantry Brigade), Defence Scheme, Part 1, Beach Defence, July 1941.

51   TNA WO 166/1038 (War Diary, 165th Infantry Brigade), 6.8.40.

52   Some 200 miles of barbed wire according to the Divisional war diary, but this included inland areas. TNA WO 166/693 (War Diary, 55th Division, CRE), 3.11.40.

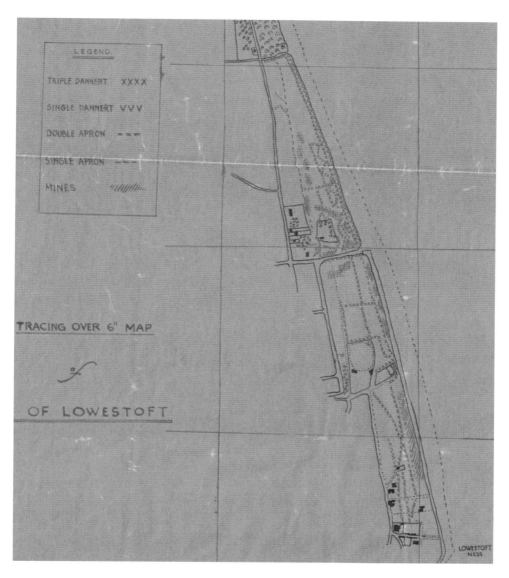

LEGEND

TRIPLE DANNERT   X X X X

SINGLE DANNERT   V V V

DOUBLE APRON   – – –

SINGLE APRON   – – –

MINES

TRACING OVER 6" MAP

of

OF LOWESTOFT

LOWESTOFT
NESS

Figure 2.12. Hand-drawn map of 1940 showing placement of barbed wire on the battalion front of the 7th Manchester Regiment at Lowestoft from the battalion war diary. A variety of entanglements and fences were used in combination in order to obstruct beach exits. (TNA WO 166/4454)

the Divisional front. Such wire did not necessarily require supporting pickets and so could be rapidly unwound to create an immediate impediment. A common practice was to combine coils in groups of three – two side by side and a third on top – with such 'triple concertina' creating a particularly off-putting obstacle for infantrymen. In addition, more conventional barbed wire fences existed, but with additional wire pinned down on one side (known as single apron) or on both (double apron).[53] Barbed wire was ubiquitous on the invasion beaches, but tended to be used in specific ways. On beaches a line of concertina was usually placed parallel to the sea just above high water mark, but in order to prevent lateral movement entanglements were added at right angles in order to create bottlenecks where contained troops could be more easily dispatched. The most sophisticated arrangements, however, were on the good landing beaches and their main exits; here combinations of concertina and double apron produced a landscape that resembled a First World War battlefield (Figure 2.12).[54]

The second principal beach obstacle was the mine. Some 17,500 mines (11,000 anti-personnel and 6500 anti-tank) were laid on the Divisional front in the three months after May 1940, in some 16 separate minefields.[55] Minefields were placed either directly on the beaches themselves or on roads leading immediately inland. It is worth emphasising that minefields were often very large. That on the seaward side of Bawdsey Radar station was over one kilometre (1100 yards) in length, while even smaller examples, such as that at Walberswick, which was 360 metres (400 yards) long, were extensive. Although they were fenced off and provided with warning signs, minefields represented a constant danger for troops anywhere near the beaches, with fatalities involving mines accounting for the majority of military deaths on the coast during the war. Such incidents unwittingly demonstrated their effectiveness, as did the occasions when deliberate testing took place: Christopher Thompson of 55th Divisions' engineers recalled that when his men dragged a lorry chassis over an anti-tank mine to determine the effect the vehicle was blown 20 feet (7 metres) in the air.[56]

Given the emphasis in Ironside's scheme on delaying an enemy advance for as long as possible, considerable effort went into restricting the movement of vehicles off beaches and then inland. As was the case elsewhere in the country, the use of natural obstacles as vehicle barriers was preferred to the creation of new defences and in the Sandlings the coastal topography favoured the defenders, as the numerous drainage ditches and channels provided an immediate source of anti-tank ditches. The Dunwich river formed an anti-tank obstacle in its own right and was by far the longest section of wet anti-tank ditch in the whole Sector. At Shingle Street an anti-

53   War Office, *Military Training Pamphlet No. 30 Part III, Field Engineering All Arms, Obstacles* (1940).

54   TNA WO 166/4454 (War Diary, 7th Manchester Regiment). Trace of September 1940.

55   TNA WO 166/693 (War Diary, 55th Division, CRE). Statement of works completed to Midnight 2/3 November 1940, 3.11.40.

56   Interview by authors with Major Christopher Thompson, 17.11.09.

tank ditch a little inland from the beach was formed by flooding a natural creek with sea water by opening the sluice at Dumb Boy House and linking it with a freshwater drainage channel newly dredged by the East Suffolk Rivers Catchment Board, resulting in a stretch of anti-tank ditch of some four kilometres (2.5 miles). Elsewhere, where drainage channels had silted up before the war these were now recut to depths of just under three metres (nine feet), subsequently reduced to two metres (six feet) in order to speed up work, with the result that, alongside inundations, the coastal wetlands became generally wetter.[57]

But, where topography was unfavourable, the chief man-made obstacle used to hinder the movement of vehicles off the beaches in 1940 was the anti-tank block: simple concrete cubes often built of local materials and constructed *in situ* which were arranged in lines to provide a static barrier. The majority of blocks in the Sector were three feet six inches (1.07 metres) square and usually spaced five feet (1.5 metres) apart. Where revealed by the action of the sea, it can be seen that in at least some cases the blocks sat upon a concrete base, whereas others were seemingly just sunk into the ground out of expediency. The simple nature of the design means that there is little in the way of variety in the blocks themselves, but most carry the marks left by wooden shuttering and the considerable variety in the shape and size of the planks used hint at their rapid construction. Just under 11,500 blocks were laid on the foreshore by 55th Division in 1940, with the majority constructed either directly by Royal Engineers or under supervision by civilian contractors and possibly in smaller numbers by infantry (Figure 2.13). Anti-tank blocks tended to be used in a number of ways. Firstly, runs of blocks were used to form a continuous barrier parallel to the beaches which often extended for considerable distances. At Felixstowe an almost unbroken line ran for five kilometres from Landguard Point north to Cobbald's Point, while that between Minsmere and Southwold ran for some 1.5 kilometres. Although in theory the cubes provided the most effective barrier when placed at an angle in the direction of the enemy, such tactical employment was either unknown or ignored, as most cubes directly face the sea. Secondly, shorter runs of blocks ran at right angles to the shoreline in order to prevent the lateral movement of vehicles in the same manner as barbed wire was used to impede those on foot. Thirdly, blocks were used to form all or part of the defensive perimeters of particularly vulnerable places, such as Bawdsey and Dunwich radar stations and ECDBs such as Pakefield, where cordons of blocks were integrated into wider defences. The most extreme example of this kind of employment was at Lowestoft, where two lines of anti-tank cubes protected the landward approaches to the town.

The second means of delaying the passage of vehicles inland was roadblocks, which were sited chiefly on roads leading away from the beaches, usually at bottlenecks, junctions or places that were otherwise suitable for ambushes. Initially these were

---

57   TNA WO 166/1038 (War Diary, 165th Infantry Brigade), 13.6.40; TNA WO 166/4433 (War Diary, 1st Liverpool Scottish), Operational Instruction No. 11, dated from daily war diary at 26.5.40.

Figure 2.13. Linear run of anti-tank cubes, Minsmere. Such long lengths of blocks parallel to the beaches were a response to the muted topography of the Sandlings.

simple sandbag arrangements or improvised with agricultural equipment, but later they tended to be replaced by steel rails placed vertically in roads to stop traffic and, occasionally, provisioned with anti-tank blocks and an adjacent pillbox.

Finally, the threat of aerial attack by paratroops or troops landed by aircraft or glider also led to a degree of obstacle construction in open areas behind beaches. Beach huts at Southwold were displaced and scattered over the common in order to prevent it being used as a landing strip, while the airstrip at King's Marshes at Orford, part of the pre-war research establishment, was put out of action by the placement of over 2000 concrete blocks on the runway.[58] Elsewhere, the extent to which the construction of bespoke anti-landing ditches took place in the summer of 1940 is unclear, as documentary evidence is unforthcoming and only a small number of contemporary aerial photographs exist. Where available, however, they suggest that in 1940 the construction of anti-landing ditches was chiefly confined to the hinterland of ports, beach exits and the larger heaths inland. Two definite examples are inland from Felixstowe around Trimley, dating to before July, and Benacre, where they were associated with the other beach defences.[59] At Aldringham a ditch system was in place by September 1940 and the same was probably true for the hinterland of Walberswick

58   J.M. Becker, *Story of Southwold* (Southwold, 1948), 155; TNA WO 166/693 (War Diary, 55th Division, CRE), 3.11.40.

59   Suffolk Historic Environment Record (hereafter HER), MXS 19236/7/8 (Felixstowe); MXS 18948 (Benacre).

and Dunwich. Although the details are unclear, there are also documentary references to open spaces having been rendered unsuitable for landings, probably with upright poles or wire obstructions, and it is probable that many inland heaths were provided with some kind of rudimentary obstacle.[60]

Infantry defence

While the construction of obstacles might slow down any invader they could do little in themselves if they were not covered by fire and so the defence of the coastline ultimately rested upon the shoulders of the men on the ground: infantrymen with rifles, machine guns and bayonets who had to physically prevent their German counterparts from gaining a foothold ashore for as long as possible. For those charged with defending the Sandlings' coastline, withdrawal was explicitly forbidden and it was anticipated that they would fight until the last man. One group of veterans later recalled that they 'expected for several weeks to be annihilated'.[61] The basic element of the infantry defence was earthwork trenches for ten-man sections, known as section posts, that were grouped together in threes to make a platoon position, with three platoon positions in turn making up a company area. According to official manuals, the process for digging a section post involved the excavation of simple pits, which could then be extended and joined up to form a larger earthwork that was known as a 'fire trench'. Such trenches were in some ways reminiscent of First World War works in that they required revetting and could be developed by the addition of firing points and dugouts, both for protection and for semi-permanent occupation; the term 'sandbagged pillbox' was used for a strongpoint that lacked the more robust materials of its concrete counterpart. The trenches on the Suffolk coast were built to this standard and war diaries could report that in some cases men were supposedly perfectly comfortable when sleeping at their posts.[62]

As archaeological monuments, section posts dating to 1940 are extremely rare. Only a handful of the hundreds originally created remain extant and all identified in this study are backfilled, rather than retaining their original depth. But those that do remain are of similar form and comprise long sinuous trenches that terminate in pillboxes (Figure 2.14). By far the best-preserved example is at Hoist Covert near Walberswick, which was the section post marking the extreme right flank of 'C' company of the 2nd/4th South Lancashire Regiment (Figure 2.15). There are three distinct elements to the position: a fire trench 20 metres long, a 10-metre length of communication trench and a concrete pillbox. Archaeological excavation demonstrated that the fire trench was originally over two metres deep and provisioned with a firestep. Given the sandy nature

60   TNA WO 166/4249 (War Diary, 4th East Lancashire Regiment), 10.1.41.
61   G.W. Robertson, *The Rose and the Arrow. A Life Story of 136th (1st West Lancashire) Field Regiment Royal Artillery, 1939–1946* (Dorchester, 1986), p. 55.
62   TNA WO 166/4680 (War Diary, 2nd/4th South Lancashire Regiment), 30.6.40.

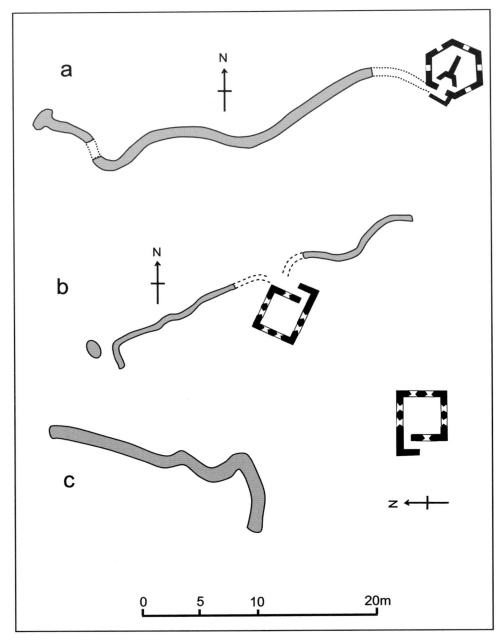

Figure 2.14. Section posts and associated pillboxes, c.1940: a) Wilford Bridge, Melton, position of 1st or 2nd Liverpool Scottish; b) Aldringham Walks, position of 9th King's Regiment; c) Sizewell, probably 9th Kings.

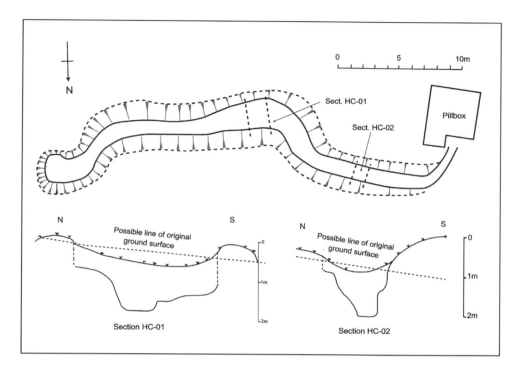

Figure 2.15. Plan of section post of 2nd/4th South Lancashire Regiment, Hoist Covert, Walberswick, 1940. Construction of this position started in May 1940, with pillbox added in July. As it was abandoned in the spring of 1941, it gives a good impression of what were originally hundreds of such posts in the Divisional Sector during the invasion summer.

of the soil and the depth of the trench, subsidence must have represented a particular problem and the presence of in situ iron pickets argues for a timber or wire revetment. The rudimentary nature of the position was suggested by the recovery of a metal lock, presumably from a door acquired locally and pressed into use to support the sides of the fire trench; war diaries recorded that poles were requisitioned from local woodland for revetments.[63] The dimensions of the trench, together with its location on a forward slope, conform closely to the prescribed form laid down in the 1936 *Manual of Field Engineering*.[64] As the unit responsible was the otherwise untrained 2nd/4th South Lancashire Regiment, it suggests that the Hoist Covert post represents green troops, in the absence of any detailed practical experience, doing it 'by the book'. The gradual evolution of the position during the invasion summer can be charted in detail from the battalion war diary. On 11 May the battalion took up its war positions and a day later 'commenced to dig in and wire', which presumably marked the construction of

63   TNA WO 166/4433 (War Diary, 1st Liverpool Scottish), Operational Instruction No. 15, 31.5.40.
64   War Office, *Manual of Field Engineering Vol. 1 (All Arms)* (1936), chapter 9; War Office, *Field Service Pocket Book, Pamphlet No. 4, Field Engineering* (1939), pp. 20–23; IMW H2699, H2702, H2703.

Figure 2.16. Artist's reconstruction of section post at Hoist Covert, Walberswick, *c.*September 1940. (Virtual Past, UEA)

Figure 2.17. Staged photograph of trenches at Great Yarmouth during the summer of 1940. Such sandbagged emplacements were a common feature of the coastal defences. (IWM H2700)

the fire trench. After six weeks the battalion's forward positions were described as being 'completed' and at the end of July it was noted that they were '*now* all finished' and that there were '*now* no less than fifty concrete pill-boxes either complete or under construction in the Battalion area' [authors' emphasis]; it follows that the pillbox at Hoist Covert (and presumably those elsewhere) was a relative latecomer and was added to the existing fire trench possibly as late as ten weeks after its initial construction (Figure 2.16). The form and character of positions seen in contemporary photographic and film evidence confirms the field evidence at Hoist Covert. A aerial photograph of Sizewell taken on 8 July shows almost exactly the same arrangement, with the sinuous line of fire trench terminating with a pillbox, and the whole position surrounded by barbed wire. A set of staged images of a mock defence of the beach at Great Yarmouth, in neighbouring Norfolk, show simple structures with sandbagged dugouts, corrugated iron and wooden revetments for trenches (Figure 2.17), while film of positions at Minsmere shows rudimentary, unrevetted trenches with sandbags.[65]

Today, it is the concrete pillboxes that mark the locations of these 1940 section posts, and the accompanying trenches are now almost entirely absent. While not all section posts were provisioned with pillboxes and not all pillboxes had accompanying trenches, pillboxes represent the best dataset for analysis for reconstructing both the locations of the infantry and the reasons for those locations at this time.

The landscape of pillboxes

The majority of pillboxes in the Sandlings are of two types: the Type 22 (a regular hexagon) and a regional variant of a square design only found in Suffolk and so known to modern observers as the 'Suffolk Square' (Figures 2.18-19). The exact reason for the latter's restricted distribution is unknown, but is almost certainly an idiosyncrasy of the Engineer Companies attached to 55th Division. According to a Divisional summary in November 1940, some 870 pillboxes had been constructed in the three coastal Sub-Sectors, of which 245 were Suffolk Squares and 625 Type 22s.[66] Field survey confirms the suggestion of the documentary evidence that the balance of the two types was uneven across the Sector: Type 22s are in the majority in Sub-Sectors 1 and 3 and Suffolk Squares predominate in Sub-Sector 2. Within these two broad typological categories numerous minor differences exist in details such as construction materials, the arrangement of blast walls, embrasures and internal shelving arrangements, all of which serves as a reminder that pillboxes reflect very local conditions.

The Type 22s and Suffolk Squares were intended to protect their occupants against small arms fire only; they were not hardened 'shell proof' structures, something

---

65   Hegarty and Newsome, *Suffolk's Defended Shore*, p. 60.

66   Although it should be noted that a proportion of these were inland and outside of the bounds of the present study area. TNA WO 166/693 (War Diary, 55th Division, CRE), Statement of works completed to Midnight 2/3 November 1940, 3.11.40.

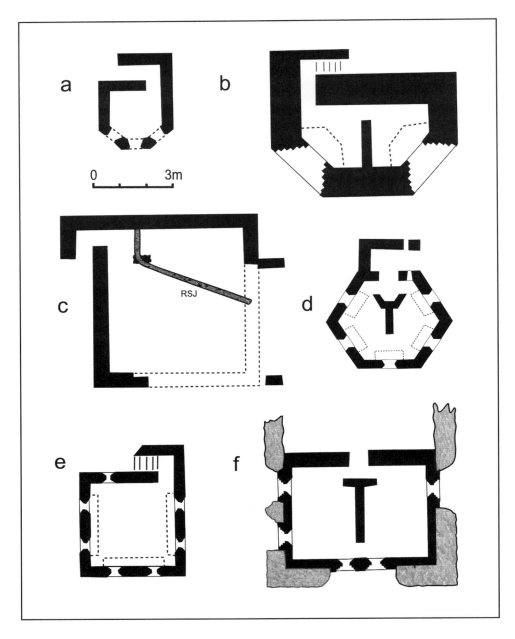

Figure 2.18. Plans of concrete structures from the Sector, 1940: a) Artillery Observation Post, Walberswick; b) Heavy Machine Gun 'shell-proof' pillbox, Blythburgh; c) emplacement for static 4-inch gun, Thorpeness; d) Type 22 pillbox, Wilford Bridge; e) 'Suffolk Square' pillbox, Thorpeness; f) pillbox in medieval 'chapel', Minsmere.

Figure 2.19. 'Suffolk Square' pillbox at Hoist Covert, Walberswick. The design was unique to 55th Division and chiefly confined to the Sandlings. The bullet marks on the face of the structure are a result of training in the mid-war period when the pillbox was used for the staging of mock attacks.

brutally exposed when two shots from a 2-pounder anti-tank gun were fired at one by 2nd Liverpool Scottish with the result that one round went clean through and the other demolished one of the walls.[67] Alongside the two dominant types a smaller number of other designs exist, with the most significant regional designs again probably originating from 55th Division's Engineers. These included a shell-proof pillbox for use with the Vickers machine gun and an air defence variant of the Suffolk Square with an additional open bay for the mounting of a machine gun. Elsewhere, other designs are fewer in number and probably represent one-offs or responses to particular circumstances. A hybrid of the Suffolk Square and a rectangular Type 23 is known from Trimley St Mary, while at Bawdsey radar station bespoke concrete works for infantry positions were dug into the cliff face in order to give a field of fire onto the beach below. As few, if any, new pillboxes were built after November 1940 (for reasons explained below), as a group they reflect arrangements from a relatively brief period in the invasion summer.

The distribution of pillboxes dovetails well with the general locations of troops given in war diaries, but adds important detail to local arrangements – this is one instance where the archaeological evidence comes into its own. In sum, the evidence indicates that the forward infantry battalions of 55th Division in 1940 arranged

---

67   TNA WO 166/4434 (War Diary, 2nd Liverpool Scottish), 28.9.40.

their four rifle companies in a 'three up, one back' formation, a practical method of maximising the battalion frontage while retaining a reserve and a degree of defence in depth. The positions of the forward 'up' companies are frequently marked out by a line of pillboxes, with arrangements particularly clear at Lowestoft, Southwold and Felixstowe. In a rare survival, an almost complete pillbox complex at Knodishall Whin represents the position of the reserve 'back' company of the 9th King's at Aldeburgh. 'Three up, one back' was a standard formation, but while a battalion in defence might expect to have a frontage of c.2200 metres at most, in the Sandlings most were significantly longer, often over ten kilometres. The result was that the distances between company areas and their component platoon and section posts were often considerable, and the mapping of pillboxes points up the often highly dispersed nature of the infantry positions. Between Orford and East Lane Bawdsey the pattern of pillboxes represents the platoon localities of the 1st Liverpool Scottish that are otherwise unrecorded in their unit war diary, but which the geography reveals were widely scattered, with significant intervening gaps between section posts.[68] With so much ground to cover, especially in Sub-Sector 2, section posts tended to be placed in a line, leaving no opportunity for defence in depth or 'all round defence', something that is crucial to understanding why they were subject to so much criticism later in the year and in 1941.

As well as the concentrations on and around the potential landing beaches, pillboxes cluster at the Sector's designated vulnerable points, such as the radar stations at Bawdsey, searchlight positions and Nodal Points such as Leiston and Saxmundham, and occasionally mark the sites of roadblocks. Where beaches were less suitable for landings or where the coastline comprised inundated marshland, fixed defences were fewer and consequently pillboxes less densely scattered. Here some of the decision-making process of 1940 reveals itself; with such long fronts to defend, in places where natural or man-made obstacles existed the density of pillboxes was correspondingly lower. In Sub-Sector 2 the relationship between landscape and pillboxes is particularly clear, with concrete structures clustered in the areas of beaches or beach exits, and at the radar station at Dunwich, and largely absent from the intervening areas, which comprised either flooded marsh or cliff. On the Minsmere levels there was only one pillbox along a five-kilometre stretch between Dunwich cliff and Goose Hill. As the area had been flooded and could be covered by fire from the higher ground to the north and south the only infantry position necessary was in the ruined medieval chapel of the former monastery, which it shamelessly used as camouflage (Figures 1.6; 2.18f).

The Sandlings pillboxes were built either directly by the Divisional Engineers or the pioneer corps, or by contractors working under the supervision of army officers. In at least one case the uniformity of the surviving examples suggests that they were built

---

68   TNA WO 166/4433 (War Diary, 1st Liverpool Scottish), 25–26.5.40.

by the same group or working party: in the hinterland of Thorpeness the similarity of the concrete blocks and minor design details of Suffolk Squares, combined with graffiti from 558 Field Company Royal Engineers, argues that they were built by the company men themselves. Elsewhere the geography of the local landscape had a direct effect on the nature of the design. A striking lack of uniformity is seen to the north of Shingle Street, where, over a three-kilometre stretch of coast from Oxley Dairy to Simpson's Saltings, of the nine extant pillboxes only three are of the exact same design, with the remainder all exhibiting significant variations. The two Suffolk Squares are both of subtly different form in order to facilitate placement on the earthwork bank marking the sea wall, while one Type 22 has a loopholed blast wall and flying buttress, presumably as a safeguard against slippage resulting from erosion. In the case of a square pillbox of 'Admiralty' design, it is the only example known in Suffolk and again is probably connected with its siting within the sea wall.

Field artillery

The final element of the coastal defences was artillery. The Royal Artillery was one of the most successful arms of the British army in the Second World War but as an element in the anti-invasion landscape its role is often curiously understated.[69] In coastal defence artillery fulfilled a number of roles, principally the engagement of hostile vessels as they neared the coast; firing directly on the shoreline and beaches, and subsequently inland as the enemy gained a foothold; and firing on any forces that had landed behind the lines. The stopping power of a defensive artillery bombardment, especially when used against troops in the open, had been clearly demonstrated during the First World War and artillery had the potential to seriously hamper any German attempt to effect a landing. In April 1940 only a dozen serviceable guns were available to 55th Division and the invasion summer was characterised by both a steady build-up of additional weapons and the gradual upgrading of the ordnance available so that by November 151 guns of all kinds were within the Sector. It is important to stress, however, that the artillery provision displayed considerable diversity and, as a fighting 'arm', was made up of different elements, each with a slightly different role and landscape context (Figure 2.20).

The artillery used in the anti-invasion landscape came in a variety of forms. Static anti-tank guns were initially placed on the coast so they could fire directly on the beaches, with improvised mobile versions, comprising 4-inch guns mounted on lorries and 6-pounders mounted on an armoured train, intended to guard the roads leading inland.[70] The bulk of the artillery support was provided by the heavier calibre guns of the Field and Medium Artillery regiments, manning either single guns that could shoot directly on the beaches or, more usually, troops of four guns (chiefly

---

69   J.B.A. Bailey, *Field Artillery and Firepower*, 2nd edn (Annapolis, MD, 2004).

70   TNA WO 166/1441 (War Diary, No. 1 Armoured Train Group).

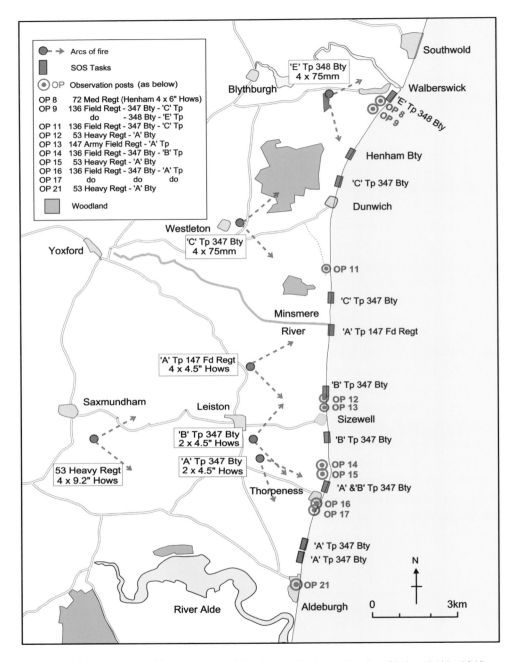

Figure 2.20. Map showing artillery landscape of Sub-Sector 2 between the river Blyth and Alde, 1940, showing gun positions for medium and heavy artillery, observation posts and SOS tasks.

6-inch howitzers and American-imported French 75mm guns) placed behind the lines to provide indirect fire. In addition, Heavy Artillery regiments (chiefly with 9.2-inch howitzers) were placed further inland in a similar role. The contribution of these guns was particularly important in 1940, as artillery was the primary mechanism by which thinly stretched infantrymen were to be supported.

The arrangement and exact siting of the guns on the ground reflected a number of factors, such as the range of the weapon concerned, the area to be defended and the need for camouflage. Those guns that were required to shoot directly on the beaches were usually sited to one side of their designated target area so that they could provide enfilade fire and so make best use of their long range. For example, five such guns (comprising 18-pounders, two of which were later replaced with 4-inch guns) were sited individually in Sub-Sector 2, each of which was intended to fire on beaches at Benacre, Kessingland, Southwold, Dunwich and Sizewell respectively. These and the small number of anti-tank guns available to 55th Division tended initially to be given sandbagged emplacements that were later replaced in concrete. The latter were often rudimentary structures; that for a 4-inch gun at Thorpeness comprised an open emplacement with little in the way of protection for the gunners (Figure 2.18 c).

Back from the coastline itself, there were, in effect, two further gun lines. Positions for the medium artillery were usually from five to eight kilometres inland, with the heavier artillery further back at approximately nine kilometres. Such locations permitted best use of the ranges of the guns concerned and the widest possible arc of fire. The general shortage of equipment meant that, as with the infantry, units were expected to cover a much greater front than normally would have been anticipated. As a consequence, the constituent troops of batteries were spread out over unusually long distances; the two troops of A Battery, 72 Medium Regiment at Wrentham and Henham were some six kilometres apart in order that together they could cover 12 kilometres of coastline. The danger from air attack meant that the preferred location for field artillery positions was in woodland. Typically gun pits were dug on the woodland edge and the guns – while in theory they could be fired from their pits – were wheeled forward and fired on open ground, so as to permit the widest possible arc of fire. Here, too, gun pits were at first hastily built sandbagged structures, although engineer diaries record that those for some heavier guns were at least partially finished in concrete, probably for floors where holdfasts were needed and where pits walls required additional revetment. Above the pits camouflage nets could be supported by a frame of poles, and photographs from 1940 show gun houses of timber generously garnished with scrim and foliage (Figure 2.21).

By September 1940 it was, in theory, possible for field artillery to cover the entire Sector front with defensive fire. Targets were determined by forward observers in observation posts who could relay information back to their guns by field telephone and, where the equipment was available, by radio. Despite the requirement to cover

Figure 2.21. Field gun position near Ipswich, 1940. The rough and ready nature of these posts is obvious enough and they tended to be replaced over time by concrete structures. (IWM H2243)

long stretches of coastline with fire, those areas that particularly required defence were singled out for special arrangements. Specific areas were pre-registered and designated as 'SOS' tasks so that fire could immediately be brought to bear on them on a given signal. The observers or the defending infantry could initiate such a task by a signal rocket, at which point shells would descend in a matter of minutes. The locations of the designated SOS tasks reveal much about how the artillery was to be employed in the event of action. Ten such tasks existed between the Blyth and the Alde and most covered likely disembarkation points on the beaches or bottlenecks where invading troops would be constrained by topography. Walberswick, Dunwich, Sizewell and Aldeburgh beaches all had SOS tasks (Sizewell had two) but the location of others evidences a concern to cover even relatively minor exits from potential beachheads.

As the artillery defence relied so heavily on the ability of the forward observers to direct their guns, the position of observation posts (OPs) and the protection of their occupants were crucial to its effectiveness. The locations chosen for OPs were those that tended to offer exceptionally wide fields of vision. Martello Towers, water towers, windmills and private houses with commanding sea views all found themselves

Figure 2.22. A concrete artillery observation post, Walberswick, dating to the summer of 1940. This structure replaced an earlier improvised post on Walberswick church tower.

pressed into use. The area's rich legacy of late medieval churches also provided ready-made positions for observation and, in defiance of the Geneva Convention's prohibition on the use of religious buildings for military purposes, the church towers at Covehithe, Reydon, Southwold, Thorpeness and Walberswick were all used as OPs during the invasion summer. In the absence of tall buildings the natural topography was exploited, as at Walberswick, where both OPs were situated on a spur overlooking the Corporation marshes. In other cases OPs were sited either very close to, or sometimes right on, the beaches themselves. At Thorpeness an OP was established at Haven House, immediately fronting onto the beach, while two similar locations were used at Sizewell, both of which visually commanded the whole beach area and the designated SOS tasks. Here, the OPs were closely integrated with the immediate infantry positions, a spatial indication of how closely the two arms were expected to work together in action. Together with the clear visual benefits of such a forward location, such positions may also have been chosen to facilitate the observer's ability to hear the approach of any invasion craft, particularly at night (Figure 2.22).[71]

71   Robertson, *Rose and the Arrow*, p. 51.

OPs display more variety in their design than infantry pillboxes. In part, many were improvised to meet specific local purposes, especially at the start of the summer, when OPs were built of sandbags or a pre-existing building was simply occupied by the men and their equipment, but from July both these options tended to be replaced by concrete structures. At Benacre Ness and Southwold two identical concrete examples are known, taking the form of structures with a single long opening for observation, while at Walberswick and Sizewell a different design – with a hexagonal front and three apertures for observation – remain extant. In both cases the designs are unusual and appear to be the only ones of their kind identified across the country; their idiosyncrasy is probably again connected to the Divisional Engineers responsible for their construction, as their structural affinity with the 'Suffolk Square' pillbox is clearly evident.

The coastal crust: regionalism and topography

The forms and functions of these various obstacles are well documented in the specialist literature on this subject and numerous local case studies exist from across the country showing how they were configured on the ground, but none has taken place at the level of the Divisional Sector. Analysis at this scale is revealing, however, as it shows that it was the grouping of different elements and their particular arrangement within a very regional environment that helped give the 55th Division's piece of coastal crust a distinctive character (Figures 2.23–2.24).

The areas that tended to see heavy concentrations of obstacles were those beaches identified in the May 1940 beach reconnaissance as vulnerable to an enemy landing: Gunton Denes, Benacre and Kessingland, Southwold and Walberswick, Sizewell, Aldeburgh, Shingle Street and Felixstowe. While less vulnerable parts of the coastline also received their share of defence works, it is only at the former that obstacles such as barbed wire, dragon's teeth, mines and anti-tank blocks were placed together. It was also in the vicinity of these beaches that the majority of infantry positions were sited. While commanders prioritised some places to defend over others, the structuring agent when it came to the arrangement of obstacles on the ground was topography. As a result, the 'spurs' identified in tactical appreciations tended to see a clustering of defences, with those low-lying intervening areas seeing relatively fewer. In some cases it is possible to see how the geography was used to facilitate the best use of specific weapons. Where there were extensive fields of fire, the range of the Vickers machine gun (four to five kilometres) could be exploited to the full, and so they tended to be used either for enfilading fire across long areas of coastline, as at the southern end of Dunwich Heath, or inland as the final line of defence against troops breaking out of the beaches, as at Walberswick and Benacre (Figure 2.25).

But the structuring hand of topography was seen in other ways. The extensive open beaches of the Sandlings did not lend themselves to easy defence, in part because of a lack of headlands or rocky outcrops that would otherwise break the coastline into

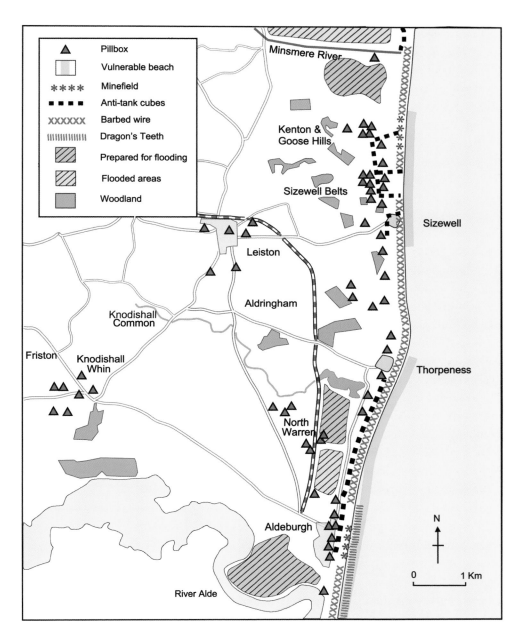

Figure 2.23. Map showing obstacles and concrete defences around Sizewell, 1940.

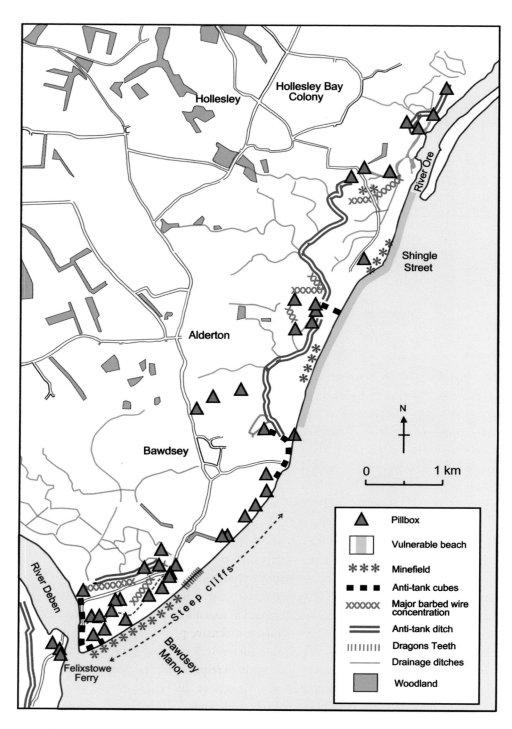

Figure 2.24. Map showing obstacles and concrete defences around Shingle Street, 1940.

Figure 2.25. Heavy machine gun pillboxes at Blythburgh, 1940. These housed Vickers machine guns, which tended to be sited in order to enfilade the long Sandlings beaches or, as here, inland to fire on the principal routes leading inland.

discrete defensible sections and impede lateral movement. In the absence of what on other parts of Britain's coastline had been provided by nature, such hindrances had to be created by man. The extensive linear runs of barbed wire, minefields and anti-tank cubes placed along the shoreline, which were such characteristic features of the coastal defences, simply ran parallel to the shore. Shorter perpendicular runs intended to prevent lateral movement tended to be found in those places where geology ensured that beaches were at their narrowest. In Sub-Sectors 2 and 3, where the topography of the coastline was relatively undifferentiated, this resulted in extensive areas of beach 'boxed in' by obstacles. In Sub-Sector 1 and in Sub-Sector 2 north of Southwold, by contrast, the existence of cliffs and bodies of water close to the shore at Easton, Covehithe and Benacre Broads meant that the lines of obstacles were correspondingly shorter, and served more to link these favourable topographic features. Here, beaches tended to be divided up into smaller compartments than further south. Man-made barriers to lateral movement on beaches, such as anti-tank blocks, tended to be shorter and only obstructed beach exits or formed a defensive perimeter for vulnerable sites. Elsewhere, the geography also worked to the defender's advantage. Stretches of cliff that could not easily be scaled or traversed by vehicles required less in the way of protection and so tended to receive fewer obstacles, although, as cliffs in the Sandlings tended to be shallow, few such places were left entirely undefended. The only place to escape the building of beach defences altogether was Orford Ness, owing to its unsuitability for an amphibious landing. While the individual obstacles were never mutually exclusive,

Figure 2.26. Rare wartime ground view of the coastal crust defences looking south from Dunwich Heath over what is now the Minsmere RSPB reserve. This image is a panorama made up from film footage shot on 27 September 1940 and shows a thin line of defences with the Minsmere levels slowly being inundated with water. Compare with similar view in Figure 1.10. (IWM AYY 41)

some combinations were less favoured than others. Only in the exceptional case of Bawdsey Radar Station do minefields ever seem to have been laid below cliffs, as the natural defence was clearly felt to be sufficient. The need to have anti-tank obstacles across as much of the Divisional front as possible clearly emerges as a priority, but there was no attempt to create any defence in depth and so it was unusual for anti-tank blocks to be used in conjunction with anti-tank ditches, as seen at Shingle Street, where blocks were absent along the front of the wet anti-tank ditch and were used only in short sections at either end to seal off the exits.

With its section posts, pillboxes, obstacles and artillery support, this, then, was the piece of Ironside's coastal crust as it came to exist in the Sandlings, and it came together in a remarkably short period of time. A detailed comparison of 55th Division's war diaries permits its chronological development to be reconstructed with a high degree of precision. As has been seen, the initial deployment of the infantry took place very quickly after 10 May and thereafter trenches were excavated, with some units preoccupied by digging and wiring for up to ten weeks; this extended period was probably accounted for in some cases by a lack of adequate entrenching

tools.[72] The third week of June began to see Ironside's scheme take shape, as it was in this month that the arrival of large quantities of barbed wire, the delivery of mines, the construction of anti-tank blocks and dragon's teeth and the building of concrete pillboxes is recorded. The speed of work was considerable as, where such statements exist, war diaries record units as having completed their defence works at the end of July (Figure 2.26).[73] A snapshot of this process is provided by an aerial photograph of Walberswick on 8 July showing considerable activity in the locations that would later have pillboxes, with newly cut gaps in hedges suggestive of an imminent structure. Furthermore, if this particular photograph shows the moment that 'C' Company 2nd/4th South Lancashires was receiving its concrete fortifications then it also gives a glimpse of the method: in this instance, the positions on the flanks were completed first, with the central part of the line subsequently filled in.[74] Across the whole of the divisional area July was the month that saw the various elements of Ironside's scheme come together. By this date a number of Stop Lines crossed the Sandlings, with Lines

72   TNA WO 166/4434 (War Diary, 2nd Liverpool Scottish), 28.5.40; TNA WO 166/4454 (War Diary, 7th Manchester Regiment), 14.9.40.

73   TNA WO 166/4452 (War Diary, 6th Manchester Regiment), 30.6.40; TNA WO 166/1037 (War Diary, 164th Infantry Brigade), 18.6.40; TNA WO 166/4679 (War Diary, 1st/4th South Lancashire Regiment), 17.6.40; TNA WO 166/4412 (War Diary, 2nd/8th Lancashire Fusiliers), 18.7.40.

74   HE (NMR) RAF Photography, RAF 2/BR11/14 Frm.34 (8.7.40).

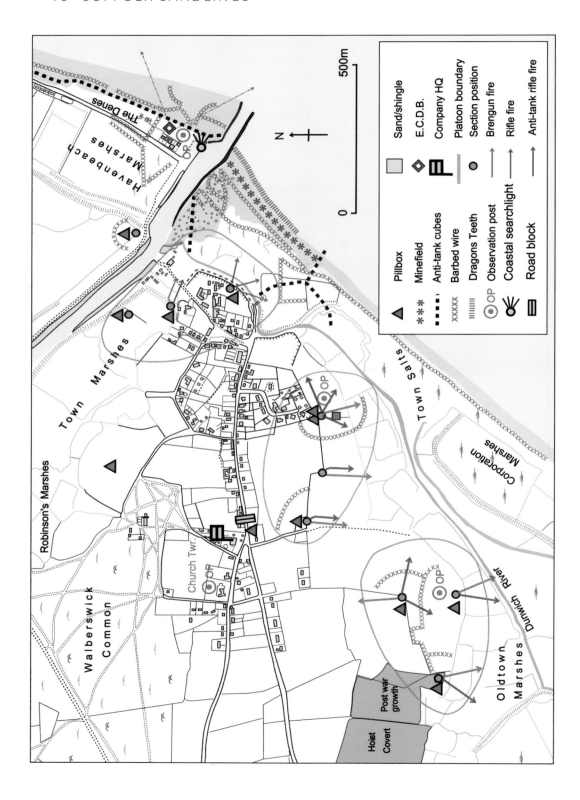

Havenbeach Marshes

The Denes

Town Marshes

Robinson's Marshes

Walberswick Common

Church Twr.

Town Salts

Corporation Marshes

Hoist Covert

Post war growth

Oldtown Marshes

Dunwich River

OP

N

0   500m

▲ Pillbox		▦ Sand/shingle	
✳✳✳ Minefield		◈ E.C.D.B.	
▪▪▪ Anti-tank cubes		▥ Company HQ	
✕✕✕ Barbed wire		▮ Platoon boundary	
▥ Dragons Teeth		● Section position	
◉OP Observation post		➶ Brengun fire	
✸ Coastal searchlight		→ Rifle fire	
▤ Road block		→ Anti-tank rifle fire	

'D', 'E' and 'F' following the course of the Orwell, Deben and Blyth respectively and the 'E–F Switch Line' running parallel to the coast along the railway between Campsea Ashe and Halesworth.[75] The towns and larger villages of the Sandlings were now designated as Nodal Points and here, as well as along the Stop Lines, concrete defences were being put into place. The process of construction had been hurried and confused, but into September the scheme envisaged by Ironside was a meaningful reality on the ground (Figure 2.27).

The coastal crust: chronology and criticism

It is perhaps ironic that after ten weeks of frantic effort and almost at the very moment when they were reaching their completion, the anti-invasion defences started to draw criticism, both from outsiders and also from those responsible for their construction. The reasons behind many of the perceived faults were not difficult to find: the speed with which the coastal crust had been completed was praiseworthy, but had led to mistakes. Pillboxes in particular were a cause for unease and, following an inspection of the coastline held by 55th Division during the first week of August by its Commander, General Majendie, he wrote to his brigadiers (Sub-Sector commanders) on the subject. His remarks are worth quoting in full:

> I am very much concerned that we are going pill-box mad, and losing all sense of proportion in the matter of siting defences. The lure of concrete is leading us away from first principles. The countryside is covered with pillboxes, many of which will never be occupied, many could never serve any useful purpose, and many face the wrong way. Much labour, money and material have been wasted. I realise that this is largely due to haste and the desire to get something done quickly … I wish to emphasise that a concrete pill-box with the weapons at our disposal cannot be regarded as forming an adequate defensive post. It should form part of a small defensive locality. On occasions it may have to stand alone – naked and ashamed – but only when local conditions make this unavoidable.[76]

Such remarks should not be taken as a commentary on the state of the Divisional Sector as a whole because, as field survey makes clear, the distribution of pillboxes was

---

75   TNA WO 166/329 (War Diary, XI Corps), XI Corps Defence Scheme, 30.6.40. The E–F Switch line was also known as the 'Back Line' from 1940, TNA WO 166/688 (War Diary, 55th Division, GS), June–July *passim*; TNA WO 166/4351 (War Diary, 2nd Kensington Regiment), 30.7.40.

76   TNA WO 166/688 (War Diary, 55th Division, GS), Appendix 1, Pill-Box Complex, 5.8.40.

Figure 2.27. (Left) Map of Walberswick showing anti-invasion defences in September 1940. By this date, Ironside's 'coastal crust' was a reality on the ground. Note how the fixed obstacles such as dragon's teeth and anti-tank blocks were on the beach itself, with the line of infantry section posts crossing the 'spur' from the river Blyth to the Oldtown marshes.

uneven. Majendie's comments probably refer to places where the numbers exceeded those of the infantry sections expected to man them, something chiefly seen at those beaches felt to be particularly at risk, such as Sizewell and Southwold, but also where section posts with a single pillbox were particularly isolated. Analysis of battalion war diaries shows that in places Majendie's inspection directly triggered changes on the ground. Alterations began immediately to add depth to the line of the 2nd Liverpool Scottish, who reported that 'The General came to see A and B Coy positions having been to see D Coy yesterday. He has unexpectedly ordered drastic changes in our own dispositions which will mean a heavy programme of work for weeks to come. We are not amused.'[77] In this particular case, it is probably significant that, to judge from the distance between pillboxes, the battalion's posts were thinly scattered as a result of attempting to cover the maximum length of coastline possible with the number of troops available. Here the coastal crust was very thin indeed.

More subtle was the suggestion that concrete was taking the siting of defences away from tactical principles and, implicitly, that the style of defence of which pillboxes formed a part was suspect. Here the national context is again important, as Majendie's comments reflected the changed mood at senior levels in the army. Ironside had been replaced as Commander in Chief by Alan Brooke on 19 July on the grounds that an officer with command experience of recent operations was a more suitable candidate to direct the nation's defence.[78] In fact, Ironside was in part a victim of some uncomfortable truths that emerged during the post-mortem following Dunkirk. The army high command was left with the task of explaining why the British Expeditionary Force had fared so badly in France and part of the blame was laid at the door of the defensive tactics employed, which owed more to the previous war than the one being fought in the present. Ideas of 'linear' defence were seen as outmoded in what was now deemed as a new age of mobile warfare and a doctrine that favoured 'all round defence' was seen as more credible.[79] Ironside's Stop Lines in particular drew criticism and Brooke immediately disassociated himself from the scheme of his predecessor in favour of a strategy based on mobile reserves. His command both reflected and influenced a more general change in military thinking concerning how defences should be engineered. Much has been written about the military politics at this time, and it appears clear that, faced with a chronic lack of equipment, Ironside had little choice but to devise a strategy based upon a static defence, whereas Brooke had the benefit of increasing numbers of men and equipment and so had the luxury of being able to turn his preferred ideal into reality. Yet if antiquity was being sought in Britain anti-invasion defences then evidence could be found aplenty. As this discussion has made clear, much of what was put in place in 1940 owed its origins to the Great War,

---

77   TNA WO 166/4434 (War Diary, 2nd Liverpool Scottish), 4–5.8.40.

78   B. Bond, 'Ironside', in J. Keegan (ed.), *Churchill's Generals* (London, 1992), pp. 17–33.

79   French, *Raising Churchill's Army*, pp. 189–90.

no more so than many of the weapons employed: the guns for the Emergency Coastal Defence Batteries, the improvised anti-tank guns and field artillery pieces were all of First World War vintage. If their arrangement on the prepared battlefield was in part reminiscent of the previous conflict, then this could only heighten the perception of a landscape laid out for a battle of the past, rather than the present. Crucially, the long thin lines of pillboxes lining long stretches of the Sandlings coast looked uncannily like a Maginot line in miniature. Little wonder that, with the new mood, Majendie looked to make changes.

The events at national level soon began to be reflected in the Sandlings. In Eastern Command Brooke's tenure had an almost immediate effect, not least in the cessation of new concrete works, with only existing contracts to be honoured. In early November 55th Division were rotated into the General Headquarters reserve and relieved of their coastal defence duties. The achievements of the summer were clearly a source of pride for those who took part, but for the veterans of 42nd Division lately returned from France who replaced them, the defensive works put in place left much to be desired, and a host of problems with the works of the summer were identified. In places pillboxes were so close together that they interfered with lines of fire, while elsewhere positions were too far apart or there were simply no defences at all; section posts were poorly camouflaged, others were inadequately drained and lacked revetting, so that they were beginning to collapse; overhead cover for such posts was often too heavy and so liable to fail; and owing to the movement of the sea the exact location of minefields was uncertain.[80] Underpinning these practical deficiencies, however, was the more deep-seated sense that the tactical principles that lay behind the 1940 works was at fault. What was termed the 'Maginot Mentality' – a short-hand for linear defensive tactics that were deemed to have failed so spectacularly in France – was the root cause of the problem.[81] The assessment of Sub-Sector 2 in particular was damning:

The defences are linear all down the beaches, and they just 'happened'. The 55 Div[ision] stuck pillboxes, gun pits, guns etc just where they wanted them. We shall have to round the area up and make it into a defensive area … when we get fixed up we shall have to re-organise these defences, but the General is of the opinion that nothing should be done until the Spring, if we did any digging now it would not be worth while.[82]

80   TNA WO 166/4393 (War Diary, 5th King's Own Royal Regiment), 5.11.40; TNA WO 166/977 (War Diary, 127th Infantry Brigade), 127th Infantry Brigade Operation Instruction No. 12, 25.11.40; 127th Infantry Brigade Operation Instruction No. 13, 3.12.40; TNA WO 166/4409 (War Diary, 1st/6th Lancashire Fusiliers), 28.1.41.

81   TNA WO 199/44 (Concrete Defences Policy), General Staff Directive on the choice of concrete or earthworks for deliberate field defence, draft paper, August 1941; TNA WO 166/975 (War Diary, 125th Infantry Brigade), Summary of Brigadier's Conference, 8.11.40.

82   TNA WO 166/975 (War Diary, 125th Infantry Brigade) Points from Brigadier's Conference, 17.10.40.

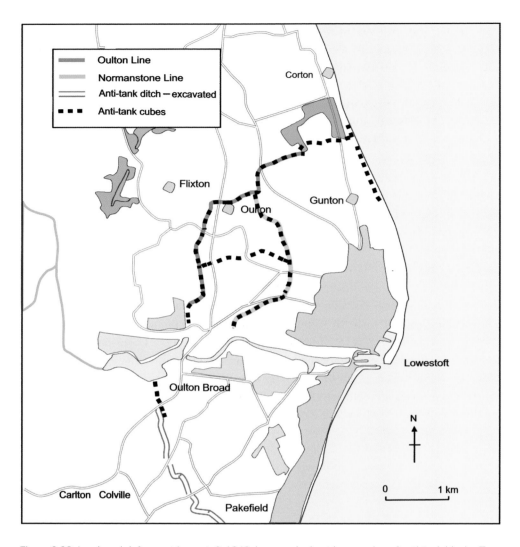

Figure 2.28. Landward defence at Lowestoft 1940, here marked out by mapping of anti-tank blocks. Two successive defensive lines, the 'Normanstone' and 'Oulton' existed to defend the western approaches to the town. Here 'all round', rather than 'linear' defence existed from the start and was facilitated by greater manpower. The anti-tank ditch to the south was probably added in 1941.

While a certain level of denigration of the coastal defences can be explained by mockery associated with the inter-unit rivalry familiar to the British army, such criticisms were bound up in the broader process of troops distancing themselves from defences increasingly seen as obsolete. The new mantra was one of 'all round defence', where posts give each other mutual support, rather than being placed in lines. But detailed study of defence plans also shows that elsewhere the Divisional front was not always quite of 'linear' form and so some of this criticism was unfair. At Lowestoft over the summer two westward-facing lines of defences – the 'Normanstone' and the 'Oulton' lines – as well as those facing seaward, were constructed so that the town had a defended perimeter (Figure 2.28).[83] Similarly, at Felixstowe a scheme to protect the rearward defences of the town by providing positions in depth was also in hand relatively early.[84] The importance of 'all round defence' can also be found in documents as early as May, but this was only viable where geography and manpower permitted such schemes to be enacted on the ground.[85]

That 55th Division's deployment should be criticised not just by their successors but also a little earlier by its own commander not only reflected a changing mood higher up the chain of command but also pointed up a certain loss of control during the initial stages of the invasion crisis. Decisions on where to site positions had been taken quickly by men under considerable stress, with the overwhelming impression given by operational orders throughout the summer one of officers at the mercy of events, rather than in command of them. The observation that 55th Division's defences had 'just happened' was uncannily near the mark, as they had indeed come about from a myriad of local decisions; even at such an important asset as Bawdsey Manor, additional defences were forthcoming only after plaintive pleas for assistance from the station commander.[86] As a result, local tactical schemes differed considerably and this localism was itself largely structured by topography. The panicked state in which it had initially come into being goes a long way to explaining why 55th Division's piece of coastal crust varied along its length. In 1940 it was the men on the ground, rather than the general above, who had had to decide how they would fight them on the beaches.

83   TNA WO 166/4454 (War Diary, 7th Manchester Regiment), 19.9.40.
84   TNA WO 166/4357 (War Diary, 13th King's (Liverpool) Regiment), 7.11.40.
85   TNA WO 166/4433 (War Diary, 1st Liverpool Scottish), Operational Instruction No. 14, 29.5.40; TNA WO 166/1052 (War Diary, 199th Infantry Brigade), Operational Order No. 1, 26.6.40.
86   G. Kinsey, *Bawdsey. Birth of the Beam* (Lavenham, 1983), pp. 57–8.

Chapter 3

Consolidation and reorganisation, 1941–42

Introduction

Under Brooke's command, Britain's anti-invasion strategy was subject to considerable readjustment, with the central principle being an active, rather than a static, defence. Formations from the field army were to defend only the most vulnerable parts of the coast, second-class divisions the remainder, with the balance of the nation's home forces held back as a mobile reserve.[1] The areas of coastline deemed to be particularly exposed to attack and so worthy of the attention of a field division were those of Kent and Sussex, facing occupied France across the Pas de Calais, and that of Suffolk, which faced the Low Countries: the Sandlings was now officially in the front line against invasion.[2]

A strategy in which mobile reserves would play the crucial role did not, however, mean that the coastal crust was to be neglected. In Brooke's scheme holding up an invasion force near their initial landing places bought time for his reserves to move forward; fighting the decisive battle close to the beaches was infinitely preferable to letting the enemy advance inland.[3] So, far from being weakened, the more problematic elements of Ironside's scheme were to be eradicated through a major reconfiguration and the coastal defences themselves were to be strengthened. This reorganisation was a process – rather than an event – that was planned in November 1940 and initiated in January 1941 by 42nd Division, continued by 15th Division until September 1941 and, finally, brought to a conclusion by 54th Division in the spring of 1942. By the time of its completion the anti-invasion landscape of 1940 had been significantly altered in a number of key respects.

The process of consolidation needs to be set alongside three additional changes. Firstly, in October 1940 the Sector's manpower was increased by 25 per cent with the permanent attachment of an independent infantry brigade. Secondly, this increase in strength facilitated a reshaping of Sub-Sector boundaries. From January 1941 an additional Sub-Sector was created between Pakefield and Southwold so that the

---

1   B. Collier, *The Defence of the United Kingdom* (London, 1957), pp. 229–30.

2   TNA WO 166/1 (War Diary, GHQ Home Forces), Military Defence of the United Kingdom, 27.11.40.

3   D. Newbold, 'British Planning and Preparations to Resist Invasion on Land, September 1939–September 1940', PhD Thesis (King's College London, 1988), pp. 367, 388.

Divisional front was now divided into four, rather than three. As has been seen, the stretch of coastline between Lowestoft and Aldeburgh had been particularly undermanned in 1940 and the new arrangements significantly reduced brigade and battalion fronts in the areas concerned, although troops across the front remained stretched. With a greater quantity of reserves inland, it permitted as many troops to be committed forward as possible, so that, by the middle of the summer, the four forward brigades of each Sub-Sector had all their battalions in a 'three up' formation. And thirdly, in accordance with changes in policy at a national level, the majority of Stop Lines that crossed Suffolk were abandoned, with the defence of the interior resting on the network of existing Nodal Points, which were to be provided with stronger defences. Only two Stop Lines escaped the cull: the Corps Line in the west of the county and, in the Sandlings, parts of the existing 'E', 'F' and the 'E–F Switch' lines, which were now extended north from Halesworth to Beccles along the course of the railway line to form what was now known as the 'Back Line'. This new defence line linked up a series of Nodal Points from Beccles to Ipswich to form a defensive belt parallel to the coast across the whole Sector and would be the first inland line met by an invader breaking out from the beaches.[4] It was within this new framework that the anti-invasion landscape was re-defined (Figure 3.1).

The principles of reorganisation, 1940–41

As early as 14 November the outline of the new scheme was set out, which was, where practicable, to be completed by the following March. Vulnerable beaches were to be strengthened so that they had three lines of 'double apron' barbed wire and two anti-tank obstacles. The most significant change, however, concerned the infantry defences. These were to be reorganised in order to give greater depth, with 'the present linear system' substituted for 'a system of strong localities capable of all round defence'.[5] Such localities were to comprise well-sited and concealed infantry fieldworks that were securely revetted, adequately drained, correctly camouflaged and surrounded by barbed wire and an anti-tank obstacle. Localities were still to be organised on a platoon basis but, rather than having section posts strung out in a line, these were to be arranged in such a way that they could offer mutual support, and so they could fire in all directions. Within the perimeter of these localities, or covered by their fire, anti-tank guns, field artillery and heavy machine guns could also be sited. Such heavily fortified positions were expected to hold up an enemy advance for a greater period of time than a platoon whose section posts were isolated. It was fully accepted that there would sometimes be considerable gaps between localities, but these were to be made

---

4   The change noted in the following maps: TNA WO 166/688 (War Diary, 55th Division, GS), Defence Scheme, July 1940; TNA WO 166/495 (War Diary, 42nd Division, GS), 42 Division Defence Scheme, January 1941; TNA WO 166/329 (War Diary, XI Corps), Operational Instruction No. 40, 14.11.40.

5   *Ibid.*, Operational Instruction No. 45, 29.11.40.

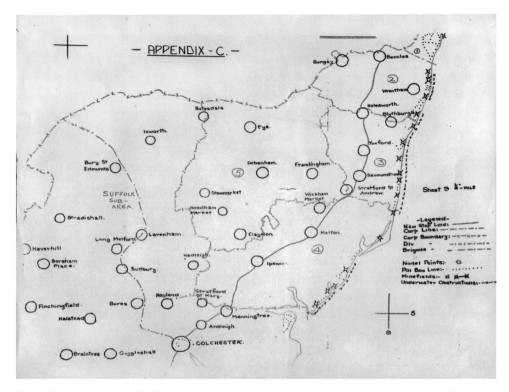

Figure 3.1. The defence of Suffolk in January 1941, showing 42 Division's new arrangement of Sub-Sectors, Nodal Points and remaining Stop Lines. From 42 Division war diary. (TNA WO 166/495)

as impassable as possible to enemy vehicles by obstructions and covered by fire from the localities themselves. The front line troops were still not permitted to withdraw and were expected to hold on to the bitter end, but in continuing to defend their positions, even when bypassed by the invading forces, they might have some hope that they would be relieved by counter-attacking reserves.[6]

An additional factor informing the new strategy was the concern that during an invasion the coastal defences would be attacked by airborne forces, either before or at the same time as a beach landing. Such an eventuality had informed British planning since late 1939, but German use of paratroopers and glider troops in 1940 furthered the expectation that a major blow would come from inland. In the light of this, when it came to placing their forces on the ground, commanders faced a dilemma. Although manpower on the coast had increased, it was not sufficient to adequately defend the coastline from east *and* west; as the commander of Sub-Sector 3 put it, he was 'facing

6   *Ibid.*, Revised Defence Scheme, 5.1.41.

a 24 mile attack from either way'.[7] In order to provide support for their comrades directly on the beaches those troops defending in depth would ideally be no more than one kilometre back, but in order to adequately defend likely drop zones and landing grounds they needed to be at least three to five kilometres inland. The solution, as worked out and tested through exercises simulating a major seaborne assault, was that the Division would concentrate on holding both the seaward defences facing east and an inner defence line facing *west*.[8] The Division's heavy and field artillery was to be concentrated between these lines, with all potential landing grounds and roads blocked or otherwise obstructed, and the Division would fight its battle from its positions in the hope that Brooke's mobile reserve would swiftly come to the rescue. While Britain now had 'mobility' at the heart of its national defence plan, on the coast it still very much meant a static defence fought on a prepared battlefield, and this is directly reflected in the field evidence. While necessarily complex to relate, the changes seen at this time brought the anti-invasion landscape to a level of elaboration that it was not to see again during the conflict.

A new landscape: forward defended localities

In contrast to the hasty siting of infantry positions that had taken place in May 1940, the placement of the new infantry localities was conducted with a considerable degree of care. It was appreciated that a significant change in dispositions would take time to complete and units were expected to occupy their existing posts until an informed decision could be taken on new locations. A measure of the importance of the impending change was the personal visit of senior officers to individual battalions specifically to discuss the 'defence problem' in the middle of December.[9] Proposed sites for the new positions were marked up on aerial photographs and late in December a Divisional Conference took place where, in all probability, final decisions were taken, to be acted upon in January.[10] Again, the contrast with May 1940 is instructive as, while battalion and company commanders were to have discretion over the exact siting of their posts, orders stressed that they were not to be allowed to depart from the agreed plan – this time defence works would not 'just happen'.[11] The construction of the new defences was concurrent with the reorganisation of Sub-Sectors, with war diary evidence indicating that work started in January 1941.[12] The 1st/6th Lancashire Fusiliers' diary recorded that 'improving and erecting new defence works in the

---

7   TNA WO 166/975 (War Diary, 125th Infantry Brigade), 125 Infantry Brigade Group Operational Instruction No. 3, Appendix B, 6.1.41.

8   TNA WO 166/977 (War Diary, 127th Infantry Brigade), 22–25.1.41.

9   TNA WO 166/975 (War Diary, 125th Infantry Brigade), Summary of Brigadier's Conference, 6.12.40.

10   TNA WO 166/976 (War Diary, 126th Infantry Brigade), 19.12.40.

11   TNA WO 166/977 (War Diary, 127th Infantry Brigade), 127 Infantry Brigade Operation Instruction No. 13, 3.12.40.

12   TNA WO 166/975 (War Diary, 125th Infantry Brigade), 1.1.41; 25.1.41.

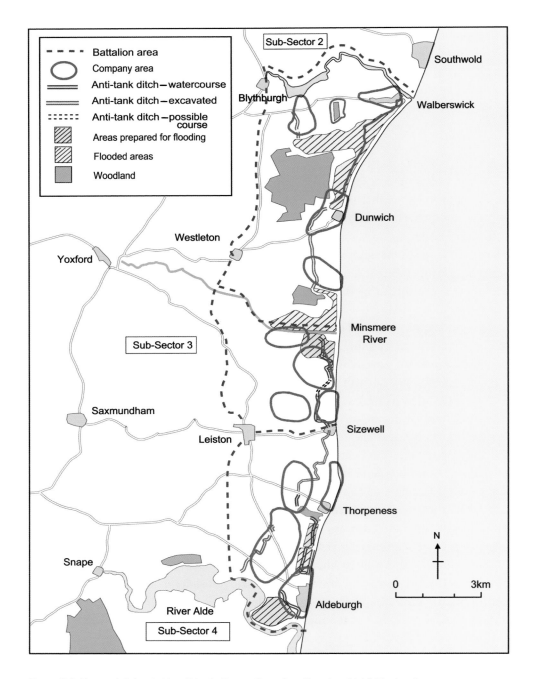

Figure 3.2. Forward defended localities in the northern Sandlings in mid-1941, showing company areas by Sub-Sector. Here the defences were concentrated on the 'spurs' between river valleys and low-lying areas. The provision for defence in depth and for a 'westward' battle is clearly apparent, especially around Walberswick.

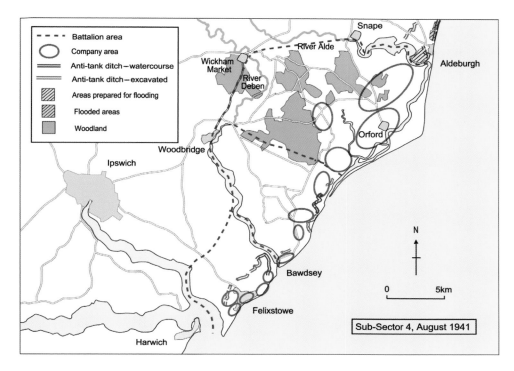

Figure 3.3. Forward defended localities in the southern Sandlings in mid-1941. Here, the topography meant that more 'linear' arrangements tended to remain.

Battalion area' took place during this month, while that of the 1st/5th Lancashire Fusiliers noted that no training had been completed during this same time – a sign that most of their time had been spent constructing fieldworks.[13] By early summer the arrangement of the infantry defences was in places radically different to that of the previous year, as new positions were created and others abandoned. A detailed series of war diaries permit their recovery in detail across the whole Sector (Figures 3.2–3.3).

Immediately apparent is the greater concern for defence in depth and, in particular, the provision for the 'westward' battle against airborne troops. In Sub-Sector 1 at Lowestoft a battalion (one-third of the infantry manpower in the Sub-Sector) was detailed to provide landward defence for the town, which involved the creation from scratch of a new line of posts four kilometres inland (see Figure 3.21). Construction took place from February 1941, with attendant frustrations from the battalion concerned regarding the necessary clearance and digging in heavy clay at what was probably the worse time of year for such an undertaking.[14] In Sub-Sectors

13   TNA WO 166/4409 (War Diary, 1st/6th Lancashire Fusiliers), January 1941; TNA WO 166/4407 (War Diary, 1st/5th Lancashire Fusiliers), January 1941.

14   TNA WO 166/4367 (War Diary, 6th King's Own Scottish Borderers), *passim*.

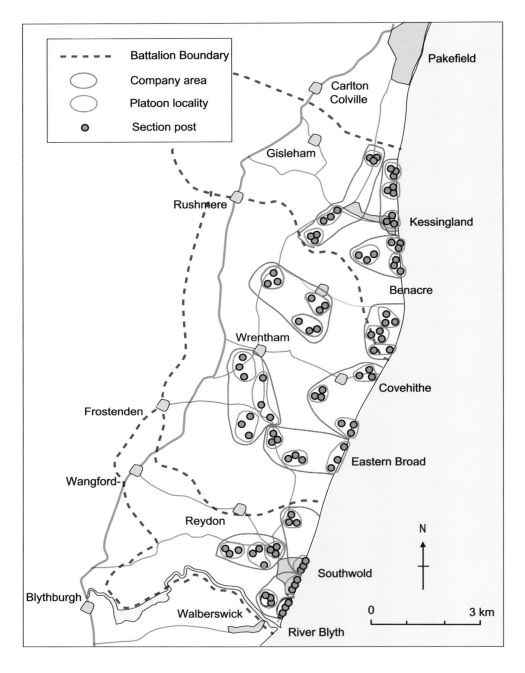

Figure 3.4. The arrangement of platoon 'forward defended localities' within company areas between Pakefield and Southwold, 1941. Within these localities section posts were staggered in order to provide 'all round defence' to the new positions.

2 and 3 units staggered the deployment of their companies to deal with threats both from inland and from the sea.[15] In the majority of cases the westward-facing positions were entirely new. Only in Sub-Sector 4 were there slightly different developments. Here, there was more short-term continuity from previous arrangements, in that one of the brigade's battalions was kept back in order to defend Martlesham and Ipswich aerodromes and was moved up to the coast only in May, when reserves were provided from the neighbouring division.[16]

At the lower reaches of the chain of command, at the level of platoon, the new localities were different from their predecessors in a number of respects. Whereas in 1940 there had been a tendency to place the three section posts of a platoon and in turn the three platoon positions of a company in a line in order to cover as much of the coastline as possible, now there was marked change. Albeit not exclusively, platoon localities and section posts were now placed in a triangular pattern or otherwise staggered in order to give 'all round defence' (Figure 3.4). In addition, no new section post established after 1940 appears to have been provisioned with a concrete pillbox; field survey for this study has found no clear-cut examples on positions started as part of the 1941 reorganisation. The absence undoubtedly reflected the wishes of higher authority as, even though stocks of concrete were available, no new pillboxes were to be built without permission from senior commanders.[17] The 'lure of concrete' was not to compromise the new arrangements.

As a result of these changes in places an altogether different defensive landscape emerged. A particularly clear example is at Walberswick, where, although still held by one company of infantrymen, dispositions were markedly unlike those of the previous year (Figure 3.5). Some two-thirds of the 1940 line was abandoned and only one position, on higher ground to the south of the village (probably a platoon headquarters and with an artillery OP) was retained, which became the focus of one of three new localities. The increase in manning levels provided by the creation of a new Sub-Sector also permitted much greater defence in depth along the 'spur' leading inland, where a headquarters and a rifle company lay in a multi-layered defence line. At the level of battalion and company, the new battlefield was not one where troops tried to cover as much coastline as possible, but rather one where a reduced front was held in greater strength. How widespread such comprehensive reorganisations were across the Sector is unclear, but where the locations of the new localities can be compared with the

---

15   TNA WO 166/975 (War Diary, 125th Infantry Brigade), 125 Infantry Brigade Group Operational Instruction No. 3, Appendix B, Appreciation of the Coast Defence, 6.1.41.

16   By the early summer the Back Line, which ran closest to the coast around Woodbridge, was sufficiently developed to provide adequate rear defence, and 42nd Division (which had by then been rotated out of the line and was now part of the general reserve) lay in close proximity and so freed up the reserve battalion to move forward.

17   TNA WO 166/494 (War Diary, 42nd Division, GS), 7.11.40; 42 Division Operational Instruction No. 24, 20.11.40.

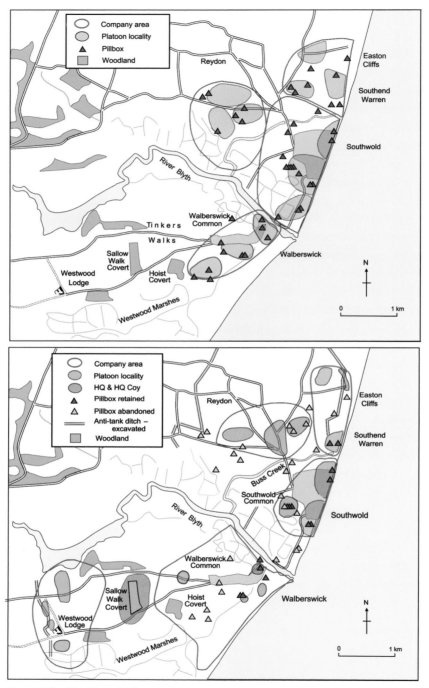

Figure 3.5 a & b. Map of military positions, Southwold and Walberswick, 1940 (*top*) and mid-1941 (*bottom*). The contrast with the previous year can clearly be seen; note the abandonment of the 1940 line south of the village and the greater defence in depth along the 'spur' leading inland, together with the appearance of anti-tank ditches.

distribution of pillboxes, Sub-Sectors 2 and 3 appear to have seen the greatest changes, presumably because it was here that 'linear' systems dominated and so required the greatest alteration. Here those section posts abandoned tended to be those that lay outside the bounds of the new localities or could not otherwise be adequately manned. As the pillboxes at these superfluous sites could potentially be used by an attacking enemy, they were to have their loopholes blocked or booby trapped.[18] The field remains show that such orders cannot have been completed systematically, but clearly were followed in some places: at Hollesley, for example, two pillboxes had the date June 1941 marked in the concrete of the blocks stopping up their embrasures; in that case, the remote position away from the newly created localities accounts for their disuse.

Forward defended localities: continuity and change

While historical studies of anti-invasion strategy tend, often rightly, to juxtapose the defence schemes of Ironside and Brooke, on the ground the archaeological evidence suggests that differences between the infantry defences of 1941 and their predecessors are more apparent than real. For all the criticism levelled at them, not all aspects of the 1940 fortifications were deficient and the changes of 1941 rested heavily upon what was already in place. That good work had been undertaken by 55th Division and was to be retained in the new schemes is noted in numerous war diaries, but comments to this effect tend to be marginalised by a focus on new works and redeployments that inevitably gives a slightly misleading impression.[19]

In particular, the frequency of the new buzzword of 'all round defence' in documents after November 1940 tends to obscure those cases where such tactical thinking had already informed schemes on the ground, especially in the defence of urban areas. As was seen in the previous chapter, at Felixstowe and Lowestoft work on the rear defences had taken place almost from the start of the invasion crisis.[20] At Lowestoft, the new westward-facing defence line was in effect an extension of the 'Normanstone' and 'Oulton' lines that was facilitated by greater manpower, rather than by improved tactical expertise. Additionally, some fieldworks constructed during the summer of 1940 were clearly well sited and adequately completed. On handing over in November 1940 the 2nd Liverpool Scottish reported that their relieving battalion 'showed great appreciation' of the level of work that had gone into defences and that its Commanding Officer 'expressed the opinion that our trenches were better than any that he saw in France'.[21] Given that the Liverpool Scottish had put works in hand to

---

18 TNA WO 166/451 (War Diary, 15th Division, GS), Operational Instruction No. 10, 16.4.41; Operational Instruction No. 41, 24.5.41.

19 TNA WO 166/977 (War Diary, 127th Infantry Brigade), 127 Infantry Brigade Operation Instruction No. 13, 3.12.40.

20 TNA WO 166/4454 (War Diary, 7th Manchester Regiment), 28.9.40.

21 TNA WO 166/4434 (War Diary, 2nd Liverpool Scottish), 30.10.40; 2.11.40.

Figure 3.6. Photograph of camouflaged Suffolk Square pillbox of 1940 at Thorpeness, retained as part of the coastal defences the following year. (IWM H11455)

improve the capability for all round defence during the previous August, it follows that the limited references to the resiting of posts by the incoming 4th East Lancashire's was because much was already of an appropriate standard.[22]

It also needs to be remembered that, while the change of overall strategy reflected shifting priorities at the highest level of military command, on the ground infantry positions – regardless of how they were arranged – continued to reflect very local circumstances. The topography of the coastline that required defending had not, of course, altered; and while those localities established inland to fight the 'westward' battle were *de novo* works, in the seaside towns and on the vulnerable beaches changes were often more subtle. Here there was inevitably a degree of continuity between defence posts, with those that were judged to have been well situated being retained and incorporated into new schemes (Figure 3.6). At towns such as Lowestoft and Southwold the evidence of maps showing the location of section posts in 1940 and 1941 indicates that there was a 'thinning out' of positions rather than wholesale

---

22   TNA WO 166/4249 (War Diary, 4th East Lancashire Regiment), 19.12.40.

abandonment, with those remaining arranged in 'linear' fashion much as had been the case in 1940, simply because they had to cover long stretches of beach. Albeit on a larger scale, this was also the case in the south across much of Sub-Sector 4 (Aldeburgh to Felixstowe) where the presence of extensive wetlands back from the beaches meant there was much less scope for change, simply because the landscape context prevented it; here the company and platoon localities were almost as 'linear' in 1941 as they had been the previous year.

In other cases, whatever new tactical scheme was desired, topography demanded that defences be arranged in much the same way as before. At Dunwich, for example, while some section posts became redundant and some pillboxes were abandoned, others became part of the new localities because they were in the only place suitable to cover the beach exit and there was no conceivable alternative; the key difference between 1940 and 1941 was the increase in manning, as there were seven rather than three platoons defending the area, each with smaller areas to defend (Figure 3.7).

Similarly, for all the criticism levelled at the 1940 works, existing trenches with accompanying pillboxes were often at the heart of the new localities, with physical evidence for their continued use readily found in minor structural modifications. An alteration commonly made to pillboxes was the blocking up of embrasures in order to facilitate more effective use and negate the problem of a multiplicity of loopholes allowing the entry of hostile bullets. The clearest support for the continued utility of pillboxes comes from the use of Turnbull mounts for use with Bren guns, the arrival of which war diaries place in the early summer of 1941: at that time, evidently, pillboxes were still a valued part of the beach defences.[23] The pillboxes that marked the line of the 1940 defences at Walberswick clearly indicate this trend, in that those abandoned in 1941 exhibit no modifications and remain as originally built, whereas the two that formed part of a defended locality from 1941 have blocked loopholes and evidence for Turnbull mounts. To some extent, then, concrete still remained king.

Moreover, field survey shows that the section posts and trenches making up the new localities were not that dissimilar to those of the previous year (Figure 3.8). In one case at Dunwich Heath a platoon locality with two of its three section posts survives remarkably intact, with trenches extant to almost their original depth. Here the position probably started by the 1st/5th Lancashire Fusiliers and completed by the 10th Cameronians took the form of fire trenches 20 metres long and almost two metres deep with fire bays at either end and in one case a cut for a 2-inch mortar. Large rectangular pits mark the remains of dugouts in each trench and the surface remains of corrugated iron suggest sandbagged roofs that did not reach above ground level, a form of construction suggested in operational orders (Figure 3.9).[24] Elsewhere,

23   TNA WO 166/4592 (War Diary, 6th Royal Scots Fusiliers), 24.5.41.
24   TNA WO 166/958 (War Diary, 46th Infantry Brigade), 46th (HLI) Infantry Brigade Operational Instruction No. 7, 11.3.41.

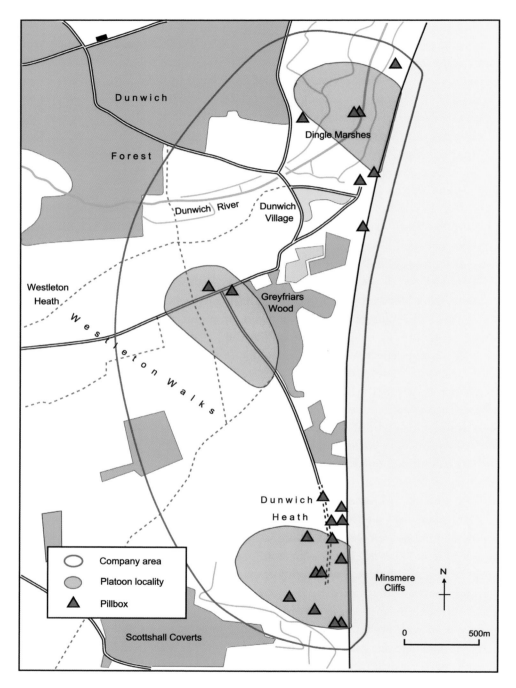

Figure 3.7a & b. Defence of Dunwich beach, 1940 and 1941. Although some positions and pillboxes were abandoned in the spring of 1941, the local topography demanded that some were retained; the real difference was the increased level of manpower.

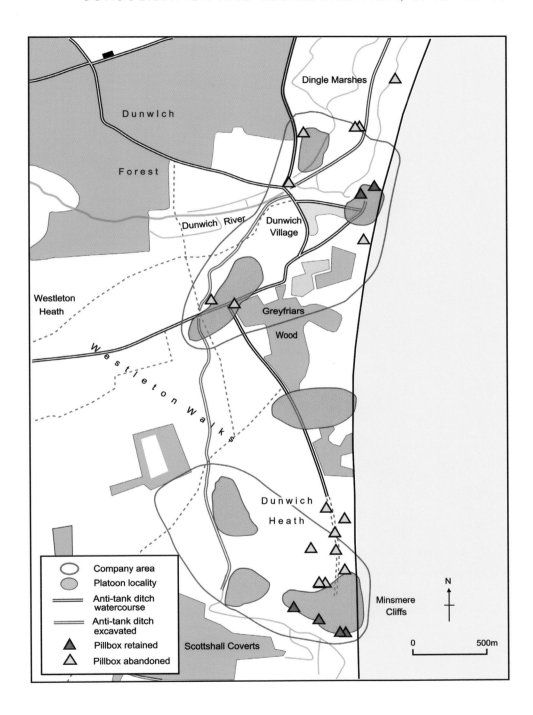

Dingle Marshes

Dunwlch

Forest

Dunwich River   Dunwich
                 Village

Westleton
Heath

Westleton Walk

Greyfriars

Wood

Dunwich

Heath

Minsmere
Cliffs

Scottshall Coverts

N

0   500m

Company area
Platoon locality
Anti-tank ditch
watercourse
Anti-tank ditch
excavated
Pillbox retained
Pillbox abandoned

Figure 3.8. Photograph showing trench system at Thorpeness, 1941. The image shows what is probably a section of communication trench terminating in a dugout that probably also served as a firing point. Despite the camouflage netting, the nature of the construction can be appreciated; field survey has shown that the arrangement of trench and dugout shown here was replicated at numerous other sites. (IWM H11462)

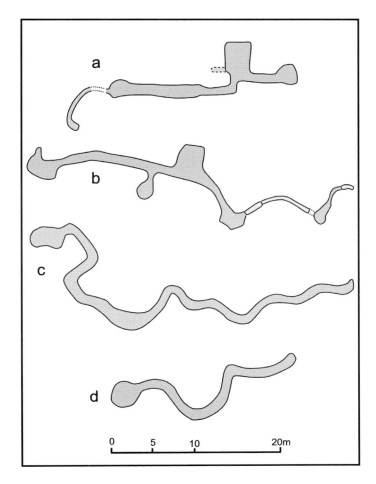

Figure 3.9. Section post trenches associated with forward defended localities: a) Dunwich Heath, 1st/5th Lancashire Fusiliers January 1941 with rectangular dug out; b) second trench from the same platoon locality, but with cut for 2-inch mortar and possible extension for the purposes of training later in the war; c) Sallow Walk Covert, Walberswick; d) Westwood Lodge, Walberswick. With the exception of an absence of pillboxes and the existence of some larger dug-outs, the trenches are not dissimilar to those of 1940; compare with Figure 2.14.

the archaeological remains suggest that sinuous fire trenches also terminating in larger circular pits were commonplace. Such trenches are, it should be noted, substantially similar in form to those trenches of the previous year, as seen at places such as Hoist Covert at Walberswick. The only appreciable difference between the 1941 fieldworks and those of the previous year is the absence of a concrete pillbox and the provision of more substantial dug outs.

Field evidence also shows a degree of diversity in the morphological form of trenches, suggesting that troops on the ground were free to adjust in order to meet their immediate local circumstances. An unusual case exists at Tinker's Walks near Walberswick, where earthworks mark a platoon position built as part of the inland defences early in 1941. Here the trench complex takes the form of a swastika, a design recommended as particularly useful for defending infantry against tanks.[25] The context

---

25   War Office, *Home Guard Manual* (1941), 79. We owe this reference to Dr Derwin Gregory.

would make sense here, lying on the northern end of the defence line and in an open area a little behind an anti-tank ditch. A similar example of a platoon position, possibly for use with an anti-tank gun, is at North Warren near Aldeburgh and was seemingly an addition to a larger training work of May 1940 (Figure 5.2). Such archaeological evidence demonstrates that, while their construction was the result of decisions made by a much higher authority and part of a planned 'top-down' reorganisation, very local circumstances governed the location and form of positions on the ground. On such occasions, continuity and adaptation are as much in evidence as change.

The protective edge: coastal batteries, scaffolding and anti-tank ditches

On the coast itself, the 1941 reorganisation also involved the construction of additional ECDBs and the appearance of new obstacles on the beaches. During the course of the year the often rudimentary existing coastal battery sites were upgraded, and weaknesses in the 1940 arrangements were identified and ameliorated (see Figure 2.7). To the south of Lowestoft significant dead space was found to exist where existing guns could not effectively protect the harbour mouth, and further down the coast the sea space around Benacre Ness could not be adequately covered by existing sites. The winter of 1940/41 had also brought difficulties. The site of the Southwold battery was found to be vulnerable to flooding, while at Covehithe eroding cliffs caused a fissure to open up in front of one of the guns and threatened collapse.[26] The response was the construction of four new ECDBs (Grand Hotel Lowestoft, Kessingland, Minsmere and Bawdsey) and two relocations (Covehithe and Southwold). All these new sites represented considerable improvements in terms of their design, with brick and concrete used from the start. The new arrangements were intended to fulfil specific local needs and, on a wider scale, eliminate areas of dead sea space along the whole coast. The Grand Hotel Battery at Lowestoft was sited so it could fire on the gap at the harbour mouth and the entry points from the South Roads, while that at Kessingland resolved the problem of inadequate cover for Benacre Ness. Finally, the relocation of Covehithe and Southwold and the construction of the Minsmere Battery served to equalise the arcs of fire of the batteries. As a group the ECDBs now gave complete coverage of the inshore approaches to land. The final phase of the construction of ECDBs occurred at East Lane, Bawdsey. During reconnaissance in 1940 a decision was taken not to site a battery here owing to the likelihood of flooding, but the considerable gap in provision as a result (it was some 19 kilometres from the batteries at Aldeburgh and Felixstowe) was evidently felt to be too long and in February 1942 the new battery at East Lane became operational.[27]

---

26   TNA WO 199/940 (Tours and Visits to Coast Defences), Notes on part of MGRA's NORFOLK Tour, 12.2.41.
27   TNA WO 166/11 (War Diary, GHQ Home Forces, Coast Artillery), 29.7.40; TNA WO 166/6020 (War Diary, Eastern Command Royal Artillery Branch), 10.2.42.

Scaffolding

On the shoreline and beaches the greatest change instigated in 1941 was concerned with the stipulation that vulnerable areas be provided with two anti-tank barriers. Across the Sector one such barrier, in the form of either anti-tank blocks or watery anti-tank ditches and rivers, already existed, and the newcomer was beach scaffolding: a framework of steel tubes that presented a vertical face on the enemy side whilst braced by angled tubes at the rear. Scaffolding, originally of naval design, was intended to sit below the high water mark to prevent invasion barges from reaching the shore. Trials at Felixstowe showed that in this role it was ineffectual, but when placed above the high water mark it was an effective barrier to slow-moving vehicles, and so it was chosen as the additional anti-tank obstacle required on the invasion beaches (Figure 3.10).[28]

Stocks of tubing were delivered from central stores and dumped along the shoreline of the Sandlings from December 1940, but delays ensued before construction started.[29] Disagreements between the army and navy and within the army itself over the exact role that the scaffolding was to play were in part to blame; the commander of 42nd Division's engineers commented that it was 'more of a correspondence source than tank obstacle'.[30] The enormity of the task meant that logistical difficulties hindered building work, which was dogged by problems including shortages of key parts, the small number of railway stations close to the coast where material could be offloaded and the dangers of construction on beaches where the action of the sea had disturbed minefields. The difficulties were neatly summarised by 42nd Division's chief of engineers again:

> Lt. Cmdr Owen, Beach Defence Officer, Landguard, is O[fficer].C[ommanding]. Tubular Scaffolding Obstacle and is responsible for indicating to the Military exactly where the obstacle has to be placed on all parts of the Div[isional]. front. He is a dammed nice fellow but seems to have no control whatsoever over delivery of the tubes in the right place, at the right time and in the right quantities, which is unfortunate.[31]

The physical work of erecting scaffolding initially lay with the Pioneer Corps and the Royal Engineers, but soon passed to the infantry; however, by May progress was retarded to such an extent that artillery, reserve troops and headquarters personnel were all required to take part.[32] As the work was delegated down the chain of

---

28   For trials at Felixstowe, see TNA WO 166/498 (War Diary, 42nd Division, CRE), 15.12.40; 6.1.41. For general policy on siting see TNA WO 166/450 (War Diary, 15th Division, GS), Defence Scheme, 9.6.41.

29   TNA WO 166/3670 (War Diary, 200th Field Company, Royal Engineers), Orders, 1.12.40; 11.12.40.

30   TNA WO 166/498 (War Diary, 42nd Division, CRE), Handing over notes CRE 42 to CRE 15 Div, February 1941.

31   *Ibid.*

32   TNA WO 166/450 (War Diary, 15th Division, GS), Operational Instruction (Beach Defence) No. 2, 5.3.41; Operational Instruction (Beach Defence) No. 14, 17.5.41.

command units constructed their allotments according to their own schedules; as a result, scaffolding appeared along the coast at different times. The initial construction probably took place between Landguard Point and the mouth of the Deben in February and in parts of Sub-Sector 3 around Aldeburgh.[33] Thereafter gaps were infilled on a piecemeal basis on the front of the unit concerned: work by the 6th Royal Scots Fusiliers around Sizewell and Minsmere started on 15 March and by the 11th Highland Light Infantry around Bawdsey on 8 May, and new work was still being initiated in July, some four months after the original deadline for all defences to be completed had passed. Construction was labour intensive, repetitive and, given the distances involved, immensely time consuming. As such, it drew complaint, especially when orders were given to construct more than originally requested, when incorrectly made sections had to be relaid and when it seemed a never-ending task; even the normally upbeat war diarist of the 11th Highland Light Infantry reported that after three months 'work on tubular scaffolding and defences is getting rather boring, the men need a change'.[34]

As would be expected, the siting of scaffolding was broadly similar to that of anti-tank cubes. In Sub-Sectors 1 and 2 scaffolding ran almost uninterrupted from Corton Cliffs at Lowestoft to Southwold, with minor gaps formed by bodies of water or minefields. In Sub-Sector 3 scaffolding, likewise, protected the beaches at Walberswick, Sizewell and Aldeburgh and ran between Walberswick and Dunwich for over five kilometres. In Sub-Sector 4, between the Alde and the Deben, lines protected

33   TNA WO 166/975 (War Diary, 125th Infantry Brigade), 8.2.41; TNA WO 166/3719 (250th Field Company Royal Engineers), February 1941.
34   TNA WO 166/4346 (War Diary, 11th Highland Light Infantry), 11.8.41.

Figure 3.10. Aerial photograph of Landguard Point in 1941 showing scaffolding and other anti-invasion defences. By this stage of the war most of the beaches in the Sandlings were provisioned with similar defences. The boom protecting the entrance channel to Harwich Haven can be seen running along the top of the photograph. (Reproduced by permission of Historic England Archive (RAF Photography))

the beach at East Lane and around part of the perimeter of Bawdsey radar station, while elsewhere it augmented the watery anti-tank ditch of the previous year. To the south of the Deben to Landguard Point, the majority of the coastline was scaffolded.

The precise course of scaffolding lines on the ground depended upon the location of the high water mark on any given piece of coastline and the position of other fixed defences, especially the line of the existing anti-tank obstacle. As a location above the high water mark was known to be effective against tanks, wherever possible scaffolding was sited accordingly, but there were exceptions. Around Landguard Point a long run was located at low water mark, probably marking the location of initial trials when scaffolding's use in an anti-barge role was under discussion.[35] Elsewhere, scaffolding might run in front of or behind the existing anti-tank obstacle, and here local circumstance was the primary determinant in siting. At Felixstowe the scaffolding line ran immediately inland of the line of anti-tank cubes at the crest of the long seaside terrace, a decision probably informed not only by topography but also by the presence of extensive minefields on the beach itself. Around Shingle Street scaffolding augmented the existing defences in a variety of ways. At East Lane Bawdsey the scaffolding line ran in front of the anti-tank cubes on the beach, but its course switched to the landward side of the watery anti-tank ditch that it followed for half its course, before a short gap, whereupon it continued on the seaward side as far as Boyton marshes. Such an arrangement was similar to the area around Sizewell, where a short section functioned as an anti-tank obstacle back from the beach and served to link the conventional anti-tank ditch and the watery ditch that ran north towards Minsmere. By contrast, at

35   HE (NMR) RAF Photography, S349/H.51.1416, 23.7.41.

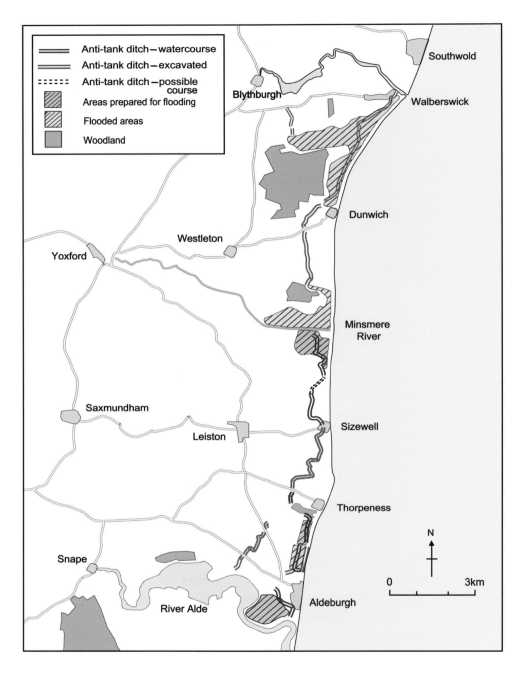

Figure 3.11. Anti-tank ditches in the central Sandlings. Ditches tended to link up water courses and flooded areas but in this part of the Sandlings were akin to prehistoric cross-ridge dykes, in that they bisected the topographic 'spurs'.

Minsmere itself the scaffolding line ran parallel to the high water mark and the gap between scaffolding and anti-tank cubes was larger than in other areas.

In a smaller number of cases, scaffolding was built further inland. A barrier existed at Wilford Bridge at Melton near Woodbridge, where in an unusual arrangement three sections formed the main obstacle of the defensive perimeter protecting the bridge itself.[36] Its comparative rarity away from the coast was probably due to a lack of manpower and logistical problems, but may also have been caused by persistent disagreements about how exactly it should be employed. The comment by 11th Highland Light Infantry that 'The Navy called and apparently took grave exception to our erecting scaffolding in land. At present a conflict rages between the Army and Navy as to who may do what with the scaffolding. I think the Navy look like winning' suggests that inter-service disagreements surrounding the use of scaffolding were never fully resolved. This, together with supply shortages, probably explains why Nodal Points and villages such as Leiston and Westleton ultimately did not receive what had originally been scheduled, and by September 1941 plans to build a scaffolding line between Orford and Alderton were shelved on the grounds of a lack of manpower.[37]

Anti-tank ditches

The second principal addition to the field defences of the coastal crust in 1941 were anti-tank ditches. While these had been a feature of the previous year's works, their construction had been limited to the use of existing watercourses and drainage ditches. New work was planned in January 1941, but owing to delays in obtaining excavators began in earnest only from April, when it was carried out by specialist army engineer companies and civilian contractors.[38] The programme saw the additional widening of watercourses and drainage channels as well as the construction of the majority of the Sector's artificial ditches (Figure 3.11).

The use of anti-tank ditches in the Sector tended to fall into two categories. First were those ditches immediately back from the beaches, which were intended to prevent vehicles breaking out soon after they had landed. Analogous to these were those on the landward side of urban areas and vulnerable points, which were intended to stop enemy vehicles that had landed elsewhere attacking from the west. Second were those ditches slightly further inland, which provided a further barrier to those forces moving in from the coastline but also marked the line of the 'westward' defences.

Regardless of the exact tactical employment of ditches, a common set of principles tended to govern their form and location on the ground. Exact siting was closely related to the location of the new infantry localities, so that most ditches could be covered by

---

36 Hegarty and Newsome, *Suffolk's Defended Shore*, p. 59.
37 TNA WO 166/4346 (War Diary, 11th Highland Light Infantry), 12.8.41. On 16 August the diarist noted that 'the Navy have won this argument with the Army'.
38 TNA WO 166/498 (War Diary, 42nd Division, CRE), 2.2.41, 28.1.41.

Figure 3.12. Extant anti-tank ditch at Walberswick excavated in 1941. This 'two-way' ditch was intended to guard against enemy vehicles either moving inland from the beaches or advancing from the west.

fire. In almost every case the preferred option was to use natural obstacles as barriers and for lengths of ditch to link up rivers, existing watery anti-tank ditches, widened drainage channels and inundated areas. At Lowestoft excavated ditches to the north and south of the town bridged the gaps between the beach defences and Fritton Lake and Oulton Broad and a similar, albeit much smaller, scheme existed at Aldeburgh, where over half of the town's ditch was made up of watercourses, with shorter runs of excavated ditch completing the circuit. Away from urban areas similar principles applied, but differed according to topography. In Sub-Sector 3, where lowland areas were already impassable to tanks because of inundation, newly created anti-tank ditches tended to lie on the intervening and slightly higher watersheds. Here they ran for longer distances north–south in order to divide the 'spurs' laterally, much in the manner of prehistoric cross-ridge dykes, as at Walberswick, where a 1.5-kilometre length of ditch connected the flooded Westwood marshes with the estuary of the Blyth (Figure 3.12). On a larger scale, almost all of Dunwich and Dunwich Heath were cut off by the inland ditch that connected the Dunwich river at Bridge Farm with the flooded Minsmere marshes three kilometres to the south. The only area not to experience ditch construction on a large scale in 1941 was Sub-Sector 4. Here, the only ditches were that of 1940 at Shingle Street and on the landward side of Felixstowe; the large inland heaths were untouched. The absence of ditches on this part of the coast was in large part connected to geography. The rivers Deben and Alde were both anti-tank obstacles in their own right and their course rendered the area inland from Bawdsey to Boyton something of a peninsular, with the neck at Campsea Ash. At this bottleneck the 'Back Line' provided the chief anti-tank defence and while a reconnaissance was made to site an additional ditch here in September 1941 this was late in the day and never seems to have been realised.[39]

In the field, anti-tank ditches could take a number of forms.[40] The major variation concerned whether the ditch was intended to function as a 'one-way' or 'two-way' obstacle: that is, whether it offered protection on one side or both. A one-way ditch required a revetment facing the direction of attack, while two-way ditches could have either a flat-bottomed or a 'V'-shaped profile; as such they did not require additional revetments, and so became the War Office's preferred form.[41] Wartime manuals also recommended that anti-tank ditches comprise straight sections of between 365 and 550 metres (400–600 yards) in a zig-zag pattern to permit enfilade fire.[42]

As field monuments, anti-tank ditches often display considerable variation along even relatively short sections. The vast majority of surviving ditches are of 'two-way' design, a morphological form that confirms a date of 1941 for their construction. The best-preserved examples conform closely to wartime manuals, that at Aldringham Walks retaining its 'V' profile and flattened banks on either side. Elsewhere, at least one section of 'one-way' ditch, at Broom Hill, Dunwich, which was intended to defend the landward side of Dunwich Heath, was built with a raised bank on the enemy side in places over four metres high.

Such variety of form is probably in part related to the process of construction. It is doubtful that there was ever a Sector 'grand plan' for the arrangement of ditches in detail; rather, as with beach scaffolding, responsibility was devolved to those on the ground. While eventually the process of construction led to an almost continuous anti-tank obstacle across the Divisional front, this was the result of piecemeal construction in sections, rather than a single sustained campaign. This process is occasionally glimpsed in war diaries. In April work was taking place at Southwold and at the beginning of May work started on a length of ditch in the Sizewell area, which was to join up with works already complete.[43] Despite the use of machines, excavation proceeded slowly; at the end of the month the 6th Royal Scots, in whose area work was taking place, noted that 'the mechanical diggers break down frequently and are always being taken for other work'.[44] Progress reports in July and September 1941 provide

---

39   TNA WO 166/958 (War Diary, 46th Infantry Brigade), 10.8.41.
40   Lowry, *20th Century Defences*, p. 89.
41   Dobinson, *Anti-Invasion*, pp. 140–42.
42   War Office, *Military Training Pamphlet No. 30 Part III, Field Engineering All Arms, Obstacles*, (1940; 1941).
43   TNA WO 166/4592 (War Diary, 6th Royal Scots Fusiliers), 2.4.41.
44   *Ibid.*, 30.4.41.

snapshots of the process and timescale of the works and, while it never seems to have been fully completed, by the end of 1941 an almost unbroken obstacle ran the length of the Divisional Sector.

The field evidence shows that War Office guidance on the staggered course of ditches was followed only to a limited extent. The chief determinant for the exact route of anti-tank ditches was the pre-existing landscape, in that ditches tended to follow field boundaries or railway lines, or skirt along roads or woodland edges. Where zig-zag patterns are apparent, it is usually because the antecedent structure permitted it; in other words, in those cases the pattern of boundaries on the ground dovetailed with tactical advantage. In more open landscapes, such as heaths, ditches tended to run relatively straight towards a pre-determined point, such as a widened drainage ditch or river. While following existing boundaries may have had benefits in terms of camouflage, these arrangements were clearly intended primarily to minimize disruption to the agricultural economy, as lines were prone to deviation in places where they crossed a farmed landscape or approached settlements. The majority of abrupt changes in direction or significant deviations were to take account of road junctions or major farmhouses. The large farm complex at Westwood lodge at Walberswick, for example, was clearly bypassed by the adjacent anti-tank ditch, as were Home Farm on Sizewell Common and Shellpits cottages at Aldringham. Only in a minority of cases across the Sector is it possible to find examples of ditches running straight across farmland. Where this does occur, it is chiefly in the most heavily farmed areas of Sub-Sector 2, where there was little alternative, and even here the pattern is mixed. While lengths of ditch cut across field boundaries, other sections also respect or follow roads and hedgerows – and, in some cases, as at Wrentham, they appear to run over the agricultural landscape only in order to avoid villages.

Inland defences

ECDBs, scaffolding and anti-tank ditches were intended to protect the seaward and western-facing edges of the coastal defences. The space between these lines also saw important changes during 1941, especially in the construction of obstacles to impede the movement of vehicles on roads, the widespread excavation of anti-landing ditches and the resiting of artillery.

While roadblocks and bridges prepared for demolition had been a feature of 1940, these were now augmented with additional static defences equipped with new weapons. An improvisation from 1940 that was maintained into 1941 was the use of naval depth charges, which were buried in roads so that they could be detonated in order to create a large hole that was impassable to vehicles; that blown by 15th Division's engineers as an experiment resulted in a gap 36 feet (11 metres) wide and 10 feet (3 metres) deep.[45]

---

45   TNA WO 166/3748 (War Diary, 279th Field Company, Royal Engineers), 7.5.41.

A second device, introduced in 1941, was the Canadian pipe mine, which comprised a length of steel tube placed into an angled hole in a road surface and then packed with explosives. When detonated, one pipe alone could create a substantial crater and multiple pipes were usually laid in order to render the road totally impassable. On 5 June one such device comprising two pipes was deliberately test fired near Westleton and left a crater 20 feet (7 metres) wide and 9 feet (2.7 metres) deep that was judged to be a 'complete tank obstacle'.[46] A further device was the flame fougasse, which fired burning fuel from oil drums sited immediately adjacent to a road; the drums were usually placed in fours in order to create a barrage that could hit a target up to 25 yards (22 metres) away.

How these weapons were intended to function within the wider anti-invasion landscape is clearly illustrated by mapping their locations across Sub-Sector 3 (Figure 3.13). Here depth charges and fougasses were used exclusively on the coast itself, chiefly on all roads leading inland from the beaches and around coastal towns. Typical was the use of a series of charges on a single road; for example, seven separate charges were laid inland from Sizewell on the road towards Leiston. A smaller, but significant, number were also placed where roads or tracks crossed anti-tank ditches, both on those ditches back from the beaches and on those of the western-facing defences. By contrast, pipe mines were reserved for the defence of the Sub-Sector Nodal Points at Blythburgh, Saxmundham and Leiston and of the 'Back Line', here running south from Halesworth, being placed chiefly in locations where slight cuttings and embankments rendered the railway line an ineffective obstacle.[47] When considered along with the bridge demolitions, the overall scheme for the Sub-Sector is clear: all roads leading inland from the coast and all bottlenecks inland were to be rendered impassable by vehicles, the only exceptions being stretches of road connecting the Back Line with Nodal Points, which presumably were to allow the movement of counter-attacking British troops towards the otherwise immobilised enemy attempting to get off the beaches.

Anti-landing ditches

The final addition to the 1941 defences were anti-landing ditches. The threat from troops landed by parachute or glider had been widely anticipated in 1940, with the chief concern not so much paratroopers themselves but rather men landed by glider or by troop-carrying aircraft using suitable terrain as grassy airstrips.[48] Here a distinction needs to be drawn between the use of troop-carrying transport aircraft and that of gliders. British calculations suggested that enemy ferry aircraft would, if possible, operate from level open spaces not less than 500 yards (450 metres) square and without high field boundaries. This was not the case for gliders, however, which needed only a

---

46 TNA WO 166/454 (War Diary, 15th Division, CRE), 5.6.41.

47 TNA WO 166/498 (War Diary, 42nd Division, CRE), November–February 1941, *passim*.

48 Dobinson, *Anti-Invasion*, p. 129.

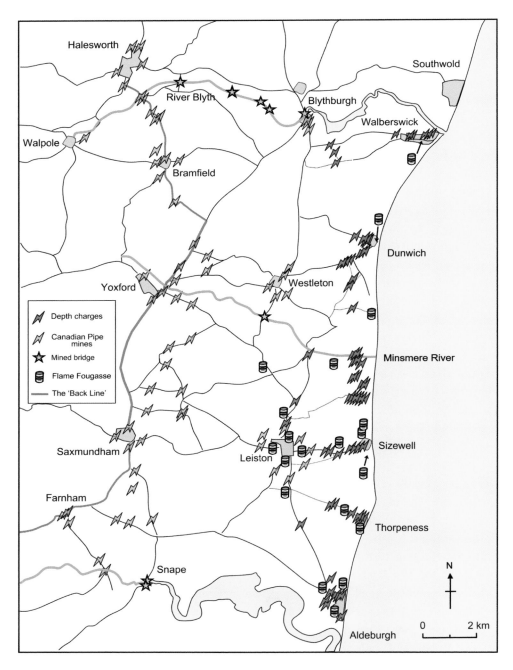

Figure 3.13. Static obstacles in Sub-Sector 3, mid-1941. Canadian pipe mines mark out the course of the 'back line' and nodal points, while depth charges, craters and flame fougasses were more common on the beaches and roads leading inland. As can be seen, even minor roads and tracks were to be obstructed.

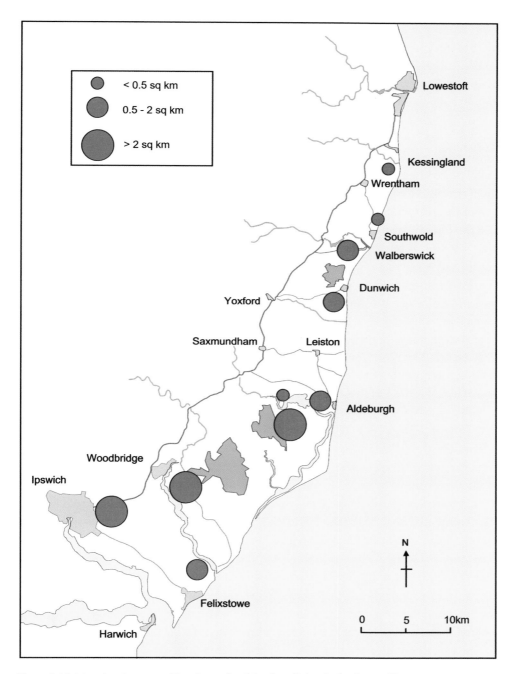

Figure 3.14. Map showing general locations of anti-landing ditches in the Sector. The greatest concentrations lay in the southern Sandlings, where there were larger expanses of heath and where the distance between the coast and the rear defences of the Back Line at Woodbridge was at its greatest.

short landing run of 40 yards (35 metres) or less. Given that it was simply impractical to construct the density of obstacles needed to prevent a glider landing, potential landing strips for use by troop-carrying aircraft were singled out for attention; the aim of obstruction was to give a high probability that planes would be damaged on landing and that any that were not would be preventing from taking off again.[49]

In the Sandlings potential landing areas did not exist uniformly across the Sector (Figure 3.14). The area from Lowestoft to Southwold was generally unsuitable owing to the presence of large bodies of water and marshes around Lowestoft, while north Suffolk's farming landscape of small, irregular fields with well-established hedges interspersed with pockets of woodland meant that a significant airborne operation would be technically difficult. In Sub-Sectors 3 and 4 the presence of coastal marshes and the forestry plantations around Dunwich, Tunstall and Rendlesham ruled out the possibility of airborne attack, but the large heaths at Walberswick, Dunwich, Iken, Sutton and Martlesham were, in contrast, ideal landing grounds.

Air Ministry advice for the obstruction of such places suggested a number of measures, of which the most relevant here was ditches 150 yards (137 metres) in length aligned in a chequerboard pattern, which made landings by aircraft impossible and had fatal consequences for gliders unfortunate enough to strike one during touchdown. The ditches themselves were four feet (1.2 metres) in width and were constructed by excavator with a drag line which left the spoil in heaps on either side, known as 'tumps', which had the effect of making the ditch all the more effective (Figure 3.15).

Such ditches were excavated in considerable numbers in the Sandlings, but their distribution needs to be related to the ongoing changes in the wider defence landscape, specifically the provision for the 'westward' battle. While a small number of ditches were excavated to the landward side of the western defence line – as on the 'spurs' at Walberswick and Dunwich – overall, even some large expanses of flat heath in the Sandlings, such as Westleton Walks, were left untouched because they were outside the main battle space.[50] Rather, potential landing grounds *between* the western line and the coast saw the heaviest concentration of anti-landing obstacles. As there was no question of placing ditches on arable land it was heath and, to a lesser extent, pasture that received attention. The pattern of anti-landing ditches across the Sandlings therefore tended to reflect, albeit not exclusively, two factors: first, the distance between the coast and the western defence line at any given point and, second, the area of open ground that needed obstruction between those two lines on the other.

In a small number of cases, ditches were created in or close to marshland close to the coastline itself, such as to the east of Felixstowe or to the north of Sizewell, but the majority were on the larger heaths. Field remains and aerial photographs show that the

---

49   *Ibid.*, p. 132.

50   An exception is at Aldringham Walks, but here it is not clear if the anti-tank ditch marking the line of the western defences was in place at the time of the anti-landing ditch's construction.

Figure 3.15. Anti-landing ditch at Walberswick from 1940/41, showing characteristic 'tumps'. Such ditches were intended to prevent areas being used as grassy airstrips (during the war the area was devoid of trees).

length and configuration of ditches were usually governed by the shape and extent of the area that required obstruction. The classic chequerboard pattern tends to be found on those larger areas where aircraft could land from any direction or where mass glider landings were feasible. Around Iken and at Sutton Common, in Sub-Sector 4, heaths were systematically covered by ditches of textbook form that extended over hundreds of acres (Figure 3.16). Here the coastline and western defence lines were furthest apart, and the muted relief of the intervening area made for perfect landing grounds. At Walberswick a less extensive system of ditches covered East Sheep Walk and extended around Sallow Walk covert; here there was less of a chequerboard pattern, as the only viable direction of a landing run was east–west. Elsewhere, smaller areas tended to receive long ditches that were crossed by shorter lengths, as this was the most efficient way of disrupting the area in question. At Dunwich, for example, the heath saw the construction of two systems, both of which comprised a length crossed by two others, with separate shorter lengths placed seemingly at random. Exactly when these works took place is difficult to establish precisely, but whatever the number of ditches excavated in 1940, the historical evidence points to the spring and summer of 1941 as a period of widespread construction, as at the end of January arrangements were

Figure 3.16. Aerial photograph of Sutton Common, 1944, showing anti-landing ditches covering the heath in classic chequerboard pattern. (Reproduced by permission of Historic England Archive (USAAF Photography))

being made between contractors and the Ministry of Transport.[51] Anecdotal evidence suggests that it was at this time that Sutton Common received its ditches, something confirmed archaeologically by an aerial photograph of 1944, which shows a section of anti-tank ditch constructed for use in a training demonstration in September 1941 overlying a section of anti-landing ditch.[52]

The artillery landscape
The creation of a zone between the sea defences and the western defence line also had important implications for the artillery landscape. The greater overall manpower in 1941 was reflected in an increased provision for artillery. In comparison with the previous year, the Sector was 'up-gunned', with nearly double the number of artillery pieces of all kinds – a greater proportion of which comprised modernised equipment – available to 15th Division in the summer of 1941.

The artillery landscape over the winter of 1940/41 was broadly similar to that established during the invasion summer, with most guns placed behind the lines and

---

51   TNA WO 166/498 (War Diary, 42nd Division, CRE), Handing over notes CRE 42 to CRE 15 Div, February 1941.

52   HE (NMR) USAAF Collection, 7PH/GP/LOC 288, 19.4.44 F24; TNA WO 166/454 (War Diary, 15th Division, CRE), 26.9.41.

firing eastward towards the coast. The requirements of the westward battle made such arrangements difficult to sustain, in part because a proportion of artillery positions were sited so far inland that they were beyond the line of the new west-facing defences. From January 1941 the valuable guns were to be placed between the coastal and the western defences, ideally close to or within the new forward defended localities. As a consequence the artillery landscape was reconfigured and a dozen gun sites were moved in order to align them more closely with the infantry defence.[53]

In places where the existing positions were adequate either no change occurred or positions were moved only a few hundred metres, but in other cases the shift was more substantial and could be up to ten kilometres. Gun positions resited at this time tended to be either those that were isolated from other defence works or those the relocation of which both afforded greater protection and permitted greater use of the guns' range or fitted more easily into the new Sub-Sector arrangements. Elsewhere, where guns were well-sited for covering particular stretches of coastline or were closer to other positions, they tended to remain in situ. A similar reorganisation of anti-tank guns also took place at this time; again, this redeployment was intended to make most effective use of the available firepower (Figure 3.17).

The general reorganisation of the anti-invasion landscape at the start of the year also included a rationalisation of methods and renewed thought as to how artillery might be used to best advantage. Much in the same way as the infantry changed their dispositions as a result of new tactical thinking, so too artillery fire plans reflected a more considered approach. As the number of guns increased there was a return to 'first principles' in order to take advantage of good fields of fire and an almost unlimited target area over the sea. Increasingly the task of the gunners was to destroy what they could when targets were offshore and then place their fire immediately in front of the beach defences, or in areas where small arms and anti-tank fire was impaired.[54]

It was necessary to take particular care not to aid enemy landings by destroying 'friendly' obstacles with defensive bombardments. The problem had arisen in 1940, but with beaches now covered with obstacles and about to be provisioned with scaffolding the issue was more acute. The solution was to concentrate artillery fire on the sea itself, ideally no less than 180 metres (200 yards) seaward of the high water mark.[55] In theory, at least, the role of field artillery was to bombard landing barges and other craft as they neared the shore, rather than hit those floundering on the beaches themselves; the latter was possible, albeit that it required observed fire. In the spring and early summer of 1941 more elaborate methods of defensive fire were devised and refined, but in essence all involved bringing concentrated fire to bear on specific parts of the

---

53 TNA WO 166/453 (War Diary, 15th Division, CRA), 15 Division Operation Instruction No. 27, Appendix A, March 1941.

54 TNA WO 166/329 (Eastern Defence References), 11 Corps Artillery Instruction No. 1, 7.4.41.

55 TNA WO 166/450 (War Diary, 15th Division, GS), Operational Instruction (Beach Defence) No. 3, 8.3.41.

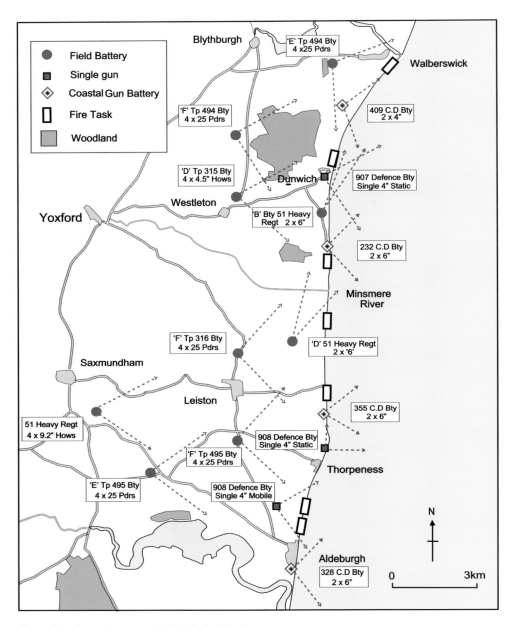

Figure 3.17. Map of gun sites in Sub-Sector 3, 1941.

coastline, usually between 500 and 180 metres (600–200 yards) offshore. Such drills were practised exhaustively in training and accuracy was remarkable. After one such test, the 22nd Royal Fusiliers were suitably impressed, recording that:

> The practice has taught Companies that Artillery fire can be relied on to fire on the exact position indicated. It was interesting to observe that shells exploded immediately on contact with the water … [one of these shots was] approximately 50 yards N of pier (Southwold) and 200 yards from the shore.[56]

The location of designated 'firetasks' again reveals both those parts of the coastline deemed to be at particular risk and differing arrangements between Sub-Sectors. In Sub-Sectors 2 and 3 the tendency was to reduce the number of places along the coastline where firetasks were required. The ten SOS tasks in 1940 between Walberswick and Aldeburgh, for example, were reduced to four firetasks by June 1941. In Sub-Sector 4 a considerable number ran offshore from Orford Ness, presumably covering the sea-space in the absence of any shore defences along this stretch of coast. In only one case, in Sub-Sector 1 around Lowestoft, were firetasks directed inland. Here a string of targets ringed the town, all on the roads leading away from the town.

The reconfiguration of the artillery landscape in 1941 is reflected in the surviving archaeology of troop and battery positions. In contrast to the abandonment of concrete as a material for infantry positions, its use on artillery sites increased in 1941, as well-placed guns were not expected to be required to move around and so permanent infrastructure could be built from the start. Artillery positions were characterised by a myriad of local variations depending on the type of weapon involved, its specific role and those responsible for construction (Figure 3.18). At Hollesley the two 6-inch guns were located in idiosyncratic emplacements open to the front and with the immediate ancillary structures behind. This was markedly different than the position at Cliff House, Dunwich, also for 6-inch guns, where gun pits were constructed, rather than emplacements, and were of concrete sandbagged construction. Unusually, part of the wider battery site survives, consisting of an underground command post and trenches and gun pits that formed part of the close defence posts. A particularly clear example of the archaeological remains of field artillery and the development of one troop position during this period is to be found at Wrentham, near Southwold. Here, a site for four 6-inch howitzers had been established in July 1940 by 'A' Troop, 'A' Battery, 72 Medium Regiment, Royal Artillery.[57] The position was due to be moved as part of the reorganisation of early 1941, but when this move was cancelled (probably because it was a good site), the site was redeveloped with gun houses of a rudimentary design

---

56   TNA WO 166/4547 (War Diary, 22nd Royal Fusiliers).
57   TNA WO 166/1935 (War Diary, 72nd Medium Regiment, Royal Artillery), 9.7.40.

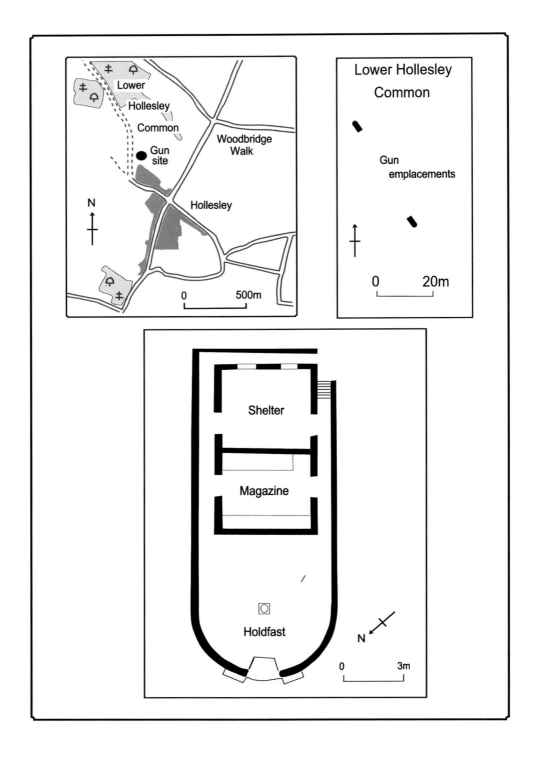

Lower Hollesley Common

Gun emplacements

0   20m

Lower Hollesley Common

Woodbridge Walk

Gun site

Hollesley

N

0   500m

Shelter

Magazine

Holdfast

N

0   3m

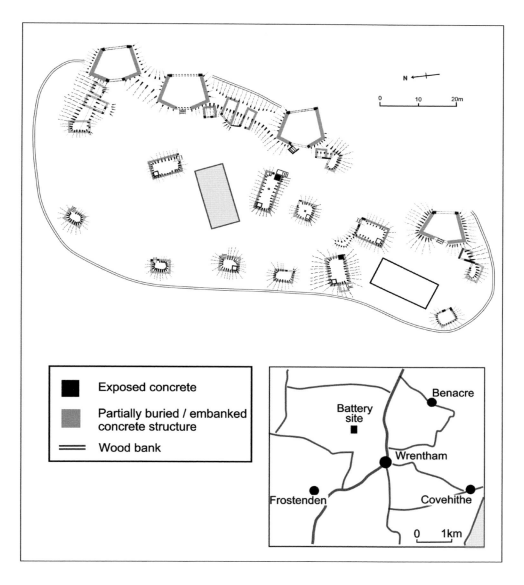

Figure 3.18 a (left) & b (above). Artillery gun sites: Hollesley Common, position for two 6-inch guns, 10th Super Heavy Regiment showing unusual form of integrated gunhouse; Wrentham, position for four 6-inch howitzers, 'A' Battery, 72nd Medium Regiment showing a more conventional layout of a troop of field guns with partially embanked gun houses, crew shelters and magazines to the rear and the probable bases of two Nissen huts.

Figure 3.19. Troop site at Wrentham. Rear of concrete gunhouse and ammunition lockers from 1941.

Figure 3.20. Anti-invasion defences at Felixstowe, 1944. This shows the defences that were completed during the summer of 1941, with two anti-tank obstacles (anti-tank cubes and scaffolding) and barbed wire. The beach was also heavily mined. (John Smith)

that are known from elsewhere in the Sector, along with crew shelters and ammunition storage completed in concrete, with work probably finished by March (Figure 3.19).

1941: ideal and reality

The cumulative changes to the anti-invasion landscape made during 1941 were therefore significant, and when 15th Division were rotated out of the Sector in November 1941 the coastal defences were altogether more formidable (Figure 3.20). Greater resources had allowed for an altogether more elaborate prepared battlefield to be made on the ground. But, despite the effort expended on their creation, the reforms initiated in January were in places unfinished, with sections of anti-tank ditch and scaffolding remaining incomplete. While the firm impression given by documents is that 1941 saw the imposition of a far-reaching new design on the Sector's anti-invasion defences, the need to defend the same places as in 1940 and the structuring force of topography meant that not all the changes taking place at this time were as radical as might be imagined. In the northern Sandlings the 'spurs' were most heavily defended and here defences tended to cluster, while in the southern part of the region a more 'linear' arrangement reflected the particular nature of the coastline and its immediate hinterland. Analysis of the 1941 works also reveals the aspects of the previous year's defences that were seen as particularly problematic. The cause of most complaints were remote section posts that were unable to give mutual support, which left handfuls of men isolated in positions that could easily be overrun in battle. That such a situation had been a response by units suddenly faced with the problem of defending an overly extended front was not necessarily fully appreciated by new arrivals who faced a slightly better situation. It is undoubtedly significant that the heaviest criticism was directed at those parts of the line that had been most undermanned in 1940 and where there was consequently little scope for defence in depth.

Reorganisation and abandonment, 1942–43

The final phase of the anti-invasion defences began in November 1941, with the replacement of 15th Division by 54th Division. The latter's time on the coast coincided with the effective ending of the invasion threat in June 1942, something anticipated in January, when the formation was put onto the 'Lower Establishment', meaning that it was not expected to serve overseas and that its trained men would be drafted off into units destined to fight abroad. As a consequence it received a low priority for new equipment, was gradually denuded of its units, especially artillery, and was eventually disbanded at the end of 1943.[58] Nonetheless, its time in the Sector is important, not least because during its period in the Sandlings it undertook a further reorganisation of the coastal defences. This latter phase in the development of coastal defences normally

---

58   M. Bellis, *Divisions of the British Army, 1939–1945* (Crewe, 1986), p. 56.

receives less attention that those of 1940 and 1941, but deserves consideration in its own right, as the changes were far-reaching.

Fifty-Fourth Division had been responsible for coastal defence in Suffolk in late 1939 and early 1940; any still in the ranks from that time were no doubt taken aback at the transformation of the defences that had taken place in the intervening time. The formation's arrival was marked by the customary gripes of incoming units about their inherited situation and almost immediately criticisms began to circulate about the organisation of the defences. The 2nd Hertfordshires noted the 'mass of confused defences' on their battalion front and the large similar quantity of 'defence plans and dug positions, many of them badly sited and fallen into disuse'.[59] A particularly instructive case was at Lowestoft, where the brigade commander described the organisation of the Sub-Sector as 'tactically unsound', citing the defended perimeter of 25 kilometres, posts up to 900 metres (1000 yards) apart and places where anti-tank obstacles were not covered by fire.[60] There were some positives to be derived from the physical state of the coastline, however. The abundance of redundant fieldworks meant that, as long as adequate camouflage and track discipline was maintained, it would be impossible for enemy aerial reconnaissance to distinguish between those posts that were still occupied and those that had been abandoned. Additionally, they might give the erroneous impression that the British had concentrated all their troops on the coast, making the defences altogether more formidable.[61]

While senior officers recognised their subordinates' natural inclination to organise the defence of their respective areas according to their own preferences, there was a general unease at the idea of undertaking a further round of major construction works.[62] The cumulative efforts of three divisions meant that the scale of defences was considerable and a clear perception existed throughout the chain of command that additional work was unnecessary; in a telling remark, Lowestoft's commander noted that, given that so much had already been built, he was 'finding it increasingly difficult to direct units or Home Guard as regards work on defences'.[63]

Yet in the early months of 1942 54th Division took up where 15th Division had left off the previous September, with a continuation of scaffolding and wiring, which presumably represented the rump of works left unfinished by their predecessors.[64] The 2nd/4th Essex at this time recorded work on the construction of machine-gun posts,

59   TNA WO 166/8725 (War Diary, 2nd Hertfordshire Regiment), 8.1.42.

60   TNA WO 166/1051 (War Diary, 198th Infantry Brigade), Defence – No. 1 Sub-Sector, 30.12.41.

61   TNA WO 166/8739 (War Diary, 8th King's Regiment), Special Directive by Commander No. 1 Sub-Sector', c.May, 1942.

62   TNA WO166/4134 (War Diary, 6th Beds and Herts Regiment), 54 Div Training Memorandum No. 5 of 1941 Winter Training 1941/42, November 1941; TNA WO 166/4156 (War Diary, 6th Border Regiment), 'Commanding Officer's Instruction No. 10, 2.12.41.

63   TNA WO 166/1051 (War Diary, 198th Infantry Brigade), Defence – No. 1 Sub-Sector, 30.12.41.

64   TNA WO166/7199 (War Diary, 232nd Coast Battery, Royal Artillery), 18.2.42.

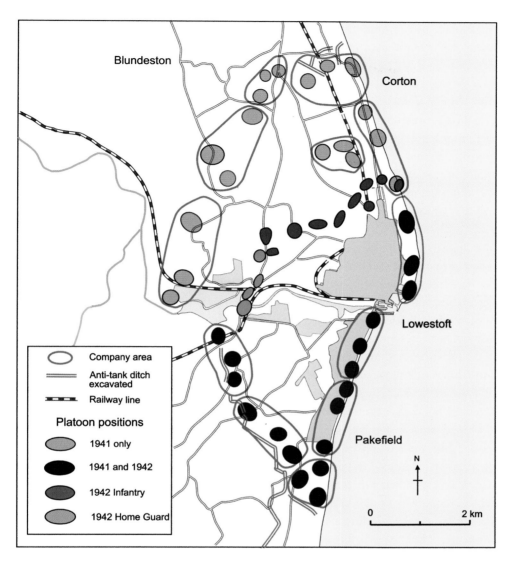

Figure 3.21. Defence lines at Lowestoft, 1941–42, showing the successive schemes to defend the landward side. That of 1941 involved the creation of a line of posts to the west of the town that extended beyond those of 1940 (see Figure 2.28), which was subsequently pulled back during reorganisation in 1942.

the strengthening of scaffolding and the laying of barbed wire and new minefields.[65] Additional lengths of scaffolding are also recorded as being laid around the Minsmere ECDB in March and April.[66] But in comparison to the previous year such works were

---

65   TNA WO 166/8671 (War Diary, 2nd/4th Essex Regiment), 15.1.42; 3.2.42.

66   TNA WO166/7199 (War Diary, 232 Coast Battery, Royal Artillery), Precis of Constructional Works, March/ April 1942.

small-scale and represented the completion of unfinished works, maintenance and repair. More significant is the cumulative evidence for ongoing lower-level changes that were codified in May in a new Divisional defence scheme that in many respects took the basic strategy envisaged by Brooke and extended it to its logical conclusion.

The 1942 reorganisation

The underlying difficulties were the longstanding ones: there were not enough troops both to adequately cover the coastline and guard inland against an initial attack by enemy forces landed by air. But the proposed method of dealing with these issues was different to that put forward in 1940 and 1941. Now the underlying principle was that troops should not be 'dissipated from the start in small packets all along the coast', as men tied to their positions were a wasted asset if they did not happen to find themselves directly confronted by the enemy. The basis of the new scheme was to retain as many uncommitted men as possible so that they could be moved to wherever the battle demanded. But, as the coast could not be left totally unguarded, localities would be retained in the most vulnerable places with their constituent positions reinforced with additional barbed wire and the defenders provisioned with the lion's share of heavy weapons so that they could hold out for as long as possible. In the words of the Divisional commander: 'Their positions will be made as impregnable as material and labour will allow, and they will stand and fight to the last.'[67] In essence, the new scheme was a major redeployment, rather than one involving major works on fixed defences, but resulted in some important changes on the ground.

The new arrangements again played out differently across Sub-Sectors. By far the most significant new construction work was in Sub-Sector 1 at Lowestoft. Here, reflecting the concerns identified the previous December, the defensive perimeter was reduced in length by withdrawing its northern and western lines back towards the town, while the sea-facing element of the defences was given over to the Home Guard (Figure 3.21). As a result, a new defence line of fieldworks and scaffolding was planned in February and constructed from March.[68] Elsewhere, the most striking aspect of the scheme was the *withdrawal* of the majority of troops from the beaches to take up concentration areas a little inland, where they were intended to act as a reserve and move to meet any threat, from either the sea or the landward side. In Sub-Sector 2 two battalions were to concentrate around Wrentham, in Sub-Sector 3 around Westleton, Minsmere and Aldeburgh and in Sub-Sector 4 around Ipswich and Martlesham and inland from Felixstowe.

This was itself not entirely new, because, as we have seen, placing a proportion of troops to face a westward battle was a feature of the 1941 reorganisation, but now there was no western-facing line to be held and so the number of troops withdrawn from

---

67   TNA 166/6380 (War Diary, 54th Division, HQ), Operational Instruction No. 15: Defence Lay-Out, 1.5.42.

68   TNA WO 166/8159 (War Diary, 249th Field Company, Royal Engineers), 6–7.2.42, 25.2.42; TNA WO 166/4156 (War Diary, 6th Border Regiment), 16.3.42; trace of 22.4.42

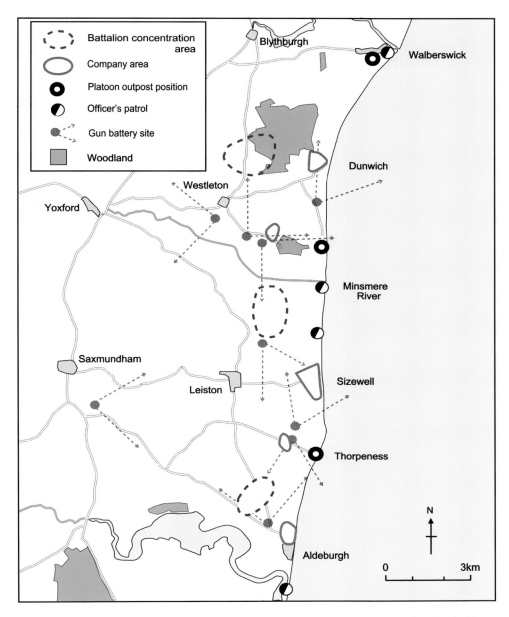

Figure 3.22. Sub-Sector 3 Defence Scheme, 1942. Here battalion concentration areas lay inland with only beach companies, outpost platoons and patrols on the coast itself. A shortage of artillery meant that, as well as firing east, guns had arcs of fire to the north and south. Compare with Figure 3.2.

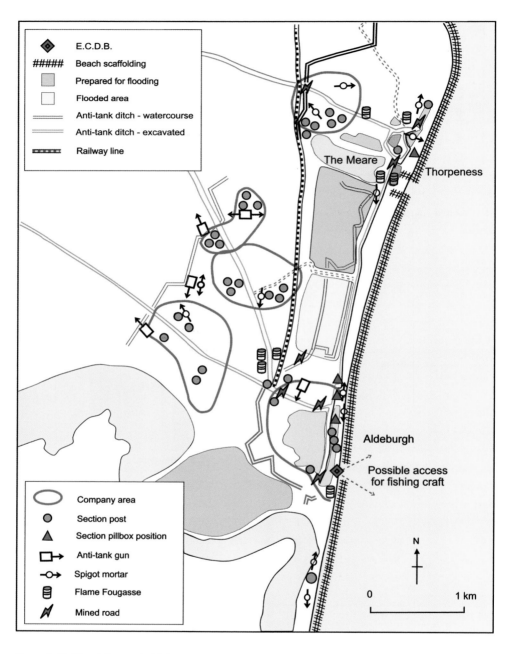

Figure 3.23. The defence of Aldeburgh, 1942. One company and one platoon held the coast, with the battalion concentration area slightly inland.

static positions was significantly greater. Extensive parts of the coastline the defence of which had been felt to be of considerable importance in the previous two years were either abandoned altogether or saw troop levels dramatically reduced. Reductions in levels of manning took place at Walberswick, Dunwich Heath and Thorpeness; at Orford, company strength deployments were reduced to platoons. Areas were entirely vacated by the infantry or were now only to be guarded by patrols commanded by an officer, as at Corton, the stretches of coast between Pakefield and Kessingland, Easton and Southwold and Minsmere and Sizewell and, most dramatically of all, in Sub-Sector 4, where, with the exception of Orford and Bawdsey radar station and Felixstowe sea front, the entire infantry defence was removed. These areas continued to maintain their coastal batteries and artillery observation posts, but the boots on the ground now had no fixed battle positions; rather, they were to concentrate and move to where they were needed.

In contrast, those places on the coast that retained their importance in the new scheme were to have their localities maintained and made stronger. These were specific locations that had always been identified as important to defend as they had good beaches and usually roads leading inland, and so 'beach companies' were retained at Benacre, Easton Wood, Southwold, Dunwich, Sizewell and Aldebugh. Even so, in total these amounted to seven companies of regular infantry on the beaches between Pakefield and Bawdsey, compared with 17 the previous year. The larger gaps that now existed where men had been pulled out of the line were to be filled with larger minefields which, when taken together with the inundated areas and static obstacles of scaffolding and anti-tank cubes, meant that the idea of localities with gaps protected by obstacles implemented the previous year was taken to its extreme (Figure 3.22).

Inevitably the changes brought about a further reorganisation on the ground as the location of positions were once again changed and defence plans altered. This is particularly clear at Aldeburgh and Thorpeness, where a trace of the positions of the 5th Royal Berkshire Regiment shows the revised military landscape in detail (Figure 3.23).[69] Here only one of the battalion's four rifle companies was actually deployed: this 'beach company' occupied the town itself, while the others and the headquarters had concentration areas either adjacent to or astride the anti-tank ditches one kilometre inland. Of these, the northern company detached one platoon to occupy Thorpeness, but the bulk of the battalion was withdrawn from the immediate coastline. Given that Aldeburgh was seen as requiring defence throughout the war, the new arrangements were not a complete break with the past, but those at Thorpeness were very different. The 'outpost' platoon, together with 20 men from the Home Guard, were the only defenders, in contrast to the whole company that had occupied fixed field positions there the previous year. While numbers of men on the coast itself may have diminished,

---

69   See two traces/documents: TNA WO 166/8851 (War Diary, 5th Royal Berkshire Regiment), Operational Instruction No. 3, 17.4.42; *ibid.*, Defence Scheme, 21.9.42.

the increase in firepower is clearly apparent. The spigot mortar became the leading anti-tank weapon for the beach companies, usually one per platoon, but sometimes more; four were placed on the Martello tower at Aldeburgh, while even small units such as the outpost platoon at Thorpeness had two 6-pounder anti-tank guns and one 75mm gun within its locality. Similar arrangements are seen elsewhere. At Southwold, the seaward side of the town was no longer defended; with the presence of cliffs and extensive fixed defences it was clearly felt that any attempt to make a landing and establish a beachhead would have been difficult. The town was instead defended from the landward side by a company whose three platoon positions occupied slightly different positions to those of the previous year, again augmented by the Home Guard. What is most apparent is the isolation of the beach company; the area to the north of the town previously held by another company was now entrusted to mobile patrols.[70] At Felixstowe a more idiosyncratic defence plan had been worked out in February and March.[71] On 'Action Stations' the company of regular troops covering the beach was to withdraw 800 metres (half a mile) inland to act as a reserve, with their place being taken by the Home Guard. In a scheme not seen anywhere else at any time during the war, in the event of an attack from the west and where there was an absence of a seaborne threat, the two flank companies were instructed to thin out their line and occupy positions to the rear, leaving the beach positions largely unguarded.

A measure of how things had changed is illustrated by the fate of pillboxes. Early in 1942 the War Office had solicited reports on those that could potentially be strengthened and in the Suffolk Sector there is evidence that the issue was discussed on the ground and a small amount of work conducted, but which ceased almost as soon as it began.[72] A list of pillboxes drawn up at this time shows that across the Sector only a minority of those of 1940 were still in use and, of these, the majority could be abandoned, as they no longer featured in the forthcoming scheme.[73] At a local level, of some 26 pillboxes in the battalion area of the 2nd/4th Essex Regiment in July 1942 only four were manned on 'Stand To', with a further two retained as secondary positions and two more used as observation posts. The remaining 18 had been stopped up and were disused, with two already demolished.[74] The contrast with 1940 could hardly be greater.

Concurrent with changes to the infantry defence were those taking place in the artillery landscape. As a Lower Establishment formation, 54th Division saw the piecemeal removal of its field artillery, which by September meant that in Sub-Sector 4 there was 'a total lack of field artillery'; while positions for them existed, there were

70   TNA WO 166/6623 (War Diary, 162nd Infantry Brigade), Defence Scheme, Appendix 3.
71   TNA WO 166/8696 (War Diary, 10th Gloucestershire Regiment), Operational Instruction No. 1, 5.2.42; TNA WO166/6645 (War Diary, 212th Infantry Brigade), Operational Instruction No. 18, 10.3.42.
72   TNA WO 166/8159 (War Diary, 249th Field Company, Royal Engineers), 5.2.42; 10.2.42; 17.2.42; 25.2.42.
73   TNA WO 99/2528 (Home Defence, Pillboxes), Pillboxes, 47/G (O) to HQ Eastern Command from Commander 11 Corps District, 21.2.42.
74   TNA WO 166/8671 (War Diary, 2nd/4th Essex Regiment), Operational Order, Appendix F, 31.7.42.

no guns to man them.[75] The change of strategy within the Sector, together with a smaller number of guns, was reflected in the number and distribution of artillery sites. The trend initiated in the spring of 1941 to move battery positions close to or within infantry localities continued and gun sites that had escaped the process that year were now relocated, while in places such as Southwold field guns were established within the areas of the new beach companies.[76] The depletion of the number of guns together with the revised strategy of mobile reserves meant that arcs of fire for field guns were altered, with a significant proportion firing either westwards or – unusually up to this point – laterally along the coast.

There is perhaps a supreme irony in the fact that – with its thin deployment on the coast itself and the majority of troops held inland as a mobile reserve – the Sector defence scheme as set down in May 1942 had a closer affinity with the J.C. Plan of 1939 than with the schemes of 1940 and 1941: an irony compounded by the fact that it was the same formation holding the coast in both periods. But the new arrangements were short-lived. In the month after 54th Division had codified its new scheme Home Forces confirmed that training was to take precedence over defences and that only those works that could be completed by that September should continue.[77]

As will be seen in Chapter 5, from this point the pattern established since 1940 of delivering training alongside building and manning defences ceased, and training became the principal activity for those units on the coast. During this time regular troops continued to guard their posts and maintain patrols, but the extent of these measures did not go beyond what might reasonably be expected of any military unit in the field during wartime.[78] From the summer of 1943 the infantry battalions of 54th Division started to vacate the Sector and were not replaced, and their billets were now occupied by troops training on the Orford Battle Area.[79] By the end of the year coast watching, as it had now become known, was carried out by the Home Guard. The extent to which the perceived threat had reduced is seen in the levels of manning. On the stretch of coast from Southwold to Aldeburgh one company of part-time Home Guard were responsible for watching what had been defended by a brigade of regular troops 18 months earlier.[80]

---

75   TNA WO 166/8739 (War Diary, 8th King's Regiment), Operational Order No. 1, 4.9.42; Appendix B, 5.10.42.

76   TNA WO 166/7247 (War Diary, 75th Medium Regiment, Royal Artillery), January 1942, *passim*.

77   Dobinson, *Anti-Invasion*, p. 51.

78   TNA WO 166/10805 (War Diary, 198th Infantry Brigade), Appendix A, issued with 198 Infantry Brigade Operational Instruction No. 3, 8.4.43.

79   TNA WO 166/12537 (War Diary, 2nd/4th Essex Regiment), March 1943 *passim*; TNA WO 166/12482 (War Diary, 5th Royal Berkshire Regiment), May 1943 *passim*; TNA WO 166/10795 (War Diary, 163rd Infantry Brigade), Location Statement, 10.6.43.

80   TNA WO 205/1092 (Assault Training Areas, Eastern Command), Correspondence C-in-C to HQ 21st Army Group, December 1943; TNA WO 199/3078 (Coast Watching, Overlord), Coast Watching 'Exercise Overlord', 23.12.43; TNA WO 166/14537 (Area War Diary, East Suffolk Sub-District), Operational Instruction, 31.5.44.

End game and raiding, 1943

The end game for coastal defence in the Sandlings lay in the arrangements made to guard against isolated raids. British expertise in operations against enemy-held coastlines led to the erroneous perception that their adversaries were capable of similar action, and a set of procedures to warn of raids, codenamed 'Bandit Alert' and then 'Bugbear Alert', were developed, which replaced the longer sets of instructions for 'Stand To' and 'Action Stations'.[81] By 1943 what was known as the 'Flood State' was issued daily; this indicated the suitability of the weather conditions and sea state for a raid either from the air or by sea where the raiders were expected to make their escape by boat, and at the highest state of alert those places thought vulnerable to sudden attack were to increase vigilance.[82] Occasionally the arrangements against raiding were the subject of specific exercises. Exercise 'Oyster', on 14 February 1943, rehearsed the counter-measures to be taken in the event of an enemy raid or reconnaissance on Orford, which was found to be capable of 'strong resistance' if attacked and whose defenders could delay the enemy until the arrival of other troops.[83] Elsewhere, the Home Guard was occasionally exercised alongside their regular counterparts to ensure that their defences were adequate, as during Exercise 'Deben', which tested those at Wilford Bridge, near Woodbridge.[84] But residual concerns about small-scale German raids or larger operations to disrupt British preparations in the lead-up to D-Day continued surprisingly late. In 1943–4 detailed schemes existed for local defence by 79th Armoured Division in the event of an airborne attack on the environs of Orford.[85]

For the first half of the war the Sandlings had been prepared to meet an invasion that never came and its landscape was transformed as a result. With hindsight the efforts made to fortify the coastline tend to look somewhat wasteful and perhaps pointless as it is now known that, had it ever happened, Operation Sealion would have been directed against Kent and Sussex, rather than East Anglia. But this is to ignore the reality at the time and the perceived nature of the threat and also neglects the fact that, although the anticipated invasion did not occur, it was not the case that the region was entirely at peace.

---

81 TNA WO 166/4156 (War Diary, 6th Border Regiment), Commanding Officer's Instruction No. 11 Beach Defence, January 1942.

82 TNA WO 166/10805 (War Diary, 198th Infantry Brigade), 198th Infantry Brigade Operational Instruction No. 3, 6.4.43.

83 *Ibid.*, Final Conference – Exercise 'Oyster' Director's Notes on the Exercise, February, 1943.

84 *Ibid.*, 12.3.43.

85 TNA WO 166/12031 (War Diary, 79th Engineer Assault Squadron, Royal Engineers), Secret Operation Order No. 23, 5.5.43; TNA WO 166/11996 (War Diary, 6th Engineer Assault Regiment), 6th Engineer Assault Troops Operational Instruction No. 1, Anti-Raid Measures, 6.7.43.

Chapter 4

The landscape of air defence, 1939–45

While the defences put in place to protect the coastline of the Sandlings were never put to the test, those intended to guard the airspace above were regularly tested – and were breached – throughout the conflict. The war in the skies was an 'active' one: with the Suffolk coast only a short flying time from Luftwaffe airfields in the occupied Low Countries and also on a flight path for hostile aircraft conducting raids on the industrial Midlands, visitations by the enemy were a common occurrence. The air war was also a part of the conflict that existed from the start until almost the very end, beginning with initial forays by aircraft in 1939 and culminating in a brief but intense period of defence in 1944 against V1 flying bombs. Those structures put in place to give early warnings of approaching aircraft and provide the means to retaliate – what is termed here the 'landscape of air defence' – comprised installations such as radar stations and airfields that were provisioned with their own air and land defences, and anti-aircraft gun batteries, barrage balloons and searchlight sites, whose role was to deter or engage enemy planes. In common with the anti-invasion landscape, that of air defence was subject to regular reconfigurations, but here changes tended to be reactive, responding to actual rather than hypothesised patterns of enemy operations. In this important way, the landscape of the air war was different to that described in the previous two chapters, in that, almost from the start, it involved direct contact with the enemy (Figure 4.1). It was also distinctive in that its structuring forces were more heavily influenced by human geography; but, as we shall see, topography was still a factor in influencing spatial patterning on the ground. The discussion here is concerned with the activities of Anti-Aircraft (AA) Command (rather than those of the RAF or the Royal Observer Corps), whose campaign against the Luftwaffe has been well documented by Dobinson, meaning that what follows is very much a regional view.[1] But it is one that is important: wartime estimates put the number of high explosive bombs dropped on east Suffolk at over 1000 and incendiaries at over 40,000, and it is clear from the evidence of oral history that

---

1   C.S. Dobinson, *Twentieth-Century Fortifications in England, vol. 1 Anti-aircraft Artillery: England's Air Defence Gunsites, 1914–46* (York, 1996) and site gazetteers; Dobinson, *AA Command*.

Figure 4.1. Bullet marks on the wartime transmitter block at Bawdsey Radar station: rare physical evidence of the air war in the Sandlings.

the experience of the conflict in the Sandlings was very much defined by the air war.[2]

The air war

The landscape of air defence was largely shaped by three factors: the location of major targets for air attack; the weapons used by AA Command; and the nature of German operations. The chief potential targets were the ports of Lowestoft and Harwich, especially the latter, as it was the site of a naval base and relevant here as its defence drew in Felixstowe, on the Suffolk side of the Orwell. Harwich's role as a Royal Navy fleet anchorage was significant in itself, but from July 1940, when passage for merchant vessels through the Straits of Dover in daylight ceased, its value increased as it became a staging post for convoy ships.[3] The significance of Lowestoft also increased over the course of the conflict as it became the main base for the Royal Navy Patrol Service, whose auxiliary craft took the lead in anti-submarine and mine-sweeping operation in home waters. Until 1944 the environs of both ports saw the heaviest deployment of AA defences. The other military targets in the Sandlings were

2   M. Bowyer, *Air Raid! The Enemy Air Offensive against East Anglia, 1939–45* (Wellingborough, 1986), p. 330; D. Shirreff and A. Sharman, *Suffolk Memories* (Sudbury, 1998), pp. 15–16; A. Sharman and P. Whyte, *Further Suffolk Memories* (Sudbury, 2001), pp. 161–4.

3   Dobinson, *AA Command*, p. 211.

its radar stations, especially in the early part of the war those at Bawdsey, Dunwich and Darsham; the Fighter Command aerodromes at Nacton and Martlesham near Ipswich; and the Emergency Coastal Defence Batteries. The anti-invasion defences were also the subject of strafing attacks, especially in 1940–41, and the region's seaside towns were easy victims for indiscriminate 'nuisance' raids intended to cause maximum disruption with minimal effort.

In order to protect these places early warning was provided by radar, and here the Sandlings held a significant place, in that before the war it was at Orford and Bawdsey that the initial technological breakthroughs were pioneered, the latter being the first working RAF radar station in the country. As the radar network expanded, further stations were established across the region as additions to the overall network and, later, in order to direct friendly fighters onto intruders. As part of national schemes to protect Britain's cities and industrial areas batteries of searchlights were placed across the Sandlings in order to illuminate targets for AA batteries and for night fighters. The direct engagement of hostile aircraft from the ground was the responsibility of AA Command, who could deploy the heavy 3.7-inch anti-aircraft (HAA) gun in either a mobile or a static version and, before it was phased out, the older 3-inch anti-aircraft gun.[4] These heavy guns were manually operated and accurate fire was labour intensive and required considerable skill, but wartime development of radar-assisted gun laying and predicting revolutionised gunnery so by the end of the conflict guns were power operated and laid automatically. HAA guns were usually arranged in four gun batteries, which were substantial sites akin to coastal batteries, with technical buildings, camp sites and structures for close defence.[5] HAA batteries were grouped together into concentrations known as Gun Defended Areas (GDAs), of which there came to be two in the Sandlings. Harwich had been designated for air defence prior to the war and remained a GDA throughout the conflict, with its reach extending to the defence of Felixstowe, Nacton and Martlesham airfields and Bawdsey radar station. As a result of successive German operations against Great Yarmouth and Lowestoft in 1941, this area also became designated as a GDA and was provisioned with heavy AA ordnance. HAA guns were intended to strike high-flying aircraft while they were on bombing runs, but were found to be of limited use against dive bombers or fast low-flying aircraft, where an engagement was often over in seconds – and, as it turned out, it was these kinds of action that predominated in the Sandlings. In these circumstances the chief means of defence were Light Anti-Aircraft guns (LAA): the 40mm Bofor, the 20mm Oerlikon and Hispano and the Lewis machine gun. The Lewis was often mounted in pairs or as quadruples and, despite initial doubts, proved effective against

---

4   P. Chamberlin and T. Gander, *Anti-Aircraft Guns* (London, 1975), p. 49; I.V. Hogg, *Allied Artillery of World War Two* (Marlborough, 1998), pp. 94–114.

5   Dobinson, *AA Command*, pp. 319–34.

such attacks.[6] GDAs were by far the most heavily defended places, with a combination of HAA, LAA, searchlights and balloons, but outside these areas air defences were a limited resource and so it was inevitable that much of the Suffolk coastline was, effectively, undefended.

The pattern of the air war in the Sandlings was set early in the conflict. German air activity chiefly took the form of minor incursions by small numbers of aircraft, usually for the purposes of mine laying, reconnaissance, strikes on shipping and opportunistic raids on land targets. Larger formations of raiders usually passed over at great height on their way to more distant objectives. In 1940 and 1941, while the intensity of raids directed against the Sandlings could never compare with the large Luftwaffe operations against Britain's cities, on a number of occasions the region's airfields were drawn into the wider aerial battles. Both Nacton and Martlesham airfields were attacked during the Battle of Britain, the heaviest raid taking place on Martlesham on 15 August 1940 by 15 bombers and fighter bombers with a fighter escort. From the spring of 1942 the Sandlings was caught up in the Luftwaffe's wider 'Fringe Target' campaign against coastal resorts, in which so-called 'tip and run' raids caused damage and loss of life out of all proportion to the number of aircraft engaged.[7] These attacks accounted for the heaviest loss of life and tended to be those remembered in post-war histories: that on 22 October 1942 killed 11 civilians in Orford; that on Aldeburgh on 15 December 1942 killed 9; while at Lowestoft on 13 January 1943 a single raider emerged from a snow storm and its four bombs killed 70 civilians and military personnel.[8]

Small-scale incidents – albeit significant enough for those caught up in them – made up the vast majority of encounters with the Luftwaffe. The ECDB at Aldeburgh was targeted three days running in the summer of 1940 and that at Sizewell was machine-gunned and bombed on 18 August, 27 October and 5 November 1940 and again in September 1942.[9] Such attacks were often vigorously pressed home at a very low level; in 1940 artillery observers in the 'The House in the Clouds' water tower at Thorpeness had the somewhat surreal experience of looking down on German aircraft flying beneath them.[10] Enemy aircraft came in with such speed that there was rarely the opportunity for air sentries to return fire, which was in any case often so ineffective that strict rules of engagement were issued so that ammunition was not wasted by men shooting blindly with little chance of success. During the Martlesham raid of 15

---

6   A.J. Cooper, *Anti-Aircraft Command, 1939–1955, The Other Forgotten Army* (Fleet Hargate, 1994), p. 125. In addition there was the UP rocket, which was developed during 1941 as 'Z' batteries, but these did not feature in any number in the Sandlings, with only a small deployment at Lowestoft and around Ipswich.

7   Dobinson, *AA Command*, pp. 351–5, 364–77.

8   TNA WO 166/7711 (War Diary, 125th Light Anti-Aircraft Regiment), November 1942; TNA WO 166/7376 (War Diary, 6th Anti-Aircraft Brigade), 15.12.42; Foynes, *Battle of the East Coast*, p. 254.

9   TNA WO 166/1835 (War Diary, 355th Coast Battery); TNA WO 166/7210 (War Diary, 232nd Coast Battery, Royal Artillery).

10   Robertson, *Rose and the Arrow*, p. 40.

August, while there were no serious casualties, severe embarrassment was caused by the fact that no warning had been given, ground fire had been futile and only one Bofor had been fired. Owing to the Luftwaffe's uncanny ability to retain the initiative and so the element of surprise, standing orders for air sentries throughout the war emphasised the need for alertness and for continuous manning of posts from dawn to dusk.[11] The reality of much AA work was monotonous hours or days scanning the skyline without incident before suddenly confronting the enemy in an engagement that lasted only a few seconds. The inability to repel intruders led to numerous appeals – usually unsuccessful – for air defence from local commanders. Pleas from a naval officer at Southwold in 1940, for example, requested anti-aircraft guns both for the coastal towns and the ECDBs, which were being attacked by single bombers and were so incapable of fighting back that he was astonished that the latter had not already been bombed out of existence.[12] The air war in the Sandlings was therefore one of a particular kind: a constant trickle of enemy activity but without any decisive outcome.

The landscape of Gun Defended Areas:
Harwich/Felixstowe and Yarmouth/Lowestoft

In contrast to the sluggish development of the anti-invasion defences during the Phoney War, this early period witnessed a flurry of activity when it came to air defences. The need to provide AA cover for Royal Navy anchorages had been agreed before the war and at Harwich activity commenced before the outbreak of hostilities, with work taking place in August 1939 to protect newly established searchlight and light machine-gun emplacements.[13] Two days after the declaration of war 3.7-inch guns in what became the Harwich GDA were reported ready for action at Beacon Hill, Dovercourt, Landguard and Trimley, while arrangements were made for the protection of gun emplacements with sandbags and camouflage. The following two months were characterised by a series of confused orders and counter-orders involving the movement of guns, the creation and abandonment of new emplacements and the posting of AA regiments to the area for as little as a few weeks before being moved on.[14] After the war, this period in AA Command's history was seen as particularly challenging nationwide and so it was in the Harwich GDA. One operation room for ten men was housed in an underground chamber at Landguard Fort which 'has one entrance and no ventilation and with temperature of mid-summer outside, the atmosphere in the "Tomb" is – well, better left unsaid.'[15] Bad weather in October caused

---

11   TNA WO 166/2229 (War Diary, 6th Anti-Aircraft Brigade), 7.9.40.

12   TNA ADM 199/66 (AA Defence of Ports and Naval Establishments), Anti-aircraft Defence against Single Bombers, 23.8.40; 29.10.40.

13   Dobinson, *Anti-aircraft Artillery*, pp. 49–52; TNA WO 166/2168 (War Diary, 6th Anti-Aircraft Division, G), List of Sites, 26.8.39.

14   TNA WO 166/2529 (War Diary, 248th Heavy Anti-Aircraft Battery), September to December 1939, *passim*.

15   TNA WO 166/2662 (War Diary, 409th Heavy Anti-Aircraft Battery), 5.9.39.

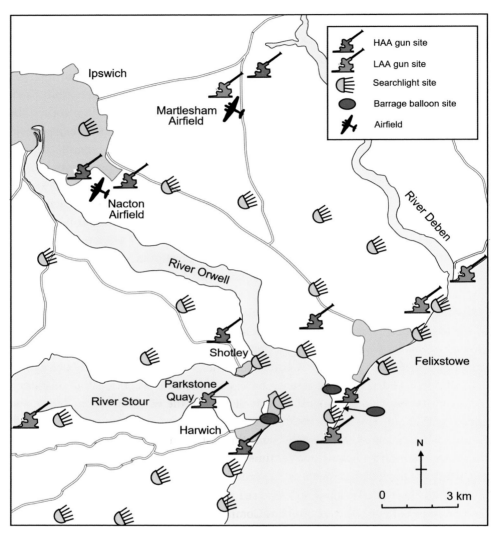

Figure 4.2. Disposition of guns in the Harwich GDA, February 1940. Heavy guns lay in a cordon around Harwich Haven, with lighter guns, searchlights and barrage balloons scattered across the area.

problems with waterlogging as positions flooded and had to be constantly pumped out, and wet ground made handling guns difficult, prompting one war diarist to state that 'the inclemency of the weather seemed to numb the wits of officers and men'.[16] Nonetheless, the first recorded engagement with the enemy took place on 17 October 1939, when two HAA sites at Trimley and Dovercourt fired some 11 rounds against a lone German raider.

16 TNA WO 166/2529 (War Diary, 248th Heavy Anti-Aircraft Battery), 28.10.39.

Work continued throughout November and December 1939 amid less than ideal material conditions. The gun site at Dovercourt in Essex was described as 'being like a wet farmyard' as permission was awaited regarding the construction of roads and paths, while 25 December, it was remarked, was 'undisturbed by alarms – A fine sunny day which with the rest and Christmas dinner appeared to be enjoyed by all, except perhaps at H-3 [Dovercourt] where the sun began to thaw the mud.'[17] But by the following month a layout for AA guns in the Harwich GDA had been agreed and the distribution of sites confirmed (Figure 4.2). A cordon of heavy 3.7-inch guns, searchlights and barrage balloons ringed the haven itself, with outlying heavy guns at Nacton and Martlesham.[18] The HAA guns were typically sited on the highest available open ground away from the area of Harwich and Felixstowe towns, with LAA guns spread a little more evenly, but with idiosyncratic arrangements reflecting the perceived vulnerability of the haven. At Parkstone Quay six Lewis Guns were mounted at each end of the pier and the pre-First World War depot and submarine repair ship HMS *Cyclops*, which was tied up and armed with two 4-inch guns and four twin Lewis machine guns, was a bespoke static gun battery in its own right.

In these early months gun batteries reported only spasmodic firing on enemy planes, whose chief activity was mine laying at night, with one operation on 21 November proving successful when the destroyer HMS *Gypsy* was sunk with the loss of 30 of her crew.[19] This incident established a pattern of an enemy operation being followed almost immediately by a British response; in this case, some 17 searchlights were moved to more suitable positions where they could illuminate the airspace being used by the mine-laying aircraft.[20] But with the exception of a small number of relocated positions and the replacement of older 3-inch guns, the basic framework of the Harwich GDA was put in place early in the war. Over time there was a general development of gunsite and searchlight facilities, with concrete structures replacing those made of sandbags, but to judge from aerial photographs and site plans these seem to have comprised local modifications of structures typical of AA Command, with batteries placing their guns in an arc with command and ancillary structures in close proximity.[21] That at Landguard in 1941, for example, shows these arrangements and with little attempt at camouflage; this was one such area where the site was intended to be seen by hostile aircraft to deter raiding (Figure 4.3). In this respect the Harwich GDA did much that was asked of it. The presence of HAA guns was a deterrent in itself and so aircraft tended to avoid flying

17 TNA WO 166/2529 (War Diary 248th Heavy Anti-Aircraft Battery), 25.12.39.
18 TNA ADM 199/66 (AA Defence of Ports and Naval Establishments), Anti-aircraft defences Harwich minutes of meeting, of 6th D.C.O.S. (AA) Sub-Committee, 16.1.40; TNA WO 166/2581 (War Diary, 309th Heavy Anti-Aircraft Battery), Order of Battle, 31.1.40; TNA AIR 16/149 (Defence of Harwich), Reconnaissance in connection with the proposed increase of balloon defences for Harwich Estuary, 21.11.39.
19 Foynes, *Battle of the East Coast*, p. 19.
20 TNA WO 166/3094 (War Diary, 74th Searchlight Regiment), Operation Order No. 2, 24.11.39.
21 Dobinson, *AA Command*, pp. 317–34; TNA WO 166/3317 (War Diary, 469th Searchlight Battery).

Figure 4.3. Aerial photograph of HAA Battery at Landguard Fort, 1941 with gun emplacements in an arc and command buildings behind. (Reproduced by permission of Historic England Archive (RAF Photography))

within range, while those that did could expect their attack runs to be disrupted. In time the absence of attacks led to an erroneous perception by those on the ground that the port was somehow being 'saved' in order that its facilities might be used in an invasion, but in reality the GDA, while registering relatively few successful engagements, arguably succeeded in its aim of deterring heavy attack altogether.

The northern Sandlings: the Lowestoft/Yarmouth GDA

In contrast to the early formation of the Harwich GDA, that at Lowestoft was established relatively late. Despite having a significant role in the internal convoy system and being the site of numerous Royal Navy shore establishments, until 1941 the port area was defended solely by LAA guns. This was, however, not for a lack of concern, as the previous October the Admiralty had notified the local naval commander that, although heavy anti-aircraft defences had been authorised for its protection, delays should be expected owing to the shortage of equipment.[22] The area was not completely defenceless, however, as the numerous small vessels using the

---

22   TNA ADM 199/66 (AA Defence of Ports and Naval Establishments), Yarmouth and Lowestoft AA defences, 25.10.40.

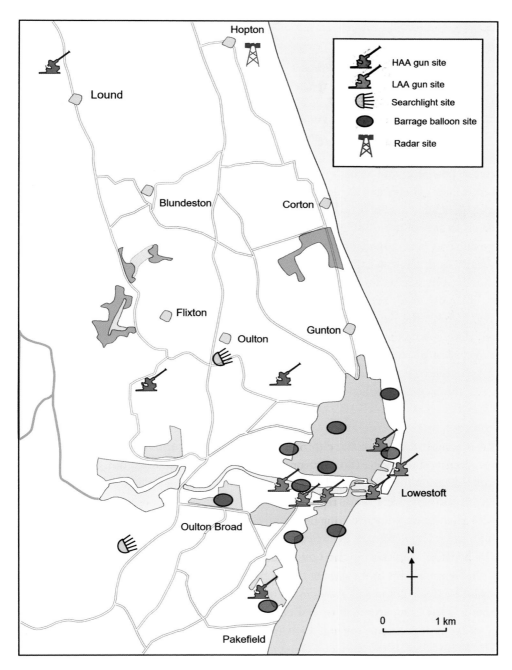

Figure 4.4. Map of the Lowestoft GDA. While smaller than that of Harwich, the same principles governed the arrangement of guns. The concentration of LAA batteries around the harbour area was a response to low-level raiding.

harbour, such as minesweepers, motor torpedo boats and armed trawlers, possessed their own ship-based anti-aircraft guns that could be used against low-flying aircraft. But, perhaps because of the presence of the GDA at Harwich, the Lowestoft area offered a softer target for the Luftwaffe and so was subject to more numerous visitations. After a prolonged period of raiding up to spring 1941, which had a cumulative destructive effect, at the end of May the Great Yarmouth and Lowestoft area was designated a GDA with two new HAA sites, one each for Yarmouth and Lowestoft respectively, each with four 3.7-inch guns.[23] The following month saw the addition of two further HAA sites at Lowestoft and a share of the 26 additional searchlights provided for the GDA as a whole.[24] The three HAA batteries ringed the town on green-field sites that could take advantage of what little high ground presented itself: at College Farm and Camps Heath to the west and at Pakefield golf course to the south. In time, the Lowestoft portion was provisioned with two more HAA sites, at Ashby near Lound and Mutford Great Wood; the exact time of their construction is not entirely clear, but they may have been built as a response to heavy raiding in May 1943 (Figure 4.4).

To judge from aerial photographs and fragmentary remains on the ground, the sites of both the Sandlings GDAs were entirely typical of those of AA Command and developed along familiar lines (Figure 4.5).[25] This included the usual upgrading of technical provision for radar and also of accommodation; and the increasing use of mixed-sex personnel, with women drawn from the Auxiliary Territorial Service (ATS), as seen archaeologically in the physical separation of huts on domestic sites.[26] While the GDAs gave a certain stability to the landscape of HAA defence, neat maps of gunsites tend to obscure a litany of minor changes to manning arrangements and also the exact distribution of the guns themselves, which were frequently moved around or redeployed elsewhere in the country. As Dobinson has pointed out, AA Command took a decision to build new emplacements whenever necessary in the expectation that even if the guns were removed they could be redeployed again, so physical gun sites were often more numerous than the actual number of batteries manning them at any one time.[27] Documentary evidence is often unhelpful when it comes to determining which places were occupied at any given point and on some sites occupation was probably transitory. In the case of the Yarmouth/Lowestoft GDA it is possible that the site at Mutford Wood was never operational in an AA capacity at all.[28] Nonetheless, whatever the exact arrangements, the permanence of the GDAs was quite different to other types of gun site elsewhere.

---

23 TNA WO 166/2525 (War Diary, 244th Heavy Anti-Aircraft Battery), Operation Order No. 11, 18.5.41.

24 TNA WO 166/2278 (War Diary, 41st Anti-Aircraft Brigade), 41 AA Brigade Operation Order No. 9, 12.7.41.

25 Dobinson, *AA Command*, pp. 319–34; Hegarty and Newsome, *Suffolk's Defended Shore*, pp. 36–9; Lowry, *20th Century Defences*, pp. 48–59.

26 Jarvis, *Fortress Lowestoft*, p. 48; Dobinson, *AA Command*, pp. 317–19.

27 Dobinson, *AA Command*, pp. 357–62.

28 Jarvis, *Fortress Lowestoft*, p. 45.

Figure 4.5. MPs watching 3.7-inch gun crew in action in the Harwich GDA in 1943. (IWM H28390)

The light anti-aircraft war

Outside the GDAs, the landscape of LAA was characterised by the defence of fixed points such as radar stations and airfields, but at these sites and in the wider landscape there was considerable fluidity. What cannot be emphasised enough is that exact configurations were subject to almost continual change owing to shifting tactics by raiders and the consequent tactical redeployment of the guns in what was described by one officer as a 'War of Movement'.[29]

The air defence of radar stations and airfields, which, as has been seen, were also fixed points in the anti-invasion landscape, was chiefly the preserve of LAA regiments. In the case of Sub-Sector 3 (from 1941, Sub-Sector 4) the presence of Bawdsey radar station and Martlesham and Nacton airfields was a major influence on the defence

---

29 TNA WO 166/7711 (War Diary, 125th Light Anti-Aircraft Regiment), October 1942.

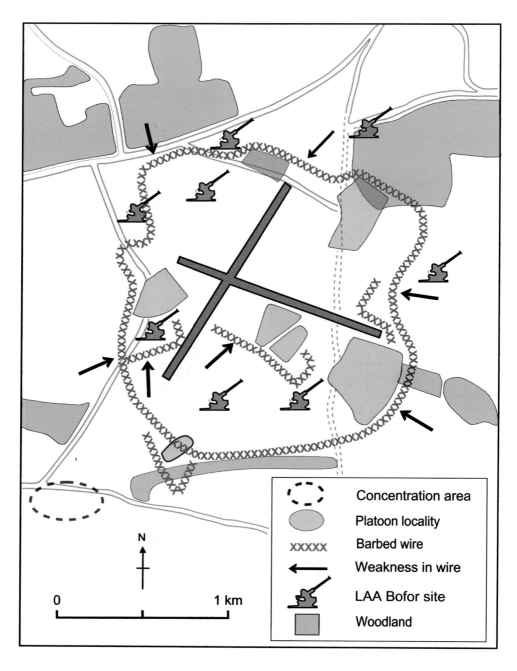

Figure 4.6. Defence of Martlesham aerodrome in 1942, showing defensive localities for the airfield garrison together with concentration areas and entry points for relieving forces from the South Wales Borderers.

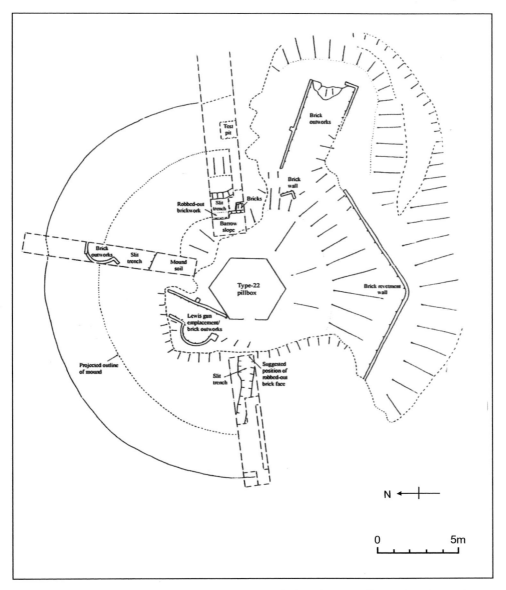

Figure 4.7. Archaeological plan of ground defences at Martlesham showing pillbox and Lewis gun pit. (Suffolk County Council)

scheme of the resident infantry brigade. These sites were provisioned with their own fixed perimeter defences and, in what is often a bewildering range of defence schemes, many of which were operational for only a short period of time, the conduct of the defence oscillated between increasing the numbers of infantrymen acting as a semi-permeant garrison and holding strong mobile reserve columns back as a relieving force.[30] One particularly elaborate plan for the defence of Martlesham in 1941 involved platoons in vehicles breaking through deliberately weakened sections of barbed wire on the perimeter fence so they could attack enemy paratroops deemed to have landed on the runways (Figure 4.6).

The broader defence of these places is important because here LAA guns were expected in the last resort to be used against enemy ground troops and so they were usually integrated with other defences. At Bawdsey in 1942 the defence of the station was formed of three AA sites, each consisting of one Bofor and one Lewis gun with eight riflemen for protection from ground attack, together with one searchlight site consisting of three Lewis guns and 14 defending infantrymen.[31] These AA sites formed part of a ring of defences that included pillboxes, section posts and an anti-tank ditch. At Martlesham, a surviving section of one of six platoon localities making up part of the airfield defences provides direct archaeological evidence for arrangements on the ground. Here a Type 22 pillbox was sited on a Bronze Age burial mound and provided with an adjacent fire trench with brick revetments – an unusual case in the Sandlings, as the infantry seemed to have used timber – alongside which was a circular brick-built Lewis gun emplacement (Figure 4.7). A short distance to the north there is a more unusual complex comprising a pillbox, a heated room and a Lewis gun emplacement. The pillbox is a variant of the Type 23 design, with an extra bay for the mounting of a LAA weapon, and the adjacent circular Lewis gun pit is revetted with corrugated iron; there is surface evidence for an additional Lewis gun pit. The presence of a square brick-built heated room between the pillbox and the Lewis gun post sheds light on the reality of how such places were used and dovetails neatly with documentary evidence for air sentries suffering from the effects of cold while on duty and crews being rotated every 20 minutes as frozen fingers could not operate guns.[32]

Elsewhere, physical evidence for LAA posts is more elusive, in part because guns were rarely in the same place for any length of time and so their mountings were often temporary. Those intended for more permanent installations, such as airfields or places otherwise expected to remain occupied for a period of time, were more

---

30 For arrangements for Bawdsey, see TNA WO 166/4433 (War Diary, 1st Liverpool Scottish), Operational Instruction No. 6, 20.5.40; TNA WO 166/688 (War Diary, 55th Division, GS), 55 Division Operational Instruction No. 2, 9.10.40; TNA WO 166/4357 (War Diary, 13th King's (Liverpool) Regiment), 9.1.41.

31 TNA WO 166/8993 (War Diary, 6th Battalion South Wales Borderers), Appendix 'B' to Operational Instruction, No. 1, 29.1.42.

32 M. Muldowney, *World War II Defences on The Swale, Brightwell Heath, Ipswich* (Ipswich, 2009).

likely to be housed in concrete emplacements, as is documented at Martlesham in July 1942, at Felixstowe that November and at Lowestoft, where an extant example comprising a simple concrete enclosure is known.[33] A small number of mountings for other light weapons such as the Oerlikon exist, but again these are found at vulnerable places, such as Bawdsey. Pillboxes containing mountings for machine guns in an air defence role exist in small numbers and again tend to be found on vulnerable sites, such as at the fixed coastal battery Beacon Hill Fort on the Essex side of Harwich Haven,[34] or on searchlight sites (see below), but not exclusively; one such site remains extant on a clifftop north of Felixstowe and was probably in a small way intended to aid the infantry defend themselves from low-level attack. At the sites of ECDBs, field gun batteries and substantial infantry positions a common arrangement was probably to site Lewis guns in circular pits surrounded with sandbags; one such structure is shown in a 1941 aerial photograph of Walberswick ECDB and such posts were no doubt once numerous.[35]

Fringe raids and tip and run

It was the LAA war that predominated in the Sandlings throughout late 1942 and into 1943, as so-called 'nuisance' raids, in which attacking aircraft varied the places where they made landfall and altered their approach runs to their targets, increased. This was part of the broader 'Fringe' campaign by the Luftwaffe and dealing with these attacks resulted in a cat-and-mouse battle that saw the movement of guns up to the coastline in order to engage the marauders directly. The redeployments of LAA to deal with these raids could be recounted at some length, but a few examples give a flavour of the overall scene. During August 1942 near-daily raids on Harwich necessitated the movement of some 18 searchlights and 12 Bofors between Boyton and Alderton.[36] During October 1942, eight Bofors were deployed in Felixstowe and four at Southwold and Landguard Fort's defences were strengthened by the deployment of Bofors to replace Lewis guns. This period also saw considerable relaxation of rules of engagement in an attempt to hit the raiders. By the end of November Bofor and Lewis gunners at Landguard, Felixstowe, Parkstone Quay, Southwold and Orford were free to immediately engage all aircraft, other than flying boats, approaching from seaward below 500 feet (150 metres) without prior recognition in daylight hours.[37]

A spate of more serious raids on the Yarmouth and Lowestoft area resulted in more permanent measures. Successive attacks in the area over 7–12 May 1943 came

---

33 TNA WO 166/7376 (War Diary, 6 Anti-Aircraft Brigade), July 1942; Jarvis, *Fortress Lowestoft*, p. 50; TNA WO 166/7711 (War Diary, 125 Light Anti-Aircraft Regiment), November 1942.

34 M. Brown and P. Patterson, *Beacon Hill Fort, Essex* (English Heritage, Archaeological Field Survey Report. Requested Survey, 1997).

35 HE (NMR) RAF Photography E2/BR260 PO6988, 7.7.41.

36 TNA WO 166/7376 (War Diary, 6th Anti-Aircraft Brigade), 18.9.42.

37 *Ibid.*, Operational Instruction No. 45, Engagement of seen targets, 5.11.42.

Figure 4.8. Barrage balloons at Lowestoft in 1943; their deployment was a response to a series of low-level air attacks that were otherwise difficult to deter. (Suffolk Record Office, Lowestoft)

in at such speed and low altitude that it proved almost impossible for defenders to engage the enemy, resulting in 32 fatalities.[38] On 13 May a 30-strong balloon barrage force was deployed to the GDA, which, together with a later reinforcement of four heavy guns and 44 light anti-aircraft guns, appeared to have been the immediate answer to the very low-level attacks from the sea (Figure 4.8).[39] The increased air defences for the town had been the cause of considerable correspondence between all three armed services in the previous months and weeks. As the nature of Luftwaffe operations had become more familiar, from March recommendations were being made that more LAA capability be made available for the Yarmouth/Lowestoft GDA and suggestions were requested on how to overcome the failure in obtaining pre-warning of attacks.[40] Almost at the same time, the naval commander at Yarmouth

---

38 TNA WO 1266/11642 (War Diary, 161st Heavy Anti-Aircraft Regiment), May 1943; Jarvis, *Fortress Lowestoft*, p. 67.

39 TNA WO ADM1/13117 (AA Defence of Gt Yarmouth and Lowestoft), *passim*.

40 *Ibid.*, 5 AA Group, AA Defence of Fringe VPs, 23.3.44.

was urgently pointing out the vulnerability of the large numbers of minesweepers and other naval craft that could be crippled in the event of a large raid. He strongly recommended that a balloon barrage should be provided, although this option had been refused in the past.[41] The real truth was that AA Command was overstretched nationally and resources did not exist to provide adequate defence for all those places the Luftwaffe might choose to raid. But the perceived inadequacy of AA Command was the subject of a somewhat cutting remark by a senior Navy commander in the days after the 12 May raid, which may have had an element of truth in it: 'since the smallest man of war or armed merchant ship maintain a standard of vigilance sufficient to prevent surprise from low flying aircraft, it should not be difficult for a coastal town situated on low lying land to do so'.[42]

The landscape of searchlights

Outside the areas covered by AA guns more passive defence was provided by decoys and searchlights. A small number of the former existed in the Sandlings from late 1940, chiefly in the south, and were intended to distract attention from Martlesham and Ipswich.[43] These might serve to deceive, but, prior to the development of adequate radar, the only way of targeting hostile aircraft at night was by physical illumination. The GDAs retained their own arrangements for searchlights in order to assist the HAA, but away from here in the early part of the war searchlights were sited individually at 6000-yard intervals, forming a grid, which allowed several beams to illuminate a target simultaneously and so aid interception by friendly fighters (Figure 4.9).[44] This was the situation in the Sandlings in the first nine months of the war; the distribution of sites was relatively even, but equipment shortages meant that numbers fell far below the required density. Those searchlights that did exist tended to be placed in isolated locations on locally higher ground and away from potential light and sound interference. The projectors were usually given a slight circular earthwork as protection, but to date no field remains of these have been located in the Sandlings and they appear only as cropmarks on aerial photographs. As part of the anti-invasion landscape, searchlight posts were intended to be responsible for their own defence and, while it is doubtful that barbed wire or even rifles were ever issued in sufficient quantities, at sites today the most obvious marker is that of a concrete pillbox.[45] Typologically a greater proportion of these are Type 23 variants for mounting a machine gun in an AA role than is seen elsewhere in the anti-invasion landscape for the obvious reason that

---

41 TNA WO ADM 1/13117 (AA Defence of Gt Yarmouth and Lowestoft), Note from Flag Officer Great Yarmouth to C-in-C, The Nore, 31.3.43.

42 *Ibid.*, Defence against low-flying aircraft, 15.5.43.

43 TNA WO 166/2229 (War Diary, 6th Anti-Aircraft Brigade), 14.9.40.

44 Dobinson, *AA Command*, p. 280.

45 TNA WO 166/2229 (War Diary, 6th Anti-Aircraft Brigade), 18.7.40; *ibid.*, Brigade Operation Order No. 51, 6.7.40.

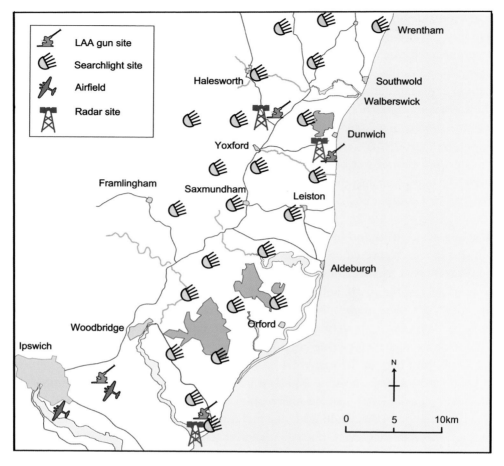

Figure 4.9. Distribution of searchlights, 1940.

operating searchlights made themselves visible targets and when aircraft fired 'down the beam' some kind of rudimentary defence could be enacted.

By the autumn of 1940 the searchlight system nationally was deemed to be failing, owing to aircraft flying at higher altitudes, the use of non-reflective paint and a suspicion that searchlights were actually helping to guide enemy aircraft to their target. In addition, equipment trials had demonstrated the benefits of using radar to control searchlights – known as 'Elsie' – which aided the guiding of several lights when projectors were drawn together in a cluster, rather than operating individually. As a result, from November 1940 a wholesale reorganisation of searchlight sites, which were now to be clustered in groups of three, took place. These new sites were formed by abandoning at least two-thirds of those already in existence and drawing their projectors together on locations ideally 10,400 yards apart, with lights arranged in a

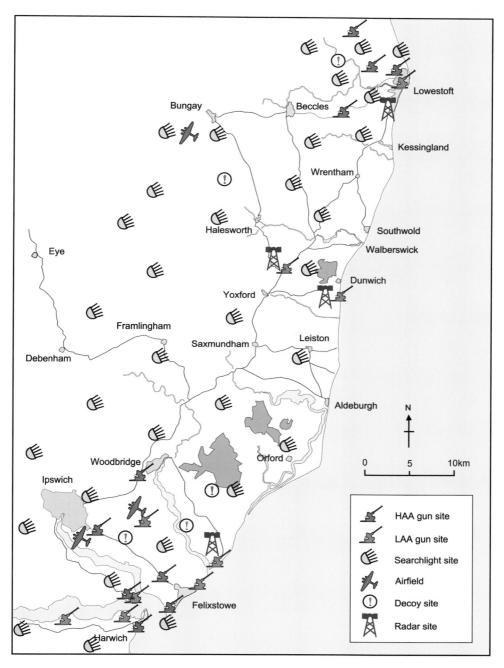

Figure 4.10. The landscape of air defence, June 1941, showing 'clustered' searchlight sites, locations of AA batteries and radar stations.

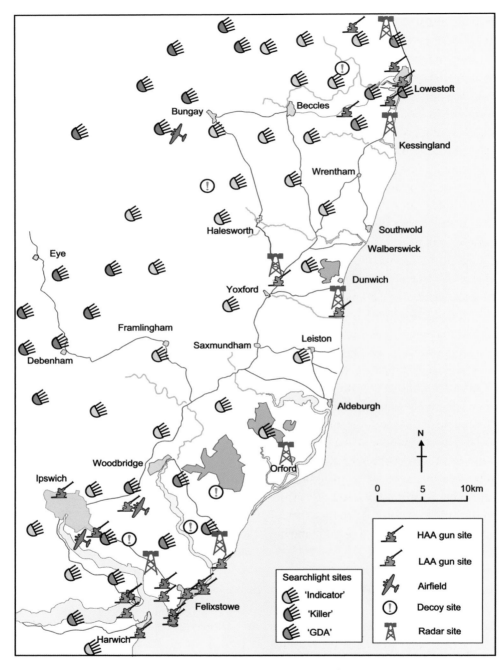

Figure 4.11. The landscape of air defence, 1942, showing 'declustered' searchlights, locations of AA batteries and radar stations.

triangle about 50 yards apart.[46] In the Sandlings 'clustering' took place in December 1940 and a new landscape emerged (Figure 4.10).[47]

But, in turn, a second reordering took place later in the year. Now it was the cluster system that was deemed to be failing because the spaces between sites was great, allowing aircraft to fly through the intervening dark areas and meaning that contacts were lost in handovers. It was replaced by a more sophisticated 'Fighter Box' system, aided by the growing availability of the 'Elsie' searchlight control radar.[48] Here, the areas outside GDAs were divided into 'Killer Boxes', with one central light forming a marker around which defending fighters could circle. This scheme, part of a wider attempt to frustrate raids on Midland England, saw the Sandlings placed outside the main 'Killer' zone as part of an 'Indicator' zone (Figure 4.11). Here the lights were placed just under ten kilometres apart; as this had been the approximate distance between the previous clusters, the reorganisation was not universal. But this second change to the searchlight layout was protracted and when it involved moving huts and laying out new sites the work involved was considerable and brought training to a standstill. The commandeer of 69 Searchlight Regiment wrote in his war diary that 'it had left its mark on the efficiency of the regiment as well as severely trying the temper, patience, spirit and discipline of all concerned. I, like the rest of you, have been groping around in the dark, trying to formulate some definite policy, living on faith and hope, and enduring charity.'[49] One consequence of this move was a greater level of infrastructure on searchlight sites; the earthwork remains of a projector bank and associated pit at Minsmere are the only definite archaeological example located during the course of this study (Figure 4.12).

So, by the middle of the war, the landscape of air defence was relatively defined, with an ordered system of searchlights and two GDAs, albeit LAA was mobile and somewhat reactive. Up to this point of the conflict the air war had been locally and regionally significant, but was otherwise on the margins of AA Command's main effort to defend cities and industrial targets. But as Fringe raids started to diminish a new aerial threat emerged – the V1 flying bomb – that thrust the Sandlings very much into the front line.

The defence against the flying bomb: Operation Diver

The threat to the UK from flying bombs had been anticipated by AA Command but the subsequent campaign against them – Operation Diver – rapidly evolved as the tactical employment of the V1, and the British response, changed. The course of the Diver campaign has been related in detail by Dobinson and so is not discussed at

---

46   Dobinson, *AA Command*, pp. 282–4.
47   TNA WO 166/3095 (War Diary, 32nd Searchlight Regiment), 13.10.41.
48   Dobinson, *AA Command*, pp. 344–5.
49   TNA WO 166/3088 (War Diary, 69th Searchlight Battery), Directive, 31.10.41.

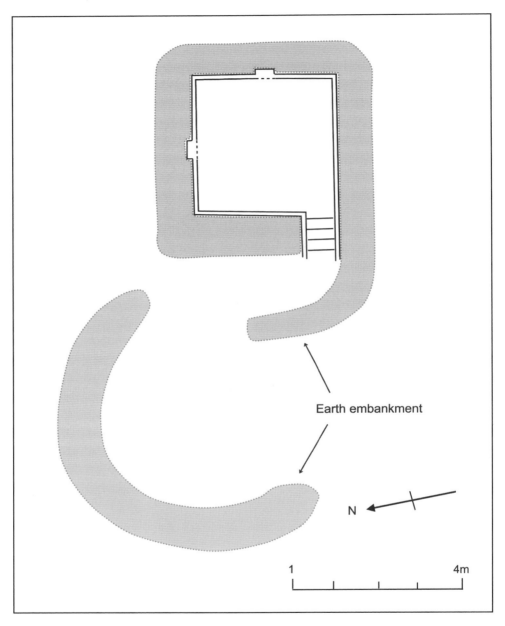

Figure 4.12. Rare archaeological survival of a searchlight post at Minsmere. The exact date of the post is unknown and it may have only been in use for a short period of time, but it was known to have been operational in 1942.

length here, but its chief elements and some of its technical aspects require sketching out in brief.[50] Diver commenced in the middle of June 1944 with the establishment of an extensive GDA to the south of London (the Kentish Gun Belt) to shoot down rockets on their approach to the capital. This proved ineffective and the guns were relocated to the south coast (the Coastal Gun Belt) and along the Thames estuary (The Diver Box), in order to allow batteries greater freedom of engagement and promote co-operation with intercepting fighter aircraft. It quickly became apparent that the static form of the 3.7-inch AA gun was most effective against the fast-flying V1, but as there was no time in which to construct the necessary concrete emplacements an improvised wooden and steel framework known as the 'Pile Platform' was developed, which went on to characterise gun sites. Advances in predicting radar and power-controlled guns, together with the use of new proximity fuses – which enabled shells to explode when in close proximity to the target, rather than when they actually came into contact with it – delivered much greater accuracy and were eventually decisive in negating the V1 threat.[51] By September 1944, with launch sites being overrun by the Allied advance across northern Europe, the German focus switched to attacking London with V1s launched at night from aircraft operating over the North Sea. These bombs made landfall over the east coast and, in response to this new direction of attack, on 22 September AA Command redeployed the guns of the Coastal Gun Belt to the 'Diver Strip', a narrow band of coastline running north from the Diver Box to Great Yarmouth and so encompassing the Sandlings in its entirety.[52] In anticipation of bombs being launched from even further north the Diver 'Fringe' was later established in Lincolnshire and Yorkshire, but, although attacks continued until March, by the beginning of 1945 the campaign was largely at an end.

Operation Diver: a regional view

The landscape of the Diver Strip reflected the recent experience gained by AA Command in dealing with flying bombs as well as the specific arrangements required to shoot down air-launched V1s. The Strip itself comprised the area between lines nine kilometres (10,000 yards) out to sea and 4.5 kilometres (5000 yards) inland, with HAA batteries placed as close to the coast as possible. This arrangement had proved effective in the Coastal Gun Belt, but successfully dealing with air-launched V1s proved to be more involved. The attacking aircraft tracked low over the sea to avoid detection then climbed slightly to release their payloads before heading for home, meaning that V1s flew significantly lower than had previously been the case. The majority flew between 500–1000 feet (150–300 metres), but some were lower; a number crashed into the sea or exploded as they hit land. These unconventional targets also represented a challenge

---

50   Dobinson, *Operation Diver* and Dobinson, *AA Command*, pp. 429–51.
51   N.W. Routledge, *Anti-Aircraft Artillery, 1914–55* (London, 1994), p. 414.
52   TNA WO 166/14617 (War Diary, 1st Anti-Aircraft Group), 22.9.44.

as the V1 was small in comparison with a conventional bomber, the exact height of approach was unpredictable and the weapons at AA Command's disposal were designed to shoot down aircraft, not rockets.[53]

As the best method of dealing with air-launched bombs was initially unclear, a number of improvisations characterised the early stages of the Diver Strip deployment. Rather than being placed in batteries of eight, as had been the case in the Coastal Gun Belt, HAA guns in the Diver Strip were chiefly grouped in more conventional groups of four. The guns themselves were adapted so they could fire at lower elevations and the left and right guns of each four-gun battery were additionally modified so that their barrels could be depressed even further. For safety reasons the two end guns were then placed a little forward of the central pair, resulting in a concave or 'arc' pattern.[54] The gun predictors were housed in 'tracker towers', which were initially improvised structures frequently made from scaffolding poles culled from the beach defences, while others were made of concrete blocks and timber.[55] Gun site radar also required the construction of 'clutter screens', which were intended to eliminate interference from the ground and – given the locations in which many sites were placed – from wave action of the sea, and these too were often improvised from scaffolding and chicken wire.[56] Each site had a Nissen hut as a command post and in the earliest stages of the operation the battery personnel were accommodated in tents.[57]

The initial Diver deployment also saw innovations in the use of LAA, both on its own and in combination with HAA. A new two-gun layout known as a 'Welter site' was introduced, which represented a combination of two 3.7-inch HAA guns but with LAA predicting equipment. In addition, 'intermediate' sites also existed, comprised either two HAA guns alongside batteries of 40mm LAA guns or four 40mm Bofor guns on their own.[58] The final component of the strip was searchlights and, although their value steadily diminished with improvements in radar, these were placed on the coastline just under three kilometres apart with the intention of giving early warning and indicating the approximate positions of V1s to gun sites.[59]

A necessary pre-requisite for understanding the nature of Diver in the Sandlings is that it was 'mired in chaos from the start', with an initial deployment expected to take four days taking four weeks and accompanied by logistical difficulties.[60] The head of AA Command, Sir Frederick Pile, described the situation at the time as

---

53   Routledge, *Anti-Aircraft Artillery*, p. 411.
54   Dobinson, *Operation Diver*, p. 91.
55   *Ibid.*, p. 110.
56   Dobinson, *AA Command*, p. 443.
57   TNA WO 166/14640 (War Diary, 5th Anti-Aircraft Brigade), Appendix A1, Construction Work, October, 1944.
58   TNA WO166/14666 (War Diary, 57th Anti-Aircraft Brigade), 29.9.44.
59   TNA WO 166/16693 (War Diary, 57th Anti-Aircraft Brigade), General Instructions, 4.3.45.
60   Dobinson, *AA Command*, p. 441.

'deplorable' and harangued his subordinates, as it 'reflects great discredit on every one of us … everywhere there is some reason for shame … everyone is trying to put the blame on someone else…'.[61] The war diaries of the units concerned give a vivid sense of events on the ground, with the arrival of personnel without equipment and lacking an adequate commissariat. One battery of 122 HAA Regiment moved into the Sandlings on 24 September, but their guns were not fully deployed until 8 October.[62] And 140 HAA Regiment, who arrived on 22 September, were not joined by their full complement of guns until 13 October, when the whole regiment finally became operational.[63] Such delays meant that, although the chronology of the establishment of the Sandlings' portion of the Diver Strip was short, it was characterised by a piecemeal build-up of ordnance. In a rare instance of a senior commander explicitly commenting upon the geography of the region it was held as partly responsible for the difficulties, with Pile later relating how 'on the narrow twisting roads in that part of East Anglia where we were redeploying, convoy of ten tonners would suddenly encounter head on convoys of three tonners. The subsequently delay and confusion were enormous.'[64] While these criticisms are a well-known feature of the Diver operation, they bear repeating here as they are important to understanding its impact on the landscape of the Sandlings.

The Diver Strip

The part of the Diver Strip that encompassed the Sandlings was divided into five sections, each manned by an AA Brigade – 63rd Brigade (Corton to Benacre); 57th Brigade (Benacre to Leiston); 5th Brigade (Leiston to Orford); 102nd Brigade (Orford to Bawdsey); and 40th Brigade (Felixstowe) –with their constituent gun sites established from late September through to November 1944 (Figure 4.13). Possibly as many as 66 HAA and 72 LAA/Welter sites were initially anticipated, but in the confusion that followed some were never established and others were occupied for only a matter of weeks. The exact number of Diver sites in the Sandlings is in fact unclear, with some 85 listed in documentary sources and 72 identified from aerial photographs.[65] The discrepancy can be explained by reference to hastily drawn-up documents listing sites that were never realised, but the precise number is to some extent unimportant, as what the statistics demonstrate clearly enough is the impact of Diver on the ground. The number of AA sites that came into existence in the late autumn of 1944 massively outnumbered those of the region's two GDAs and totally changed the nature of the air defence landscape.

---

61   Pile quoted by Dobinson, *AA Command*, p. 442.
62   TNA WO 166/14784 (War Diary, 122nd Heavy Anti-Aircraft Regiment), 24.9.44; 8.10.44.
63   TNA WO 166/14798 (War Diary, 140th Heavy Anti-Aircraft Regiment), 22.9.44; 13.10.44.
64   Pile quoted by Hegarty and Newsome, *Suffolk's Defended Shore*, p. 74.
65   *Ibid.*

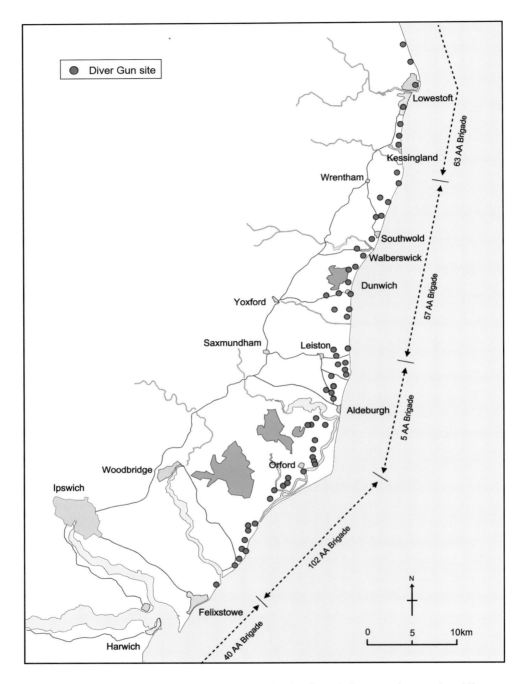

Figure 4.13. Distribution of Diver battery sites across the Sandlings. As it was not known where V1s would make landfall the whole coastline required defending, and so the pattern of sites was reminiscent of that of pillboxes in 1940.

Figure 4.14. Diver site at Orford, 1944. This staged photograph shows the nature of such sites when they were situated in favourable locations; on the marshland a little to the south of where this photograph was taken, conditions were very different. (IWM H 40431)

Diver was in many respects a self-contained operation that constituted a small war in its own right. In the Sandlings it was a brief, but intense, period of military activity that left a distinctive archaeological legacy. As a hurried response to an unexpected threat, it also draws comparison with events of the summer of 1940. In a regional context, the development of the Strip is best seen as a refortification of the coastline, albeit one directed against a specific kind of attack. But in a way that had not characterised the landscape of air defence up to that point, the influence of topography came to the fore in how the Strip was configured.

The Strip took shape through the provisioning of the existing GDAs at Yarmouth/ Lowestoft and Harwich with additional HAA and LAA batteries, with the intervening coastline progressively infilled as guns were redeployed from the Coastal Gun Belt. All HAA sites in the Sandlings were equipped with four 3.7-inch guns, with the exception of one in the Yarmouth/Lowestoft GDA that was equipped with eight guns and a new site at Lowestoft that comprised six.[66] The HAA sites themselves conformed to a particular pattern. Photographs show that the pits in which the Pile Platforms were placed were backfilled with hardcore sometimes to form a slight mound, and often rounded off with a line of sandbags with improvised ammunition lockers (Figure 4.14).[67] The few archaeological remains of gun platforms that exist tend to

66   TNA WO 171/1165 (War Diary, 139th Heavy Anti-Aircraft Regiment), 23.9.44; 1–19.10.44.
67   IWM H40430–40438, 9.10.44.

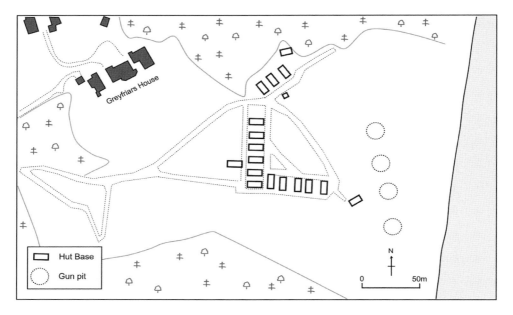

Greyfriars House

Hut Base

Gun pit

N

0   50m

Figure 4.15. Plan of Diver site at Dunwich showing the four gun positions marked by shallow mounds and hut bases of camp site to the rear.

comprise shallow mounds approximately nine metres in diameter (Figure 4.15). But at four-gun sites an important morphological distinction existed, with the guns being placed either in an arc or in a straight line. As has been seen, the 'arc' arrangement was initially introduced as a way of facilitating the engagement of low-flying bombs, but this guidance was rescinded on 29 October in favour of a straight line on all new sites, as this facilitated the engagement of all four guns of a battery when using proximity fuses.[68] As is seen below, this difference in morphology in part reflected the chronological development of the Strip.

The use of Welter sites and LAA was transient, however; the construction of Welter sites was discontinued at the end of October and LAA was completely withdrawn the following month.[69] Their deployment resulted from the initial uncertainty about how to successfully engage air-launched V1s, but they soon became redundant as it became clear that flying bombs could be effectively engaged by four-gun batteries using proximity fuses, and so their continued operation was unnecessary. As 5th AA brigade put it on 17 October, 'it is now becoming noticeable that as HAA shooting improves the LAA get little firing, the FBs are destroyed out of the range of the LAA

68 On new sites the angle at which the guns were to be laid out would be determined to allow all guns to open fire on the approach of the target. This practice was continued on sites in the Diver Fringe.

69 TNA WO 166/14666 (War Diary, 57th Anti-Aircraft Brigade) Ops Order No. 8, 17.11.44.

guns'.[70] The absence of Welter and LAA sites on aerial photographs and a lack of physical remains on the ground mean that establishing the nature of these positions is difficult. The field evidence for LAA sites in the Diver Strip is almost non-existent, but one rare case suggests that the guns were also placed in an arc and, unusually, also mounted on Pile Platforms.[71] On these short-lived sites the infrastructure was probably insubstantial; 83rd LAA Regiment, for example, moved into the Sandlings on 26 September to man Welter batteries but were withdrawn pending disbandment on 13 November, and so any facilities were probably rudimentary.[72] In other cases there is documentary evidence that what was in place was removed when the site was vacated; in November 5th AA Brigade explicitly ordered that with the withdrawal of LAA all structures and stores were to be dismantled.[73] An additional reason for the apparent absence of Welter sites is that those not earmarked for abandonment were to be converted to conventional four-gun HAA sites and in such cases the earlier arrangement is therefore masked by what came later. All this said, while HAA sites are normally highly visible on aerial photographs taken in August 1945, the situation with Welter sites is almost the opposite: of the six Welter sites between Southwold and Minsmere listed in war diaries five appear to have left no evidence whatsoever, while the existence of the sixth is open to question. On balance, this suggests that a proportion of the planned Welter sites were never actually realised on the ground, as even those in action for as little as a month might reasonably be expected to show evidence of the gun emplacements or command buildings. The Diver war rapidly became one exclusively of HAA.

The consolidation of the Diver Strip associated with the conversion of Welter sites and the withdrawal of LAA represents an important chronological marker, as it is at this time that the documentary record becomes more reliable and can be reconciled with the evidence from 1945 aerial photographs. Within each AA Brigade sites were identified by a prefix letter and a number, but the numbering sequence is often irregular and reflects the changing circumstances in which the Strip originated and developed.[74] Converted Welter sites, for example, tended to receive higher numbers than those four-gun batteries already in place, or were distinguished by an additional letter in their prefix. But, by comparing these lists with the pattern of sites on the ground and the information from aerial photographs, a certain amount of detail about how the Strip originated and developed can be recovered.

---

70 TNA WO 166/14640 (War Diary, 5th Anti-Aircraft Brigade), 17.10.44.

71 Diver Site SC 17, David Thurlow, pers comm.

72 TNA WO 166/14728 (War Diary, 83rd Light Anti-Aircraft Regiment), November 1944.

73 TNA WO 166/14640 (War Diary, 5th Anti-Aircraft Brigade), Appendix to War Diary, November 1944.

74 From north to south: 63rd Anti-Aircraft Brigade unusually designated sites by double lettering with the prefix Y; 57th Anti-Aircraft Brigade prefix T; 5th Anti-Aircraft Brigade prefix S; 102nd Anti-Aircraft Brigade prefix G; 40th Anti-Aircraft Brigade prefix K.

Topography and distribution

At the start of the Diver operation the original intention was to place four-gun HAA sites at approximate intervals of one kilometre (1100 yards), as close to the coast as possible and sited to provide low radar cover. Across the Sandlings, while the overall density of gun sites did indeed accord with the ideal, this was subject to a degree of local variation. As there was no way of knowing where exactly V1s would make landfall the AA screen needed to cover the whole coastline and here a familiar pattern emerged, in that the distribution of Diver sites was broadly analogous to that of the 1940 defences, which had themselves attempted to cover as much coastline as possible. In the northern Sandlings the existence of the 'spurs' with intervening wet or marshy ground tended to structure the placement of sites, which clustered on the higher ground around Walberswick, Dunwich Heath, Sizewell and Aldeburgh. A furthering structuring influence was the presence of the seaside towns, over which firing was not permitted, and so here sites were usually placed to one side. But in order to give coverage over the intervening marshland or inundated areas gun sites were placed as close to the coastline as topography permitted and came inland where they skirted around marshes and bodies of water. Thus in the area between Walberswick and Dunwich sites T1–T3 overlooked the flooded Dingle and Corporation marshes and at Aldeburgh sites S5, 7 and 8 hugged the higher ground around the marshes to the north of the town. The same was true of the southern Sandlings, with clifftop locations and necks of promontories exploited, but here the geography and land use presented a problem, in that the extensive marshes that made up much of the immediate coastal hinterland were far from suitable places for the siting of heavy batteries.

But in order to be as close to the sea as possible and, crucially, to meet the requirement for low-angle radar cover, such locations had to be pressed into use. Here battery sites tended to be placed in something of a liminal zone, where the marshes met harder ground, usually the closest site to the marsh thought to be viable. This was especially the case between the Alde and the Butley river, with a string of sites lining the edge of the marshes. An additional problem was the isolated nature of many such sites, which were a considerable distance from a metalled road. The presence of an existing road along which relevant equipment could be transported was clearly a factor in choice of site, but those roads that accessed marshes were dirt farm tracks which vehicle use soon rendered a quagmire. Although 50 tons of hardcore was in theory allocated to each HAA site at the start of the operation considerably more was necessary in many cases owing to boggy ground.[75] Compounding this difficulty was the fact that such places often lay in areas that had not previously seen military use, so were defined by a lack of infrastructure, which meant that camp sites soon deteriorated.

---

75 TNA WO 166/14640 (War Diary, 5th Anti-Aircraft Brigade), Appendix A1, Construction Work in 5th Anti-Aircraft Brigade, October 1944.

War diaries provide an illuminating commentary on the attempts to establish Diver batteries in the early period of deployment, especially along this southern part of the Sandlings coast, with that of 189 HAA Regiment a particularly candid record of events, as the diarist tended not to pull his punches. For a week after their arrival the regimental headquarters lacked electric lights and telephones, and the siting of positions was carried out by commanders touring their areas and pegging them out largely on their own initiative. During October inspections revealed the nature of the conditions. Sites G1 and G2, at Orford, drew the comment 'mud everywhere and want at least 100 tons of hard core per site'; G3 was 'a sea of mud'; and G4, at Gedgrave Marshes, was so bad that access was impossible. The situation was no better in November and a new hutted camp at site G16, again at Gedgrave Marshes, was reported as 'in a dreadful state owing [to] water [all] round'. At sites G5 and G6, on Boyton Marshes, the lack of roads and the distance to the gun sites meant the 'same old difficulty shortage of everything but hardcore the real stumbling block'.[76] It was similar issues that probably accounted for the relocation of sites G7, G9 and G13, as their initial location simply proved unviable.[77]

The way in which the Strip developed can also be seen to some extent in the numbering of sites within each AA brigade. Analysis of the sequences coupled with evidence from war diaries tends to confirm the suggestion that sites that appear out of numerical sequence were either additions to an initial scheme or were redesignated Welter sites. In the case of 5th AA Brigade, between Leiston and Orford, the sites are in numerical order from north to south, with the exception of site S16, which was a converted Welter site, and S15, which was an unusual two 3.7-inch gun site and appears to be the only case where a Welter site survived and retained its two guns after the move to four-gun sites. Further south, between Orford and Bawdsey, the numbering of sites for 102nd AA brigade seems to reflect two successive 'waves' of deployment, the first involving G1–G7 from Orford to East Lane Bawdsey, with G8–G13 then overlapping and extending the line south from Shingle Street to Bawdsey Point (Figure 4.16). Here an exceptionally detailed war diary confirms that the siting was a two-part process, albeit with one following closely on from the other. By contrast, the numbering of sites of 57th AA brigade in the area between Benacre and Leiston is very much out of sequence and seems to reflect particularly complex changes in a short space of time. Here the density of sites was greater than elsewhere, which may reflect a large number of LAA and Welter sites in the initial deployment. While the war diary evidence is unclear, it is possible that this part of the Sandlings was the first area between the Lowestoft and Harwich GDAs to be 'infilled' from late September. If this was the case then the conversion of two-gun Welter sites to four-gun sites would necessarily have been more involved, simply because the former probably existed in greater numbers.

76   TNA WO 166/14841 (War Diary, 189th Heavy Anti-Aircraft Regiment), October–November, *passim*.

77   TNA WO 166/14679 (War Diary, 102nd Anti-Aircraft Brigade), 7.11.44; 11.11.44; 18.11.44.

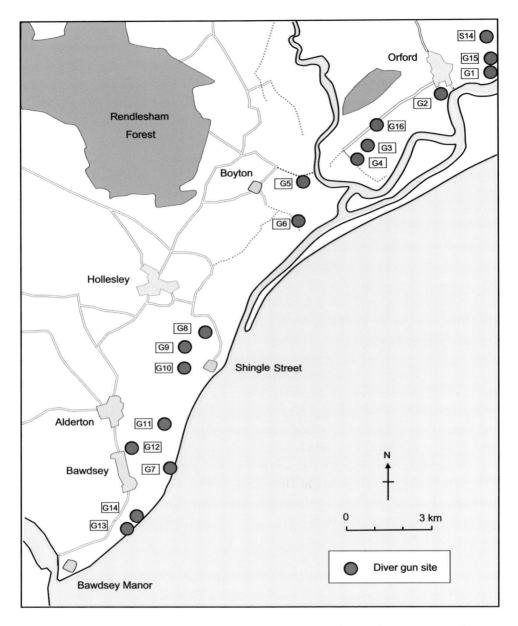

Figure 4.16. Distribution of Diver sites south of Orford. Here the numbering of sites suggests at least two phases of deployment, with higher numbers marking relocated or converted Welter sites.

But to some extent the numbering might reveal the early phases. Sites T1–8 all lie on higher ground and were close to good roads, while T9–11 represented an extension to the north on less suitable and more isolated sites. In addition, some positions in this area seem to have moved to more favourable locations. Around Easton, for example, the high-numbered sites T17 and T19, which were slightly inland and close to roads, would seem to have been preferable to neighbouring T10 and T11, which lay on the edge of eroding cliffs; while the relevant war diary is not detailed and so cannot confirm the issue, the numbering suggests a straightforward case of replacement.

Analysis of aerial photographs also confirms the suggestion that variations in the form of Diver sites are in part linked to chronology. As has been seen, from September guns were to be placed in an arc, but this was changed to a line at the end of October. Where they can be plotted from aerial photographs, those sites with guns in an 'arc' were in the majority, with 30, as against 17 where the guns are in line.[78] By cross-referencing the numbering sequence in each brigade against the form of gun sites themselves, the broad conclusion reached is that those with higher numbers tend to have their guns placed in a line (and were thus presumably constructed after October), whereas those with lower numbers tend to have the form of an arc, and were presumably constructed earlier. One particularly clear case comes from Orford, where Sites G1 and G15 lie in close proximity and where the detailed war diary of the regiment concerned confirms that the former was in the first wave, whereas its higher-numbered counterpart came later (Figure 4.17).[79] But this is in no way to be dogmatic; such were the circumstances of the early phases it is possible that some very early sites took the form of the straight line familiar to the Coastal Gun Belt, and this might explain why some sites with low numbers have this arrangement.

The nature of the Diver conflict brought with it a particular kind of routine. As V1s tended to be launched at night Diver sites were not manned during the day and training was allowed only during the morning, with compulsory rest in the afternoon. However, by night all sites had to be ready to engage targets within ten seconds of a warning, with 50 per cent of the manning detachments ordered to stay awake.[80] Air-launched V1s brought with them a host of challenges: rockets were launched so that they intermingled with returning friendly bombers, which meant that warnings of approach sometimes came too late; bombs crossing the coast at 100–200 feet (30–60 metres) made engagement impossible; heavy rain could cause severe radar clutter, making it very difficult to engage the hostile target, and it was under such circumstances that a battery at Gunton shot down a friendly fighter on 14 November; the Luftwaffe were prepared to take risks and in one case an aircraft plotted as friendly and showing navigation lights approached to within 2000 yards (1800 metres) of the coast just south

---

78   Based on Diver entries in Suffolk Historic Environment Record.

79   Confirming the suggestion in Hegarty and Newsome, *Suffolk's Defended Shore*, p. 75.

80   TNA WO 166/14640 (War Diary, 5th Heavy Anti-Aircraft Brigade), 29.9.44.

Figurer 4.17. Aerial photograph of 1945 showing Diver sites G1 and G15 near Orford. Site G1 has its guns placed in an arc, while the higher-numbered (and later) site of G15, at the top of the photograph, has its guns in line. Here the topography of the site dictated a 'linear' domestic camp arrangement. (Reproduced by permission of Historic England Archive (RAF Photography))

of Lowestoft, where it launched its bomb too close for guns to engage.[81] While it came late in the conflict, during Diver the level of engagement with the enemy was higher than at any other point in the war. Over the period 11–18 October 5th AA Brigade, for example, engaged 11 flying bombs, of which nine were destroyed, with 1071 rounds of HAA ammunition and 496 rounds of 40mm ammunition expended.[82] These difficulties notwithstanding, the Diver campaign was a victory for AA Command. Between September 1944 and January 1945, of the some 495 V1s that had crossed the English coast 320 were shot down. A little over 50,000 rounds were fired, which indicated an average 'kill' rate of 156 rounds per flying bomb. During this period, just 13 flying bombs reached London.[83] This concentrated period of activity has left surprisingly little archaeological trace, especially at the sites of guns themselves; the majority of physical remains comprise concrete access roads and domestic buildings at camp sites.

---

81 TNA WO 166/14671 (War Diary, 632nd Anti-Aircraft Brigade), 4–23.11.44.

82 TNA WO 166/14640 (War Diary, 5th Heavy Anti-Aircraft Brigade), 11–18.10.44.

83 Routledge, *Anti-Aircraft*, p. 418.

Camp sites and winterisation

As it became clear that Diver would be an ongoing operation, the unforeseen logistical difficulty of accommodating personnel necessitated a 'winterisation' building programme, ordered in October.[84] In a throwback to 1940, those troops accommodated in tents soon found these were insufficient, something brutally exposed when the first storms hit in November. The war diary of 189th HAA Regiment reported on 28 November: 'Torrential rain all night. Gale as well. Expect half the canvas blown down.'[85] As battery personnel were required to be close to their guns, those on remote sites soon found that facilities were inadequate. The exceptions were those situated close to existing GDAs, ECDBs and vacated camps, where accommodation was already in place, but in the majority of cases domestic sites and camps had to be constructed from scratch.

Building was pushed forward with such rapidity that it was deemed a logistical success in its own right. The construction of hutted sleeping accommodation for all troops was to be followed by canteens, drying rooms, a command post rest-room and dining rooms, cookhouses and messes, with mixed-sex batteries having priority for works.[86] Essential road construction also took place, with roads on dry sites to be constructed from Sommerfeld Track – a metal mesh netting with steel rod reinforcements intended for temporary airfields with an overlay of chestnut paling – with metalled roadways provided for especially damp gun positions. The progress of hutting can be closely followed in war diaries. By October 1944 working parties had been allocated to each Diver site, consisting of 20 tradesmen from AA Command Construction batteries and 80 unskilled men from LAA Searchlight Regiments. By the end of November 5th AA Brigade between Orford and Leiston reported that the shells of huts were erected on nearly every site. They were still to be floored and in several cases units were carrying out this work themselves; paint was to be supplied to all units so that they could carry out internal decoration for themselves. But units were still waiting for an adequate supply of precast paving slabs and roads within the hutted camps and to the guns, and command posts were still to be completed.[87] The war diary of 140th HAA Regiment, deployed in the Hollesley/Bawdsey area, recorded that construction teams arrived in the last week of October and during November made so much progress that by the end of December work was nearly complete, with similar reports on road construction.[88]

The vast majority of the buildings themselves have been removed, so the archaeological evidence is usually confined to concrete hut bases and the sewerage

---

84   Dobinson, *Operation Diver*, p. 94.

85   TNA WO 166/14841 (War Diary, 189th Heavy Anti-Aircraft Regiment), 28.11.44.

86   Dobinson, *Operation Diver*, p. 71.

87   TNA WO 166/14640 (War Diary, 5th Anti-Aircraft Brigade), Construction work in 5th Anti-Aircraft Brigade November 1944.

88   TNA WO 166/14798 (War Diary, 140th Heavy Anti-Aircraft Regiment), November–December 1944, *passim*.

systems, along with pickets used to secure Sommerfeld Track. The archaeological remains that do exist show a degree of regional variation in building forms and also in the morphology of camp sites. In the case of domestic huts, the principal buildings were the standard six-bay Nissen hut and the curved asbestos hut (Asbestos Nissens), which had a slightly greater width.[89] The distribution of the two hut types was in part based on their specific transport demands. A dismantled curved asbestos hut could be transported in one lorry, while it took one and half loads to carry the Nissen. In order to reduce congestion on the Sandlings' road network, the ten mixed-sex sites in 57th AA Brigade were allocated the asbestos variety, which explains their restricted distribution at camp sites between Southwold and Leiston, evidenced today by hut bases.[90]

Morphologically, across the Diver Strip camp sites also tended to fall into two broad categories: 'linear', where the huts were arranged along a road, and 'square' where the huts were placed around a central open space akin to a parade ground. These types almost certainly followed central designs, but were clearly adopted according to specific local requirements.[91] War diary evidence indicates that the exact type of camp was decided at the level of the Commanding Officers of regiments, in liaison with their brigadiers and the relevant senior office of the Royal Engineers, and this decision-making process, while not totally clear, can be mapped on the ground. From Dunwich Heath to Leiston all Diver sites have 'square' camps, which probably reflects a single decision by an individual commander. But here the landscape also probably played a part, as such camps are typical of those found on open areas or heath where there was little in the way of antecedent structures; with open ground to hand, a certain formality was clearly seen as desirable. By contrast, 'linear' camps tend to be found in places where the gun sites were remote and there was only one point of access. Here road construction probably consisted of metalling the surface of the farm track leading to the site in question; it was expedient to simply place the huts on either side of the road, and so camp sites were strung out over longer distances.

Epilogue: the Cold War

The final phase of Diver saw the threat of a new generation of ground-launched V1s, expected to cross the coast between Orfordness and the Isle of Sheppey. AA Command moved guns southwards to the new vulnerable area from January through to March, with HAA sites abandoned and left in the care of maintenance parties.[92] This was the endgame of the war in the Sandlings, but the region could claim one last event of national importance: the final V1 attack took place on 29 March 1945, with the bomb

---

89   Dobinson, *AA Command*, pp. 93, 263.
90   Dobinson, *Operation Diver*, p. 95; TNA WO 166/14666 (War Diary, 57th Anti-Aircraft Brigade), 22.9.44.
91   Dobinson, *Operation Diver*, p. 188.
92   *Ibid.*, p. 118; TNA WO 166/16693 (War Diary, 57th Anti-Aircraft Brigade), 22.1.45; *ibid.*, Ops Order No. 10, January 1944; 3.3.45.

Figure 4.18. Machine gun pillbox reused as Royal Observer Corps post at Benacre. In a small number of cases, Second World War defences found a new role during the Cold War.

concerned shot down off Orford Ness.[93] Diver officially ceased on 24 April 1945, the end of the campaign being recorded in 63rd AA Brigade's war diary in the following words: 'Diver activity considered to have ceased, therefore the Diver Gun Strip and all rules pertaining thereto are suspended.'[94] In early May the HAA defences of the Great Yarmouth/Lowestoft GDA became non-operational and LAA defences were dramatically reduced, tending to be retained only at radar and airfield sites.

But there was an important epilogue to this aspect of the conflict. The meaningful militarisation of the Sandlings began with air defence in 1939 and it was this part of the conflict that had the greatest longevity. While the anti-invasion defences of barbed wire and pillboxes were being removed, those of airspace were maintained into the Cold War. The Sandlings lay within what was known as the 'Main Defended Area': it continued to face the direction of strategic threat, albeit that this now came from the Soviet Union rather than Germany, and Harwich remained an asset important enough to be defended.[95] A small number of new works were constructed, usually to defend against attack from the air, and at Trimley the site of the wartime HAA battery was demolished in 1946 and replaced by a new battery immediately adjacent for the new 5.2-inch AA gun. From the 1950s active air defence from the ground switched from

93   Dobinson, *AA Command*, p. 450.
94   TNA WO 166/16695 (War Diary, 63rd Anti-Aircraft Brigade), 24.4.45.
95   B. Clarke, *Britain's Cold War* (Stroud, 2009).

the use of guns to missiles that were fired from sites located inland, but in the late 1970s a launch site for Bloodhound II missiles was established at Bawdsey, to the north of the radar station. The wartime system of monitoring air defence was retained after 1945 until, in the 1950s, the ROTOR radar programme saw only two of the Sandlings' Second World War radar stations – Hopton and Bawdsey – retained and upgraded. Visual watching of the coastline continued by the Royal Observer Corps and some wartime monuments were given a new role as observation posts (Figure 4.18). As the nuclear threat developed a network of fallout monitoring posts was established, of which eight were in the Sandlings, but by far the most significant pieces of Cold War infrastructure were at Orford Ness. From 1953 the southern part of the spit was used by the Atomic Weapons Research Establishment as a test site for components for nuclear weapons; six of the characteristic 'pagodas' were constructed for testing.[96] In 1968 construction started on the northern part of the Ness of a short-lived Anglo-American 'over the horizon' radar station known as Cobra Mist, tasked with giving early warning of a nuclear strike and whose antenna fan visually dominated the immediate coastline. This presence not only reflected continued militarisation but, as is seen in Chapter 9, was also important in developing the post-war sense of place.

---

96 W. Cocroft and M. Alexander, *Atomic Weapons Research Establishment, Orford Ness, Suffolk. Cold War Research & Development Site. Survey Report* (English Heritage Research Department Report Series, No. 10, 2009).

Chapter 5

Training and defence works, 1940–43

Since antiquity military commanders have recognised that in order to function efficiently on the battlefield soldiers require not only individual proficiency in the use of weapons but also skill in collective activities.[1] As a consequence, armies throughout history have placed great emphasis on training both to directly increase the chances of success in battle and also to raise morale and foster *esprit de corps*. By the eighteenth century the range of gunpowder weapons and a greater number of troops involved in exercises meant that the British army habitually required large areas of land upon which to practise.[2] With the advent of industrialised warfare and the 'citizen armies' of the twentieth century, demand increased on an unprecedented scale and in 1944 some 9.8 million acres across Britain were in use as training grounds.[3] Even without the existence of an invasion threat, it was probably inevitable that the Sandlings would have seen intensive military use during the Second World War. The British army had an established tradition of placing newly raised or inexperienced units on coastal defence duties in order to provide a more meaningful context for training and the open landscape of the Suffolk heathland made it eminently suitable for the unrestricted movement of men and vehicles.

The use of coastal areas for army training deserves greater attention, not least in areas such as the Sandlings, where it took place throughout the conflict. This chapter deals with the period 1940–43 and is concerned with the training regimes of those formations (55th, 15th and 54th Divisions) that successively occupied the Sandlings, paying particular attention to how the demands of coastal defence and training were reconciled. It is important to note, however, that the experiences of these three divisions were not uniform; while 55th and 15th Divisions built and manned defences, by 1942–43 this requirement no longer existed and so 54th Division, while ostensibly defending home territory, spent the majority of time training in what was still technically the coastal defence zone. The following chapter discusses the period

---

1   Flavius Josephus famously commented on the Roman army that 'their exercises [were] unbloody battles, and their battles bloody exercises': *Wars of the Jews* (Pantianos, n.d.), Book 3, 4, 1.

2   J.A. Holding, *Fit for Service: Training of the British Army, 1715–1795* (Oxford, 1981).

3   Schofield, *Modern Military Matters*, p. 7; Dobinson, *Supplementary Study*. TNA WO 277/36 (Training in the British Army, 1939–1945).

from late 1943, when the character of the training landscape changed considerably during intense preparations for Operation Overlord. To date, no overview of training within one Divisional Sector has been attempted and the aim of this chapter is to offer a more nuanced view of the impact of coastal defence duty on army training via a close analysis of units on the ground.

For the purposes of analysis a useful distinction can be made between those troops stationed on the coast primarily for defence duties and those units from outside that rotated in and out of the area to take part in exercises. For the former, training took place alongside the construction and manning of defences, while for the latter time on the coast was more transient and simply involved undertaking their allotted tasks on one of the Sandlings' designated training grounds before moving elsewhere. The practice of moving other units in and out of the coastal zone for exercises continued throughout the war, but increased specialisation in training meant that some units came to be based on the coast solely for this purpose.[4] In general terms, as the conflict progressed the move was towards larger, more elaborate exercises that more closely reflected the actual operations that troops were expected to undertake in the field. As a consequence, not only was there an increase in the amount of land used for training but the activities that took place tended to leave a more tangible trace in the landscape.

The archaeological evidence for training reflects activities ranging from small-scale tactical drills involving only a handful of troops through to large formal exercises with hundreds of soldiers. The study of such 'training archaeology' is of value not just because it can offer important insights into the nature of the activities themselves (something documentary sources do not always relate in detail) but also because it informs wider debates concerning the nature of Britain's Home Army in the period from Dunkirk to D-Day. The quality of army training was the subject of much criticism both during the conflict and subsequently by historians, with what has sometimes been seen as a lacklustre performance by British troops on the battlefield, especially in the Normandy campaign, in part explained by inadequate preparation at home.[5]

Training and defence works, 1939–42

Perceptions of the period 1939–42 are bound up with the idea that coastal defence took valuable time away from training, was ultimately pointless as an invasion never happened and so was pernicious and retarded the development of units. This view finds particular expression from 1942, when it was invoked by a number of Divisional commanders in the Home Army to explain deficiencies in their formations.[6] Historians

4   As is the case for 49th Infantry and 79th Armoured Division and discussed in the following chapter.

5   T. Harrison Place, *Military Training in the British Army, 1940–1944, From Dunkirk to D-Day* (Oxford, 2000).

6   TNA WO 205/1C (General Paget's Conferences as Commander in Chief Home Forces) Reports on State of Training of Field Force Formations, 22.4.42; significantly, those formations citing coastal defence as reasons for backwardness tended to be independent brigades, rather than divisions.

have tended to follow this lead and consequently made some damning judgements, which at their most extreme argue that 'coastal … duties … made collective tactical training quite impossible for months at a time' and that they were 'deleterious' for units.[7] When presented in such exaggerated terms these statements are simply erroneous, as the evidence discussed here shows: training was a constant feature of coastal defence duty from the earliest part of the war. While building and manning defences of course reduced the potential time available for training it did not mean that it ceased entirely. The evidence at brigade and battalion level presented here shows that while the peculiarities of their situation was one factor in dictating what *kind* of training took place, for units undertaking coastal defence it was a more common activity than might otherwise be supposed.

Between 1940 and 1944 the Home Army suffered from a myriad of deficiencies the cause of which actually lay elsewhere, but it was easy for troops undertaking somewhat unglamorous anti-invasion duties to see this as the main reason for a variety of complaints. For senior officers frustrated at the progress of their formations, coastal defence provided at least one reason why their troops were not up to the standards they demanded or expected. But, even here, close analysis reveals a more complex picture: Divisional commanders frequently reported that relief from coastal defence duties would speed up the process of bringing their formations up to war proficiency, but the duties themselves were not in themselves always identified as a reason for backwardness. Rather, the root causes of poor training were the high turnover of junior leaders, a lack of instructors and umpires for exercises, weapon and ammunition shortages and a lack of firing ranges.[8] Significantly, coastal defence started to be invoked as an issue as far as training was concerned from 1942, a time when the invasion threat had passed and the Home Army was tentatively beginning to plan for offensive action.[9] When a genuine invasion threat was believed to exist, however, the requirement to defend sovereign territory took priority and much of the grumbling by officers in 1940–41 was connected with the overall quality of their troops and shortages of equipment rather than defensive duties per se.

The training landscape

While the creation of the coastal defence zone resulted in a contiguous strip of land over which troops could potentially train, in practice the army did not have an entirely free hand. The military's requirements had to be balanced against other needs, especially those of agriculture, and so were carefully managed. Training was a case in point, and the coastal landscape was not a 'free fire zone' where troops could do

---

7   Harrison Place, *Military Training*, pp. 41, 43.

8   TNA WO 205/1C (General Paget's Conferences as Commander in Chief Home Forces), 'Paget to Divisional Commanders', 19.5.42.

9   TNA WO 199/2623 (Army's Commander's Personal Memorandum No. 2), 21.3.42.

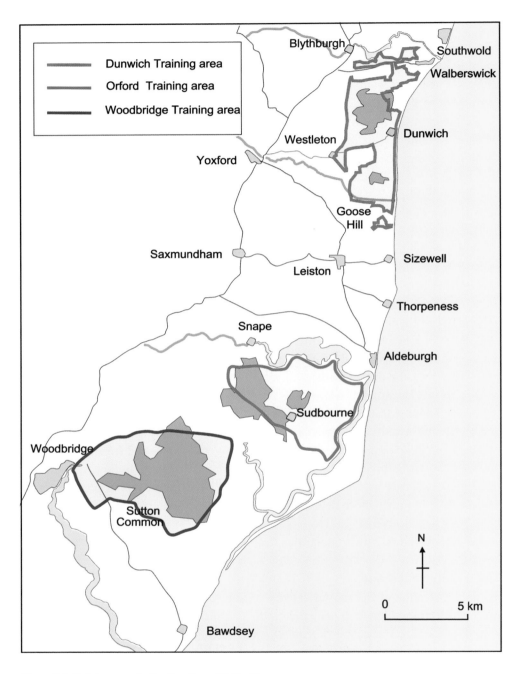

Figure 5.1. Training areas in the Sandlings, 1940–42.

whatever they wished wherever they liked. Rather, specifically designated training areas were established where live firing and the movement of vehicles could take place with little in the way of restriction. In the adjacent countryside, while albeit still under military control, soldierly activities were curtailed. Differing arrangements in the use of the coastal zone originated with the authority of Defence Regulations (DR) 51 and 52, created under the auspices of the Emergency Powers Act of 1939.[10] Under DR 51 the military could requisition land with seven days' warning without risk of appeal and subsequently deny the owner and civilians access. Where these powers were invoked for training purposes this resulted in heavily militarised landscapes where exercises with live ammunition could be carried out with impunity. While land requisitioned under DR 52 gave the military right of use, the landowner and sometimes other civilians were still permitted to enter, so allowing continued occupation and farming. The training that took place in these areas therefore tended to be less intense and more likely to involve instruction in fieldcraft, tactical movement and the use of blank ammunition.

The Phoney War

The earliest training grounds in the Sandlings were established in or very soon after November 1939, with the military build-up associated with the J.C. Plan (see Chapter 2). By April 1940 what was known alternatively as the Dunwich or Westleton Training Area had been requisitioned under DR 51, the core of which comprised a 775-hectare (1900-acre) block of wetland and common around the Minsmere levels and Westleton Walks. In addition, a much more extensive area of 1400 hectares (3500 acres) to the north was taken under DR 52, which encompassed other parts of Westleton Walks, Dunwich Forest and a large tract inland from Walberswick.[11] Although the exact circumstances of its origin are unclear, a further training area was established at Woodbridge, which had at its heart Sutton Common and Hollesley Heath. Marginal land elsewhere across the Sandlings also appears to have been used at this time, albeit the exact legal mechanisms governing its military control are lost (Figures 5.1).[12]

The landscapes chosen for the Dunwich and Woodbridge Training Areas lay on some of the most freely draining and acidic soil on the Sandlings and chiefly comprised heath, plantations and rough grazing. The soil's incompatibility with arable farming meant that these areas were thinly populated and could be taken by the military while avoiding significant damage to the agricultural economy; Woodbridge, for example, lay on the particularly intractable sandy soil of the Newport 4 Association and so contained relatively few working farms. The extent to which agriculture affected the

---

10　TNA WO 277/36 (Training in the British Army, 1939–1945).

11　TNA HO 207/1182 (Dunwich–Sizewell Battle Training Area).

12　TNA WO 166/688 (War Diary, 55th Division, GS), Training Instruction No. 10, April 1940, Appendix B to Training Instruction: Sheet 1 Westleton Training Area; TNA HO 207/1180 (Battle Training Areas), File I, Part 3, Map c.April 1942.

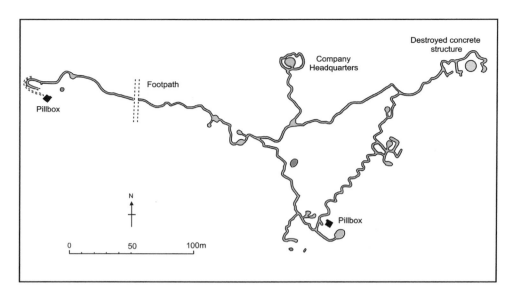

Figure 5.2. Plan of earthworks at North Warren. This complex earthwork site probably originated as a training work, but the existence of pillboxes indicate that it was reused in 1940 and the 'swastika' trenches to the east probably date to 1941, when it formed part of a platoon locality. The destroyed concrete structure, probably a pillbox, is almost certainly a legacy of pre-D-Day training.

geography of the training landscape is neatly illustrated by the irregular bounds of the Dunwich Training Area, which chiefly followed those of pre-war heath, rough pasture and plantation and tended to avoid those areas shown as arable on the 1930s Land Utilisation Survey. The relationship between the military and the agricultural landscapes is most clearly seen in the area around Westwood Lodge at Walberswick, where the farm and its adjacent fields form an 'island' surrounded by land requisitioned for training.[13] The well-drained land that comprised these areas also had the advantage that it could be used by tracked vehicles throughout the year and, given that newly mobilised units were charged with coastal defence in this early part of the war, there was also probably a certain utility in providing dedicated training areas immediately adjacent to the coastline they were nominally defending.

North Warren

The creation of designated training areas is a reminder that in the early stages of the war the purpose of the Home Army was to train recruits so they could be drafted overseas. In the brief period between the laying down of the J.C. Plan and the invasion crisis, there is archaeological evidence that the kind of training that took place was broadly similar to that undertaken during the First World War. At North Warren near

---

13 TNA HO 207/1182 (Home Office Civil Defence Regions. Dunwich–Sizewell Battle Training Area), Dunwich Battle Area, May 1943, shows earlier requisitions.

Figure 5.3. View of trench system and pillbox, North Warren. The trench system probably dates to the spring of 1940 and was excavated during the 'Phoney War' for training purposes, with the pillbox added later in the year when it was part of the coastal defences.

Aldeburgh a highly unusual earthwork comprising a series of sub-circular positions connected by long ribbons of communication trench suggests that at least part of this training involved constructing earthworks (Figures 5.2–5.3). A possible context is provided by a 55th Division instruction from April 1940 stating that units in the area were to dig both battalion and company positions.[14] The suggestion that the North Warren trench system dates to the earliest part of the war comes from its distinctive form, which corresponds closely to the layout of a company position given in the 1925 *Manual of Fieldworks*.[15] In particular, the arrangement of the detached company headquarters that formed the 'keep', which in turn connected three platoon positions, appears to be heavily based on the textbook example. Such designs were a throwback to the First World War and did not survive long into the Second, suggesting that the North Warren system is unlikely to date from after the summer of 1940. Although primarily an exercise in training, the resultant trench systems were to face towards the coastline should circumstances ever arise which required them to be held against an enemy landing. Seen in this light, the North Warren trench system makes a great deal of sense, lying as it does behind the forward line of the company of the 9th battalion the King's Regiment at Aldeburgh, the unit presumably responsible for its construction.

14   TNA WO 166/688 (War Diary, 55th Division, GS), Training Instruction No. 10, April 1940.
15   War Office, *Manual of Field Works (All Arms)* (1925).

If the North Warren trench system was indeed a response to a training memorandum from April 1940 then it is good evidence of the kind of activity that troops were engaged in immediately before the invasion crisis. It is analogous to the activities undertaken by the British Expeditionary Force in France over the winter of 1939–40, but also to similar schemes during the First World War, when substantial networks of training trenches were excavated in order to provide practical experience in the digging of fieldworks and to replicate the kinds of conditions soldiers would face when they eventually moved into the front line.[16] That the North Warren position might have been intended for broadly comparable purposes is also indicated in the training instruction, which talks about leaving areas of 'No Man's Land' between battalion and company positions.[17]

Training and coastal defence, 1940–41

Whatever the provenance of trench systems such as that at North Warren, the events of May 1940 quickly removed the opportunity for troops to spend their time creating elaborate earthworks solely for the purposes of practice. Most modern historians have rightly seen a tension between the demands of coastal defence on the one hand and training on the other, but what has not been sufficiently acknowledged is that while the fortification of the coastline represented a considerable effort, it did not put an end to training altogether.

Brigade and battalion war diaries make it clear that units on the coast adopted a carefully managed and pragmatic approach to integrating their activities. Even during the height of the invasion crisis, not all time was spent building defence works. In the case of the 2nd/4th South Lancashires, as early as June 1940 one platoon from each company (that is, one-third of the battalion's manpower) was released per day in order to take part in exercises. During the following month more elaborate training

---

16   B. Bond, 'The British Field Force in France and Belgium, 1939–40', in P. Addison and A. Calder (eds), *Time to Kill: The Soldier's Experience of War in the West* (London, 1997), pp. 40–49 at 42; Appleby *et al.*, *The Home Front in Britain*, pp. 45–9.

17   TNA WO 166/688 (War Diary, 55th Division, GS), Training Instruction No. 10, April 1940; if excavation was started soon after 10 April, it would be tempting to link what would appear to be unfinished elements of the North Warren system with the invasion crisis on 10 May, when the 9th King's hurriedly redeployed. It is also significant that the 9th King's known war positions did not include North Warren; the battalion's reserve company was some miles inland, at Knodishall Whin, where there was a major pillbox complex. The possibility that the proposed training trenches ordered a month earlier might have to be used during actual conflict seems a little prophetic, given that an invasion crisis did indeed break four week later, but the subsequent construction of three pillboxes on the site suggests that during the summer of 1940 North Warren was intended as a secondary position to be used in the event of men falling back after Aldeburgh's capture. Given the tactical importance of the location at this local level, it is unsurprising that it became a platoon position in 1941–42 and it is probable that the 'swastika' earthworks date to this time, especially as an almost identical example dating to 1941 exists at Walberswick. If this was indeed the case, then it would mean that most of the site had by that time been abandoned, strengthening the case that its original purpose was redundant.

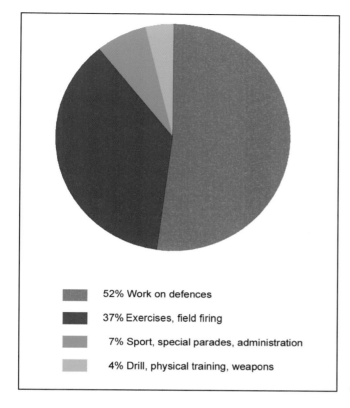

52% Work on defences

37% Exercises, field firing

7% Sport, special parades, administration

4% Drill, physical training, weapons

Figure 5.4. Pie chart showing time spent on training and on defence works by 6th Royal Scots Fusiliers, June–September, 1941. From schedules in battalion war diary.

took place in conjunction with neighbouring units. On 20 July the Headquarters Company undertook joint exercises with the 66th Anti-Tank Regiment, with the carrier and motorcycle platoons of the 2nd/4th providing the enemy. By the end of July it was deemed appropriate for the full battalion to train for a whole day, with a practice counterattack on enemy-held Walberswick forming the main objective. While the exact details of such exercises remain unclear, they were of 'two-sided' form and used live ammunition, as it was during such an exercise in September that the battalion took their only casualty of their time on the coast, when a private died from a gunshot wound.[18]

The pattern of training taking place alongside the construction of defence works established during the summer of 1940 continued the following year and a detailed run of weekly work schedules from 6th Battalion Royal Scots for three months in the summer of 1941 permits harder evidence to be brought to bear on the question of the extent to which the building of defences interfered with training regimes (Figure 5.4).[19] This evidence shows that, while work on defences made up the majority of work for the battalion's rifle companies, training was always a significant feature of the weekly

18 TNA WO 166/4680 (War Diary, 2nd/4th South Lancashire Regiment), 11.9.40.
19 TNA WO 166/4592 (War Diary, 6th Royal Scots Fusiliers), June–September, 1941, *passim*.

routine. Across the period for which schedules exist, each company of the battalion spent approximately 52 per cent of their time on defence works compared with approximately 40 per cent in training of all kinds. These figures do require qualification, however. They represent the situation during a summer that saw considerable variation in the pattern of work. This period coincided with a concerted effort to erect beach scaffolding and so it is to be expected that totals for the construction of defences would be high. When fully underway, scaffolding often took priority over everything else: in the week beginning 14 July some 83 per cent of time was taken up in this way, with only 16 per cent taken up with training. On only one occasion at the end of July did defence works entirely compromise training, when some 95 per cent of the working week was put into defences. But, by the same token, when the defences were nearing completion the balance swung the other way. In the week beginning 29 September some 76 per cent of time was devoted to training, with only 15 per cent to work on defences; a fortnight later, 100 per cent of the working week was listed as training. While it is undeniably the case that time building defences represented a considerable investment for the troops involved, the idea that it made training impossible should clearly not be pushed too far. Regardless of the time that went into defence works, it rarely resulted in a complete cessation of training. The standard routine for the 6th Royal Scots was for at least one day per week to be designated for training and, when this was scheduled for the same day for all four rifle companies, it permitted the opportunity for battalion level exercises. Units on the coast did not, therefore, suffer particularly from a lack of training time; rather, routines were structured in order to ensure that it was integrated alongside the building of defence works.

The evidence from schedules notwithstanding, it would also be unwise to draw a binary distinction between defence works on the one hand and training on the other because coastal defence duty constituted a form of training in its own right. Throughout the war there was a general agreement among senior officers that purposeful training with a clear aim produced the best results and, especially in 1940, the urgent need to fortify the coastline coincidentally provided such an obvious and immediate purpose. The role played by defence works as a surrogate for aspects of basic training in the early part of the war is easily underestimated, as it meant that soldiers newly arrived in the ranks engaged in collective activity, completed allotted tasks under orders, underwent considerable physical and sometimes mental stress and became accustomed to military routine and to long hours of work. On occasion, tactical necessity was deliberately exploited for training purposes, such as laying barbed wire at night simply for the sake of practice, and officers were encouraged to promote the idea that work on defences was not fatigue duty but rather field training in preparation for future operations.[20]

---

20 TNA WO 166/975 (War Diary, 125th Infantry Brigade), Summary of Brigadier's Conference, 8.11.40; TNA WO 166/977 (War Diary, 127th Infantry Brigade), 127 Inf Bde Operation Instruction No. 14, 3.12.40; TNA WO 166/4156 (War Diary, 6th Border Regiment), Commanding Officer's Instruction No. 12, 10.2.41.

That building defences was undertaken for a genuine military reason and sometimes under air attack arguably only added to the realism. As is seen in Chapter 8, the rapid adjustment to a wartime state of readiness brought with it attendant problems of morale and discipline, but also a sense of camaraderie. Particularly in 1940, war diaries reported with satisfaction that manning the coast during a time of crisis had galvanised their otherwise inexperienced units. The 2nd/4th Lancashires, for example, reported in November of that year that the summer had seen training brought up to a standard that pre-war regulars would have envied and that the summer's activities 'may be said to mark a definite stage in the career of this B[attalio]n'.[21] It is perhaps ironic that the operational task for which 55th Division was employed that summer was actually the chief mechanism by which the formation became anywhere near fit for war service. Although an unplanned and in many respects far from ideal method of instruction, coastal defence was, especially in 1940, perhaps best described as 'on the job' training.

Once the immediate invasion crisis of 1940 had passed, units habitually prepared for action as part of their normal routine. The chief mechanism for this was the 'manning exercise', which practised the drills to be followed on 'action stations' and involved the rapid deployment of troops and equipment from billets to their battle positions. These weekly exercises also tested communications, the relaying of orders, ammunition resupply and casualty evacuation, and frequently involved live firing from defensive posts.[22] At their most elaborate these were full-scale brigade- and occasionally Divisional-scale dress rehearsals for all personnel; one such exercise in 1941 took place over two days. Manning exercises also involved co-operation between the various elements responsible for beach defences; it was when calling on artillery fire on one such exercise that a junior officer of the 6th Royal Scots was wounded by shrapnel.[23] It is probable that on these occasions basic skills were inculcated and practised, as some standing orders stated that all weapons that covered beaches actually had to be fired during manning.[24] The results of such exercises were recorded, including information on how long it took troops to get into position and how well they had scored in shooting, no doubt with a view to improvement but also to maintain standards; in any event, the weekly practice was clearly a part of the training routine.[25]

While aspects of coastal defence duty provided opportunities for particular forms of training, its peculiar demands also imposed specific constraints. The most

---

21 TNA WO 166/4680 (War Diary, 2nd/4th South Lancashire Regiment), Summary end of October 1940.

22 TNA WO 166/977 (War Diary, 127th Infantry Brigade), 127 Inf Bde Operation Instruction No. 13, 3.12.40; TNA WO 166/958 (War Diary 46th Infantry Brigade), 21–2.4.41; TNA WO 166/4592 (War Diary, 6th Royal Scots Fusiliers), 1.4.41, 2.2.41; TNA WO 166/4537 (War Diary, 22nd Royal Fusiliers), 2.2.41; TNA WO 166/4346 (War Diary, 11th Highland Light Infantry), 29.9.41.

23 TNA WO 166/4592 (War Diary, 6th Royal Scots Fusiliers), 22.4.41.

24 TNA WO 166/977 (War Diary, 127th Infantry Brigade), 127 Infantry Brigade Operation Instruction No. 13, 3.12.40; TNA WO 166/4346 (War Diary, 11th Highland Light Infantry), 26.3.41.

25 TNA WO 166/977 (War Diary, 127th Infantry Brigade), 127 Inf Bde Operation Instruction No. 13, 3.12.40.

obvious was the need for troops to be in proximity to their war positions in order that they could meet an attack if it came. Preparedness for attack was something of a badge of honour, as one colonel could boastfully report that his whole battalion was on 30 seconds' notice at all times.[26] But for training purposes the disposition of the men on the ground was unhelpful; with battalions spread out over considerable distances, concentrating men for collective activity was logistically inconvenient. In addition, the necessity for at least part of each unit to 'Stand To' at dawn and dusk (see Chapter 8) and be able to man their posts at short notice between these times meant that training at company and platoon level was administratively easier than at the level of the battalion and brigade. Geographical restrictions put limitations on lengthy route marches, inter-unit co-operation and co-operative training between the Division's fighting arms. Compounding the practical difficulties of drawing off men from their war positions was the limited availability of training infrastructure. The two designated areas for live firing at Dunwich and Woodbridge were comparatively small and had to be shared with outside units. Even when use of Dunwich or Woodbridge was possible, petrol shortages meant that moving troops onto training areas was prohibitive; route marching to training grounds was routine, which, while providing some benefits for physical conditioning, cost time.[27] A further difficulty was the need for training not to interfere with agriculture, which ruled out the use of farmed areas in the hinterland of the defences. Company training by the 9th Cameronians in May 1941, for example, was specifically to avoid taking place over cultivated fields and plantations.[28] While spatial constraints clearly did not stop training altogether, they were an additional factor in encouraging units to concentrate their training locally and on a small scale.

But underpinning such difficulties were two linked and more deep-seated problems: shortages of equipment and a lack of proficiency in basic skills among the rank and file. The real issue for units on the coast was not so much a lack of time for training or areas upon which to train but, rather, inexperience; the inadequacies of the private soldier were a constant problem for officers. These problems were not confined to those formations in the Sandlings, but existed nationwide.[29] The need to make good deficiencies in training and equipment in the rank and file are constant themes of war diaries and far outnumber complaints about the time spent building defences. While coastal defence imposed practical restrictions, its removal would not have immediately provided a solution to much deeper-rooted difficulties.

It is difficult to underestimate the standard of training and lack of equipment in some units in the first two years of the war, and one anecdote relating to 348 Battery, Royal Artillery's defence of Ipswich stands for many and is worth quoting at length:

26   TNA WO 166/975 (War Diary, 125th Infantry Brigade), Summary of Brigadier's Conference, 16.12.40.
27   TNA WO 166/4346 (War Diary, 11th Highland Light Infantry), March 1941.
28   TNA WO 166/4180 (War Diary, 9th Cameronians), 21.5.41.
29   French, *Raising Churchill's Army*, pp. 185–6.

Throughout the Regiment rifles were still in short supply and only enough to arm one man in three. Ammunition was equally short – five rounds a man. Those without rifles were told to provide themselves with pieces of wood which were to be fashioned into clubs. Shortly afterwards, to the amusement of all, there was an issue of pikes! They were bayonets of Great War pattern welded into the ends of steel tubing. They proved to be quite dangerous to the user. The wags claimed the idea was to show the pikes to the invading forces who would then die laughing.[30]

Such anecdotal evidence explains why training was deemed so important for units on the coast, even at a time of military crisis: putting unprepared men behind sandbags rendered the effort put into building defences almost useless.

While shortages of equipment were in part responsible for such difficulties, wider problems associated with mass mobilisation, together with the fact that the events of May 1940 were wholly unexpected, were equally significant. The experience of 164 Infantry Brigade, who held Sub-Sector 2 during the summer of 1940, is instructive. All three of the brigade's constituent infantry battalions were Territorials embodied on the eve of the war. At the heart of each was a cadre of pre-war servicemen who had the responsibility of bringing together the larger numbers of less experienced men filling the ranks. A small proportion of the officers and senior NCOs were First World War veterans, but the vast majority of the private soldiers had found their way into the army as a result of the first and second conscription drafts following the outbreak of hostilities. When it came, the invasion crisis led to a substantial proportion of men being posted to units before they had completed their recruit training and so they were, effectively, raw troops. Throughout the summer there was an almost constant piecemeal turnover of personnel, as new intakes were received from Infantry Training Centres while others left for new postings or were weeded out as unfit for service. The training regime comprised route marching and basic shooting courses for rifle and Bren gun, with further instruction in the use of the anti-tank rifle and gas masks. Such training was not far short of what was normally taught to recruits before they were posted to their battalions and focused on the British Army's core training principles of physical fitness and use of equipment; what was unusual, however, was that such basic instruction was not intended to be given to men on the front line and under threat of invasion.[31]

The general problem of inexperience in the ranks persisted down to 1943 and was compounded by the constant drawing off of seasoned officers and NCOs to elsewhere in the army, which denuded units of experienced soldiers at the time when they were

---

30 Robertson, *Rose and the Arrow*, p. 39; later in the summer the Regiment received French 75mm guns, but with no instruction manuals, so technical information was obtained by borrowing a book from Lowestoft library, *ibid.*, p. 48.

31 D. French, *Military Identities: The Regimental System, the British Army and the British People, c.1870–2000* (Oxford, 2005), Chapter 3, esp. pp. 61–75.

most needed.[32] One of 15th Division's Field Engineer Companies completely changed its complement of officers in less than five months.[33] In such circumstances continuity of training programmes suffered and exercises were below par when officers were absent from their commands, even if only for short periods.[34] As a consequence, evidence for poor levels of attainment in the ranks is plentiful in war diaries. In late 1940 the commander of 125 Infantry Brigade in Sub-Sector 3 ordered that troops were to receive additional war proficiency pay only if they passed the army's elementary training test. In the case of the 1st/5th Lancashire Fusiliers only soldiers who had attained suitable standard of marksmanship on ranges could proceed to field firing exercises, a sign of how even in a veteran BEF unit influxes of new men had diluted the overall skills base.[35] In terms of the kind of training undertaken, as well as soldiers' expertise in basic tasks, the experience of the 11th Highland Light Infantry during the spring and summer of 1941 is typical. In March one Company was found to be 'not quite up to expectations' when practising platoon attacks, while another undertaking the same drill drew the comment that 'it is obvious that individual training and weapon training are badly needed'. Similar exercises the following month were unsuccessful owing to the absence of both of the company's senior officers; whatever events were taking place, the battalion's war diarist's comment that 'B Coy did training, what is was they were doing is best known by themselves' does not suggest that they were productive. Regular visits to firing ranges meant that the shooting of the battalion was observed to improve, albeit with variation; in April it was noted that 'shooting wasn't too bad, apart from one man who hit a four foot target two away from his own at 100 yds with monotonous regularity'.[36] A response to the twin problems of lack of experience and equipment by commanders on the ground was to enact a series of pragmatic initiatives intended to meet the training needs of their men alongside the requirement to build and man defence works.

A standard procedure was to draw off for intensive training experienced or particularly able individuals who could then act as junior leaders. In the case of 125 Brigade, for example, arrangements were made for cadres of picked men to undertake specific training courses so that they could then pass on their skills to their immediate subordinates.[37] Where expertise was in short supply it was not uncommon for better-trained troops to be brought into units for the purposes of demonstration: the 1st/4th South Lancashires engineered the services of a platoon of Guardsmen for practical instruction in platoon attacks and night patrols.[38] Other strategies included the

32   TNA WO 199/808 (Land for Training – Formation Battle Training Areas General]), February 1942.

33   TNA WO 166/3748 (War Diary, 279th Field Company, Royal Engineers), 10.9.41.

34   TNA WO 166/4346 (War Diary, 11th Highland Light Infantry), 1.4.41.

35   TNA WO 166/975 (War Diary, 125th Infantry Brigade), Points from Brigadier's Conference, 17.10.40.

36   TNA WO166/4346 (War Diary, 11th Highland Light Infantry), entries for April–September 1941, *passim*.

37   TNA WO 166/4407 (War Diary, 1st/5th Battalion, Lancashire Fusiliers), Battalion Orders, 25.11.40.

38   TNA WO 166/4679 (War Diary, 1st/4th Battalion South Lancashire Regiment), 22.5.40.

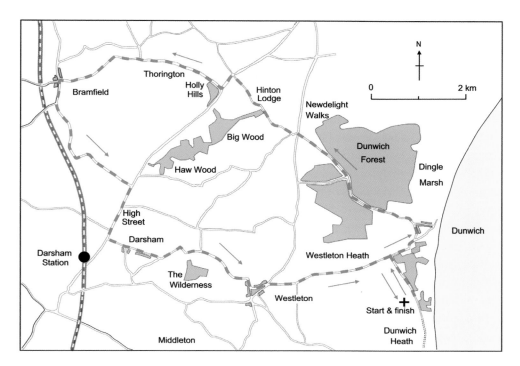

Figure 5.5. Training in the coast defence zone. Although troops may not have been able to move too far away from their battle positions, this did not prevent activities such as route marches, which were simply kept close to the coastline. This map shows such a march undertaken by the 10th Cameronians in 1941.

hoarding of training ammunition so that it could be used more effectively, rather than expended on a piecemeal basis. To alleviate the problem of distance to prescribed training areas the immediate vicinity of the coastal defences was exploited to the full; as these places were already under military control and cleared for fields of fire, they were in many respects ideal for low-level training (Figure 5.5). The war diary of the 6th Royal Scots reveals these arrangements in unusual detail. Live firing, for example, took place on open areas in front of the battalion's positions in April 1941, in a manner probably similar to a more elaborate field firing session in June involving target boats standing in for German barges; the shooting session was curtailed by the sinking of the towing boat on one day and bad weather the next.[39] The beach zone could also be used to improve training infrastructure; in one instance, a battalion rifle range was created to the front of one of the rifle companies' positions.[40]

Perhaps the most important technique, however, was the practice of rotating units out of the line for specific periods so that training could be delivered in concentrated bursts. This can be seen across the chain of command, with companies rotating

39   TNA WO 166/4592 (War Diary, 6th Royal Scots Fusiliers), 1.4.41; 2–4.6.41.
40   *Ibid.*, 31.7.41.

their platoons, battalions their companies and so on, up to the level of brigade. The arrangements of 198 Brigade in Sub-Sector 1 in the winter of 1941 are a case in point. Here each of the brigade's battalions was relieved for one month in order to undergo a programme of 'stepped' training, which over four weeks built up from individual and section work to that of a battalion-level exercise. The month's training programme chiefly comprised weapon training and fire control orders, formations and movement, night routines, obstacle crossing, a route march followed by an attack and co-ordination between the battalion's different elements and attached field artillery.[41]

The detailed analysis of war diaries shows, therefore, that it is mistaken to suggest that coastal defence made collective training impossible; while exercises above the level of company may have been administratively challenging, with planning they were evidently possible. But the fact that so few such large exercises were conducted was not because it was too difficult, but because they were of limited benefit. A more realistic approach to training was to concentrate on individual proficiency in technical skills and tactically on low-level drills at a platoon and company level, because this was where troops were deficient. The key point is that, even without the additional task of building and manning fortifications, there were limits to what units on the coast could have achieved. It was for reasons of necessity, rather than due to the demands of building defences, that the majority of training took place up to company level. Confirmation that this was the case comes from the fact that, over the course of 1941, when work on defences gradually diminished, training *still* took the form of instruction in basic soldiering skills, physical conditioning, fieldcraft and section and platoon battle drills. The experience of 'B' Company the 10th Cameronians stands for many. In the five weeks from the end of September to the beginning of November 1941, when construction of defences ceased, training comprised cross-country and route marching, platoon and section attacks, field firing, grenade throwing, map reading and searching ground. Larger-scale exercises at battalion or higher level were still comparatively rare; during this period only one day was spent exercising with the other rifle companies.[42]

It is significant to note that in the unit documentation for 55th, 42nd and 15th Divisions from the spring of 1940 to the winter of 1941/42 there are relatively few complaints about defence works, as there was a clear perception that they were required. Murmurings to the contrary date to mid-1941, when war diaries start to contain entries suggesting that such works were burdensome. By this time the perceived threat of German invasion was starting to reduce and, perhaps importantly, there was no end in sight to the construction of defences. The shift in mood was reflected in the diary of 11th Highland Light Infantry:

---

41   TNA WO 166/4516 (War Diary, 6th Border Regiment), Commanding Officer's Instruction No. 9, December 1941.

42   TNA WO 166/4181 (War Diary, 10th Cameronians), 14.10.41.

B Coy carried out individual training in their Coy area at Alderton. Training in this unit is not nearly up to the standard it ought to be. The reason being that some 10 months have been spent on beach defence, which means field works practically the whole time, and men become dirty and ill-disciplined unless they are chased the whole time.[43]

Complaints such as this and others from 15th Division reflect an easy eliding of poor performance with coastal defence; similar statements about discipline could be applied to units across the Home Army or the empire that were free of the requirement to build and man fortifications. But such remarks tended to be made when a unit had had an uninterrupted period of building defence works and when officers thought that time could be better spent elsewhere – and became louder when it became clear that the war was taking a different course. It is telling that less than six months after 15th Division's spell in the Sandlings was over the formation was reported as being 'physically very fit and the fighting spirit is excellent' with the only concern about potential performance being that the Divisional staff required more practice.[44] It would follow that either the rank and file had made truly enormous strides once they were relieved of the burden of coastal defence duties or that its training on the Suffolk coast had not been as inadequate as might otherwise be thought.

The reformation of the home army: battle schools and Orford Training Area

In addition to the reorganisation of Britain's anti-invasion landscape that was discussed in Chapter 3, Alan Brooke's tenure as Commander in Chief Home Forces also witnessed significant changes in training provision.[45] Over the course of 1942 there was a nation-wide expansion of practice grounds, a relaxation of safety measures in order to permit greater use of live ammunition and the establishment of 'Battle Schools'. The latter were the chief mechanism by which deficiencies were to be rectified, principally by giving troops instruction in 'Battle Drill', a set of tactical principles intended to improve the fighting capability of the infantry in particular.[46] The summer of 1942 also saw a major reorganisation of Britain's land forces, with the Home Army reverting to its traditional role of home defence and the training of men for drafting to what would become front-line units. All of these measures had a direct impact on the landscape of the Sandlings.

As has been seen, early in 1942 54th Division was put onto the Lower Establishment and so effectively became a training formation.[47] The division's activities in the 18 months

---

43   TNA WO 166/4346 (War Diary, 11th Highland Light Infantry), 1.5.41.

44   TNA WO 205/1C (General Paget's Conferences as Commander in Chief Home Forces), Reports on State of Training of Field Force formations, 22.4.42.

45   French, *Raising Churchill's Army*, pp. 205–7.

46   Harrison Place, *Military Training*, chapter 4; T. Harrison Place, 'Lionel Wigram, Battle Drill and the British Army in the Second World War', *War in History*, 7 (2000), pp. 442–62.

47   TNA WO 205/1C (General Paget's Conferences as Commander in Chief Home Forces), Paget to Divisional Commanders, 19.5.42.

Figure 5.6. Aldeburgh Battle School, 1942. During intensive instruction troops undertook live firing and were exposed to live ammunition. (IWM H27338)

before disbandment are not without interest, however, as they provide both a case study of the changing character of the exercises such formations undertook and also reveal in great detail how the Sandlings' training areas were actually used. This latter point might sound banal, but is more important than it first appears, as such micro-studies of training grounds are, as yet, comparatively rare. By 1944 Britain's home-trained army was ready to bare its teeth, but how it got to that point is rarely discussed from the perspective of view of landscape history. In general terms, while training at platoon and company level continued unabated, from the mid-war period exercises in the Sandlings tended to be more elaborate and to involve greater numbers of troops and vehicles, and were increasingly geared towards the 'break in' phase of battle.[48] Memoranda from mid-1942 indicate an increasing concern to undertake exercises at battalion and brigade level that rehearsed communications and inter-arm co-operation as well as tactical drills. As one

---

48   TNA WO 166/6138 (War Diary, XI Corps), Corps Training Instruction No. 10, 8.4.42.

soldier from the 2nd/7th West Surreys recalled, 'it was now large exercises – marching and movement. Presumably the senior command were learning all the time but didn't mean much to us – we only knew that we had to march from there to there'.[49]

In April 1942 54th Division established a 'Battle School' at Aldeburgh, with successive waves of men undertaking demanding programmes of 'toughening up' and intensive instruction in fieldcraft skills and minor tactics. Training films and photographs indicate a regime of rigorous physical training and practical education in battle drill delivered through exercises with live ammunition (Figure 5.6).[50] Platoons, then companies and finally battalions undertook a variety of exhausting training tasks that accord well with the military stereotype; in one letter home the author Alun Lewis, who was a subaltern in the South Wales Borderers, described his time at the Aldeburgh School as 'an ordeal that carries on all night as well as by day'.[51] In an anonymous piece for the *New Statesman* Lewis gave a vivid description of the nature of the activities:

> Divided into sub-sections we stalk each other in the scrub. Instructors fire over our heads and yell their slogans at us. Remember Hong Kong. Remember Singapore. Get him before he gets you. It might be your sister. Bang. Rat-tat-tat. Woomph. Guts. Guts. On, On, On. Sweat saves blood. Kill. Kill. The little yellow bastard's after you. Get him before he gets you. Remember Hong Kong.[52]

The war diaries of 54th Division's constituent units demonstrate that in the months after the School's establishment there was a cumulatively significant process whereby individuals (usually officers and junior leaders) completed general courses and more specific programmes. The majority of the School's activities took place in the area around its headquarters at Aldeburgh, being facilitated through additional requisitions of land under DR 51 for live firing at Ash Wood and Goose Hill, to the north of Sizewell. The anti-invasion landscape was now reused as a training ground, with troops forced to cross wet anti-tank ditches and attack redundant pillboxes, albeit that this environment brought with it attendant dangers; during a three-day route march a party of men from the 5th Royal Berkshires was killed when they strayed into a minefield (Figure 5.7).[53]

Increased numbers of better-trained troops permitted more ambitious exercises and in April 1942 Eastern Command established a new battle training area in the hinterland of the long loop of the river Alde at Orford. The requirements of the new training areas were more precise than had hitherto been the case and reflected the

---

49   IWM Oral History 18254 (Interview with L.C.H. Dodd, 2nd/7th Royal West Surrey Regiment).

50   IWM (War Office Film Unit) AYY 340/3 (54th Division Battle School Infantry Training in Assault Tactics), 15.2.43.

51   A. Lewis, 'A Sheaf of Letters from Alun Lewis, 1941–1943', *Wales*, 28 (1948), pp. 410–31.

52   Anon., 'Battle School', *New Statesman*, 24/595 (1942).

53   TNA WO 166/8851 (War Diary, 5th Royal Berkshire Regiment), 24.9.42. IWM Photographic Archive H27328–27355 (Battle School Training), 15–17.2.43.

Figure 5.7. Training in the invasion landscape, 1942. Here a drainage channel between Aldeburgh and Thorpeness widened in 1940 to form an anti-tank ditch is reused as a training aid. (IWM H27347)

broader shift towards training for offence, rather than defence. In order to give greater realism to training, units and formations were to operate in full battle scale on the ground, which required contiguous areas of countryside upon which to deploy and manoeuvre. More significantly, an emphasis on 'battle inoculation', which sought to give troops an insight into the sights and sounds of the battlefield by the greater use of live ammunition (to be fired by and fired at exercising soldiers), called for the exclusion of civilians.[54]

At 2850 hectares (7000 acres) requisitioned under DR 51, the Orford area was then the second largest training ground in Eastern Command. The decision to create a new area at Orford, rather than enlarge those already in existence at Dunwich and Woodbridge was the result of a number of factors. By this stage of the conflict the army was in competition for land with other services and government agencies, and large-scale requisitions were far from straightforward. The presence of the airfield at RAF Butley (Bentwaters), together with proposed locations for what would become RAF

---

54   TNA WO 199/808 (Land for Training – Formation Battle Training Areas General).

Leiston and RAF Woodbridge, meant that expanding the Woodbridge area would be problematic; in the event, a portion of the Woodbridge Training Area was given over to the RAF and army made do with the remainder. At Dunwich expansion could have taken place only at the expense of productive farmland and at this stage of the war this option was resisted; moreover, the presence of the still manned anti-invasion defences risked deaths from friendly fire. While not perfect, Orford fulfilled a number of needs. As the only part of the Sandlings' coastline not suitable for an amphibious landing, its anti-invasion defences were slight, meaning that training troops could fire unhindered over the sea. The proposed area was judged to be made up of 'poor arable land, heathland & salt marshes', and liaison with the War Agricultural Executive Committee had shown that, while appropriation by the military would lead to disruption of food production, in the final analysis it was the least worst option.[55] The population density in the proposed area was also low; with fewer than 500 inhabitants, chiefly in the villages of Sudbourne and Iken, there would be only limited displacement of civilians. It was in this latter respect that the formation of the Orford Training Area marked an important change in the militarisation of the Sandlings. Earlier requisitions under DR 51 had occurred in places with little or no civilian settlement and so had been relatively uncontentious. The nature of the change at Orford can be seen where the new training area ran along the coast and where there was already a military presence. Sudbourne had been occupied for the previous two years, with Sudbourne Hall serving as a company headquarters, the army co-existing alongside the village community without difficulty. In June 1942 the building became the command centre for the new training area and the residents were evacuated at short notice in what was the largest compulsory displacement of civilians in the Sandlings during the conflict. The establishment of the Orford area meant that, from the mid-point of the war, all the significant heaths of the Sandlings were now in use as training grounds, something particularly noticeable between the Alde and the Deben, which was now devoted almost in its entirety to training.

This general expansion of training infrastructure continued into the following year with the establishment of three anti-tank gun ranges for infantry, artillery and tanks at Benacre, Easton and Boyton respectively: all places where the muted topography, modest anti-invasion defences and bodies of water or marshland meant that troops could fire towards the sea.[56] The archaeological remains of the tank range at Boyton show the investment that was now being made in specific facilities (Figure 5.8).[57] Tanks drove around a triangular roadway that enabled the crews to shoot at moving targets from different angles during the course of a single 'run'. A series of 'pop up' targets for the tank machine gunner would appear at a range of about 500 metres and were controlled from two small concrete buildings, from which the number of hits could

55   *Ibid.*, 'Formation Battle Training Areas', 7.4.42.
56   TNA WO 166/10649 (War Diary, 54th Division, HQ), 3.1.43.
57   Hegarty and Newsome, *Suffolk's Defended Shore*, p. 68.

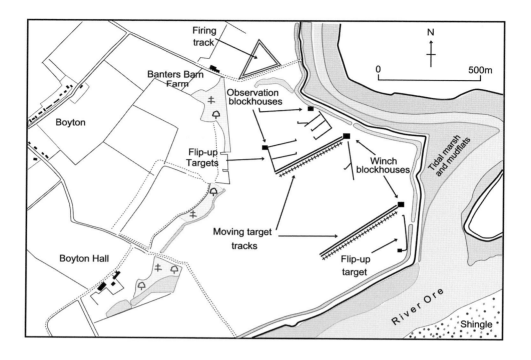

Figure 5.8. Tank gunnery range, Boyton Marshes. The scale and complexity of the site show the investment being made in training infrastructure from the mid-war period (Suffolk County Council).

also be recorded. Further along the range were two large earthwork banks with larger concrete blockhouses that functioned in a similar manner to their smaller counterparts, but here they operated large tank-shaped targets for the tank's main gun. These targets were winched along a narrow gauge railway that ran behind the earthwork bank and permitted crews to engage at ranges between 500 and 1000 metres. Various armoured units rotated through the facility and it was here that tank crews learnt basic gunnery tactics before developing their training on much larger tank ranges elsewhere in the country; this in itself represented an important development, with dedicated sites now serving a national requirement, rather than a regional one.

Training for offence

As a result of battle school movement and the expansion of training grounds, 54th Division had greater numbers of more competent soldiers and more space upon which to practise. In broad terms, the kind of training undertaken by 54th Division in 1942–43 comprised two elements: periodic large-scale exercises designed to test co-operation between arms, especially in the attack; and continual low-level instruction in minor tactics. Two exercises that took place on the Orford area – 'Tunstall' and 'Tommy' – are representative of the broader kind of training taking place at this time and illustrate the extent to which its character had changed.

Exercise 'Tunstall'

The exercise at Tunstall was officially entitled 'Demonstration of the Passage of Artificial Obstacles' and took place in November 1942 (Figures 5.9–5.10).[58] This was a large-scale manoeuvre in which a mixed force of armour, engineers, infantry and artillery practised a deliberate assault against a static enemy. It took a familiar form, whereby the troops involved trained for a final demonstration in which they showcased their new-found proficiency to an assembled party of senior ranking spectators. The objective in this case was to demonstrate the breaching of obstacles that might be expected to be encountered around enemy defensive positions. The scenario was that the enemy had been successfully attacked on 'Grandstand Ridge' on 11 November and, suitably weakened, had fallen back to 'Forest Ridge', where their positions on the forward slope were protected by a variety of obstacles. The defensive position was protected by barbed wire, an anti-tank minefield, a drainage ditch, an anti-tank ditch, more barbed wire and a second minefield, and was to be attacked at first light the following day.

The final demonstration took place on 12 November and comprised two phases. The first was a 'night' operation where lanes were opened in the first minefield. The drainage ditch was crossed by infantry with wooden bridges, while vehicles crossed by breaches partially created by explosives and then ramped down by hand. In the second

---

58 TNA WO 166/6380 (War Diary, 54th Division, HQ), Demonstration of the Passage of Artificial Obstacles held on the Battle Training Area, 13.11.42.

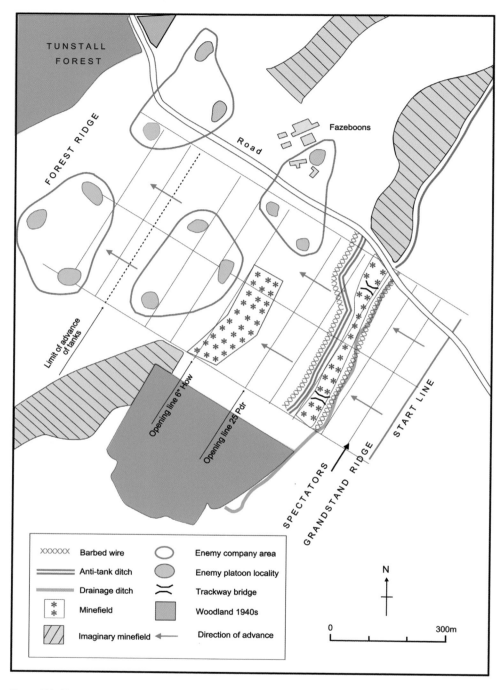

Figure 5.9. 'Demonstration of Obstacle Crossing', Exercise Tunstall, plan of demonstration. The configuration of engineers, tanks, infantry and artillery showcased the Home Army's doctrine in attacking a dug-in enemy.

Figure 5.10. An anti-tank ditch built for use in Exercise Tunstall, 1942.

phase a 'dawn' assault saw tanks crossing the main anti-tank ditch using specialised bridging equipment and lanes cleared through the barbed wire and minefield using explosives. The infantry followed through the successful breach with the tanks acting as support for the final attack on the enemy position. The assault was supported by a 'creeping' artillery barrage that protected the attackers as they moved in to breach the obstacles. On the day, the demonstration was executed faultlessly and was well received by observers.

The praise for the demonstration was probably in part because the methods accorded with the War Office's revised doctrine on combined attacks against an enemy sheltering behind obstacles and published in 1943 as Army Training Instruction No. 2 *The Co-Operation of Tanks and Infantry*. This instruction, in part based on practical experience gained in North Africa, emphasised strong co-operation between tanks and infantry and placed great stress on the requirement for minefields and other anti-tank obstacles to be breached before the tanks went forward to engage the enemy.[59] The exercise's preoccupation with the obstacles was a response to the tactical problems of the 'break in' phase of battle; in effect, the Tunstall demonstration was 54th Division's attempt at the level of a brigade at what the Eighth Army was undertaking concurrently during the Battle of El Alamein.

---

59   TNA 231/282 (The Co-Operation of Tanks and Infantry), 1943.

Tunstall shows clearly how training had changed from the previous two years of the war. The exercise was much more ambitious than those previously undertaken by 54th Division; over 1000 men took part and consequently the physical area was much bigger, at some 150 hectares. What could be termed the infrastructure of the training landscape was also more involved, with a considerable array of obstacles constructed in order to make the passage of the crossing meaningful. Archaeologically the exercise is of significance as the anti-tank ditch probably represents the first example in the Sandlings where an attempt was made to reproduce enemy obstacles on the ground for the purposes of practice. The practicalities of the exercise also extended to the construction of a dummy section of anti-tank ditch a little to the north-east of the main line of obstacles upon which troops could undertake preparatory training and a scaffolding tower 20 feet high built to act as an artillery observation post to aid the firing of the barrage.

At the same time the Tunstall exercise points up continued deficiencies. The exercise took place at a much reduced scale to that intended; it was supposed to mimic a brigade attack but, owing to shortages of ammunition and tanks, the demonstration took place on a battalion front with non-existent units on the flanks. The scenario was also somewhat vague, being intended simply to present a situation that might confront troops in 'modern battle', and was resourced with a meagre issue of training ammunition.[60] The sense of realism was restricted; as a 'one sided' exercise there was no enemy or hostile fire and some of the troops involved wore dark glasses in order to give a sense that the opening part of the attack was intended to take place at night. The level of thought given to the nature of the enemy position was also limited; the ground chosen for the demonstration was picked in order to given the spectators a good view, rather than to reflect tactical realism. Some six scaffolding stands with tarpaulin roofs, each with room for 120 onlookers, were built and it was in one of these that the one fatality of the live firing occurred, when a major was hit by a stray bullet. The importance of the Tunstall exercise and others like it here is that it represented the kind of training that was to become more commonplace as the war progressed, involving as it did live firing and close co-operation between the various fighting arms of the army: infantry, armour, engineers and artillery.

Infantry training: minor tactics

In war diaries it is chiefly the larger or more involved exercises, such as Tunstall, that are recorded in detail. Less information is usually given for minor exercises or the practising of routine skills, which are often glossed over in diaries with the term 'normal training', which in the case of the 2nd/4th Essex Regiment comprised section attacks, grenade practice, map reading, route marching, assault courses, battle drill, movement at night and weapon training (Figure 5.11).[61] Where details of this kind of training are occasionally revealed, they show the considerable efforts

60   TNA WO 166/8608 (War Diary, 7th Border Regiment), Demonstration of Obstacle Crossing, 13.11.42.
61   TNA WO 166/12537 (War Diary, 2nd/4th Essex Regiment), April 1943, *passim*.

Figure 5.11. The majority of 'minor training' is passed over in war diaries, but this official War Office photograph from 1942 of the 2nd/4th Essex regiment on the Orford Battle Training Area shows the kind of activity that was commonplace. (IWM H25860)

made to instil tactical realism. In February 1943, for example, the 1st Bucks used the hinterland of Walberswick for advanced weapon drills, which involved scenarios such as Bren gunners moving covertly to a position from which they could fire on an enemy machine-gun nest equipped with live rounds 350 metres away.[62] Such details are significant, as they shed light on unglamorous but important routine elements of training in which individuals were both given instruction in the skills that were required to take part in more elaborate operations and inculcated with the expertise that could make the difference between life and death on the battlefield.

62 TNA WO 166/12496 (War Diary, 1st Bucks Battalion, Ox and Bucks Light Infantry), Advanced Weapon Handling Tests, 16.2.43.

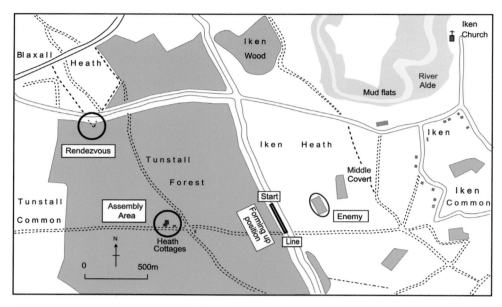

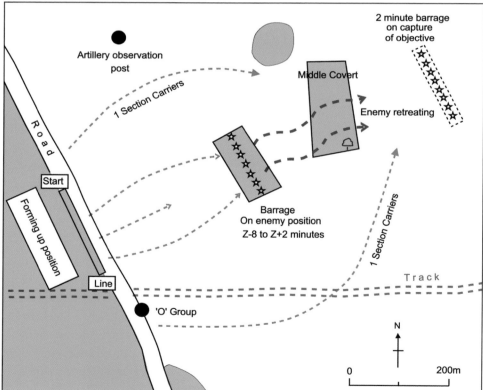

Figure 5.12. Exercise Tommy. A typical example of small-scale infantry training that took place on the Orford area. Here soldiers learned the practice of their craft through dozens of such exercises.

One such field firing exercise, the details of which are recorded in detail, is Exercise 'Tommy', which took place on 18 January 1943 and involved two successive rifle companies of the 8th King's Regiment (Figure 5.12).[63] The object was to practise deployment from a wooded area and the engagement of a retiring enemy. The scenario involved a friendly reconnaissance troop leading an advance that had been badly shot up, and a detachment of enemy that were in a wood and holding up the general move forward. One company was to clear the way as quickly as possible with the support of Bren Gun carriers, mortars and one troop of artillery. The exercise called for rapid deployment and the co-ordination of the various arms for a fast frontal attack on the wood and exploitation beyond the enemy position until the defenders were completely driven off.

What makes Tommy unusual is the detail given about the training infrastructure and the umpiring arrangements; such preparations are often referred to obliquely in war diaries but rarely in any depth. Live small arms ammunition, artillery and mortar rounds were used with wooden targets and straw-filled sandbags placed in front of these targets for bayoneting. Although a one-sided exercise with no 'live' enemy, umpires were provided, but, critically, their role was not to adjudicate on what tactics were used or narrate the course of the action; rather, it was a reporting role, which involved written feedback on tactical expertise such as the conduct of the attack; whether the troops bunched or remained correctly spaced out; and whether the final closing on the objective was conducted 'flat out' by the troops involved and the dummies were bayonetted. This was Brooke's 'battle inoculation' in practice. It was on these occasions that the infantry practised their battle drill and they did so on dedicated areas, with commanders being inventive about how they used the terrain. Such evidence is important, as it offers a corrective to the idea that training in minor tactics was 'exceptional' and that it had a low priority at this time; rather, the evidence is that this kind of training made up the bulk of that undertaken by 54th Division.[64]

A training dichotomy? Teller and Teller II

A consideration of the variety of training being undertaken at this time brings into focus the broader question of how the infantry skills practised in smaller exercises such as Tommy were integrated with the more elaborate set-piece attacks, such as Tunstall, where the emphasis was on all-arms co-operation. A strong argument exists that in such large deliberate attacks the minor infantry elements of the action, such as firing onto the objective and clearing positions, were excluded on the grounds that the infantry would not need their battle drill as they would get onto their objective behind the covering fire of an artillery barrage. By contrast, in circumstances where there was no such barrage the infantry would use their own firepower and skill to get themselves onto, and then take, their objective. The failure to integrate the two methods has been

---

63 TNA WO 166/12589 (War Diary, 8th King's Regiment), Exercise Tommy, January 1943, *passim*.
64 Harrison Place, *Military Training*, pp. 43, 46.

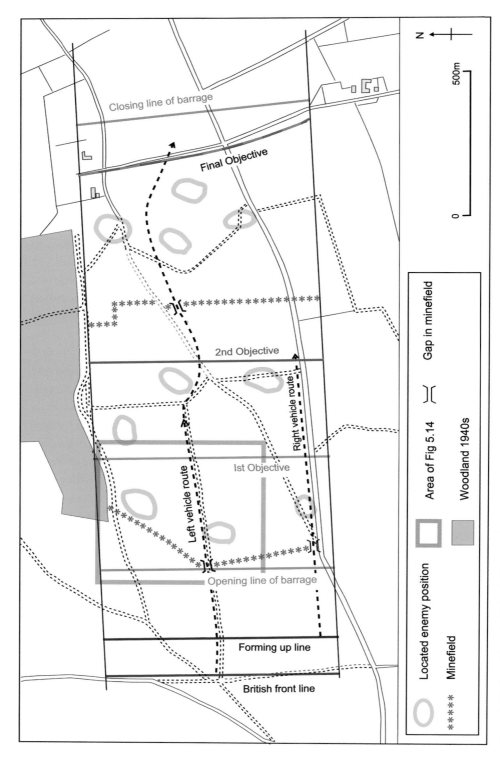

Figure 5.13. Plan of Exercise Teller II. This practised a large-scale attack on a prepared enemy position and was typical of the larger exercises carried out by 54th Division in 1943.

seen as one of the major shortcoming of infantry training in the Home Army.[65] But close analysis of documentary and field evidence suggests that this bi-fold division was not always clear cut, something suggested in 54th Division's case by two linked exercises – Teller and Teller II – held in June 1943 that represent the last large-scale manoeuvres in the formation's training before it vacated the coastal zone.[66]

The paired 'Teller' exercises were at brigade level and were intended to practise a night attack on a strongly defended enemy position (Figure 5.13). The scenario was that the British were advancing east towards an enemy force that had been in place for some ten days and so had had time to build strong fieldworks strengthened by barbed wire and minefields.[67] The objective of Exercise Teller (23–24 June) was to practise the forming up of a battalion that was to capture by night the forward positions of the German defended area. The troops involved were to practise the drills involved in reaching and marking a minefield and clearing lanes for vehicles to pass through. The attack on this position, followed by exploitation beyond it, was to take place in Teller II (29–30 June), and involved the first attack by the brigade (by two forward battalions) at night, the reserve battalion passing through at first light and then the supporting elements moving through the gaps created by the attacking troops. The first attack began with the opening of the artillery, mortar and then machine gun barrage and the movement of the infantry to their forming-up point. The creeping artillery barrage was to move 100 yards (90 metres) in four minutes, allowing four attacking companies of two forward battalions to take the first objective on Cuttens Hill. A second barrage at the same movement rate was then to open up and cover the reserve companies of infantry as they moved forward to take the second objective on the reverse slope. These reserves were themselves to consolidate with the aid of anti-tank troops. The third battalion of the brigade moved through the newly won ground and continued the advance, again behind a barrage. Once they had taken the final objective they were to hold with the support of anti-tank guns. As the attack progressed the machine guns, mortars and an advance Brigade Headquarters were themselves to move up along pre-determined routes. As a deliberate attack by infantry with artillery, mortar and machine gun support, it adhered strongly to the principles endorsed by the War Office's *Military Training Pamphlet No. 2 – The Offensive*, which codified current doctrine.

While illustrating how far training had evolved in the previous 18 months, the 'Teller' exercises also draw attention to familiar limitations. While the Dunwich area was large enough to accommodate an attack on a two-battalion front, it was far too small to permit the movement to the battle zone and forming up; for this reason, on the commander's own admission, Teller was to be 'looked upon largely as a drill' and took place on the Woodbridge

65   Essentially the argument in Harrison Place, *Military Training*, see esp. chapters 5 and 10.
66   TNA WO 166/10649 (War Diary, 54th Division, HQ), August 1943.
67   Taken from TNA WO 166/10805 (War Diary, 198th Infantry Brigade); TNA WO 166/12494 (War Diary, 6th Border Regiment).

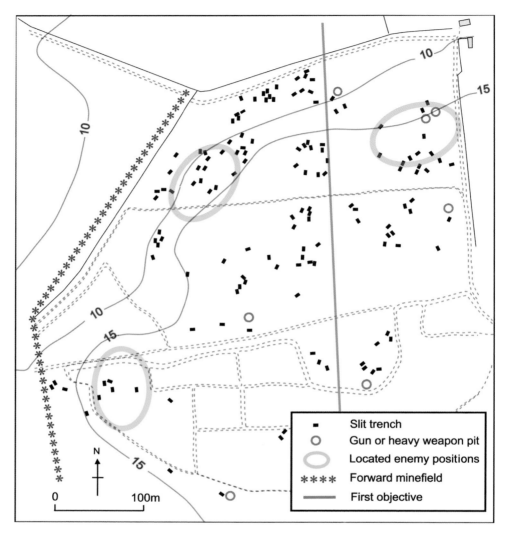

Figure 5.14. Plan of military archaeology on Cuttens Hill, Westleton. The distribution of slit trenches reflects the repeated use of the area for training, but the locations of some relate so closely to the objectives of Teller II that they can be linked to this exercise with some confidence.

area, which meant that it was accompanied by a certain artificiality. The arrangements for enemy forces included using blue and white flags on Bren gun carriers to indicate hostile tanks, with the artillery barrage represented by torches and banging tins, mines represented by bricks and an absence of pyrotechnics owing to the dangers of fire. There was also a scheduled delay of several days between the two exercises, largely on account of the administrative effort required to get all the troops onto the Dunwich area for Teller II.

But the training battlefield of Teller II was subtly different. A greater emphasis was placed on the ground over which the attack took place; the central objective was the high ground of Cuttens Hill, which not only was one of the natural high points in an otherwise muted terrain but also allowed troops to gain familiarity with an enemy that positioned itself not just on high ground but also on the reverse slope, practising defence in depth. Greater attention was also paid to the nature of the German defences. References in war diaries to troops having to undertake preparatory work prior to the exercise and also to the dismantling of barbed wire around 'enemy' positions at the end of the exercise indicate that an attempt was made to replicate the battlefield.[68] Orders also show that advancing troops were to hold their gains by digging in. While the earthwork remains of training in this area represent a palimpsest from across the war, in what seems too precise to be a coincidence groups of slit trenches on the line of the first objective for Teller II appear to mark the consolidation of the newly won ground, in accordance with the instructions laid down in the exercise's orders (Figure 5.14). In one case a rough circle of slit trenches for an 11-man infantry section in 'all round defence' occupies the crest of Cuttens Hill, precisely where the forward troops were to dig in. This appearance of earthworks and 'permanent' fixtures in routine exercises (rather than a demonstration such as Tunstall) was an important development that prefigured the practices seen in pre-D-Day training, discussed in the next chapter.

The existence of semi-permanent features in exercise such as Teller II carries with it another implication. As mentioned above, one of the chief criticisms levelled at infantry training for deliberate attacks was a failure to adequately marry the respective roles of the artillery barrage and the firepower of the infantry themselves.[69] A dichotomy existed whereby infantry were taught through battle drill that they could use fire and manoeuvre onto a target with the weapons at their disposal, but that in large attacks the artillery barrage that preceded the assault would get them onto the target with little difficulty. The result, it is argued, was that during the Normandy campaign assaults faltered in part because when the barrage did not work infantry failed to use their own battle skills and firepower as they ought. This was in some measure down to inadequate training, which encouraged a distinction between infantry attacks led by the barrage and those where minor tactics assumed greater importance; in short, the army should have practised fire and manoeuvre in barrage-led attacks.

The archaeological existence of 'enemy' positions gives additional insight into this problem. The location of the 'enemy' during an exercise could be shown with flags or markers; to go to the trouble of digging positions and surrounding them with field defences suggests a further motivation or particular purpose, which might be to supply an increased sense of realism, inasmuch as it gave troops a greater visual sense of what they might expect on a future battlefield. Although it might seem an obvious point, the physical construction of enemy positions presupposes that they were going to be taken

---

68 Note that in the exercise's papers it was noted that the enemy to be encountered had dug in but there was little or no concrete.

69 Harrison Place, *Military Training*, chapter 5.

during a practice assault and form the objective for specific drills; otherwise a less ephemeral structure would suffice. In this case, it presupposes that during Teller II the mock enemy positions were to be forced and cleared, as they would be in a smaller-scale exercise such as 'Tommy', where 'battle drill' would be the method employed.

In this particular case, it is undoubtedly important that the attacking battalions in Teller II were to undertake field firing in the period between the two exercises – and the war diary for the 6th Border Regiment is clear that this was conducted with live ammunition and in full battle order.[70] Two possible interpretations follow. The first is that taking enemy positions via battle drill tactics was not to take place in Teller II, as the exercise was not designed to test this. If this were the case, then the field firing was to train troops in what they would be expected to do in reality, but which was tested outside of the direct confines of Teller II itself. If so, then presumably the soldiers concerned ran past the enemy positions and it was assumed that they followed the appropriate procedures. The second interpretation is that the field firing was directly connected to Teller II and was designed to give troops practice in the skills they would undertake in the following days. Here, the enemy positions would be taken by fire and manoeuvre and, to give greater authenticity to the exercise, the positions were given physical form and surrounded with obstacles. If this is the case, it would indicate that the perception of a clear division between the use of 'barrage' and 'battle drill' methods of attack during training may not be entirely accurate.

A hedgehog on the heath: Exercise Kruschen

Exercise Teller II was the high water mark of 54th Division's training in the Sandlings, as the formation was disbanded soon afterwards. But in one other respect its period of training on the coast was of much wider significance, because in the spring of 1943 one of its brigades was responsible for one of the Home Army's most important field trials.

Although undertaken at a time when the final form of Operation Overlord was far from set in stone, preparations for the D-Day landings arguably began in the Sandlings in January 1943, when the Dunwich Training Area was the setting for a major one-off exercise ordered by the War Office, codenamed Kruschen.[71] In what was one of its last major exercises before disbandment, 54th Division was tasked with taking forward one of the most significant problems facing Allied planners: how to successfully break the German Atlantic Wall defences.[72] Such a task was a necessary pre-requisite for the successful landing of a large invasion force, as had been shown during the Allied raid on Dieppe four months earlier, where the inability to breach

---

70   TNA WO 166/12494 (War Diary, 6th Border Regiment), Field Firing, Dunwich, 24.6.43.

71   For a longer discussion, see R. Liddiard and D. Sims, 'A Hedgehog on the Heath: The Second World War Landscape of Exercise "Kruschen", Dunwich, Suffolk', *Archaeological Journal*, 169 (2012), pp. 519–49, but with the results of additional fieldwork related here.

72   For the problem in the context of the conflict as a whole, see Kennedy, *Engineers of Victory*.

the beach defences was one of the leading causes of the operation's failure.[73] Kruschen was specifically intended to test the methods and equipment required to assault a heavily fortified enemy position. The choice of 54th Division for the exercise was probably connected with a well-received obstacle-crossing demonstration at Tunstall the previous November. The allocated troops comprised an all-arms force of one of 54th Division's infantry brigades with additional units drawn from elsewhere in the Division and the wider field army.[74] Kruschen would eventually run for four months and, although technically an exercise, was more a series of ongoing field experiments using a variety of techniques and equipment.

The centrepiece of the exercise was at Westleton Walks, where a purpose-built mock German defensive position for an infantry company – nicknamed a 'Hedgehog' – was built in order to replicate in detail the field fortifications of the Atlantic Wall. Such positions, called *Stützpunkte* 'Strong Points', were made up of *Wiederstandnest* 'Resistance Nests', each with either an anti-tank gun or a machine gun post together with infantry trenches and air-raid shelters.[75]

As the exercise's commanding officer, Brigadier O.H. Wales explained in his final report:

a full scale typical GERMAN 'HEDGEHOG' was constructed … [which] includes the following:- Concrete pillboxes. Deep Shelters. Weapon Pits and communication trenches. Gun-Pits. The whole defensive locality is enclosed within an obstacle consisting of:- Wire. Minefields. Tank ditch. Escarpments.[76]

The site of the hedgehog is exceptionally well preserved archaeologically and its form can be reconstructed in detail. Geographically it extended over five hectares and was bounded on its northern and western sides by a newly excavated anti-tank ditch more than eight metres wide and over two metres deep. The eastern boundary was formed by a reused anti-tank ditch originally excavated in 1941. On the southern and western sides the rolling topography was utilised as an obstacle by cutting away the base of the escarpment to produce a vertical wall two metres high, a form of anti-tank obstacle known to the Wehrmacht as a *Panzerhindernis*.

The main defences were spread out in an arc over approximately 400 metres and comprised two groups of concrete bunkers each with a subterranean concrete-roofed

73   T. Robertson, *Dieppe, the Shame and the Glory* (London, 1965).

74   The main Kruschen complement was a composite infantry company picked from across the Brigade (5th Royal Berkshire Regiment, 2nd/4th Essex Regiment and 1st Buckinghamshire Regiment (Oxford and Buckinghamshire Light Infantry)); one squadron from 141 Royal Tank Regiment; one troop 148 Battery 92 Anti-Tank Regiment; 80 Assault Squadron Royal Engineers; one platoon of Ronson carriers, Princess Louise Fusiliers; 168 Field Regiment, Royal Artillery; one platoon, 4.2 inch mortars 9th Manchester Regiment.

75   C. Partridge, *Hitler's Atlantic Wall* (St Peter Port, 1976), pp. 20–21; A. Saunders, *Hitler's Atlantic Wall* (Stroud, 2001), pp. 29–36.

76   TNA WO 166/10975 (War Diary, 163rd Infantry Brigade), Exercise 'KRUSCHEN' – Final Report, 16.4.43.

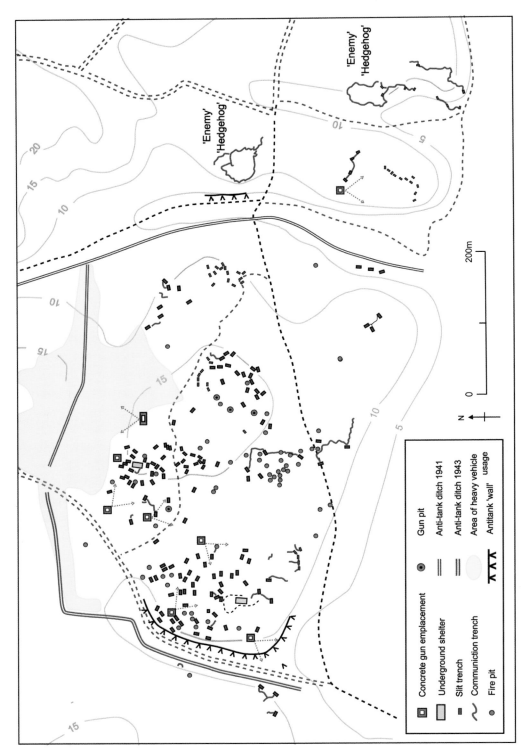

Figure 5.15. Exercise Kruschen: plan of 'hedgehog' and associated archaeology. (After Liddiard and Sims 2012, with alterations)

Figure 5.16. Remains of Kruschen 'German' Pillbox at Westleton Walks.

structure (Figures 5.15–5.16). Each concrete bunker with its earthworks replicated a *Wiederstandnest* for a machine gun or small anti-tank gun, with the subterranean structures mimicking air-raid shelters for defending infantrymen. The bunkers were themselves associated with fieldworks comprising shallow trenches running in sinuous lines or zig-zags for up to ten metres at a time, generally following ridgelines or on forward slopes. Typically, these interconnected with pits that were often rectangular in shape and up to four metres in length and two metres wide, with the spoil heaped up on one side to make a small parapet. Such earthworks represented firing positions for infantrymen, dubbed *Russenloch* by German soldiers, that were linked together by communication trenches. In the centre of the site were three low circular ringworks, almost certainly replicating gun pits for anti-tank guns, which were generally situated away from the main defences in the centre of a strongpoint and sited to fire along a pre-determined line. Film footage and photographs show minefields and further defences of barbed wire entanglements arranged in a manner known to the Germans as *Koppelzaune*.[77]

Additional mock German structures were built away from the hedgehog site. On neighbouring Dunwich Heath at least one 'stand-alone' *Wiederstandnest* was constructed, along with two additional hedgehogs, albeit without concrete defences, which comprised long circular ribbons of communication trench interspersed with firing points.[78] The shallow valley that separated Dunwich Heath from Westleton Walks was also scarped in order to create a second *Panzerhindernis*. At least two other concrete buildings

77   IWM (Film Archive) AYY387 (Exercise Kruschen, War Office Film Unit, 14.4.43); IWM Photographic Archive H29035–29069 (Eastern Command Exercise, 14.4.43).
78   G. Rottman, *German Field Fortifications, 1939–1945* (Oxford, 2004).

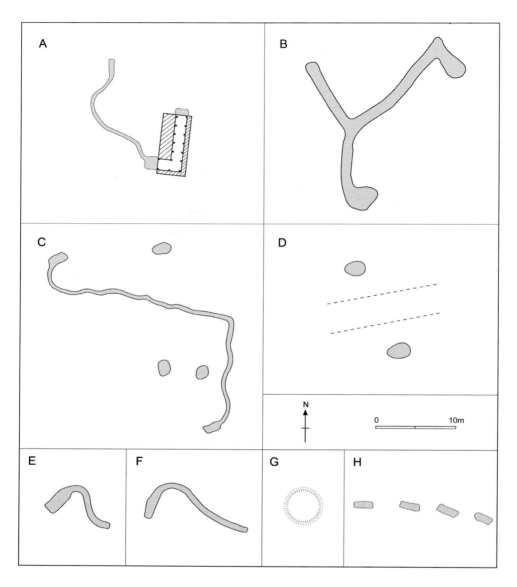

Figure 5.17. Earthworks on Kruschen site: a) shelter, communication trench and weapon pit; b) weapon pit linked via communication trench; c) long ribbon of communication trench linking rectangular weapon pits, with circular weapons pits in close proximity; d) pair of circular weapons pits reminiscent of the firing points of German 'Ringstand'; e–f) rectangular weapon pit with shorter sections of communication trench; g) circular gun emplacement for anti-tank gun; h) rectangular slit trenches, possibly British training trenches. (After Liddiard and Sims, 2012)

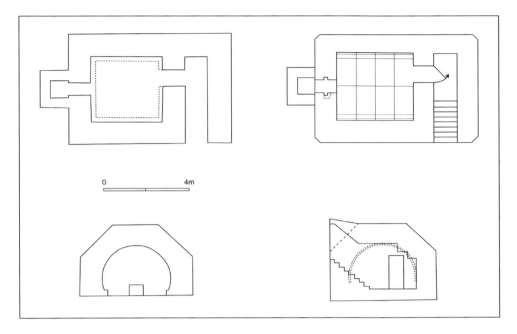

Figure 5.18. Comparative plan and internal elevation of concrete structure to the south of the main Kruschen site showing extant remains (left), with the structure listed as 'Group Shelter' in *German Fieldworks* (right), drawn at the same scale. (After Liddiard and Sims, 2012)

Figure 5.19. Tank crossing an anti-tank ditch as part of the final demonstration of Exercise Kruschen on Westleton Walks, 1943. (IWM H29041)

were constructed at Sheepwash Lane, one kilometre to the south-east, to replicate *Gruppenunterstand* or 'Group Shelters' for German infantrymen (Figure 5.17–5.18).[79]

The tactical elements of the exercise broke down into two linked elements. The first was the breaking of the anti-tank obstacle that bounded the hedgehog and the second concerning the dispatch of the enemy within. The overarching objective was to test how engineers could co-operate with tanks and infantry in a successful assault. When Kruschen was completed in May 1943 it was judged as considerable success, as it yielded technical solutions to the problem of breaching heavily defended positions (especially in the deployment of fascines from tanks and mine-clearing devices such as the Snake) and a prototype tactical drill that could be taken forward by others in further training (Figure 5.19). The morphology of the training landscape sheds some light on the organisation of the exercise. The surviving archaeology indicates that specialist training took place in discrete pockets across the landscape, with infantry training, obstacle breaching and vehicle manoeuvres geographically separated. The main hedgehog was used for a 'live run', when the disparate elements were brought together (Figure 5.20).

In many ways Kruschen marked a significant change in training methods and infrastructure. First, the extended geographical area over which Kruschen took place set it apart from what had gone before. While ongoing, the exercise monopolised training in a large part of the Dunwich area and stocks of live ammunition; the other units of the Division were told to get on with their training as best they could.[80] One surviving oral testimony records sweepstakes on how many machine gun rounds would be fired by tanks during attacks.[81] The second major change was the level of detail of the enemy defences. While previous set-piece demonstrations held previously, such as that at Tunstall, had involved the creation of obstacles, they had not involved the detailed replication of an enemy position in the field, especially not at one-to-one scale. The design of the concrete bunkers, air-raid shelters and Group Shelters were taken directly from a War Office intelligence dossier on the Atlantic Wall defences based on aerial reconnaissance, information from underground resistance groups and British experience of German fortifications in the Mediterranean, with the earthwork elements corresponding to those in Wehrmacht manuals.[82] Kruschen took the idea of a training landscape to a greater level of realism, with those taking part encountering structures that bore a close resemblance to those they could expect in action. Third, the landscape

---

79 Classified as VF2a by Rolf: R. Rolf, *Atlantic Wall Typology* (Middlelburg, 2008), pp. 74–5.

80 TNA, WO 166/10649 (War Diary, 54th Division, HQ), Training Memorandum No. 25, March 1943.

81 Bovington Tank Museum, E2009, 1964: L.A. Wells, *Projectors to Petards. A Sapper's Tale, 12 September 1940–10 May 1946* (unpublished typescript).

82 TNA WO 195/4617 (Ministry of Supply, Advisory Council on Scientific Research and Technical Development), Anti-Concrete Committee, German Fieldworks Notes No. 1, June 1943; TNA WO 195/4618 (Ministry of Supply, Advisory Council on Scientific Research and Technical Development), Anti-Concrete Committee, German Fieldworks Notes No. 2, June 1943; Anon., *Bildheft Neuzeitlicher Stellungsbau* (1942), reprinted as *German Fieldworks of World War II* (Bracknall, 1969).

Figure 5.20. *Exercise Kruschen*, watercolour on paper, Edward Bawden, 1943. This contemporary painting shows a mid-way point in the exercise, with troops constructing fascines and flamethrowers crossing the anti-tank ditch. (IWM ART LD2890)

selected for the Hedgehog was chosen for tactical considerations, again a departure from previous practice at Tunstall, where the ground over which the demonstration took place was for the benefit of spectators. Brigadier Wales was explicit about this, reporting that he put himself into the shoes of a defender and sited the defences accordingly in order to make sure that the exercise was a meaningful trial.[83] In addition, an important break with established norms was the experimental nature of the training itself: Kruschen did not

---

83   O.H. Wales, 'Exercise Kruschen', in *Conference on Landings Assaults, 24 May–23 June 1943* (US Assault Training Centre), pp. 1–2.

train troops in rigid procedures as larger exercises, such as Teller II, usually did; rather, trial and error was employed in order to arrive at a suitable drill for assaulting positions. Here the siting of the Hedgehog bunkers for mutual support not only was intended to imitate German practice but also encouraged troops to use their initiative when it came to carrying the positions.[84] This final point is important, as it suggests not the stereotype of an inflexible organisation merely rehearsing its troops in a prescribed doctrine but one actively seeking solutions to the problems it expected to face in the field.

Kruschen, while not up to that point the largest exercise in terms of soldiers engaged, was nonetheless the most conceptually ambitious. The ethos of the exercise, together with its supporting infrastructure, marked a distinctive break in training in the coastal zone, setting as it did the tone for the larger, more involved exercises that characterised the late war period. It was also significant in that many of its distinguishing principles were subsequently taken up by other formations, especially by 79th Armoured Division, as discussed in the next chapter.

Conclusion

Analysis of the training regimes of the three divisions that rotated through the Sandlings during 1940–43 clearly points up the broad shift from a landscape of defence, to one of preparing for the offense. The account presented here is also more positive about early and mid-war training practices than is sometimes found elsewhere. This is by no means to suggest that training in this period was perfect; rather, it is to say that more took place when troops were on coastal duty than might otherwise be imagined and that its relationship with the construction of anti-invasion defences is more complex than has sometimes been suggested in the past. The widespread appearance of 'training archaeology' in the mid-war period did, however, mark a watershed and was associated with larger and often more specialist exercises with a greater sense of realism and which were intended to inculcate specific skills. Here the experience of the Sandlings was not unique, but the choice of the Dunwich area for the setting for exercise Kruschen was significant in a national context. It is also important to appreciate the wider topographic frame in which training took place. Marginal landscapes such as the Sandlings had a long tradition of use as army practice grounds, but even here those areas initially pressed into use tended to be on interfluves characterised by the poorest soils. The training landscape of the late war period was slightly different however. The military demand for land in the lead up to the D-Day landings was such that from late 1943 training areas were again expanded and those already in existence witnessed more intensive use. By late 1943 and early 1944 the Sandlings was no longer a landscape that had to be fortified against invasion, but was one in which thousands of men were to be trained in order to take the war to occupied Europe.

---

84   Wales, 'Exercise Kruschen', p. 4.

Chapter 6

Preparing for Overlord, 1943–44

The planning of Operation Overlord was an undertaking of such magnitude that it has left a distinctive archaeological legacy in its own right.[1] In the lead-up to the D-Day landings training in the British army reached a new intensity as practice grounds were expanded and new ones created, while exercises became more purposeful and reflected the presumed character of the battles that troops would be expected to fight for real.[2] Within the Sandlings these broader developments were reflected in an increase in the amount of land taken by the army for training and in the appearance of specialised training facilities. From mid-1943, when 54th Division vacated the coast, the Sandlings was occupied principally by units from two formations: 79th Armoured Division and 49th Infantry Division. The former holds a particular place in the history of D-Day as the specialised formation equipped with modified tanks that played a significant role in breaching the German beach defences in the British and Commonwealth Sectors on 6 June 1944.[3] In addition to undertaking their own training programmes, 79th Armoured spent a brief but important period in co-operative exercises with elements of 50th Infantry Division, one of the 'assault' divisions that would spearhead the landings on the Normandy beaches. Forty-Ninth Division, by contrast, was a 'follow on' formation expected to move inland from the Normandy beaches after the successful lodgement made by the assault divisions.[4] Analysis of the physical evidence of training in the Sandlings, along with details of specific exercises in war diaries, offers important insights into the preparations for Operation Overlord, especially in terms of the eventualities that were anticipated and the responses expected from troops. In this respect, the evidence presented here has a much wider currency, as it sheds light on the extent to which the perceived inadequacies of British troops in the Normandy campaign reflected poor training.

---

1   Dobinson, *Operation Overlord*; J. Schofield, 'D-Day Sites in England: An Assessment', *Antiquity*, 75/287 (2001), pp. 77–83. In this chapter the term Overlord is used to describe the Normandy landings in their totality, including the beach assault of 6 June 1944, rather than Operation Neptune, which constituted the amphibious phase of operations.

2   N. Scarfe, *Assault Division* (London, 1947).

3   D. Fletcher, *Vanguard of Victory. The 79th Armoured Division* (London, 1984); R.C. Anderson, *Cracking Hitler's Atlantic Wall. The 1st Assault Brigade Royal Engineers on D-Day* (Mechanicsburg, PA, 2010).

4   E.W. Clay, *The Path of the 50th* (Aldershot, 1950); P. Delaforce, *The Polar Bears* (Stroud, 1995).

Hedgehogs on the marsh: Orford and Hobart's Zoo

The contribution of 79th Armoured Division to Operation Overlord is well known, but will be related in brief here.[5] The division was reconstituted as an all-armoured formation in March 1943 under the command of Major General Percy Hobart, an idiosyncratic character who became synonymous with a range of highly successful modified armoured vehicles dubbed 'Funnies', which were designed to undertake specialised tasks such as reducing concrete fortifications and breaching obstacles.[6] While Hobart did not invent the machines with which his division was equipped he was the driving force behind training in their use and their tactical deployment. The Divisional Headquarters was on the edge of the Sandlings at Saxmundham, but, owing to the specialist nature of their operational role, its component units carried out bespoke training across the country at designated facilities.[7] The region was particularly significant to the formation's overall programme of training, however, because in May 1943 it was granted exclusive use of the Orford Battle Training Area, which subsequently became the practice ground and experimental site for its Divisional engineers (1st Assault Brigade) and 43rd Royal Tank Regiment, the unit that trialled many of the Funnies.

The allocation of Orford to 79th Armoured Division was the result of a number of factors. Initially Hobart expressed an interest in taking over the Dunwich Training Area, presumably because it was already furnished with Exercise Kruschen's mock hedgehog. On reflection, Hobart felt that Dunwich was too small for what he had in mind and that the existing military presence on the heath could potentially interfere with his Division's activities. Orford, by contrast, was larger and the physical landscape better suited for the range of training envisaged. Hobart's personal obsession with secrecy also played a part, with the area's geographical isolation seen as advantageous for the maintenance of security. In the final event, however, the choice of Orford was also utilitarian; one of the Division's Engineer units and a tank regiment were already in close proximity and so taking the area was simply expedient.[8] Importantly, this training did not begin in a vacuum. Hobart was ordered to take up the techniques developed in Exercise Kruschen and continuity was maintained by seconding men who had taken part in order that they could pass on their expertise.[9] The task was to produce units that had the equipment and the necessary tactical drills to breach the defences of the Atlantic Wall during the initial phase of the Normandy landings

---

5   N. Duncan, *79th Armoured Division: Hobo's Funnies* (Windsor, 1972); Fletcher, *Vanguard of Victory*; R. Doherty, *Hobart's 79th Armoured Division at War* (Barnsley, 2011).

6   K. Macksey, *Armoured Crusader* (London, 1967).

7   Anon., *The Story of 79 Armoured Division*.

8   TNA WO 205/417 (79th Armoured Division Training Areas, General), 27.4.43, 22.5.43.

9   TNA WO 205/624 (79th Armoured Division Organisation, Equipment, Training Part I), Decisions taken by Commander-in-Chief at a meeting with Commander, 79th Armoured Division, 15.4.43; TNA WO 205/417 (79th Armoured Division Training Areas, General), 18.6.43.

and open up beach exits to allow the Allied armies to penetrate inland. To this end, the bulk of the work at Orford was concerned with obstacle crossing, the clearance of minefields and barbed wire, passage through or over walls and anti-tank ditches and the destruction of concrete defences with explosives. Much of the equipment needed to undertake these tasks was developed during training at Orford itself, with considerable effort put into the specialist engineer tank the AVRE (Armoured Vehicle Royal Engineer), armed with its concrete-breaking spigot mortar, known colloquially as the petard or 'flying dustbin'.[10] The sometimes unconventional training methods of the Division are familiar enough from post-war histories, but although photographs of their activities have graced numerous publications – usually those showing tanks undertaking unorthodox manoeuvres – the environment in which these took place is less well understood. While it is well known that mock German fortifications were built at Orford for the purposes of practising drills and trialling equipment, to date there has been no systematic investigation of how the training landscape was configured and how the physical infrastructure was actually used on a day-to-day basis.

Orford, the anatomy of a training ground

Post-war clearance and agricultural use have removed the overwhelming majority above-ground trace of 79th Armoured's training facilities at Orford, so the analysis that follows is based upon evidence from contemporary air and ground photographs and information in war diaries. This evidence does, however, point to the conclusion that, as had been the case at Dunwich during Exercise Kruschen, the Orford area was zoned, with specific activities tending to take place in particular areas (Figure 6.1). Sudbourne Hall and park, together with the adjacent Sudbourne Great Wood, served as the headquarters for 43rd Royal Tank Regiment and for the Divisional development unit.[11] To the north-west, the area around Fazeboons Farm was the setting for the trialling of equipment and technical experimentation, with the farmhouse itself an administrative headquarters for a training cadre. Here trials of explosive devices were carried out in the vicinity of the farm, with several full-scale 'German' concrete structures built and then blown up in order to test the quantity of explosives required to render them inoperable.[12] It was also at Fazeboons that equipment was showcased for senior commanders; the first petard the Division received was demonstrated to Hobart here on 29 February 1944.[13] On the open ground to the south-west of the

---

10   Anderson, *Cracking Hitler's Atlantic Wall*, chapters 1–2.

11   TNA WO 166/11096 (War Diary, 43rd Royal Tank Regiment), 28.5.43.

12   See run of photographs in IWM Photographic Archive H34455–34472 (79th Armoured Division, Development Unit, Home Forces), 'The Jones Onion' and 'German Type Pillbox', esp. H34458; H34461; H34464.

13   TNA WO 171/1816 (War Diary, 617th Assault Squadron, Royal Engineers), 29.2.44. For evidence that obstacle crossing took place at Fazeboons, TNA WO 171/1806 (War Diary, 77th Assault Squadron, Royal Engineers), 14.1.44.

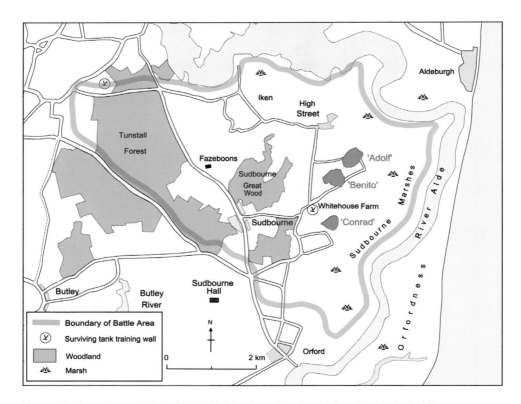

Figure 6.1. General map of Orford Battle Training Area, showing the location of principal features mentioned in the text.

farm, on the site of 54th Division's 'Tunstall Demonstration' in November 1942, four substantial sections of concrete wall were erected for the purposes of ramp trialling with fascines and artificial bridges; it was here that some of the well-known photographs of tanks scaling obstacles were taken.[14] The symmetrical arrangement of these walls suggests that they were not intended for tactical training, as they do not resemble field positions; rather, it suggests they were for initial experimentation and testing of procedure (Figure 6.2). On the wider expanse of open heath to the north-east of Fazeboons, around Blaxhall Common, anti-tank ditches and an earthwork anti-tank wall were constructed, along with, almost certainly, practice minefields.[15] This area had seen the widespread construction of anti-landing ditches in 1941 and, as aerial photographs show considerable disturbance around and across many of these

---

14 HE (NMR) RAF Photography, RAF 106G/UK/832/RP.3180 (23.9.45); TNA WO 166/12029 (War Diary, 77 Assault Squadron, Royal Engineers), November 1943 and 6.11.43; 9.12.43.

15 On occasion live mines were used during exercises, something confirmed by incidents when vehicles struck them and were damaged (TNA WO 171/1816 (War Diary, 617 Assault Squadron, 27.6.44)), but a preferred training procedure was for mines to be laid with detonators only; the resulting detonation was sufficient to show that a mine had been exploded, but without the attendant damage of a live mine.

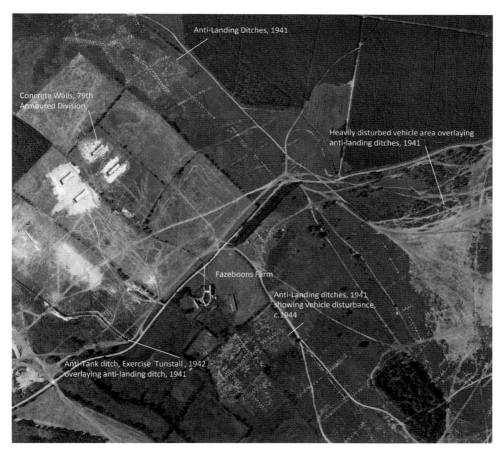

Figure 6.2. Aerial photograph from 1944 of the area around Fazeboons Farm, showing concrete walls overlying the site of earlier Exercise Tunstall and disturbance over the site of anti-landing ditches. (Reproduced by permission of Historic England Archive (RAF Photography))

Figure 6.3. AVRE using 'Goat' equipment to place explosive charges against a section of mock-sea wall at White House Farm on the Orford Battle Area in 1944. The explosives (here visible as cylinders) were held by a frame that was delivered by the tank and detonated either by electronic signal or by a pull igniter once the vehicle had backed off. (IWM H37467)

features, it is likely these were reused as minor obstacles into which fascines could be dropped, while wider areas were used for minefield clearance with Flail tanks. Away from the vicinity of Fazeboons, at least one other location was used to practise the scaling of walls. At White House Farm, near Sudbourne, in what is a rare archaeological survival, a section of concrete sea wall is built into the scarp of a natural slope; aerial photographs show it continuing as a free-standing section that no longer survives. Photographic evidence shows that this wall was used for bridging with the Churchill Ark and also for the placing of explosive charges direct from tanks via a device known as the Goat (Figure 6.3).[16]

Hedgehogs on the marsh

But by far the most elaborate part of 79th Armoured's training infrastructure at Orford were three 'German' Hedgehogs, codenamed Adolf, Benito and Conrad, on the eastern side of the area. All three were on high ground, with Adolf and Benito lying adjacent to one another on a long spur that terminated near Ferry Farm overlooking the marshes alongside the river Alde, while Conrad lay a little to the south. Each hedgehog was similar to that built for Exercise Kruschen, but all were larger and more sophisticated in their design. The perimeter in each case was marked by a multiple barbed wire fence, with sections made more formidable by the presence of lengths of anti-tank ditch, concrete anti-tank walls and minefields. Within these defended areas were numerous concrete structures and trenches (Figure 6.4).

In comparison with the hedgehog built for Exercise Kruschen, those at Orford represented a clear step up in terms of technical complexity. A greater number and range of enemy structures was present (ten in Conrad, for example), with emplacements for field, anti-tank, flak and heavy machine guns, along with earthwork weapon pits, trenches and concrete personnel shelters. The spatial configuration of the elements was also more coherent: unlike at Kruschen, where one side of the hedgehog was left open, those at Orford extended through 360 degrees, albeit with one side more heavily defended than the others. The Orford hedgehogs also bore a much closer resemblance to actual German strongpoints along the Atlantic Wall, probably as a result of Hobart's insistence that he was provided with the strongest available intelligence.[17] Photographic evidence and oral history confirm that at least some of these structures were full-scale replicas built from reinforced concrete and provisioned with either captured or mock German heavy weapons.[18] Other structures were described as 'superior mock

---

16   IWM Photographic Archive H365920–36602 (Special Assignment for 79th Armoured Division), 11.3.44; *ibid.*, H37465–37469 (Special Assignment for 79th Armoured Division), 31.3.44–6.4.44.

17   In the early summer of 1943 Hobart almost demanded that the General Staff supply him with relevant information: TNA WO 205/417 (79th Armoured Division Training Areas, General), 4.5.43.

18   See IWM Photographic Archive H37032, which probably shows part of Conrad, in which concrete emplacements are clearly visible.

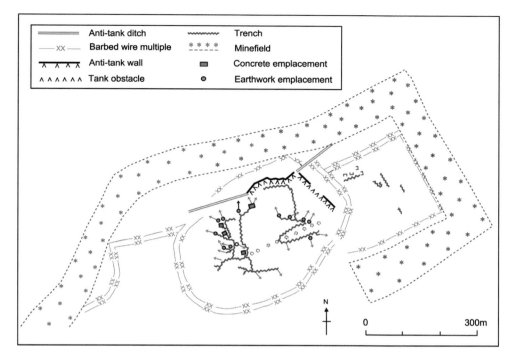

Figure 6.4. Plan of Hedgehog Adolf. One of three full-scale German 'hedgehogs' built on the Orford area for the use of 79th Armoured Division.

ups', a term that probably indicates corrugated iron and weaker grades of concrete construction or simple metal frames covered with netting. As oral history indicates that live rounds were fired into bunkers during exercises, the latter construction method was possibly a way around the problems implicit in destroying structures during training that would then need to be rebuilt.[19] War diary evidence shows that the hedgehogs were built by 79th's own engineer companies, with work probably proceeding concurrently on all three; Adolf was sufficiently complete to be in use on 10 September 1943, while much of the construction of Conrad was carried out in the period 14–17 September by three Troops from 81 Assault Squadron working continuously in shifts to build a ditch, shelter and 275 metres (300 yards) of trenches.[20] Work continued into October, with men from 80 Assault Squadron spending the second half of the month on individual training and being 'employed on works'.[21]

While it would be unwise to be too dogmatic about each hedgehog's specific function, there is evidence to suggest that at times they were employed for different purposes. Conrad's physical separation from Adolf and Benito is suggestive of a

---

19   I. Hammerton, *Achtung! Minen! The Making of a Flail Tank Troop Commander* (Lewes, 1991), p. 54.

20   TNA WO 166/12033 (War Diary, 81st Assault Squadron, Royal Engineers), September, *passim*.

21   TNA WO 171/1808 (War Diary, 80th Assault Squadron, Royal Engineers), 14–31.10.43.

Figure 6.5. Part of the perimeter of Hedgehog Conrad, 1944. A range of 'German' beach obstacles, such as these anti-tank blocks, mimicked the strongpoints of the Atlantic Wall. (IWM H37032)

slightly different role and, while Conrad was attacked by training troops in the same way as its two counterparts, it also appears to have served an additional purpose as an experimental area. Ground photographs show large numbers of different types of German beach obstacles, such as Belgian gates, Rommel's Asparagus and dragon's teeth built at full-scale and placed alongside each other on the western side, where there was also a discrete section of concrete wall outside the main hedgehog perimeter, which appears to have been a 'stand alone' structure upon which wall crossings were practised (Figure 6.5).[22] This arrangement suggests an area where the technicalities of breaking specific obstacles were trialled, rather than a strictly accurate replica of a defensive position, and it might also be significant that Conrad was located closer to the section of concrete sea wall at White House Farm where photographic evidence confirms that equipment testing was conducted. Adolf and Benito, by contrast, are more reminiscent of field fortifications whose primary purpose was simply to be attacked, an interpretation supported by a sketch plan of Adolf for use in an exercise the details of which were deemed to have come from reconnaissance.[23] Notwithstanding differences in emphasis in how each hedgehog was used, the spatial configuration

22   Ground photographs: IWM Photographic Archive H37029–37042 (Special Assignment for 79th Armoured Division), 29.3.44; aerial photograph: HE (NMR), RAF 106G/UK/832/RS/4167 (23.9.45).

23   TNA WO 166/10710 (War Diary, 79th Armoured Division, G), Exercise Hedgehog I, 26.7.43.

of the three permitted a degree of flexibility during exercises. Mock attacks could be varied according to demand or specific drills could be conducted against a particular point in the defences. The proximity of Adolf and Benito meant that in larger exercises they could be worked as a pair, with a successful attack on one followed by exploitation through to the other.

Training 79th Armoured: technical and tactical training

In common with the training areas of other armoured formations, the infrastructure of the Orford area was intended to meet both technical and tactical requirements.[24] Technical training involved the norms of driving, gunnery and radio work, but additionally in this case the operation of specialist equipment and explosive devices. In June 1943, for example, 80 Assault Squadron spent time undertaking mine laying and recording; reconnaissance; the laying and removing of booby traps; field firing; bivouacking; map reading; and practice drills for placing explosive charges on wall obstacles.[25] Tactical training was more concerned with how this expertise was deployed in the field to best effect, but for 79th this aspect was complicated by the fact that their operational role demanded co-operation not only between their own specialist vehicles of various types but also with troops from other units.[26] The character of the formation's training at Orford was also subject to change over time. Over the course of 1943 and early 1944 much is best characterised as 'proof of concept', as it was unclear which technical devices might work in practice and what tactical methods might or might not be feasible. From the spring of 1944, however, as the place of the Funnies in the assault plan for Overlord was confirmed, greater emphasis was placed on working with the units that elements of 79th were now expected to work alongside in the actual beach landings.

While the training that took place on the Orford area rightly assumes a prominent place in discussions of the formation, the results of field survey and war diary evidence from the lower levels of the chain of command show that the battle area had an extensive hinterland and that the archaeological 'footprint' of 79th Armoured's training was more extensive than has previously been supposed (Figure 6.6). As the formation's engineer (1st Assault) brigade came together from a variety of separate field companies only in October 1943, much time was initially spent in gaining technical proficiency in the fundamentals of their craft, such as the use of explosives and deployment from vehicles. At least some of this work took place elsewhere in the Sandlings. This is most readily seen archaeologically in destroyed concrete structures from the anti-invasion landscape, especially pillboxes, which found a new role at this time as surrogates for German fortifications. This was particularly the case for those parts of Ironside's coastal

---

24   J. Buckley, *British Armour in the Normandy Campaign 1944* (London, 2004), p. 82.

25   TNA WO 171/1808 (War Diary, 80th Assault Squadron, Royal Engineers), June 1943, *passim*.

26   TNA WO 205/417 (79th Armoured Division Training Areas, General), 10.9.43.

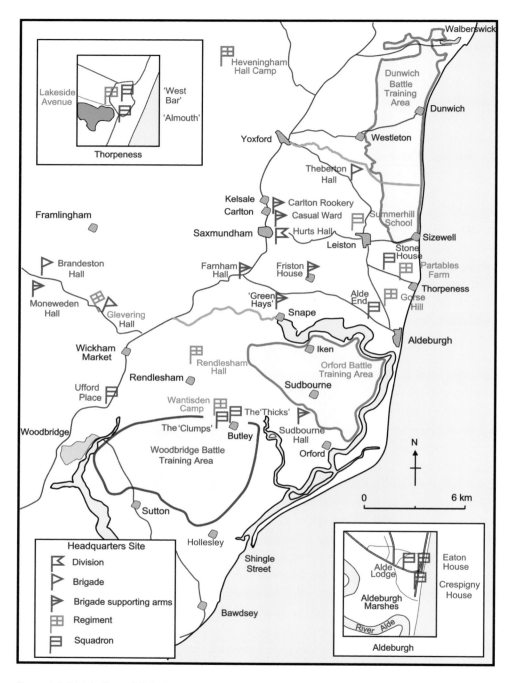

Figure 6.6. 'Halo' effect of Orford area; units training on the area clustered around its edges and made use of their immediate hinterlands for training.

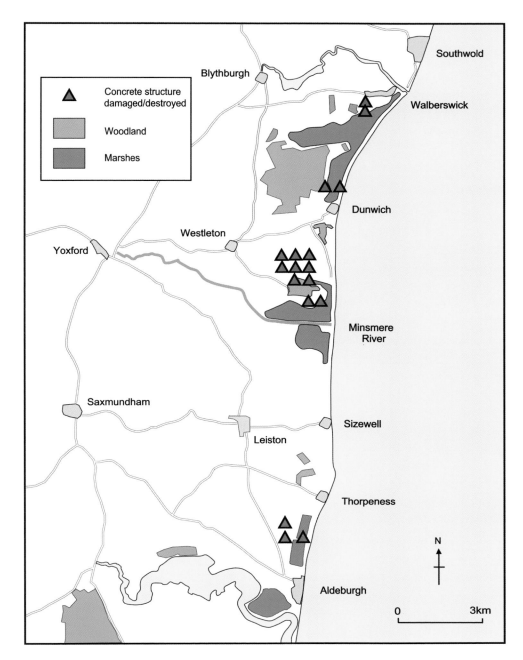

Figure 6.7. Distribution map of extant remains of destroyed concrete structures in the Sandlings. This map shows only those examples that can be seen today; documentary sources indicate that many more pillboxes were destroyed by 79th Armoured Division in late 1943 and early 1944.

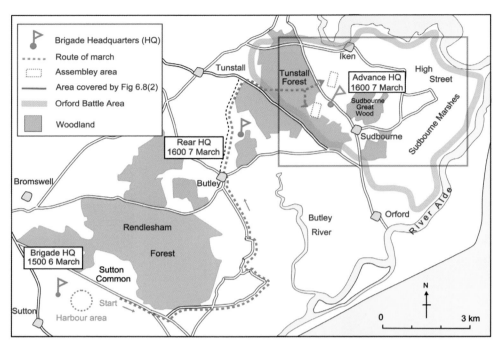

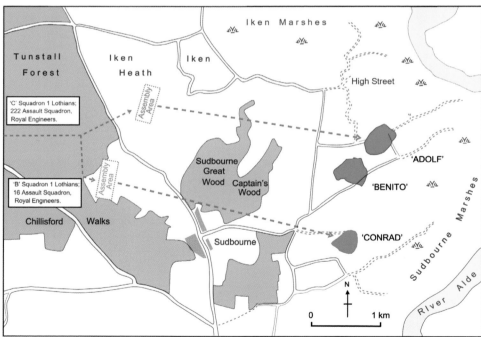

Figure 6.8. Exercise 'Gobetter': this was typical of the minor exercises undertaken on the Orford area by 79th Armoured Division. The Lothians were equipped with the Sherman flail or 'Crab' tank to clear minefields and this exercise was to test co-operation with the AVRE in assaulting a fixed strong point.

crust that had been abandoned early in 1941 and where the pillboxes had been unused for nearly two years. War diary evidence confirms demolition work being undertaken by 79th Armoured's Assault Engineers in late 1943 as a method of familiarising troops with explosive handling. That of 77 Assault Squadron, for example, records that on 6 December 1943 'troops marched to and from "Hitler" pillbox near Dunwich, which was blown up by WADES and beehives' – the latter being types of concrete-breaking explosive device.[27] In the case of the Kruschen hedgehog, the concrete bunkers were destroyed systematically by 79th engineers in November 1943 (Figure 6.7).[28] Other archaeological evidence also relates to technical training. At Thorpeness an almost complete circuit of concrete roads and ramps that survives in a former extraction pit was a tank driving area in which tank drivers practised negotiating a 30 degree slope while keeping the vehicle under control with the foot brake.[29] In addition, specialised facilities such as firing ranges were in almost constant use, with war diaries detailing the day-to-day intensity: squadrons of the 22nd Dragoons, for example, undertook field firing at Orford or on the Boyton tank gunnery range nearly every day between January and May 1944.[30]

At Orford itself, the training infrastructure was put to a variety of uses. A continual focus was the methods of crossing concrete walls in the area around Fazeboons and White House Farm, with the hedgehogs used for rehearsals with specific equipment. Much of this work was conducted on a small-scale basis at Squadron or Troop level. On 10 September 1943, for example, 81 Squadron attacked Adolf with snakes and fascines.[31] A similar exercise was the suggestively named 'Gobetter', a two-day exercise in March 1944 that practised battle procedure for a rapid deployment of two squadrons each of Flail tanks and AVREs which ended in an attack on Adolf and Conrad (Figure 6.8).[32] For the participants, the nature of these activities was gruelling. Driver/Mechanic Isley recalled that

> our training on the battle area at Orford was very intensive with inter-troop and inter-squadron competitions, everyone trying their best to shave seconds from getting in and out of the Churchill tank side hatches, dummy loading and firing Petards, crossing and climbing obstacles … my overriding memory of those days was the feeling of tremendous fatigue.[33]

27   TNA WO 166/12029 (War Diary, 77th Assault Squadron, Royal Engineers), 6.12.43.

28   TNA WO 205/419 (79th Armoured Division Training Areas), 27.4.43; TNA WO 199/811 (Assault Training Area, Southwold), 'Letter to 79th Armoured Division from General Staff, Eastern Command', 5.11.43.

29   Bovington Tank Museum, E2009.142 (79th Armoured Division Training Instruction No. 7 July 1943).

30   TNA WO 171/841 (War Diary, 22nd Dragoons), *passim*.

31   TNA WO 166/12033 (War Diary, 81st Assault Squadron, Royal Engineers), 10.9.43.

32   TNA WO 171/1805 (War Diary, 42nd Assault Regiment, Royal Engineers), 6–8.3.44.

33   Quoted in P. Delaforce, *Churchill's Secret Weapons. The Story of Hobart's Funnies* (London, 1998), pp. 78–9, 81.

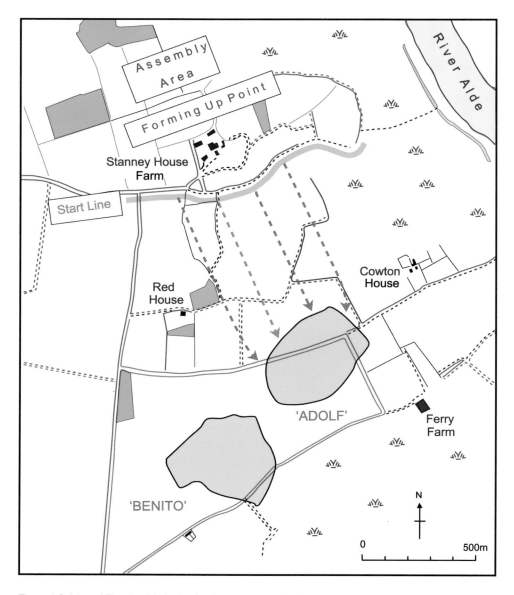

Figure 6.9. Map of Exercise 'Hedgehog': a five-stage exercise designed to develop and test procedures for attacking a heavily defended German strong point.

The tactical training at Orford took place alongside infantry and artillery units drawn from other formations. One of the earliest larger-scale exercises, which established a pattern for the future, was Exercise Hedgehog, which took place over a number of occasions between August and November 1943.[34] The exercise was broken down into five numbered components gradually increasing in complexity, ranging from Hedgehog I, which comprised a TEWT (tactical exercise without troops), through to Hedgehog V, an attack by an all-arms force on 'Adolf' while hampered by smoke (Figure 6.9). Exercise Hedgehog represented one of the first attempts to choreograph the arrangements for such an attack, and its objective was to test the drills required to successfully complete the assault. While the planning elements proved valuable, the nature of this early training was described by subaltern Julius Neave, who later commented that his unit took part in

> a series of extremely dull, and as it turned out, unrealistic exercises against a dummy west wall, known as Exercise Hedgehog. It was a 'set-piece' show in the most literal sense and all arms took part … every sort and kind of specialised armour was represented, Armoured Vehicles Royal Engineers (AVRE), Flails (anti-mine device), Crocodiles (flame throwers) and all manner of gadgets and devices. Each day we would solemnly proceed according to a minutely worked out timetable across an open piece of ground, onto a complete replica of the German channel coast defences.[35]

The Hedgehog exercises represented initial thoughts being worked out on the ground. By January 1944 solutions to the problem of breaching beach defences had developed to the point where they were beginning to be enshrined in drills. From this time, while 79th continued to conduct its own in-house training programmes, the focus began to switch to larger co-operative exercises, which saw more realistic practice attacks with troops with whom they would land in Normandy.

D-Day training: 49th and 50th Division

The two formations that trained alongside 79th Armoured at Orford were 49th and 50th Divisions. Individual units, usually battalions, were rotated on a piecemeal basis through a series of exercises of the same name in order that each was given an opportunity to undertake the required drill. As is discussed below, in the case of 49th Division training took place across Eastern Command, but a specific requirement was to practise deliberate attacks against defended strongpoints where special equipment would be needed to clear obstacles. This need was met in exercises such as 'Moose' and 'Elk', where single battalions undertook a deliberate attack on a single hedgehog alongside AVREs and Flail tanks from 79th Armoured. The practice assault was

---

34   TNA WO 166/10710 (War Diary, 79th Armoured Division, G), Exercise Hedgehog, 26.7.43.

35   Bovington Tank Museum, Neave, *The War Diary of Julius Neave*, pp. 23–4.

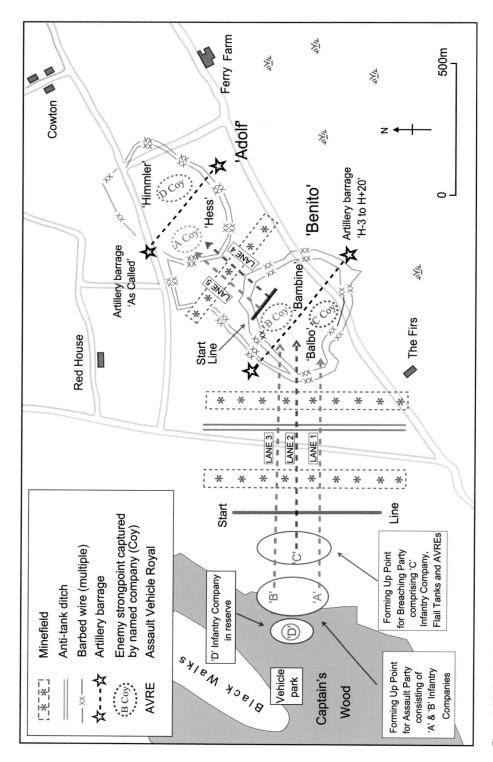

Figure 6.10. Exercise Bullshead: this was intended to give practice to troops who would land in the first wave on D-Day in working with 79th Armoured Division's specialised armour. Such exercises were some of the most complex to take place on the Orford area.

normally only one part of the exercise, which also involved forming up procedure, preliminary night work and reconnaissance.[36] Elements of 50th Division made short but significant use of Orford as part of their specific designation as an 'Assault' division; their time in the area was part of a wider programme of intensive training in the period after their return from the Mediterranean. Some two weeks were spent in the Sandlings before undertaking beach landing drills in Scotland and final rehearsals on the south coast.[37] The purpose of the training at Orford was specifically to practise co-operation with 79th Armoured's specialised units in deliberate attacks on strongpoints where minefields, anti-tank ditches and other obstacles had to be crossed before the main hedgehogs could be assaulted. Each of 50th Division's infantry brigades rotated through in exercises Kangeroo, Bullock and Bullshead in February and March 1944. Typical of these was Bullshead, which was carried out three times in March 1944 by 151 Infantry Brigade. The objective was to assault, capture and consolidate hedgehogs Benito and Adolf (Figure 6.10). Within each hedgehog there were two minor objectives: Balbo and Bambine in Benito and Hess and Himmler in Adolf. The operation was carried out in five phases: forming up, the breach, the assault on Benito, the assault on Adolf and the reorganisation. Two extensive minefields and an anti-tank ditch protected the approach to Benito, with a further minefield to be negotiated before the attacking troops reached Adolf.[38] The exercise itself involved the attacking troops forming up in Captain's Wood, with a breaching party from 79th Armoured and one infantry company a little further forward. From here, the troops crossed several hundred metres of open ground that contained the minefields and anti-tank ditch. The breaching party of Flail tanks, AVREs, pioneers and infantry cleared three lanes, after which the vehicle elements supported the main body of infantry as they moved in to take Benito, with one company each taking Balbo and Bambine. From here, a further two lanes were opened up so that the reserve company of infantry could exploit forward and capture Hess and Himmler in Adolf. In one small corner of the Sandlings D-Day was rehearsed in miniature.

49th Division: infantry training and new training areas

In the summer of 1943 it had been anticipated that East Anglia would become the principal training ground for 49th Division, a formation that was part of the 'follow on' force that would land in France after D-Day. The expectation was that the Division would undertake large-scale exercises in order to bring it up to war proficiency. More space than was then

---

36 TNA WO 171/1797 (War Diary, 1st Assault Brigade, Royal Engineers), January–February 1944, *passim*.

37 Clay, *The Path of the 50th*.

38 TNA WO 171/1291 (War Diary, 9th Durham Light Infantry), 25.3.44. The documentation for the exercise also reveals the nature of the interior, which comprised a range of weapons, concrete emplacements, weapon pits and shelters with concrete walls two metres thick. The whole attack was expected to take in the region of 50 minutes. The minefields were laid with British mines that were fitted with detonators only and the attacking troops were given blank ammunition. The enemy were probably given blank ammunition and thunderflashes, while artillery support was imaginary.

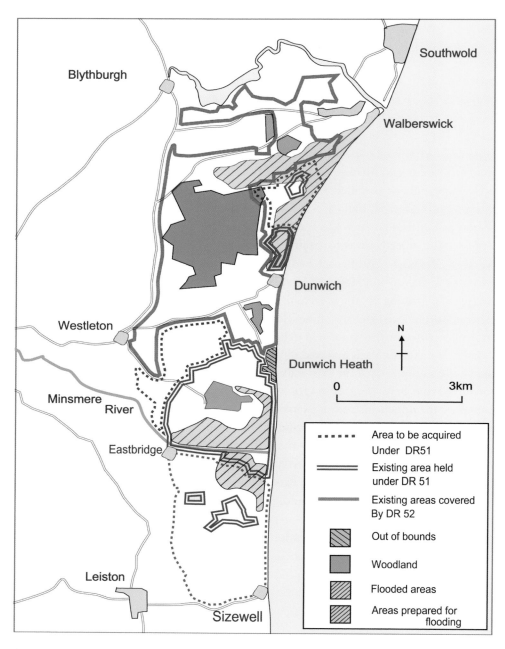

Figure 6.11. The expansion of the Dunwich Training Area, 1943.

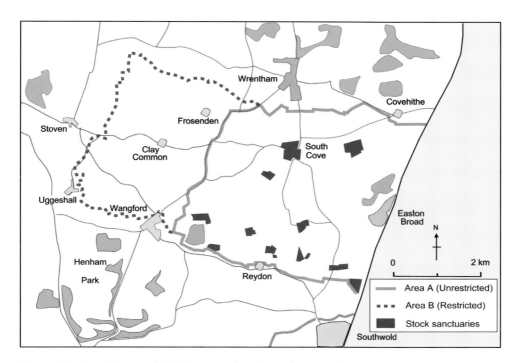

Figure 6.12. Map of Southwold Training Area, showing stock sanctuaries.

available was required for the scale of the anticipated manoeuvres and, while piecemeal acquisitions of land by the military took place on an ad hoc basis throughout 1943, the problem could be made good only by a round of large-scale requisitions (Figure 6.11).[39]

In the summer of 1943 the Dunwich Training Area was expanded, an option that had been rejected in the previous year owing to the detrimental effect on agriculture. This concern was now laid to one side as the army's requirement for additional land began to bite. The new intakes were requisitioned under DR 51 and, as had been the case at Orford, the civilian population was compulsorily evacuated. Marshland around Dingle House was commandeered, which had the effect of filling a gap left by earlier patterns of requisitioning in 1940, probably in order to create additional space over which live ordnance could be fired. An area of heath and arable adjacent to the existing training area on its western side was also taken, as well as the marshes, heath and arable to the south as far as Leiston. The result was that the Dunwich area was increased by one-third and now formed a contiguous block from Leiston to Walberswick; at 3225 hectares (7969 acres), it was the largest training area in the Sandlings.

The scale of activities envisaged also prompted the creation in late 1943 of a short-lived but extensive training area at Southwold, which comprised 2650 hectares (6550

---

39 A grenade range on Southwold Common in July 1943, for example: SRO (Lowestoft) 491/12F/28 (Requisition of Land and Property), Southwold Grenade Range, 19.7.43.

acres) inland from the coast between Southwold and Covehithe (Figure 6.12). This stretch of coastline had initially come to the attention of the military because of its potential for practising amphibious landings but, perhaps ironically, it was felt that the existence of dragon's teeth and minefields would make it unsuitable for landing craft drills.[40] The physical resemblance of this part of coastal Suffolk's hinterland to that of Normandy did, however, mean that it was eminently suitable for 49th Division, who were expected to fight further inland, rather than on the beaches themselves.

But this was the northern Sandlings, with a landscape not made up primarily of heath and marsh, but one which contained a greater proportion of arable, which led one requisitioning officer to report with a sense of foreboding that if it came to taking it 'considerable agricultural interests were involved', which would inevitably bring objections from the Ministry of Agriculture.[41] In the event, in contrast to Dunwich and Orford, at Southwold a more conciliatory approach to the agricultural interest was adopted. As the area would be used only for a short period and for a specific purpose, so long as the military's immediate training needs could be met a series of pragmatic concessions to civilian agencies, especially when it came to farming, were considered expedient. Agricultural objections were limited by a series of measures to curb the worst excesses of military use.[42] Live firing was permitted in only one part of the area and designated 'stock sanctuaries' were established so that cattle and sheep could be impounded while exercises were taking place. A complicated set of standing orders existed which extended to such details as the barring of the use of live rounds or smoke near the area's extremities in order to avoid civilian damage. Within the area itself, however, pillboxes and barbed wire were allowed to be destroyed as part of training and requisitions of houses were made in order to practise street fighting.[43] In the final analysis, it was concluded by army planners that '[it] has suited us extremely well as it is a very good area indeed for 49 Division to train upon'.[44]

The military landscape of late war infantry training

The constituent units of 49th Division began to arrive in East Anglia in January 1944 and, as would be expected of an infantry formation, the training regime was one of almost continual small-scale drills, usually up to company level (especially field firing), interspersed with much larger exercises. Oral history and post-war memoirs are unanimous that exercises in this period were more intensive than what had gone before: Corporal Cowie from the 1st Tyneside Scottish recalled that 'the hard work'

---

40 TNA WO 205/1092 (Assault Training Areas, Eastern Command), Coastal Area for Landing Practice, 20.12.43.

41 TNA WO 205/1088 (Reports on Assault Training Areas), 7.7.43.

42 TNA WO 199/811 (Assault Training Area, Southwold), *passim*.

43 TNA WO 199/805 (Assault Training Areas).

44 TNA WO 205/1088 (Reports on Assault Training Areas), 27.8.43.

Figure 6.13. A typical British 'slit' trench dug as part of training on the Dunwich area c.1944.

started when the Division moved into East Anglia and that 'training became far more realistic, with Brigade and Divisional exercises, nearly always using live ammunition'.[45]

This late war infantry training has left its own archaeological signature in the form of trenches excavated during exercises, which, as a group, are the most numerous military earthworks of any kind in the Sandlings today. These trenches were chiefly simple fieldworks that could be dug in a short period of time with a personal entrenching tool and were intended to give infantrymen only basic protection from enemy fire. As laid down in the War Office's manual on infantry training – published in 1944, but which encoded existing practice – the standard infantry trench was a two- or three-man 'weapon slit' – colloquially known as a 'slit trench' – that comprised a rectangular pit some two feet (0.6m) wide at the bottom, with vertical sides and no parapet, so as to give a better field of fire.[46] A variant on this design came under the classification 'hasty defences', which potentially comprised three stages: first, the excavation of the smallest possible hole that could provide an individual with protection; second, the continuation of this hole to a depth sufficient to allow the soldier to kneel; and, third, the excavation of a pit deep enough for an individual to stand up.[47] Here the spoil would out of necessity be heaped up over the sides. In the field, the form of trenches, either of textbook slit or hasty defence type, varied: photographic evidence from Eastern Command exercises from 1943 onwards show trenches suitable for from one to four men and of different

45   K. Beaverstock, *Breaking the Panzers* (Stroud, 2002), p. 16.
46   War Office, *Infantry Training Part VIII Fieldcraft, Battle Drill, Section and Platoon Tactics*, 4.3.44, Chapter 5, Defence, Section 176 'Design and Siting'.
47   *Ibid.*, 'Hasty Defences'.

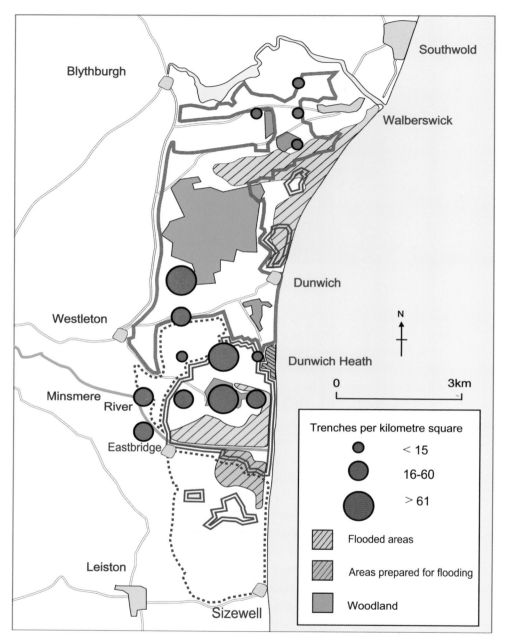

Figure 6.14. Distribution map of training trenches on the Dunwich Training Area. This map shows all training trenches known from field survey, including fully excavated slit trenches and 'hasty' defences. Those that lie in the expanded area relate to the training of 49th Infantry Division from early 1944.

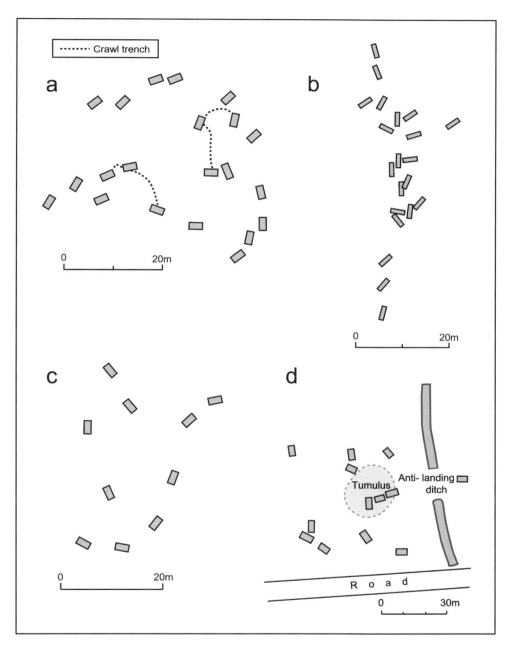

Figure 6.15. Typical training works on the Dunwich Training Area: a) slit trenches at Clay Lane, Minsmere; b) 'hasty' defences at Walberswick common; c) 'hasty' defences at Weslteton Walks; d) 'hasty' defences at Tinker's Walks, Walberswick. All represent the remains of low-level infantry training, most of which probably took place in the months before D-Day.

depths.[48] The archaeological evidence from across the Sandlings confirms a lack of uniformity. Extant examples range from those excavated to full depth for two or three men from which the spoil has been removed elsewhere through to hasty defences dug to first stage and second stage only, with the excavated soil banked up to one side (Figure 6.13). The evidence from field survey shows that the majority of such works were of 'hasty defence' type for a single infantryman. Archaeologically, these chiefly comprise rectangular or sub-oval pits, usually no more than 1.0m by 0.5m, usually with a slight parapet on one side where the soil has been heaped up. It is clear from their physical form that many were excavated to a depth of 0.5m or less, confirming that they permitted the occupant only to squat or remain prone. This observation helps explain some post-war comments from veterans of 49th Division that during training proper slit trenches were not dug at all.[49]

As archaeological features it is almost impossible to date training trenches precisely, but evidence from a number of sources suggests a dating range between mid-1943 and the spring of 1944. Analysis of the war diaries of 54th Division's infantry battalions does not suggest that the digging of trenches during training was common place and the first documentary record of such an event was during Exercise Teller II, described in the previous chapter. By contrast, the war diaries from 49th Division contains numerous memoranda that refer to the form that excavated defensive positions were to take, some of which bear close comparison with what can be observed on the ground.[50] Moreover, the distribution of training trenches that survive today on the former Dunwich Training Area shows that some examples lie on land requisitioned during the mid-1943 expansion and so they are almost certainly the work of 49th Division.

Slit trenches in general, but 'hasty' defences in particular, are ephemeral monuments, only ever used for the immediate occasion that prompted their construction. Their slight form means that survival occurs only under the most sympathetic conditions and, even where land use aids preservation, they are frequently only just discernible as faint scrapes in the ground. For this reason, in areas subject to post-war ploughing or Forestry Commission planting such trenches do not survive, meaning that in all probability literally hundreds of examples will have been removed. But where post-war land use has resulted in large-scale survival – at Cuttens Hill and Westleton Walks – the hundreds that are extant give some idea of what must originally have been a much wider distribution (Figure 6.14). Here the density of surviving examples undoubtedly represents cumulative activity by successive waves of exercising troops, rather than a one-off event, although, as we seen in the previous chapter,

---

48   IWM Photographic Archive H20999, H21000, H21002, H21008 (Eastern Command Divisional Exercise), 27.6.42.

49   Beaverstock, *Breaking the Panzers*, 16.

50   TNA WO 166/10782 (War Diary, 146th Infantry Brigade), drawing of all-round defended platoon position, December 1943.

in some cases it is possible that some examples can be related to specific exercises. Where the topography favoured practising particular drills the same location found itself continually reused, and war diaries confirm that the same ground was often used by units within days of one other. Given the muted terrain of the Dunwich training area, any exercise that involved attacking high ground was necessarily limited to a small number of locations; the number of slit trenches on Cuttens Hill, for example, suggests that it formed the focus for numerous practice assaults. In other cases the distribution of slit trenches is more arbitrary, structured by patterns of attrition and by the otherwise unknown vagaries of the exercises of which they formed a part. It is here that the archaeological evidence is invaluable as a record of events, as such small-scale practices are rarely, if ever, recorded by war diaries.

At a very local level there is a tendency for certain patterns in slit trenches to recur (Figure 6.15). It is common that slit trenches lie in small circular clusters and in some cases positions for ten-man sections can be identified on the ground. On the site of Exercise Kruschen, for example, a pattern of ten slit trenches exists incongruously in the middle of the Hedgehog – they are probably not connected with Kruschen itself, but presumably relate to a different exercise in which an infantry section was required to rapidly dig in. Another, similar example lies at Tinker's Walks, Walberswick, where a Bronze Age round barrow has been reused as a defensive point; ten slit trenches were dug around its base and another three into the top, perhaps representing a section surrounding the base with a three-man mortar team or platoon headquarters in the middle.[51] Another such group exists at Clay Lane, near Minsmere, where trenches lie scattered, in a pattern that would be explicable as a section digging in and providing for 'all round defence'.

A slightly different example exists at Walberswick Common, where some 21 trenches of 'hasty' type lie in a linear 'herringbone' pattern; here a conceivable interpretation is that this marks the place where a patrol or line of advance in single file stopped just long enough to make digging worthwhile before moving on. The number of trenches would correspond to an officer and 20 men (the recommended strength for a fighting patrol in the War Office's infantry training manual of 1944), with the pattern of archaeology on the ground bearing a close resemblance to the suggested technique of infiltration by single file.[52] The broad context for the creation of these trenches is clear from war diaries, which show 49th Division engaged in intensive low-level infantry training with platoons and companies undertaking field firing, fighting patrols, standing patrols and general fieldcraft. A particularly clear exposition comes

---

51 Platoon light mortar sections were of three men at this period, although the platoon headquarters were of four.

52 War Office, *Infantry Training Part VIII Fieldcraft, Battle Drill, Section and Platoon Tactics*, 4.3.44; Section 25 (Movement Before Contact), sub-section 95 (Platoon Movement Across Country), 51 referring to troops in single file; Section 133 (Patrols which are prepared to fight to achieve their objective), pp. 80–81.

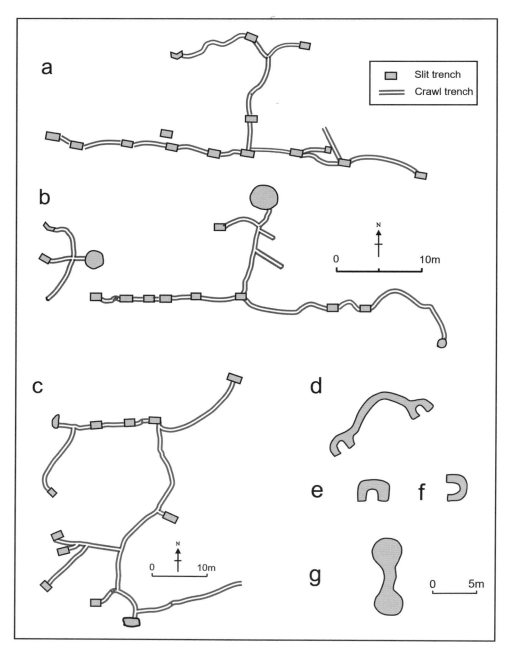

Figure 6.16. Probable 'German' earthwork positions on the Dunwich Training Area: a–b) Coney Hill, Minsmere; c) Clay Lane, Minsmere; d–g) East Sheep Walk, Walberswick.

from a training memorandum from the 5th East Yorkshire Regiment, where platoons or companies were to undergo a route march followed by an attack at dusk, after which defensive positions were to be dug and the consolidation routine practised.[53]

In addition to slit trenches, a second group of earthworks exists in the study area, but here interpretation is less straightforward. This group can be divided into two categories. The first comprises rectangular pits broadly similar to slit trenches, but interconnected by long lines of shallow communication trench, creating an earthwork with a characteristic sinuous outline. A well-preserved example lies at Clay Lane, Minsmere, where the site extends over 100 square metres and contains 12 linked rectangular pits, many of which are cut into an existing boundary bank reused as a defensive feature. A similar example exists at Coney Hill, Minsmere, where the majority of a dozen pits are connected by shallow sinuous trenches that terminate in larger circular hollows. The second, but clearly related, category takes the form of two pits or two pairs of pits connected by a length of trench to create a distinctive dumbbell shape (Figure 6.16). Interpreting these features is difficult, as they cannot be related to any kind of British defence work connected with the anti-invasion landscape, nor do they resemble the known examples of British training trenches. While they are clearly not the characteristic slit trenches, sites such as Clay Lane and Coney Hill could conceivably represent 'hasty' trenches connected by lengths of communication trench. The digging of such positions is briefly mentioned in the 1944 infantry training manual, but with the caveat that the length of such crawl trenches should be kept to a minimum – a comment that is clearly incongruent with the archaeology.[54] The 'dumbbell' earthworks do not bear any kind of resemblance to works discussed in British training manuals. An alternative, perhaps more likely, interpretation is that they represent 'German' positions that were to be attacked by troops in training, probably from 49th Division, during the exercises in which the slit trenches were created. Support for such a conclusion comes from comparable sites in the Sandlings, where the closest approximations are the earthworks found at 'German' hedgehogs. The shape of the weapon pits is almost identical with those constructed for Exercise Kruschen, the only difference being the length of the communication trenches, which in the case of Clay Lane are much longer, at over 20 metres. Similarly, the arrangement of one rectangular pit at Clay Lane with its associated run of communication trench is almost identical to earthworks at the site of hedgehog Conrad at Orford. This interpretation is strengthened by the fact that, as is the case with the four hedgehogs known to exist, the site at Clay Lane occupies high ground, while at Coney Hill the site

---

53   TNA WO 171/1398 (War Diary, 5th Battalion East Yorkshire Regiment), Training Instruction No. 2, 24.1.44.

54   War Office, *Infantry Training Part VIII Fieldcraft, Battle Drill, Section and Platoon Tactics*, 4.3.44; Section 178. 'Hasty Defences'. The idea that works such as those at Clay Lane represent such positions is also unlikely, owing to the wide spacing between the individual slits, which are placed much further apart than on comparable 'British' sites.

backs onto a substantial area of inundated marsh: an ideal position to be attacked by troops training with live ammunition, as it allowed the shot to fall over water.

The archaeological evidence for slit trenches and 'German' positions reflects at least some of the kind of training usually blandly recorded in war diaries as 'field firing', but gives an insight into its character, which was clearly more elaborate than laconic diary entries suggest. By contrast, more co-operative exercises involving the integration of tanks and artillery required a greater level of planning and the resultant documentation ensures that their form can often be reconstructed in detail. Two such exercises, 'Apple' and 'Bump', are typical examples of the medium- and large-scale exercises for which the Dunwich area was being used in the months before D-Day.

Combined training: Exercise 'Apple'

Exercise Apple took place in January 1944, with a scenario that three weeks after D-Day 49th Division was some 50 miles inland from the Normandy invasion beaches (as it turned out, the Division was engaged in Operation Martlet, part of the battle of Caen) and attacking an enemy that was withdrawing but resisting strongly. On the ground Apple was a relatively modest affair – a company field firing exercise to practise a deliberate attack against a dug-in enemy by one company of infantry and a squadron of tanks, preceded by an artillery and mortar barrage. The rapid consolidation and anti-tank measures were also to be tested (Figure 6.17).[55] In an attack of two phases a company of the 1st Tyneside Scots were to take woodland to their south that was held by the enemy. The first objectives were to be secured by the infantry and tanks, with the latter then waiting in a consolidation area until they were relieved, before then supporting an attack on the final objective. The advance would take place under cover of smoke and behind a mortar and artillery barrage, but when the objective was taken the artillery would switch and fire in expectation of an enemy counter-attack. The whole exercise was undertaken according to a set procedure, with the timings largely set by the needs of the bombardment that the attacking infantry were to follow. The objectives were clearly delineated beforehand, with the exercise representing a controlled and limited attack. In these respects it was entirely typical of dozens of such exercises that were carried out in the Sandlings by 49th Division and which inculcated operational procedures by continual practice.

But Apple, and others like it, is also of interest because it demonstrates that even minor tactical exercises were not ignorant of enemy tactical procedure. The ground over which the attack took place was clearly chosen to respond to what was termed the 'reverse slope' problem: a favoured German defensive tactic in which a thin screen of troops held the immediate front line on high ground while larger forces held back on a reverse slope out of view. When the high ground was conceded the

---

55   What follows is taken from TNA WO 171/1383 (War Diary, 1st Tyneside Scottish), 21–22.1.44.

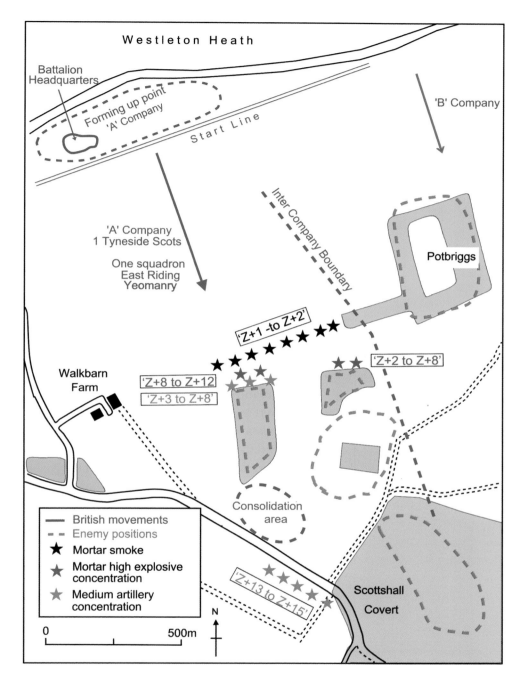

Figure 6.17. Map of Exercise 'Apple', showing principal objectives, enemy positions and line of advance from Z 'Zero' hour. A key element was the switching of the artillery barrage beyond the line of the objective in order to disrupt an anticipated counter-attack; when taken with the topography of the exercise, this was in order to negate the 'reverse slope' problem.

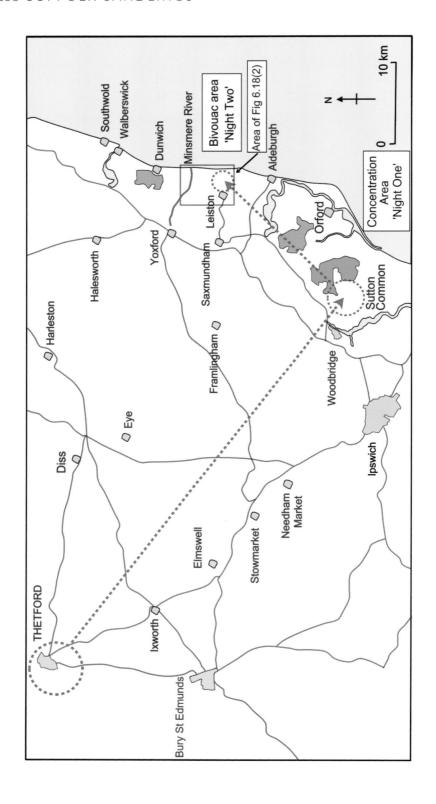

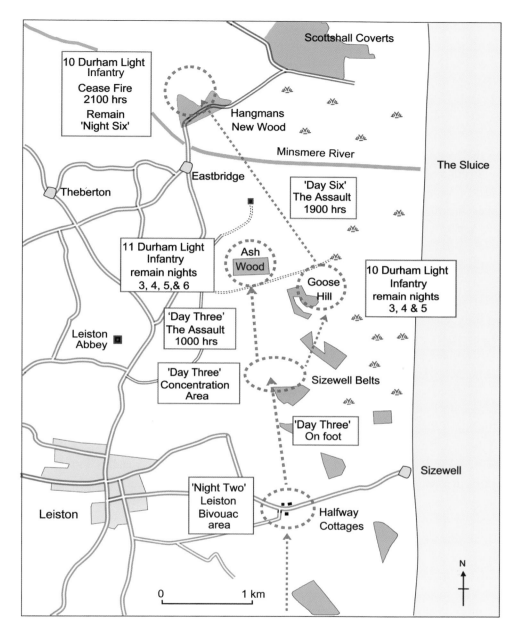

Figure 6.18. a (left) & b (above) Map of Exercise 'Bump', showing forced move from Thetford area and line of advance over Dunwich Training Area.

reserves immediately counter-attacked and retook the position at the moment when the attacking force was off balance and lulled into a mistaken sense of victory.[56] Means of countering this tactic had been considered in the Home Army since 1941, but it remains unclear how widespread practical instruction to deal with it extended across the whole organisation. In the case of Apple, there is no doubt that it formed part of the focus of the exercise, so showing in the clearest way that 49th Division were being trained to respond to enemy tactics in the field. The 'German' front line position was on the crest of one of the few major escarpments in the Dunwich Training Area, with a considerable 'reverse slope' behind. The exercise timetable, in which the artillery barrage was to switch onto this reverse slope the moment that the enemy position was taken in order to negate the oncoming counter-attack, was clearly intended to deal with what would be expected in battle. The archaeological remains in the area in which Apple took place are conceivably those of the exercise itself – or, if not, one very similar that took place over the same ground. The 'German' defence line is marked by a series of earthworks with 'hasty' defences alongside, conceivably where some of the attacking troops dug in after their initial success. Further 'dumbbell' earthworks were situated on the route of advance to the second position, beyond which a concentration of hasty works might conceivably relate to the consolation phase.

Large-scale combined training: Exercise 'Bump'

In addition to numerous exercises like Apple, 49th Division also undertook more infrequent but much larger manoeuvres that were intended to practise the general conditions that existed in the field during extended campaigning. The most important of these on the Sandlings was 'Bump', a seven-day exercise that took place in April 1944 and involved two of the division's brigades as friendly and enemy forces.[57] The chief purpose was to practise rapid movement into a battle area and administration in the field before preparation for a major attack (Figure 6.18). The exercise started with a forced move from the Stanford Training Area at Thetford to a concentration area in Woodbridge. The following day further movement took place to a bivouac area close to Leiston and then onto the Dunwich Training Area. From then on the exercise saw the attacking brigade pushing northwards, culminating in a major attack over the Minsmere levels four days later. In the intervening time the constituent battalions undertook minor attacks and day and night patrolling, dug trenches to consolidate their positions, were harassed by the enemy, dealt with prisoners and practised casualty evacuation.

---

56 See Harrison Place, *Military Training*, chapter 3.

57 TNA WO 171/499 (War Diary, 49th Infantry Division); TNA WO 171/653 (War Diary, 70th Infantry Brigade); TNA WO 171/664 (War Diary, 146th Infantry Brigade); TNA WO 171/1292 (War Diary, 10th Durham Light Infantry); TNA WO 171/1293 (War Diary, 11th Durham Light Infantry); TNA WO 171/1314 (War Diary, 2nd Princess Louise Kensingtons).

The exercise was a mixture of one- and two-sided form, with the 'enemy' passively responding to the exercise's timetable but also subjecting the attacking troops to live fire; realism was added when a company headquarters was spared casualties from artillery shells landing short only because it had dug excellent slit trenches.[58] The culmination was a brigade-level attack in which considerable quantities of live ordnance were fired over the Minsmere levels. Bump was at the edge of what was possible from a two-sided exercise with live ammunition; the 'enemy' were withdrawn only when attacks were made with live rounds, which, in the words of one war diarist, made the exercise 'as realistic as practical';[59] the 10th Durham Light Infantry commented that the battalion 'benefitted in many ways from the Ex[ercise] which was as near active service conditions as tr[ainin]g areas at home will permit'.[60] The war diarist's comment neatly sums up what the expansion of training areas the previous year was intended to achieve: it was now a place where an infantry brigade could train in full battle scale, fire live rounds and expect to see some in return.

Training for D-Day: 21st Army Group

It would be possible here to give a much fuller account of the exercises that took place in the Sandlings from the beginning of 1944, but all would tell the same story: one of troops endlessly practising the same drills in either small-scale or large-scale mock engagements. Of greater interest is the fact that the region was the leading training area for two divisions that saw extensive service in the Normandy campaign, meaning that any observations drawn from an analysis of their training patterns has a wider relevance to debates over the preparation of the Home Army for the D-Day landings. In order to fully assess the significance of the Sandlings evidence it is first necessary to briefly consider the wider historiographical context.

The battlefield performance of the British troops in the Normandy campaign has been the subject of widespread post-war criticism. In order to explain a supposed lack of fighting ability on the part of British troops historians have variously pointed the finger at brittle morale, inferior equipment, inadequacies of command, poor training and an inability to adequately adjust to the kind of fighting that took place in the Norman *bocage*. That they emerged victorious at all was partly down to the enormous superiority of resources enjoyed by the Allies, especially in the quantities of firepower that could be brought to bear on their opponents.[61] More recent surveys have

---

58 TNA WO 171/506 (War Diary, 49th Division Reconnaissance Regiment); TNA WO 171/1293 (War Diary, 11th Durham Light Infantry), 15.4.44.

59 TNA WO 171/653 (War Diary, 70th Infantry Brigade), Exercise Bump, 11–17.4.44.

60 TNA WO 171/1292 (War Diary, 10th Durham Light Infantry), Monthly Summary, April 1944.

61 The literature on this subject is vast, but for criticisms see C. D'Este, *Decision in Normandy* (London, 1983); J. Ellis, *Brute Force: Allied Strategy and Tactics in the Second World War* (London, 1990); and for discussion: S.T. Powers, 'The Battle of Normandy: The Lingering Controversy', *Journal of Military History*, 56 (1992), pp. 455–72; J. Buckley (ed), *The Normandy Campaign 1944. Sixty Years On* (London, 2006).

attempted to rehabilitate the British army's reputation, however, instead suggesting that exploiting a massive advantage in material and firepower was a logical solution for a small army largely made up of civilian soldiers. Moreover, importantly, it has been argued that Britain's army was faced with two overriding demands – casualty conservation and maintenance of morale – that directly structured its operational technique.[62] In order to guarantee its status as a European power Britain needed to be seen to be on the winning side and this required a certain number of boots on the ground at the end of the war. But, faced with a manpower shortage, the British army could ill afford significant casualties that would diminish not only its ability to fight but also to help shape the peace. In addition, senior commanders harboured doubts about the abilities of their conscripted and unblooded men and were mindful of the need to avoid a repeat of the slaughter of the First World War.[63] The conservation of morale therefore came to exercise the minds of senior planners, especially as it was itself closely linked to casualty conservation. The approach of Britain's 21st Army Group, as espoused by Montgomery, was to inculcate a specific method of fighting that involved set-piece battles intended to deliver successful results with the minimum of casualties, and to do so in a way that ensured morale remained intact. Such battles emphasised the role of firepower, especially artillery, in the assault. Such an approach also helped offset a lack of direct battlefield experience and dovetailed with a pre-war doctrinal view that machines should do the work of men. While perhaps open to the charge of being unimaginative, Montgomery's method was straightforward and rested upon a clearly defined approach that sought to maximise his army's advantages and negate its inherent weaknesses.

The place of training in this broader debate has assumed greater significance as historians have looked more closely at the preparations at home for Operation Overlord.[64] Criticisms have taken a number of forms. Earlier commentators stressed the failure of army chiefs to ensure consistency in training and blamed the lack of centralisation on a long-standing policy of letting subordinates develop their own methods in response to local circumstances.[65] More recently, major failings in the training of infantry and armour and in the area of co-operation between the two arms have been identified. Some of the doctrine developed by the Home Army was

---

62 For what follows see S. Hart, *Colossal Cracks. Montgomery's 21st Army Group in Northwest Europe, 1944–45* (Mechanicsburg, PA, 2007); J. Buckley, *Monty's Men. The British Army and the Liberation of Europe* (New Haven, CT, and London, 2013); for a reiteration of the fighting ability of British troops in the Normandy campaign more generally see R. Neillands, *The Battle for Normandy, 1944* (London, 2002).

63 G. Sheffield, 'The Shadow of the Somme: The influence of the First World War on British Soldiers' Perception and Behaviour in the Second World War', in A. Calder and J. Crang (eds), *A Time to Kill: The Soldier's Experience of War in the West, 1939–1945* (London, 1997), pp. 29–39.

64 For an early discussion of the role of training in explaining battlefield performance see J.A. English, *The Canadian Army and the Normandy Campaign* (Mechanicsburg, PA, 1991).

65 W. Murray, 'British Military Effectiveness in the Second World War', in Williamson Murray and A.R. Millet, *Military Effectiveness*, Vol. 3 (Boston, MA, 1988).

good, some was bad, while some of what was known to be good was countermanded by Montgomery.[66] Elsewhere, judgements have been more favourable. French, for example, characterised pre-Overlord training as 'probably the most extensive and thorough … programme the British army in the UK had ever undertaken'.[67] In the light of this debate two questions can be asked of the evidence from the Sandlings. Firstly, what kind of training took place and why? And, secondly, what light does the landscape evidence shed on the issue of adequate preparation more generally?

D-Day training: analysis

The areas focused on by critics of the British army's performance have tended to be those where it showed itself to be weak: aspects of infantry and armoured training, infantry–tank co-operation and the exploitation phase of battle. Less attention has been given to those areas where it performed well, such as the infantry in defence or in specialised engineering. While criticisms of the infantry and armoured formations are plentiful, those of the other principal fighting arms, the artillery and engineers, are notable by their absence, in part one suspects because shortcomings are more difficult to identify.[68]

As a case study in its own right, 79th Armoured Division acts as an important counter to the more blanket interpretations of British training being deficient. Even for those historians critical of British armour during the conflict, 79th Armoured stands as an example where pre-war training and operational success blended seamlessly. But at the same time the formation's training was clearly unusual, especially in its deliberate policy of encouraging problem-solving from junior officers and others ranks. This aspect was set out explicitly in training instructions, and in oral history this appears as one of its defining features, as one subaltern commented:

> one special feature of our training and development which has always impressed me greatly was the weekly meeting in each squadron where ideas were discussed and sifted. It was a most democratic affair – anyone could offer suggestions as to how me might improve our tactics or devise some gadget which might help surmount some problem we had encountered.[69]

Arguably, thus, the British policy of delegating training doctrine constituted an advantage, as Hobart was free to develop his own methods, which were laid out in

66   Harrison Place, *Military Training*, passim.

67   D. French, 'Invading Europe: The British Army and its Preparations for the Normandy Campaign, 1942–44', *Diplomacy and Statecraft*, 14/2 (2003), p. 281.

68   The reputation of the Royal Artillery in particular is high: S. Bidwell and D. Graham, *Fire Power: The British Army – Weapons and Theories of War, 1904–1945* (Barnsley, 2004).

69   TNA WO 166/11995 (War Diary, 5th Assault Regiment, Royal Engineers), CRE Training Instruction No. 16, 7.5.43; Hammerton, *Achtung! Minen!* p. 54.

two substantial manuals on the best ways of assaulting heavily defended positions.[70] In operations, far from being rigid in their approach, 79th specialised units found themselves capable of working alongside both the British, with whom they had trained, and the Americans, with whom they had not. At the end of the war the Division's final report concluded that 'the principles established during training in England proved to be sound', with the techniques espoused subsequently taken up during the Cold War.[71] The archaeological remains at Orford – which are certainly unorthodox – are therefore best interpreted as reflecting a particular *kind* of approach to training, which in part explains their idiosyncratic character.

The evidence from 49th Division, by contrast, shows a more formulaic approach. From war diary evidence it is clear that the formation retrained from January 1944 in 21st Army Group's operational procedure, which was practised endlessly in small-scale exercises such as Apple and larger ones such as Bump.[72] The archaeological evidence from the Dunwich and Southwold training grounds does, however, illustrate a number of wider issues. The earthwork remains show that 49th Division clearly did not train for the kind of static warfare that they were to encounter in Normandy; rather, a more fluid campaign was expected, with an enemy mounting a determined resistance, but on the back foot. Such an observation explains the ubiquity of 'hasty' defences across the areas over which its units trained. To judge from their programme of exercises, British 'follow on' troops, while expecting to attack enemy strongpoints, were chiefly preparing to fight those who had neither the opportunity nor resource to build concrete defences. At the same time, British troops were not expecting to be staying in one place for any length of time.

But if in some aspects British training was imaginative, it was at the same time prescriptive. Troops were drilled in what was required for them to fulfil their operational role and little else. Thus those elements of 50th Division that trained on the Orford area with 79th Armoured did so because their designation as an Assault division required it, while 49th Division trained in 21st Army Group's operational procedure because this was expected of them in the field. But in both cases training was methodical and repetitive. In exercises such as Bullshead and Apple troops rotated through set-piece drills that were intended to practise specific procedures only, with all ranks versed in set operational methods. In this way, familiarity with operational tasks and the means by which they would be achieved – be it a company-level infantry attack or an assault on a German strongpoint – would arguably instil some confidence in success. Here the utilitarian approach to training at home was

---

70   TNA WO 171/1797 (War Diary, 1st Assault Brigade, Royal Engineers), Assault Engineers Methods of Breaching Obstacles, May 1944; Assault Royal Engineers Equipment and Training, May 1944.
71   TNA WO 205/1159 (79th Armoured Division. Final Report, 1945), Appendix O Team and Breach Technique for Land Assault on Fortress.
72   See Harrison Place, *Military Training*, pp. 147–50.

undertaken not just to raise proficiency but arguably also to breed confidence in procedure for those taking part.

Similar thinking arguably informed the construction of mock German defences. Because part of the purpose of training was to inoculate those taking part to the sights and sounds of operations, the construction of such enemy positions not only familiarised participants with what later became their real objectives but also gave them confidence that they had the expertise available to execute their orders. The design of hedgehogs on the Dunwich and Orford areas and the range of obstacles built by 79th Armoured, also suggest that British training was intelligence driven. While technical information on German fortifications was a necessary pre-requisite to mastering how they were to be breached, for those troops training to overcome them this was probably also important for the purposes of morale. Ian Hammerton, a Flail tank troop commander, later wrote about the technique of 'posting letters' that he learnt on the Orford area, which

> involved driving up to within about 30 feet of a gun emplacement and the tank commander sighting the 75mm gun through the barrel at an embrasure. The gun was then loaded, fired, and the shell went straight inside the pillbox. At this close range, it was not possible to use the gunner's telescope owing to its distance to the right of the gun barrel. I later had good reason to be grateful for this trick.[73]

The degree of reassurance that training could lend to operations is seen in the comment concerning the attack on Le Havre in September 1944 which involved several of 79th Armoured's unit, where it was likened to training:

> Here at last was a situation for which the training at Orford earlier in the year had amply prepared us. We should be repeating the pattern of many exercises aimed at the mock strongpoints *Adolf* and *Benito*. Commanders and crews attended numerous planning conferences with the confident air of men who know precisely what to do and how to do it.[74]

The pre-war idea that machines would do the work of men, and the importance of this to morale, was exemplified by Hobart's Funnies. The decision by Montgomery to take experienced but, perhaps, battle-weary formations from the Mediterranean to lead the assault on D-Day provoked a certain amount of consternation from the troops involved, who well understood the situation they would face, and even the usually sober regimental histories attest to the reassurance provided by the Funnies that those taking part would not be embarking on a suicide mission.[75] That of the 8th

---

73   Hammerton, *Achtung! Minen!* p. 54.

74   Quoted from Doherty, *Hobart's 79th Armoured*, pp. 105–6.

75   P.J. Lewis and I.R. English, *Into Battle With the Durhams. 8th DLI in World War II* (London, 1949), p. 236.

Durham Light Infantry commented that the fact that the troops were able to see these new secret weapons considerably helped morale, while Geoffrey Picot, a subaltern in the 1st Hampshires later recalled how 'our eyes widened and our imaginations soared' when the unit was given a demonstration of the vehicles in Southwold.[76]

In a number of ways, then, training fulfilled the utilitarian need to provide troops with the means and methods by which to achieve their tasks, and did so in an environment that replicated as much as possible realistic conditions; but it arguably also served the wider remit of convincing largely unblooded units that they had a realistic chance of winning and living to tell the tail. Oral history suggests that, to some extent, this was successful. By the end of his pre-D-Day training Alan King, from the 1st East Riding Yeomanry, recalled that 'we knew exactly what we going to be told to do', while Corporal Cowie of the 1st Tyneside Scottish said that 'We all now felt that we could not have been better trained for the job in hand. Morale was sky high.'[77]

The evidence for training practices presented here therefore supports the broad observation that 'the British Army excelled at planning for foreseeable eventualities'.[78] The formations discussed intended to succeed through the most thorough preparation and relentless repetitive practice. The other side of the coin, however, was that 'it was the unforeseeable, or rather unpredictable, eventualities that caused the problems'.[79] Testing the validity of this statement through an analysis of training is difficult, not least because, as it played out after 6 June, the kind of fighting that characterised the Normandy campaign was not what had been anticipated beforehand. The Funnies proved themselves throughout the whole European campaign, but arguably this was because they were used in their intended 'break in' role in assaults, an aspect of battle in which British armoured forces were generally competent.[80] The case of 49th Division is mixed. In the Norman *bocage* infantry/tank co-operation remained problematic and procedures practised in England were rapidly re-evaluated.[81] As with other formations, 49th Division speedily adopted more suitable drills. At the beginning of September 1944 Montgomery considered that the 49th, like others trained in England over the previous four years, was now one his best formations.[82] Improved performance arguably occurred because, as a 'follow on' formation, it had unwittingly received training more suited to the campaign it was actually required to fight.

---

76 G. Picot, *Accidental Warrior. In the Front Line from Normandy Till Victory* (London, 1993), p. 37.

77 Trooper Alan King, 1st East Riding Yeomanry, interview with authors, January 2015; Beaverstock, *Breaking the Panzers*, p. 18.

78 Harrison Place, *Military Training*, p. 173.

79 *Ibid.*

80 Buckley, *British Armour*, p. 13.

81 *Ibid.*, chapter 4.

82 French, 'Invading Europe', p. 290.

One area in which the British Army did not draw criticism was its abilities in defence, an aspect in which it is generally deemed to have excelled. Several of the units that trained hard on the Dunwich area in January and February 1944 went on in June to distinguish themselves in defensive actions in Normandy against some of the best German troops at the battle of Raurey. Yet, curiously, this is an aspect of training upon which war diaries are generally silent, although provision against counter-attack was clearly part of exercises such as Apple. It is the evidence of slit trenches, even if as earthworks they were not always excavated to full depth, that speak most clearly of section, platoon and company drills in the defence. In Normandy, such practice clearly worked.

Conclusion

The remains of late war training in the Sandlings therefore tend to confirm some of the more recent conclusions of military historians, but also suggest that, in some respects, training was perhaps more dynamic than has hitherto been thought. The landscape archaeology of D-Day training is one of a purposeful and very particular approach that largely succeeded in its aims. This is not to suggest that the approach taken was correct or incorrect; rather, it was a response to the problem of training a largely untried force to conduct an operation the scale of which had never been seen before.

Training in the coastal landscape was at its most intense in the six months before D-Day. If the build-up had been a slow process, its end came abruptly. The training grounds were abandoned in June and July 1944 and, while release back to civilians took several years to complete, some clearing up commenced almost immediately. While Operation Diver was yet to be played out, the use of the Sandlings by infantry and tanks was over. But, of course, while the changes brought about by military use are important for their own sake, they do not just reflect changing ideas of defensive strategy or training needs. In modern archaeological language, the military landscape was also 'inhabited' by those who built and experienced it. It was lived in and 'experienced' by soldier and civilian alike, and it is these aspects that form the basis of the next two chapters.

Chapter 7

The face of battle

Then with great suddenness the battalion got orders to move to an unknown destination. Everyone believed this meant foreign service and a great breadth of exhilaration inflated the camp … before dawn it was well known, in that strange jungle process by which news travels in the ranks, that they were not going into action but to 'coastal ----ing defence'. The battalion was charged with the defence of seven miles of inviting coastline, and they entered with relish into the work of destroying local amenities.[1]

A major development in the writing of military history since the 1970s has been the discussion of conflict from the point of view of the individual soldier. As a result, numerous studies of the 'experience' of front line combat during the First and Second World Wars now exist.[2] While the battlefield is comparatively well researched, fewer analyses have been conducted of home service.[3] The reasons for this are unsurprising. In comparison with the activities of men involved in operations, those of units waiting for a battle that never came, or preparing for one elsewhere, seem somewhat uneventful and dull. But, as numerous studies have demonstrated, even on active operations soldiers do not spend the majority of their time fighting and so an absence of combat is not a reason to disqualify analysis. Moreover, in a period when the bulk of the British Army was at home, the Sandlings' war of anti-invasion duty, training and airspace defence is arguably more representative of army life in the four years between Dunkirk and D-Day than are the experiences of those units based abroad.

This chapter is concerned with soldierly 'experience' in the Sandlings, with an emphasis on coastal defence duty. Here the firm impression given in post-war accounts, oral history and sometimes in contemporary evidence is one of boredom

---

1   E. Waugh, *Put Out More Flags* (London, 1942), in which one of the main characters finds his desire to serve his country translating into a series of baffling and meaningless home defence and training duties.

2   The classic study, J. Keegan, *The Face of Battle* (London, 1976), and seminal work on the Second World War, J. Ellis, *The Sharp End: The Fighting Man in World War II* (London, 1980); more recently, J. Bourke, *An Intimate History of Killing: Face to Face Killing in Twentieth-Century Warfare* (London, 1999).

3   The most in-depth account of the army as a social institution is J.A. Crang, *The British Army and the People's War, 1939–1945* (Manchester, 2000); in the most recent discussion that covers many themes, home defence is curiously understated: A. Allport, *Browned Off and Bloody Minded. The British Soldier Goes to War 1939–1945* (New Haven, CT, 2015).

and inaction, often tinged with the idea – albeit with hindsight – that the activity was ultimately pointless, as the expected invasion never happened. Such sentiments all have a basis in reality, but can be overstated. While as early as the autumn of 1941 some officers and men believed that an attempt to test their defences was a remote possibility, in earlier periods, when the threat of an invasion or substantial raid was deemed to be real, the need to man the coast was rarely questioned. While this was undoubtedly boring for personnel – a boredom that was often drawn out over long periods of time – life was not necessarily uneventful. While it was clearly not akin to being on a battlefield, coastal defence did bring with it the possibility of death and injury, both through accidents and by enemy action. In any event, the army made sure that the rank and file were kept busy; troops did not spend their time sitting around idly waiting for German barges to appear over the horizon. While some soldiers were eager for a change of theatre and a chance to experience action, a tour 'on the beaches' also brought with it some positives: it represented the closest approximation to the front line that troops stationed at home could expect, and its daily routines were an alternative to a different kind of monotony in camp or barracks.

Manning the line: the daily grind

While on anti-invasion duty, the rhythm of day-to-day life was governed by the measures put in place to ensure that the coastline was adequately defended. The chief method was to place men in their battle positions at the most dangerous times of the day, during alarms or during unfavourable meteorological conditions such as fog, when enemy craft might come close to the shore unobserved. This was achieved by 'Stand To', a throwback to the trenches of the First World War, where posts were manned for an hour at dawn and dusk – the periods that were most likely to see enemy activity. Outside of these times units watched their front by maintaining sentries and observation posts and by patrolling. Commanders had to judiciously balance the requirement to keep enough men at their posts while at the same time freeing up manpower to build defences or undertake training. As a result, manning arrangements were subject to considerable change, especially in the summer of 1940, as officers wrestled with the problem of how to occupy positions during the night, when invasion was expected to take place, yet retain enough capacity to work on building defences during the day. The experience of 2nd Liverpool Scottish was typical, in that their daily routine was changed six times in ten weeks.[4] Initially, the whole battalion 'Stood To' twice a day, but after a fortnight fatigue necessitated changes; by the end of May the war diary reported blandly 'everyone dead tired'.[5] In June the practice of manning positions during minor air-raids was discontinued because men were simply losing too much

---

4   TNA WO 166/4434 (War Diary, 2nd Liverpool Scottish), May–August 1940, *passim*.
5   *Ibid.*, 26.5.40.

sleep.[6] By August the proportion of men required to 'Stand To' each day was reduced to one-fifth in the evening and two-thirds at dawn.[7] The situation in early 1940 was atypical, however, and reflected inexperienced units responding to unexpected events. From the winter of 1940 units developed more pragmatic and workable routines and, by 1941, battle positions were occupied at full strength only during manning exercises or as a result of specific alarms. While the majority of troops had to be in close proximity to their posts, only a small proportion of the unit's strength was required to 'Stand To' and, outside of these times, positions were manned and patrolled by the minimum number of troops thought necessary to maintain adequate watch. In July 1941 eight men per company of the 11th Highland Light Infantry were to maintain an observation post and patrol the company front each day, with a duty officer with attendant runner responsible for raising the alarm in the event of emergency.[8] In this way, the bulk of a unit's manpower was released either to make up working parties or to undertake training. Over time there was a gradual lessening of the state of readiness as the threat of invasion diminished, so that by 1942 coastal defence was in effect simply coast watching.[9]

The run of daily schedules for the 6th Royal Scots discussed in Chapter 5 can also be used to quantify what troops actually did on a day-to day basis during the summer of 1941, when a clear routine existed.[10] The length of the working week varied between just under 40 hours to over 50, but averaged around 45. The working day was also subject to variation, but a typical weekday in the summer of 1941 might comprise an 0830 session of PT, drill or weapon training for anywhere between 30 minutes and 1.5 hours, followed by an extended work period up to 1700, which often comprised work on defences. The schedules do not show the time taken up with a soldier's personal administration, meals both before and after 'work', movement from one location to another and evening lectures or training, so in reality the working day was longer, but they do give an indication of the typical duties of a private soldier in a rifle company (Table 7.1).

---

6   TNA WO 166/4433 (War Diary, 1st Liverpool Scottish), 7.6.40.

7   TNA WO 166/4434 (War Diary, 2nd Liverpool Scottish), 27.5.40, 6.8.40.

8   TNA WO 166/4346 (War Diary, 11th Highland Light Infantry), State of Readiness, 21.7.41.

9   The cumulative evidence from war diaries is that manning exercises ceased around March 1942; that of the 7th Royal Berkshires was on 19 March (TNA WO 166/8853).

10   TNA WO 166/4592 (War Diary, 6th Royal Scots Fusiliers), Training Programmes, June–November 1941, *passim*. For each week, the routine of the four rifle companies in the battalion was broken down on a daily basis, with timings given for each activity. Internal evidence suggests that they were drawn up on a short-term basis, according to the immediate requirements of the battalion, rather than being a long-term, idealised vision of what each company would be doing at any time. When the schedules are checked against the battalion war diary the prescribed activities did take place as stated, albeit sometimes subject to variations on account of the weather, changes in the priority of work or unforeseen circumstances. Although the information should therefore be treated with a certain amount of caution, it offers the best chance to see what troops were doing on a daily basis over the four-month period.

Table 7.1 Weekly Schedule for 'A' Company, 6th Battalion Royal Scots April-May 1941. TNA WO 166/4592 (War Diary, 6th Battalion, Royal Scots Fusiliers).

28.4.41–3.5.41	08.30–10.00	10.00–17.00	
Monday	Drill and Weapon Training	Work on Defences	
Tuesday	Two-Inch Mortar Training	Work on Defences	
Wednesday	Drill and Weapon Training	Work on Defences	
Thursday	Battalion Exercise	Battalion Exercise	
Friday	Drill Competition	Work on Defences	
Saturday	Football Match	10.00–12.00 Work on Defences	12.00–17.00 Half Day
Sunday	Free Day		

The overwhelming impression is of the repetition of a limited number of activities. Drill, PT and weapon training occurred frequently but were usually of limited duration, often at the start of the day. The bulk of time was taken up with either training or work on defences. Within these broad categories were a myriad of duties such as erecting scaffolding, different kinds of training and field firing, but at the company and battalion level the prescribed routine was not one characterised by diversity. The clear structure of the working day also extended to weekends. Sundays were normally a 'free' day, but with compulsory church parade in the morning. Saturday afternoons were also classified as free time and it was then that organised sport took place (see below).

The sea

But, unlike barracks, where routine was dictated by the whims of commanders, the ultimate arbiter in coastal defence duty was the sea itself. Tides and seasonal conditions dictated states of readiness; the need for men to be positioned close to remote beaches overrode the logistical convenience of the availability of billets; the movement of water brought objects to the shoreline; it was the sea that would bring the enemy and it was from over the horizon that hostile aircraft usually appeared. While the land could be fortified and made into a killing zone, the sea could not be controlled and as an elemental force its presence was felt in a number of ways, the most obvious of which was the physical disruption and destruction of defences. Where defence posts were directly on the beaches themselves, high tides and surges rendered them vulnerable to damage and occasionally destruction. As early as August 1940 exceptionally heavy seas disrupted barbed wire entanglements, exploded mines and washed-away posts of the

2nd/8th Lancashire Fusiliers to the south of Lowestoft.[11] In times of severe inundation, the coastal landscape, already in places covered with water by deliberate flooding, was made impassable; after floods in the winter of 1941 one of the searchlights for the ECDB at Dunwich was cut off and access was possible only by boat.[12] The sea also brought the unexpected. The recovery of flotsam and jetsam was a regular occurrence, with an eclectic range of objects washed up and reported. Over two days in January 1941 the 9th Lancashire Fusiliers recovered a raft from a Danish ship *H.H. Petersen* that was full of food and rum; two metal objects; a conical object; a 15-foot masted boat with slightly rusting engine; a German sailor's hat; part of a hammock; and part of an object resembling a marker buoy.[13] On occasion the sea brought with it refugees from the war. In September 1941 eight Dutchmen landed at Orford Ness lighthouse in a motor launch and were taken into custody by Ipswich police and then under escort to London.[14] A more immediate reminder of the conflict was the washing up of bodies of Allied or Axis airmen and sailors who had lost their lives over or in the North Sea. Bodies were normally handed over to the police after recovery and, in the case of German personnel, taken away for examination in the event that their effects could provide intelligence. It was such incidents that probably fed rumours of failed German landings or raids, but the war diary evidence is clear on this point: the only bodies washed up were the victims of the fortunes of war. War diaries tended to laconically record such incidents, underlining the bodies' status as only one of a litany of things brought in by the sea and which required attention: 'Body of German washed up at Hollesley. Been 10 days in water. Body of German airman and some wreckage washed up at Bawdsey.'[15]

Perhaps ironically for those charged with defending them, the beaches themselves represented the greatest threat to life. The most hazardous aspect of coastal defence for troops was proximity to minefields, in which small numbers of soldiers were killed on a regular basis. Fatalities in minefields usually occurred in one of two situations. The first was the laying and maintaining of the fields themselves, tasks which carried with them attendant risks. The second was where they were inadvertently entered by troops, as happened at Benacre in November 1941 when a corporal of the 1st Hertfordshires was killed after straying into a minefield while on a night patrol.[16] But deaths also occurred when troops took unauthorised access routes across beaches; with infantry positions often far apart, it was no doubt tempting to take a short cut in order to avoid a long walk back to billets or to a neighbouring post.[17] It was because of the frequency of fatal incidents that over time more stringent requirements were made of officers

11   TNA WO 166/4412 (War Diary, 2nd/8th Lancashire Fusiliers), 24.8.40.

12   TNA WO 166/1885 (War Diary, 58th Heavy Regiment, Royal Artillery).

13   TNA WO 166/4413 (War Diary, 9th Lancashire Fusiliers), 10–11.1.41.

14   TNA WO 166/451 (War Diary, 15th Division, GS), 4.9.41.

15   TNA WO 166/1038 (War Diary, 165th Infantry Brigade), 30.10.40.

16   TNA WO 166/4340 (War Diary, 1st Hertfordshire Regiment), 25.11.41.

17   TNA WO 166/4434 (War Diary, 2nd Liverpool Scottish), 4.9.40.

to ensure that their men knew the location of minefields and that carelessness on the part of individual soldiers was classified as a breach of duty. Before taking over their new positions in late 1941 54th Division instructed its units that all ranks were to be told about the dangers of taking short cuts through fences and that men were to 'beat the bounds' of minefields under the direction of an officer, so that their location was known.[18] By the start of 1942 further steps were taken by some units; the commanding officer of the 6th Border Regiment went so far as to make it a requirement that all men must sign to acknowledge that they had been shown the location of minefields in their area.[19] A persistent problem with minefields was the potential for the action of the sea to move either the enclosing fences or the mines themselves. This situation was altogether more dangerous, as it rendered extensive, but otherwise indeterminate, sections of beach potentially lethal and so interfered with patrolling, routine maintenance and access to beach positions, as well as meaning that troops could stick diligently to safe areas and marked paths but still run the risk of being killed. Where the sea moved large quantities of mines there was little that could be done and, in the event, access to some areas was effectively written off for periods of time: in December 1942, for example, heavy seas had caused so much damage to minefields that all beaches in Sub-Sector 3 were placed out of bounds pending clearance by Engineers.[20]

Infantrymen in particular, therefore, were right to be fearful of beaches and soldiers were either ordered, or took it upon themselves, not to investigate suspicious objects that were washed up on their front, but rather simply report their existence up the chain of command. One such incident took place at Bawdsey in January 1941, when the 4th East Lancashires stated that 'Two conical float mines blown up by 250 F[iel]d Co[mpan]y R[oyal] E[ngineers] on Bawdsey beach'. The Royal Engineers concerned took a different view of the same incident, however, and, in a jibe at the infantry, ironically noted their own officer's contribution to the operation: 'as regards Mr J.S.W. Bennett, personal dissection of highly lethal objects washed ashore at Bawdsey, including: 1. Civilian metal respirator container 2. Keg of grease 3. Empty packing case 4. Floats. 4th E[ast] Lan[cashire] R [egiment] were terrified by all these but not Mr Bennett.'[21]

Window on the war

While an analysis of daily routines shows units engaging in manual fatigues duties and training, it was not the case that those in the Sandlings were isolated or immune

---

18   TNA WO 166/4134 (War Diary, 6th Beds and Herts Regiment), 54 Div Training Memorandum No. 5 of 1941 Winter Training 1941/42, November 1941.

19   TNA WO 166/4156 (War Diary, 6th Border Regiment) Commanding Officer's Instruction No. 13, February 1942.

20   TNA, WO 166/10649 (War Diary, 54th Division, HQ), Training Notes, No. 33, 17.3.43.

21   TNA WO 166/3719 (War Diary, 250th Field Company, Royal Engineers), January 1941.

from the effects of the conflict. As was seen in Chapter 4, attacks by single or small numbers of aircraft were commonplace and the defence of airspace remained 'active' almost until the end of the conflict. For many units, it was on the coast where they first encountered the enemy, took their first casualties and fired their first shots of the war, with the historical significance of these events usually marked with suitable solemnity in war diaries.[22] Initial encounters with the enemy often drew extensive comment and so attest to their significance at the time. In the case of 2nd Liverpool Scottish a long account was provided of their first real meeting with the Luftwaffe during the heavy raid on Martlesham in August 1940:

> 1500. Today we had our first glimpse of enemy A/C activity apart from single planes. A loud hum like a swarm of bees growing louder was heard at Bn HQ at Broxted. 15 or 20 enemy A/C passed overhead in formation. Three or four minutes later we could see them dive bombing Martlesham Aerodrome, causing clouds of black smoke. The warning was not sounded there until the bombs dropped. AA fire broke up the formation, and the Boche flew about a bit among the puffs of bursting AA shells. Alas, forward platoons mistook these for parachutists, and we sent platoon and motor-cyclists to deal with them! … It was an interesting afternoon and we fervently hope we will avoid the mistake about parachutists again. Previously we had not seen anything of the terrific air battles every day on the south coast.[23]

Despite the frequency of low-level air attacks the chances of death while in the Sandlings were statistically remote. Given that positions in the field were so far apart it was a fluke if a bomb scored a direct hit. While there were numerous near misses and cases of livestock being killed, there were few military fatalities.[24] Deaths were more likely to occur in built-up areas and here the chances of being killed by the enemy, while still low, were higher; it was raids on Lowestoft and Aldeburgh that accounted for the greatest loss of personnel.[25] Nonetheless, such incidents underline the fact that if troops needed a reminder that they were working under a genuine threat, then plenty existed. One NCO of the 1st Liverpool Scottish, when asked in later years if it was thought that an invasion would take place, remarked that 'well having been strafed by a couple of 110s, yes we did'.[26]

In addition to direct confrontation with the enemy from the air, the possibility of a raid, invasion and the actions of saboteurs was a constant pre-occupation. Concern over fifth columnists was intense and 2nd Liverpool Scottish reported in

---

22 TNA WO 166/1529 (War Diary, 117th Field Regiment, Royal Artillery), 5.6.40; TNA WO 166/1052 (War Diary, 199th Infantry Brigade), 29.9.40.
23 TNA WO 166/4434 (War Diary, 2nd Liverpool Scottish), 15.8.40.
24 TNA WO 166/977 (War Diary, 127th Infantry Brigade), 17.11.40.
25 TNA WO 166/8851 (War Diary, 5th Royal Berkshire Regiment), 15.12.42
26 IWM Oral History 14129 (interview with Sidney East, 1st Battalion Liverpool Scottish).

May 1940 that 'The stage is now that of seeing mysterious and suspicious looking individuals all over the place'.[27] In the fevered atmosphere of the invasion summer the otherwise trivial demanded investigation. Figures as senior as the Brigade Major and Intelligence Officer of 199 Infantry Brigade went to Oulton Broad in order to watch for suspicious lights that had been constantly reported, none of which were seen due to rising marsh mist.[28] In January 1941, in the aftermath of a bombing raid, reports circulated of the ringing of church bells in Woodbridge, but on investigation the sound turned out to be the unloading of scaffolding by Royal Engineers in the town.[29] Such a febrile environment was a fertile breeding ground for rumour. Heavy bombing was interpreted as the forerunner to a sea-borne attack, but its absence also caused speculation: the 13th Kings reported in November 1940 that Harwich was 'generally immune from attack which is strange because there is considerable concentration of naval craft there. Rumour has it that it is being left alone by the enemy because they might use it for a base in the event of an invasion'.[30] Even at this stage of the year, when sea states and gales meant that the conditions for an attack were worsening rapidly, the invasion 'rumour' recurred – which by this stage had become an entity all of its own.[31] By far the most important of such scares was the issuing by GHQ Home Forces in September 1940 of the code word 'Cromwell', which signalled that invasion was imminent. In the Sandlings reports of paratroops and landings by small boats circulated and units manned their battle positions. But while the signal precipitated a genuine invasion scare elsewhere in the country, to judge from the war diaries of units in 55th Division, it was not unusually significant and simply one of a number of such false alarms. In the aftermath the 2nd Liverpool Scottish called it 'just another jittery flap'.[32] So, although the coast defences were never tested and while watching the North Sea was more peaceful than watching the Straits of Dover, the 'active' war was a constant backdrop to the daily routine, neatly expressed in an intelligence summary report from 1941:

> About noon on Tuesday 8th Apr[il], a convoy of about 60 ships sailing north was attacked
> … by bombers – '50 plus'. Wonderful day with bright blue sky and sparkling sea. Bosche
> flew so high they only hit the sea. A.[nti[A[ircraft] from the ships and shore only hit the
> air. Due to an unfortunate 'time lag' in the receipt of the warning, fighters from Martlesham
> A'drome arrived about ten minutes too late. They didn't hit anything either. They did,
> however, have a good game of hide and seek about 30,000 ft up and laid on some pretty

27   TNA WO 166/4434 (War Diary, 2nd Battalion Liverpool Scottish), 13.5.40.
28   TNA WO 166/1052 (War Diary, 199th Infantry Brigade HQ), 11.10.40.
29   TNA WO 166/977 (War Diary, 127th Infantry Brigade), 13.1.41.
30   TNA WO 166/4357 (War Diary, 13th Battalion King's (Liverpool) Regiment), 15.11.40.
31   *Ibid.*, 26.11.40.
32   TNA WO 166/4434 (War Diary, 2nd Liverpool Scottish), 10.9.40.

vapour trails for the benefit of the interested spectators. Pleasant interlude from digging and wiring.[33]

Strung out

One respect in which coastal defence duty was distinctive was the wide geography of deployment. The military reasons behind this were discussed in Chapters 2 and 3, but scattered dispositions impacted in a number of ways upon the nature of day-to-day life. In a practical sense it created logistical difficulties in billeting and supplying troops, especially in remote parts of the coastline that lacked adequate roads; in such areas there were occasionally shortages of rations.[34]

Extended dispositions also caused problems when it came to physically getting men from their billets into their battle positions, with the need to rehearse procedures in part explaining why manning exercises were so frequent. Where units were located in urban areas or had accommodation close to their posts moving to actions stations in an adequate period of time was not difficult, but in more remote areas it was more challenging simply because of the distances involved. In cases where ammunition or heavy weapons had to be manhandled out to far parts of the line, it could take troops supposedly at 30 minutes' notice double that time to reach their war positions.[35] The knowledge that men simply could not physically get to where they were required within designated times drew the frustrated comment from the 6th King's Own Scottish Borderers in May 1941 after one such manning exercise:

> The moving of HQ Coy was not satisfactory partly owing to transport difficulties. This is always likely to occur when the coy are billeted in various houses in one area, the trucks and some drivers are in another, others and the carriers are in theirs and this two mile from the coy officers and without telephone communication, and finally the QM [Quartermaster] two miles from anyone also without a 'phone. Application for phones to meet these difficulties has constantly been made to higher authorities but to no avail.[36]

A week later the battalion's commanding officer was personally chastised by his brigadier over poor standards in his unit and in particular the high use of petrol, an accusation he countered by pointing out that the battalion was more scattered than most in the Brigade.[37] The unusually long distance between posts comes through in other sources. The 9th Cameronians joked that their new Regimental Sergeant Major's

33 TNA WO 166/958 (War Diary, 46th Infantry Brigade), 46th High Light Intelligence Summary No. 3, 15.4.41.
34 TNA WO 166/4434 (War Diary, 2nd Liverpool Scottish), 22.7.40; TNA WO 166/1529 (War Diary, 117 Field Regiment, Royal Artillery), 1.6.40.
35 TNA WO 166/4357 (War Diary, 13th King's (Liverpool) Regiment), 28.11.40.
36 TNA WO 166/4367 (War Diary, 6th King's Own Scottish Borderers), 9.5.41.
37 *Ibid.*, 15.5.41.

voice was so loud that it was a waste of public money to provide another for their neighbouring battalion when it was a mere 15 miles away, while James Kelly of the 10th Cameronians saw his time in the Sandlings characterised by motorbike training, enabling him to send messages between isolated positions.[38]

As well as creating logistical difficulties, the geographical isolation of their men presented officers with a particular issue over the enforcement of discipline. Unlike in barracks or camp where formal drill, parades and inspections were routine and minor infractions could be spotted and the culprit reprimanded, scattered dispositions meant that men could spend considerable periods of time away from the direct gaze of their superiors. Such a situation brought with it considerable potential for the disregarding of procedures and minor insubordination. It was with a sense of puzzlement that one Brigade Commander in December 1940, after one month of beach defence, wrote of the saluting of staff cars:

> This has deteriorated rather badly of late, and I do not quite know why. We got it remarkably good a short time ago, and it must be brought back to that standard again … I am referring to men and often senior NCOs of units of the Bde who see the flag approaching from a distance and either do nothing about it at all or salute after it has gone past.[39]

By 1941 there seems to have been a clear perception on the part of senior officers that coastal defence brought with it particular difficulties of petty disobedience. When 54th Division were moved back onto the beaches that November a memorandum anticipated the consequent effect on saluting and turnout:

> With units split up, it will be necessary to keep an even stricter eye on these points. Only the 100% standard must be acceptable … . Saluting must be above reproach by all arms. This refers especially to those more static units on the beaches. Flagged cars will be saluted at all times.[40]

Occasionally more fundamental concerns over effective command are explicitly recorded. In November 1940, for example, the Commanding Officer of the 13th King's Regiment opposed the movement of his battalion to Shotley in part because 'The Bn would be widely scattered with consequent loss of control by the Commanding

---

38 Low Parks Museum, Hamilton, South Lanarkshire, *The Covenantor*, September 1941; IWM Oral History 20007 (interview with James Kelly, 10th Battalion the Cameronians).

39 TNA WO 166/977 (War Diary, 127th Infantry Brigade), Bde Comd's Training Instruction No. 30, 3.12.40.

40 TNA WO 166/4134 (War Diary, 6th Beds and Herts Regiment), 54th Div Training Memorandum No. 5 of 1941 Winter Training 1941/42, November 1941.

Officer.'[41] Further down the chain of command the same sentiments were expressed by the adjutant of the 11th Highland Light Infantry, whose war diary was normally upbeat; however, after a particularly poor performance in individual training by one company in May 1941 he felt the need to record that beach defences involved constantly chasing men up for breaches of discipline.[42]

Such comments reflect the view of officers; the men of 136 Field Regiment Royal Artillery, on the other hand, clearly perceived benefits in the slightly unusual situation that coastal defence presented. About the isolated existence manning single guns in 1940 it was recollected that

> To serve on these lone guns was a much sought after privilege by all the gunners. To be perched close to the sea during the summer months and be isolated from the discipline and fatigues of the Battery and Troop positions was generally considered to be as an ideal a life as could be hoped for in those days. The fact that one was very much in what might any day become the front line added a touch of spice to life.[43]

Evidence such as this offers a valuable corrective to the official record: while officers felt that, if not checked, coastal defence could breed sloppy habits among their men, for those in the ranks it presented an opportunity to get away from some of the 'bull' of barrack life.

Experiencing coastal defence

While coastal defence may have brought with it some small advantages, it was also characterised by hard manual work, exposure to the elements, physical isolation, long watches and boredom. Post-war oral history and written accounts tend to emphasise long periods spent manning positions or on sentry duty, with those from 1940 highlighting the lack of equipment (Figure 7.1). Tom Abram, a private with the Liverpool Scottish in 1940, recollected that

> there was a profound lack of action … . In June and later on we had Stand To from sunset to dawn with orders to hold on at all costs. It must be remembered that in those days we had no wireless, never saw a newspaper, never received information from our superiors, and never saw any road signs or maps. We simply lived from day to day and did as we were told.[44]

---

41   TNA WO 166/4357 (War Diary, 13th King's (Liverpool) Regiment), 17.11.40.

42   TNA WO 166/4346 (War Diary, 11th Highland Light Infantry), 1.5.41.

43   Robertson, *Rose and the Arrow*, p. 47.

44   Quoted in J. Hayward, *The Bodies on the Beach. Sealion, Shingle Street and the Burning Sea Myth of 1940* (Dereham, 2004), pp. 89–92.

Figure 7.1. Staged photograph of a sentry at Minsmere Battery, 1941. (IWM H4335)

Sidney East, also from the Liverpool Scottish, later recalled

> we were defending the coast itself. Stand To every morning, oh dear me. And all we had
> were 50 rounds per man and we also had a Bren gun which fired 50 rounds and then they
> were on wooden bullets. We used to have wooden bullets for training. We were that short
> of ammunition.[45]

Conditions can be glimpsed obliquely in a series of three reports in the *Glasgow
Herald* in November 1941, following a visit by journalists to 15th Division. Although
mediated through the lens of wartime censorship, what drew particular comment was
the isolated nature of the deployment, with soldiers 'doing duty in lonely places where
the middle aged "chain" smoker would consume 400' and hours of coast watching that
made the men 'as blue-eyed as sailors'.[46] The sense of boredom was such that route
marching, it was claimed, was a welcome distraction from sentry duty, while the

---

45   IWM Oral History 14129 (interview with Sidney East, 1st Battalion Liverpool Scottish).
46   *The Glasgow Herald*, 'Scots Division in England', 13.11.41; *ibid.*, 'Soldier's Saving Campaign', 14.11.41; *ibid.*,
     'Rest House for the RSF', 15.11.41.

weather, it was noted, could be as inclement in southern England as further north.[47] Remarks about the English weather underscore the fact that there was a seasonality to coastal defence duty. Manning positions in winter was physically uncomfortable and permission was often obtained to issue rum, something usually reserved for men on the battlefield.[48] When war diarists felt the need to record incidents of cold weather, the reality on the ground was one of men shivering at their posts. Prolonged periods of wet weather led positions to become waterlogged, caused them to collapse, and meant constant running repairs. Keeping large numbers of men in the field over the winter caused logistical difficulties right through the conflict; it was the onset of winter that was the immediate trigger of hut-building programmes in 1940, 1941 and 1944. While the logistical challenges of accommodation were largely met, it does serve to underline the point that material conditions were often rudimentary; in February 1940 a sick rate of over 20 per cent was reported by 54th Division, largely as a result of influenza spread as a result of cramped living conditions.[49] In a letter home in January 1942, subaltern and poet Alun Lewis summed up his situation neatly by saying

> Isn't it COLD? … we've been erecting miles of barbed wire fencing round an aerodrome
> this last fortnight, hands bleeding and chapped. The men don't get enough to eat, they have
> to buy woollen gloves from the quarter master, and 50 per cent of them have leaky boots.
> It's a really poverty stricken battalion.[50]

While not necessarily wholly applicable to all the units that found themselves in the Sandlings over the course of the conflict, such comments probably reflect a wider reality.

As war diaries were not intended to be vehicles for complaint, where they record dissatisfaction it is probable that this reflects a widespread mood, rather than simply an individual writer sounding off. While outright disdain for coastal defence work is hard to find, the boredom that went with it was clearly an issue, especially from 1942, when men knew that with the bulk of German forces occupied on the Eastern Front the chances of an invasion of Britain were much diminished. The response by commanders was to emphasise the potential for attack, especially the likelihood of small-scale raids, something at which Allied forces were themselves becoming increasingly adept. The instruction of the Commanding Officer of the 6th Border Regiment on beach defence in January 1942 candidly laid out the problem:

47 *The Glasgow Herald*, 'Scots Division in England', 13.11.41; *ibid.*, 'Soldier's Saving Campaign', 14.11.41; *ibid.*, 'Rest House for the RSF', 15.11.41.
48 TNA WO 166/2529 (War Diary, 248th Heavy Anti-Aircraft Battery), 19.10.39; TNA WO 166/975 (War Diary, 125th Infantry Brigade), Summary of Brigadier's Conference, 8.11.40.
49 TNA WO 177/412 (ADMS, 54th Division), 4.2.40.
50 Lewis, 'A Sheaf of Letters'.

I realise that the great difficulty is to keep up enthusiasm and alertness among men, who, quite naturally, feel that nothing has happened all these months and that therefore the chances of enemy action during the night they are on duty is almost non-existent … scrupulous attention to duty by officers and NCOs will go a long way towards ensuring alertness but what may be more effective is that they men should fully understand the position and appreciate, however boring it may be, they are carrying out a vital duty.[51]

The cause of most irritation was long uninterrupted periods of the same activity. After a protracted spell of moving and stockpiling beach scaffolding the adjutant of the 11th Highland Light Infantry cheerfully wrote of his immediate colleagues in HQ Company, who were 'still complaining about the fatigues they have to do, ah well even the best of us complain at times'; while a long period of guarding Martlesham aerodrome led to the comment by the 13th Kings that they were 'stuck here for good'.[52] A particular cause of complaint was beach scaffolding, the construction of which went on for weeks during the summer of 1941, involving long hours of repetitive work in the sea. It exposed those working to the twin hazards of exposure and sunburn as well as enemy air attack and, in one case, friendly fire, when two men were wounded by training Hurricanes. The 6th Royal Scots lamented the time being expended on scaffolding and the advent of a six-week training programme was heralded as 'a great relief from the endless work on the defences'.[53] The annoyance was clearly evident when the battalion was told later that their scaffolding required alteration, the blame being placed on the advising Naval Officer.[54]

In addition, incidents of petty or bureaucratic mismanagement caused clear frustration. Movement orders being changed or cancelled at the last moment, lack of information from higher commands and different working patterns of outside units were the cause of the majority of the dissatisfaction expressed in war diaries.[55] One incident, recorded by the 2nd Liverpool Scottish, is typical of the pointless actions that resulted in physical difficulties on the ground: 'Slight flap … and extra vigilance required. About 2315 the jitters increased, and everyone had to sleep in their posts fully dressed. As their tents in most cases are ten yards from their posts, this just causes

---

51   TNA WO 166/4156 (War Diary, 6th Border Regiment), Commanding Officer's Instruction No. 11 Beach Defence, January 1942.

52   TNA WO 166/4346 (War Diary, 11th Highland Light Infantry), 2.4. 41; TNA WO 166/4357 (War Diary, 13th King's (Liverpool) Regiment), 6.3.41.

53   TNA WO 166/4592 (War Diary, 6th Royal Scots Fusiliers), 18.7.41, 22.8.41.

54   *Ibid.*, 3.10.41.

55   The comment by 117 Field Regiment is typical: TNA WO 166/1529 (War Diary, 117 Field Regiment, Royal Artillery), 10.6.40: 'Owing to expectation of many red alarms in the immediate future, Corps Commander directs that as far as possible, units will work by night and sleep by day, in order to have sleep while it is possible. This system commenced today and caused some confusion over meals, a good deal of tiredness and not much work being done. Offices did a 24 hrs day, as Bde HQ did not try the new system, nor, of course, did outside people, RASC etc.'

completely unnecessary discomfort.'[56] Complaints such as this had little to do with coastal defence per se; rather, they were directed at failings of management. While such incidents appear trivial, the fact that they warranted recording is telling enough.

The somewhat negative themes that frame the 'experience' of coastal defence all find expression in the poetry of Alun Lewis.[57] In common with much of his writing, the overarching themes are loneliness and reflection, which sat easily with the routine of coastal duties. *Dawn on the East Coast* (1942) relates the thoughts of a soldier at what seems to be 'Stand To', being interrupted by daybreak and in so doing breaking the author's hopes for the future, with the physical backdrop of the wartime landscape a key component of the scene.

> From Orfordness to Shingle Street
> The grey disturbance spreads
> Washing the icy seas on Deben Head
> Cock pheasants scratch the frozen fields
> Gulls lift thin horny legs and step
> Fastidiously among the rusted mines[58]

It is important, however, to set a series of other observations against these complaints. Undertaking coastal defence during a genuine invasion brought with it a certain sense of excitement. The onset of protracted German air attacks in August 1940 changed the mood of the 2nd/8th Lancashire Fusiliers and led the war diarist to comment that 'The general tendency amongst the t[roo]ps appears to be one of renewed interest and vigour at the signs of increasing enemy activity.'[59] The diarist of 117 Field Regiment Royal Artillery was more explicit when, on leaving the area, he recorded that 'the men enjoyed the work in Suffolk, which was a taste of something approaching nearer to warlike activity than anything so far experienced.'[60] While coastal defence brought with it a sense of tedium and monotony, this was not the exclusive preserve of such duties, but was something shared across the Home Army. Moreover, in some respects, it was preferable to being in barracks; the 6th Royal Scots Fusiliers contrasted coastal defence in Suffolk unfavourably with barrack life in Colchester, with the move to the beaches noted in an unusual comment by the diarist of the 11th Highland Light Infantry at the end of the month: 'Good bye March, you played quite well.'[61]

---

56 TNA WO 166/4434 (War Diary, 2nd Liverpool Scottish), 22.9.40.
57 J. Pikoulis, *Alun Lewis: A Life* (Bridgend, 1984), pp. 142–69.
58 A. Lewis, 'Dawn on the East Coast', in I. Hamilton (ed.), *Alun Lewis, Selected Poetry and Prose* (London, 1966), p. 86.
59 TNA WO 166/4412 (War Diary, 2nd/8th Lancashire Fusiliers), 31.8.40.
60 TNA WO 166/1529 (War Diary, 117th Field Regiment, Royal Artillery), 4.7.40.
61 Anon., *The 6th Battalion Royal Scots Fusiliers, 1939–1946* (Ayr, 1946), pp. 49–50; TNA WO 166/4346 (War Diary, 11th Highland Light Infantry), 31.3.41.

Given that Suffolk had been a holiday destination before the war, to be on the coastline in summer was different and not in itself unpleasant. In 15th Division the arrival of spring brought about a clear change in mood, with the diarist of the 11th Highland Light Infantry writing upliftingly at the end of March and contemplating the future: 'All the bulbs are out now, the woods are full of daffodils, tulips, hyacinths, crocuses etc. are all appearing, what will spring bring this year, certainly not another Dunkirk.'[62] An outdoor existence in the summer drew comment from the Regimental Magazine of the 9th Cameronians to the effect that, if they were given leave, it would be assumed that they had been 'Out East' owing to their appearance as 'suntanned Adonis's'; and bathing parades were clearly enjoyed by those taking part.[63]

A similar emotional attachment to army life in part engendered by living in the field for an extended period is apparent elsewhere. For men drawn from the towns and cities of the north-east, the posting to rural East Anglia in 1940 brought about an unexpected comfort:

> apart from all the difficulties which this period thrust upon us was a discovery of something rather pleasing and comforting – the dawn chorus of the birds, who were very numerous in that unspoilt countryside. I doubt whether many of us had known of its existence before and probably still fewer that had ever consciously experienced that gentle 'reveille'.[64]

For all the attendant isolation and hard work, some troops clearly made attachments to their local landscapes. The drawdown of the Minsmere battery, whose unit, unlike rotating Divisional troops, had spent an uninterrupted period in the same place, occasioned a certain amount of sentimentality in the official record on the part of its commanding officer: 'The end of the chapter, the passing of a good battery and the breaking up of comradeship that had existed two years. I am proud to have had the honour to command it.'[65]

Material conditions and the boundaries of perception

So, on a daily basis, for most soldiers in the Sandlings, life existed in a curious limbo between action and inaction: on the one hand it meant actively preparing to meet a mostly unseen enemy, while all the time that eventuality never occurred those concerned were otherwise in a non-combat environment. Day-to-day existence was therefore shaped more by relatively mundane but essential concerns over the quality of material life, especially standards of accommodation, food and drink, recreation and leave arrangements. As studies elsewhere have shown, these are crucial for the

---

62   TNA WO 166/4346 (War Diary, 11th Highland Light Infantry), 31.3.41.

63   Low Parks Museum, Hamilton, South Lanarkshire, *The Covenantor*, September 1941.

64   Robertson, *Rose and the Arrow*, p. 41.

65   TNA WO 166/7199 (War Diary, 232nd Coast Battery, Royal Artillery), January 1943.

maintenance of morale not just when troops are in battle but arguably even more so when they are not in action.[66] The second part of this chapter therefore discusses the material conditions of soldierly life in the Sandlings and how these impacted on soldiers' morale, discipline and self-perception.

Billets

Most troops on coastal defence duty in the Divisional Sector were accommodated in requisitioned civilian buildings, rather than in hutted camps, although the latter became more widespread as the war progressed in order to house the large numbers undertaking training. For headquarters units from division down to company level, larger houses, either requisitioned or made available by their owners as part of the war effort, were particularly useful, in that there were usually substantial outbuildings and parkland that could be used for hutting, tented camps and vehicle parks. At Ashfield Thorpe Hall, for example, the house remained in private occupation but the park was taken over as a regimental headquarters.[67] The three largest country seats in the Sandlings – Benacre, Henham and Sudbourne – saw heavy use by the military; all served as headquarters, with Benacre and Henham also having battle positions in their parks, while Sudbourne became the centre of the Orford Training Area. But the Sandlings is not characterised by a particularly high density of large houses, and so more minor seats, such as Theberton, Orwell Park and Woolverstone, played an important role, as did numerous smaller halls or manor houses, such as Scott's Hall, Minsmere; a breakdown of locations for 54th Division indicates that buildings of this sort were used for battalion and company headquarters (Figures 7.2–7.3). While the image of the military headquarters lodged in a stately home is a familiar one, what often escapes attention is the considerable use made of municipal buildings. Large schools, orphanages, care homes and workhouses also fulfilled the needs of the military, with the added advantage of facilities such as baths, showers and connections to mains sewerage that immediately solved a series of practical difficulties associated with accommodating significant numbers of personnel. These characteristics were shared by hotels and holiday camps and so these also tended to be used for headquarters and for larger sites such as ECDBs.

Accommodating the rank and file, especially of those units that needed to be close to the coastline, presented practical difficulties. In Lowestoft the army had to compete with several Royal Navy shore establishments and so there was more pressure on the available accommodation; here billeting arrangements seem to have been a particular bugbear for officers.[68] In parts of the countryside where there were only small numbers of farms the stock of potential accommodation was restricted and, even where such

---

66   Buckley, *British Armour*, pp. 183–98.

67   TNA WO 166/4462 (War Diary, 1st/7th Middlesex (Machine Gun) Regiment).

68   TNA, WO 166/4412 (War Diary, 2nd/8th Lancashire Fusiliers), 29.9.40.

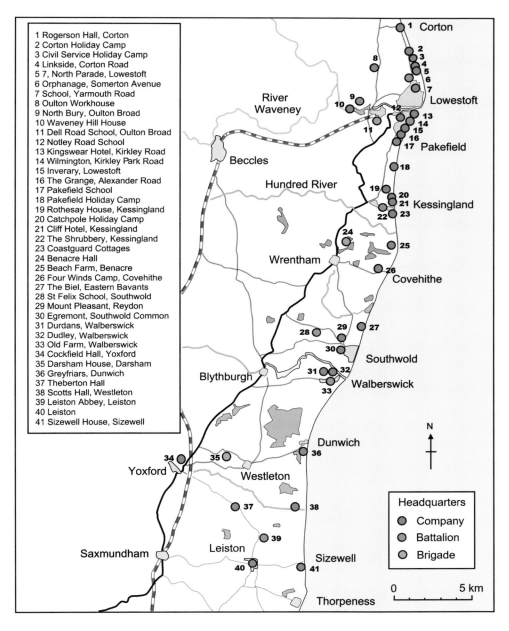

1 Rogerson Hall, Corton
2 Corton Holiday Camp
3 Civil Service Holiday Camp
4 Linkside, Corton Road
5 7, North Parade, Lowestoft
6 Orphanage, Somerton Avenue
7 School, Yarmouth Road
8 Oulton Workhouse
9 North Bury, Oulton Broad
10 Waveney Hill House
11 Dell Road School, Oulton Broad
12 Notley Road School
13 Kingswear Hotel, Kirkley Road
14 Wilmington, Kirkley Park Road
15 Inverary, Lowestoft
16 The Grange, Alexander Road
17 Pakefield School
18 Pakefield Holiday Camp
19 Rothesay House, Kessingland
20 Catchpole Holiday Camp
21 Cliff Hotel, Kessingland
22 The Shrubbery, Kessingland
23 Coastguard Cottages
24 Benacre Hall
25 Beach Farm, Benacre
26 Four Winds Camp, Covehithe
27 The Biel, Eastern Bavants
28 St Felix School, Southwold
29 Mount Pleasant, Reydon
30 Egremont, Southwold Common
31 Durdans, Walberswick
32 Dudley, Walberswick
33 Old Farm, Walberswick
34 Cockfield Hall, Yoxford
35 Darsham House, Darsham
36 Greyfriars, Dunwich
37 Theberton Hall
38 Scotts Hall, Westleton
39 Leiston Abbey, Leiston
40 Leiston
41 Sizewell House, Sizewell

Figure 7.2. Locations of 54th Division Headquarters sites in the northern Sandlings, 1941. The units stationed in the Sector were spread out over highly unusual distances.

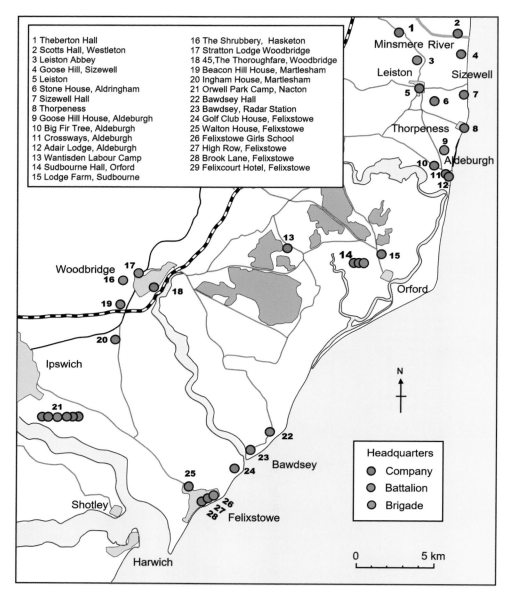

1 Theberton Hall
2 Scotts Hall, Westleton
3 Leiston Abbey
4 Goose Hill, Sizewell
5 Leiston
6 Stone House, Aldringham
7 Sizewell Hall
8 Thorpeness
9 Goose Hill House, Aldeburgh
10 Big Fir Tree, Aldeburgh
11 Crossways, Aldeburgh
12 Adair Lodge, Aldeburgh
13 Wantsden Labour Camp
14 Sudbourne Hall, Orford
15 Lodge Farm, Sudbourne

16 The Shrubbery, Hasketon
17 Stratton Lodge Woodbridge
18 45,The Thoroughfare, Woodbridge
19 Beacon Hill House, Martlesham
20 Ingham House, Martlesham
21 Orwell Park Camp, Nacton
22 Bawdsey Hall
23 Bawdsey, Radar Station
24 Golf Club House, Felixstowe
25 Walton House, Felixstowe
26 Felixstowe Girls School
27 High Row, Felixstowe
28 Brook Lane, Felixstowe
29 Felixcourt Hotel, Felixstowe

Headquarters
● Company
◉ Battalion
◉ Brigade

Figure 7.3. Locations of 54th Division Headquarters sites in the southern Sandlings, 1941. In the absence of a high density of large country houses, more minor county seats and a range of municipal properties tended to be used for Headquarters.

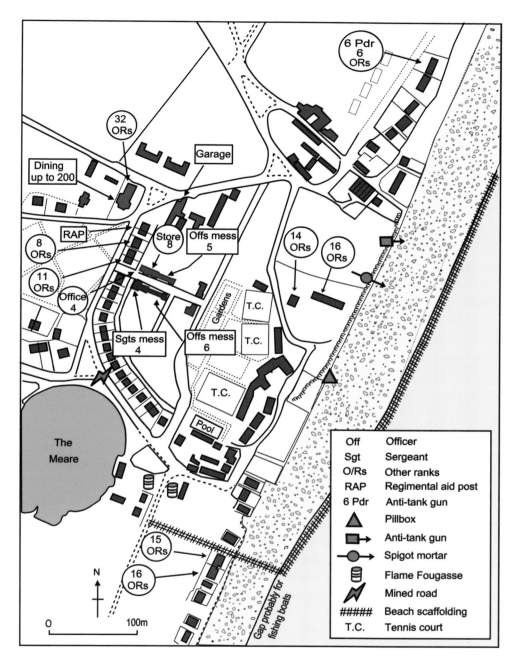

Figure 7.4. Dispositions of billeting areas, Thorpeness, 1941. Spatial arrangements were dictated by a range of factors, but the military hierarchy was evident in the location of billets and requisitioned houses.

buildings could be taken, the dispersed pattern of settlement meant that units often found their facilities strung out over a wide area.[69] Here infrastructure was often lacking and so weekly travel to the closest facilities – usually the nearest town – for a hot bath or shower was a common occurrence.[70] In seaside resorts there was less pressure, however, and finding suitable lodgings was consequently easier. The collapse of the tourist industry meant that holiday lets, vacated homes and hotels all provided ready sources of accommodation in close proximity to the beaches. The majority of infantrymen on coastal defence duty in the Sandlings found themselves living in small requisitioned properties.[71]

Particularly clear arrangements can be reconstructed at Thorpeness in 1941 showing how one company of the 9th Cameronians arranged themselves in their respective area (Figure 7.4).[72] The majority of men were scattered in penny packets of just over a dozen individuals in houses throughout the village, with the officers' and sergeants' messes clustered together with the company office and stores in one distinct space. Patterns such as these reflected a number of concerns, such as the availability of buildings, the need to disperse in order to prevent heavy casualties in the event of bombing, messing facilities and the hierarchical structure of the unit. Elsewhere, the chain of command was usually reflected spatially on the ground, with officers and senior NCOs physically separate. Officers' messes tended to occupy the chief buildings of a locality – not just country houses and estate centres, but the more exclusive pre-war places such as the golf course at Aldeburgh. These also tended to be spatially distinct from those seaside houses inhabited by the rank and file, and had a superior standard of accommodation. In the case of Easton Wood ECDB, the details of the electricity circuit show that, apart from the Fort canteen (the largest building on the site), the most generously supplied and well-lit space was the officers' mess.[73] The division between officers and men is also reflected, albeit to a slightly lesser extent, in field positions. Structures such as artillery command sites, in which officers could spend a greater proportion of their time either in exercises or in battle, tend to exhibit more fireplaces than pillboxes manned by the rank and file.

Such arrangements for accommodation had been worked out during the early part of the war. In 1940 the immediate logistical pressure had initially been met by putting troops under canvas, either in temporary camps or in tents immediately adjacent to

---

69   TNA WO 166/4367 (War Diary, 6th King's Own Scottish Borderers), 24.2.41.

70   TNA WO 166/4524 (War Diary, 5th Royal Berkshire Regiment), Battalion orders, 27.11.41; TNA WO 166/7199 (War Diary, 232nd Coast Battery, Royal Artillery), 25.4.42; TNA WO 166/3748 (War Diary, 279th Field Company, Royal Engineers), 4.8.41.

71   TNA WO 166/4357 (War Diary, 13th King's (Liverpool) Regiment), 7.10.40.

72   TNA WO 166/4180 (War Diary, 9th Cameronians), Appendix A, November 1941.

73   TNA WO 192/56 (Fort Record Book, Easton Wood Battery).

Figure 7.5. Soldier's canteen at Easton Battery, 1942. This building was constructed by the men of the battery themselves; when units were in one place for a length of time it facilitated a gradual improvement in material conditions. (IWM H23553)

their battle positions.[74] Such arrangements were not suitable for winter, however, and from late autumn there were considerable problems arising from waterlogged tents, overcrowding in billets and consequent worries of epidemic disease. On 4 November 1940 the 1st Border Regiment reported that owing to heavy rainfall tents were no longer adequate and that the interior of pillboxes were wet on account of a lack of drainage; then, three days later, the diary recorded that it had been forced to evacuate its tents and that some pillboxes were flooded.[75] Moves such as this put greater pressure on occupied buildings and in December 1940 125 Infantry Brigade reported that owing to

---

74   TNA WO 166/4434 (War Diary, 2nd Liverpool Scottish), 22.9.40; TNA WO 166/1529 (War Diary 117th Field Regiment, Royal Artillery), 7.6.40.

75   TNA WO 166/4153 (War Diary, 1st Border Regiment), 4.11.40; 7.11.40.

a scarcity of beds nearly 1500 of its men were sleeping on stone floors.[76] Responses took the form of additional hutting, the purchase of wood for bunk beds and a relaxation of regulations that forbade the use of top floors for accommodation owing to the dangers of bombing.[77] These were expedient measures and in the following year, from late summer, there was a determined campaign of constructing hutted camps in the Sector in order to alleviate the problems encountered 12 months earlier.[78] Over time, the problems experienced earlier in the war were largely overcome, so that from the middle of the war there were fewer complaints about the standard of accommodation. At fixed sites such as the ECDBs, which were less subject to unit rotations, mains sewerage, electricity, gravel paths and piped hot water became commonplace, and here material conditions seem to have been superior to those of the infantry (Figure 7.5).

The geographical horizon of troops

While their positions might have been spread over unusually long distances, the geographical bounds of soldiers' lives were still very much governed by those of their unit. Restrictions were placed on the areas in which troops were allowed to circulate and personnel were required to have an official pass in order to leave their battalion area.[79] Orders that censured the practice of vehicles moving out of designated areas offer evidence both that soldiers' lives were lived within prescribed boundaries and that such regulations were routinely flouted by troops (Figure 7.6).[80] Around billeting areas and camps there were designated 'walking out' areas where troops could move freely and, where these can be mapped, they highlight that, while unit boundaries may have been unusually large, movement within them was restricted (Figure 7.7).[81] These geographical boundaries were not uniform, however, and displayed subtle differences. Officers enjoyed more freedom than other ranks, while soldiers in headquarters companies tended to be inland and in more spacious surroundings. Here material comfort was often better and walking out areas more attractive, especially if they included a town. It was clearly from the point of view of the headquarters company that the diarist of the 2nd Liverpool Scottish wrote with trepidation 'The CO went to tea with the Brigadier. We are so comfortable at Woolverstone that we dreaded that a move was in the air.'[82] For infantrymen in rifle companies or those manning searchlight stations, gun sites or aerodromes situated in more remote parts of the Sandlings, opportunities were more limited. In September 1940 for example the 2nd Liverpool

---

76   TNA WO 166/975 (War Diary, 125th Infantry Brigade), Summary of Brigadiers Conference, 6.12.40.
77   *Ibid.*, Summary of Brigadier's Conference, 15.11.40; TNA WO 166/3670 (War Diary, 200th Field Company, Royal Engineers), 5.11.40.
78   TNA WO 166/3698 (War Diary, 229th Army Field Company, Royal Engineers), *passim*.
79   TNA WO 166/4180 (War Diary, 9th Cameronians), Operational Instruction No. 4, 22.2.41.
80   TNA WO 166/4341 (War Diary, 2nd Hertfordshire Regiment), Battalion Orders, 29.12.41.
81   TNA WO 166/8725 (War Diary, 2nd Hertfordshire Regiment), 14.1.42.
82   TNA WO 166/4434 (War Diary, 2nd Liverpool Scottish), 22.5.40.

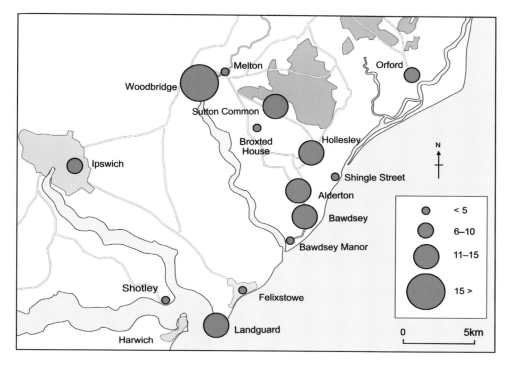

Figure 7.6. Battalion area of 11th Highland Light Infantry 1941, showing frequency of places mentioned in the unit war diary. The dominance of Woodbridge reflects the fact that this was the battalion headquarters, with company areas also strongly represented. Sutton common and Landguard Fort were regular venues for training, with Felixstowe and Ipswich favoured destinations for those on short-term leave. The majority of troops spent their time on the coast within such prescribed bounds.

Scottish set out billeting areas in which troops were free to move without a pass, and for the forward companies this included only the nearest village.[83] Such arrangements naturally focused routine activity within certain defined limits and for infantrymen it was the level of the company and below that defined most day-to-day experiences. It was through the company that messing arrangements were usually arranged and training undertaken. It was probably only during larger training exercises and off-duty periods that soldiers on coastal defence duty experienced what it meant to be part of a larger unit. Probably for many, the exact reasons for their situation or the 'bigger picture' were not elaborated in great detail. As Fredrick Perkins of the 5th Royal Berkshires put it:

> We were stationed in a small place called Aldeburgh, a village type town. We were a beach defence battalion expecting the Germans to land. We were a battalion on the dunes with a

83   *Ibid.*, 25.9.40.

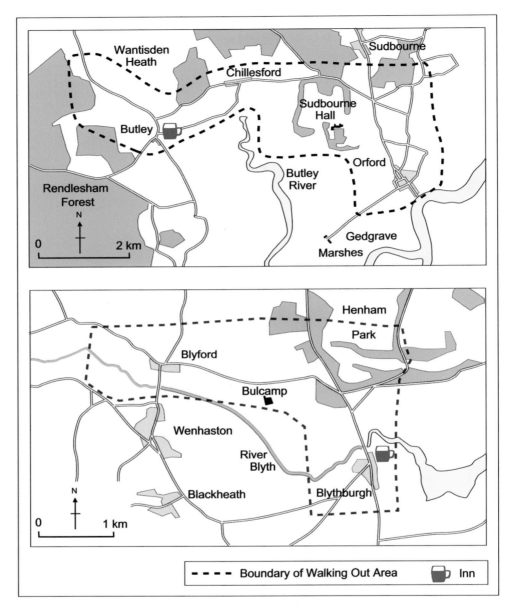

Figure 7.7. Walking-out areas around Blythburgh and Sudbourne Camps, 1942 as recorded in the battalion war diary of the 2nd Hertfordshire Regiment. Here troops were permitted to move freely and the inclusion of public houses within both areas was probably deliberate.

few anti-tank guns. Not a lot really, a few mortars and a few machine guns. Basically that was it – a few pillboxes about. We thought they would get ashore as we were still poorly equipped after Dunkirk.[84]

A similar picture of hasty improvisation early in the war followed by a more settled administrative routine pertains to other aspects of unit administration. The importance of food to the morale and well-being of soldiers in the field is well known and, where evidence exists, it suggests that the commissariat largely succeeded in this respect, supplying meals from cookhouses in requisitioned buildings and field kitchens. Usually three hot main meals were served per day. The range of food was limited and meals were based around carbohydrates, with a typical day comprising porridge for breakfast, meat and vegetables at midday and a similar meal for supper. The troops' diet was therefore sufficient but unremarkable and the lack of variety, coupled with general shortages, galvanised efforts by units to procure additional foodstuffs. The most obvious method, which was encouraged by the army generally, was for troops to cultivate vegetables themselves, and there is evidence for what are described as large garden plots being cultivated at several ECDBs and by units stationed on the coast during the summer months.[85] The acquisition of meat was more difficult, but it was clearly possible to augment rations, albeit on a small scale. On the light Suffolk sands rabbiting was possible and it was during what was clearly an organised hunting party that a gunner was killed by a mine at Coney Hill near Minsmere.[86] A more opportunist event was related by the 11th Highland Light Infantry in April 1941 when 'A Heinkel flew fairly low over D Coy at Bawdsey. This gave them the excuse they were waiting for and a cock pheasant in a field found itself en route to the cookhouse.'[87]

Rest and recouperation, leave, recreation and esprit de corps

As has been seen, a soldier's weekly routine included the equivalent of one day off duty a week and commanders on the ground were keenly aware of the disciplinary issues that could be encountered if men were left entirely to their own devices. This problem was compounded in the Sandlings because many troops were some distance from recreational facilities available in urban areas and those that did exist were not necessarily inspiring. As one war diarist put it, there was a 'lack of entertainment in this part of the country'.[88] Consequently, units put various schemes into place to ensure that time off was meaningful. These chiefly concerned ensuring a degree of flexibility

---

84   IWM Oral History 14252 (interview with George Perkins, 5th Royal Berkshire Regiment).
85   TNA WO 192/72 (Fort Record Book, Kessingland Battery), April 1942; TNA WO 166/4592 (War Diary, 6th Royal Scots Fusiliers), 28.2.41.
86   TNA WO 166/957 (War Diary, 45th Infantry Brigade), Intelligence Summary, 31.5.41–31.7.41.
87   TNA WO 166/4346 (War Diary, 11th Highland Light Infantry), 1.4.41.
88   TNA WO 166/1036 (War Diary, 163rd Infantry Brigade) 25.12.41.

in the timing of leave arrangements, facilitating transport to places away from battalion areas and organising in-house facilities for entertainment.

The experience of the 2nd Liverpool Scottish is a particularly clear example of how units balanced the needs of manning positions and providing off-duty periods. Friday and Saturday afternoons were tabled as half days and a bus was provided for personnel to travel to Ipswich, with Sunday classed as a working day; these schedules presumably reflected the fact that Friday and Saturday were preferred as off-duty days.[89] In addition, the battalion had a local leave bus for men from each company to travel to Ipswich at weekends.[90] Outside of these times soldiers were to be indoors by 22.30 hours each night, but evidence that many were not is provided by orders relating that only those men billeted in public houses were to remain there after this time.[91] Being tied to billeting areas was clearly enough of an irritation to warrant complaint, with the unit's war diarist grumbling in November 1940 that 'Still only 20% of the Bn are allowed out, and after nightfall they are all at ½ hours notice.'[92] The tendency over time was to reduce the proportion of men tied to their billets each night, which allowed those not rostered on for night duty to have more time off. Again, the discretion of commanders was key here; it was after a conversation between the Commanding Officer of the 13th King's Regiment and his Brigadier in November 1940 that the percentage of men confined to billets at night was reduced from 75 per cent to 25 per cent.[93] This flexibility is also seen in leave arrangements. In 125 Infantry Brigade each man received one whole day per week off, as it was felt that a half day was of only limited value, and one journey per fortnight of not more than 20 miles was permitted, with men contributing a nominal sum for petrol.[94] In addition, units clearly instigated their own arrangements as they saw fit; in at least one infantry and one artillery regiment a further 2.5 per cent of men were permitted to be on leave for 48 hours above the officially permitted 7.5 per cent at the weekend providing that they stayed within 90 miles of their railway station of departure.[95] Clearly the weekend was the best time to attempt an amphibious operation against the Sandlings coast.

Anecdotal evidence, albeit cumulatively significant, suggests that soldiers, either through choice or necessity, spent short off-duty periods within their company or battalion areas.[96] Outside battalion areas the favoured destinations were the larger population centres, with their greater numbers of pubs, organised dances and cinemas.

89   TNA WO 166/4434 (War Diary, 2nd Liverpool Scottish), 9.10.40.

90   *Ibid.*, 24.8.40.

91   *Ibid.*, 20.9.40.

92   *Ibid.*, 3.10.40.

93   TNA WO 166/4357 (War Diary, 13th King's (Liverpool) Regiment), 18.11.40.

94   TNA WO 166/975 (War Diary, 125th Infantry Brigade), 8.11.41.

95   TNA WO 166/1935 (War Diary, 72nd Medium Regiment, Royal Artillery), 25.11.40; TNA WO 166/4409 (War Diary, 1st/6th Lancashire Fusiliers), 26.11.40.

96   For soldiers in village pubs, Mass Observation Archive, File Report 170, Suffolk Village Report, 6.6.40.

Where research can ascertain the locations of off-duty soldiers it confirms that troops tended to gravitate, albeit not uniformly, towards the nearest urban centre in their Sub-Sector, chiefly Lowestoft, Ipswich, Woodbridge and Felixstowe. The war diarist of the 11th Highland Light Infantry commented that on their half day there was a 'general exodus' to Felixstowe, and it was in the same town that two (presumably inebriated) men of the battalion were 'apprehended in a powerless condition' in March 1941.[97] A companion of subaltern Alun Lewis later commented that they held conversations on the sea front (probably at Felixstowe) which were 'full of Wrens talking at the tops of their voices about the RAF officers that had taken them out'.[98]

While units were undeniably flexible in their approach such flexibility was of only limited value. Off-duty arrangements had to be choreographed so that enough men were available to fulfil their military obligations and the majority of men remained close to their billets and battle positions. Even the granting of 48 hours' leave was inadequate in cases where a soldier's family were a considerable distance away, as was the case from April 1940 to November 1941, when 55th Division (West Lancashire) and 15th (Scottish) Division manned the Sector. A response to this particular difficulty was the creation of rest and recreation rooms, either in billeting areas or slightly behind the lines. These rooms were furnished from local houses and provided with boardgames, books and newspapers, either donated or acquired from local libraries.[99] This provision followed army practice in the First World War, when such places had been seen as invaluable for troops recently taken out of the line. The 6th Royal Fusiliers had a recreational hut a little behind their front line at Leiston and in the summer of 1941 this was augmented by a house in Saxmundham. Visiting journalists from Scotland noted with approval the benefits of such facilities for men who, it seems, appreciated a quiet area away from the daily routine. When set against the evidence for a typical working day the report's comment that the facility was valued by those using it because it meant that they could sleep for as long as they wished seems credible. The money for both these facilities had been gifted by the North Ayrshire Farmers Association and, while the official public reporting stated that the idea had been suggested by the troops themselves, the war diary of the 6th Fusiliers was perhaps more truthful when it stated that the Saxmundham house had been procured for the use of 'men on short leave who cannot afford railway fares'.[100]

In the face of limited geographical horizons and limited access to urban areas troops frequently took it upon themselves to provide entertainment. While army mobile film shows and the army theatre unit (ENSA) toured the Sector with a degree

97   TNA WO 166/4346 (War Diary, 11th Highland Light Infantry), 2.3.41, 27.3.41.

98   Pikoulis, *Alun Lewis*, p. 155.

99   TNA WO 166/4357 (War Diary, 13th King's (Liverpool) Regiment), 20.11.40; TNA WO 166/7199 (War Diary, 232nd Coast Battery, Royal Artillery), 24.2.42.

100 TNA WO 166/4592 (War Diary, 6th Royal Scots Fusiliers), 25.8.41.

of regularity, evidence from war diaries tends to support the widespread feeling at the time that ENSA did not tend to visit more remote parts of the country.[101] Clearly this complaint was hard felt, and 2nd Liverpool Scottish summed up the situation from their point of view: 'ENSA were to give us two cinema shows to-day, the first we have had literally for months. In the end they could only give one, and they were two hours late for that.'[102] The battalion took it upon themselves to start their own concert party, 'The Liver Birds', which seems to have been a marked improvement on what was otherwise provided.[103] Other battalions held weekly dances, usually at the weekends, and it is here that the social side of units appears to have been most readily expressed. In addition, units spent a good deal of time encouraging, or compelling, sporting activities of all kinds, such as cross-country, soccer, boxing and cricket, but with rugby predominating. Inter-unit competitions were held, as well as matches against neighbouring military units and civilian teams. The most obvious recreational activity on the coast during the summer months was, of course, swimming and during the summer of 1940, when the beaches were still relatively clear, troops clearly took advantage. As the beaches became littered with obstacles and were closed off, access for the military for the purposes of bathing continued, but as part of unit-sanctioned and organised 'bathing parades' that probably also had exercise and hygiene benefits.[104]

When it came to promoting unit *esprit de corps*, the tried and tested institutional methods familiar to the British Army were encouraged, possibly all the more so given the number of citizen soldiers in the ranks. Regimental traditions were promoted, as on Minden Day 1940, when the 2nd/8th Lancashire Fusiliers bedecked their caps and vehicles with red and yellow roses taken from gardens and the men were given complimentary cigarettes, cake and a pint of beer from the Regimental Institute.[105] Great efforts were made by units during Christmas and Easter periods, with an emphasis on obtaining fresh meat. The 1st/6th Lancashire Fusiliers reported that Christmas 1940 was

> Declared a holiday. The Battalion had a very enjoyable day in the existing circumstances. 75 Turkeys were bought for Xmas dinners by the PRI [President of the Regimental Institute]. These were cooked in a bakery in Lowestoft and brought by unit transport to the cookhouse.[106]

101 J.A. Crang, 'The British Soldier on the Home Front: Army Morale Reports', in P. Addison and A. Calder (eds), *Time to Kill: The Soldier's Experience of the War in the West, 1939–1945* (London, 1997), p. 63.

102 TNA WO 166/4434 (War Diary, 2nd Liverpool Scottish), 16.8.40.

103 *Ibid.*, 11.10.40.

104 *Ibid.*, 23.7.40.

105 TNA WO 166/4412 (War Diary, 2nd/8th Lancashire Fusiliers), 1.8.40.

106 TNA WO 166/4409 (War Diary, 1st/6th Lancashire Fusiliers), 25.12.40.

Such occasions also saw a relaxation of the normal movement restrictions, the same battalion holding dances with relaxed curfews at the Pier Pavilion at Southwold on New Year's Eve and New Year's Night.[107] None of this suggests that officers were flippant or unaware of the difficulties that their situation presented; rather, they took steps to manage the peculiarities of their circumstances.

Discipline and morale

The attitude of those in the ranks to their situation can be addressed to an extent through an analysis of morale, although, as studies elsewhere have pointed out, this is far from a straightforward exercise.[108] As was seen above, coastal defence brought with it opportunities to disregard petty regulations, but this was different from serious insubordination leading to a breakdown of order. Nowhere in this study is there any evidence that low morale was ever a major problem or that troops ever raised such objection to their duties that it jeopardised discipline; rather, the overwhelming impression is that the majority of soldiers complied with instructions with relatively little complaint, albeit utilising strategies to play the system. It was only during 1940 that a sufficient proportion of men in the ranks were seemingly dissatisfied enough with their situation that commanders felt a need to underline military authority. A case in point concerns the 7th Manchester Regiment, the Commanding Officer of which wrote an open letter on 8 July to be read by officers to all ranks. It is worth quoting at length:

> Here … we find ourselves in what is actually the front line, and it is apparent that while some of you realise the position, others are endeavouring to 'rationalise' their own behaviour by blinding themselves to the fact that at any moment they may have to fight and stay fighting – no withdrawal – where they are. It is for this reason only that you are being put to work hard and regularly, why you cannot have leave when you want it, except for the gravest reasons, and why we cannot allow you to be further away from your posts than will enable you to return to them in five minutes … . I must emphasise that anyone who, at this serious time, may seek questionable means to evade his responsibilities and to obtain by unfair methods the privileges necessarily denied to his comrades is little less than a traitor to his comrades. Any man who at such a time goes absent, who applies for leave on grounds shown by the Police to be non-existent, who applies for a transfer for reasons no more compelling now than in our earlier peaceful periods, who goes sick unnecessarily – any such individual is at this stage little better than a deserter in the face of the enemy … .[109]

---

107 TNA WO 166/4407 (War Diary, 1st/5th Lancashire Fusiliers), Battalion Orders, 24.12.40.

108 D. French, '"Tommy is No Soldier": The Morale of the Second British Army in Normandy, June–August 1944', in B. Holden-Reid (ed.), *Military Power. Land Warfare in Theory and Practice* (London, 1997), pp. 154–78; Crang, 'British Soldier', *passim*.

109 TNA WO 166/4454 (War Diary, 7th Manchester Regiment), Essential knowledge for all personnel, 9.7.40.

Such difficulties were perhaps inevitable, given that 55th Division contained an overwhelming proportion of citizen soldiers new to the ranks who had been posted to the other side of the country in the midst of an invasion crisis. Dissatisfaction with the lack of leave at this time was not confined to the 7th Manchesters: 117th Field Regiment, while reporting that their men seemed to relish the prospect of action, noted in the same time that 'the lack of leave is being felt, however; there has been no leave since early May'.[110] The absence of leave clearly remained an issue in the case of 7th Manchester – so much so, in fact, that some dependants apparently took it upon themselves to bring an end to the separation, as by October the battalion war diary reported that soldier's families who had arrived within the battalion area should leave.[111]

Attempts to gauge morale can also be made by examining the frequency of offences tried at court martial and the rate of desertion. Where there is evidence, it shows that serious offences against military discipline were rare. In eight months the 7th Manchester held 12 courts of inquiry and six Field General Courts Martial, and had one soldier tried in a civil court.[112] The offences in the latter two categories are not listed but courts of inquiry were usually held to establish the cause of injuries, chiefly whether they were self-inflicted wounds. Such cases did occur; for example, two privates from 2nd Liverpool Scottish were charged with smashing their hands on leave in order to avoid military service.[113] The national register of charges for General Courts Martial for 1940 lists only 14 cases for Suffolk, mostly cases of theft, insubordination, absence without leave and loss of property.[114] Where war diaries appear to consistently list incidents of desertion, the rates are tiny: in eight months the 7th Manchesters listed only two, while over a five-month period the 6th South Wales Borderers had only one.[115] While these recorded incidents are few, it is possible that they are masking other instances that were dealt with internally and not recorded. A similar lack of evidence for field punishments means that it is almost impossible to get an accurate picture of the kinds of charge soldiers commonly faced. Many lesser breaches of discipline were dealt with in-house by the units concerned and tend not to enter the documentary record. In the one case in this study where 'daily orders' exist and do show the kinds of infraction that crossed the commanding officer's desk, the majority of punishments were fines or confinement to barracks for cases of absence without leave, minor deficiencies in kit and petty insubordination. In April 1943, for example, of some 27 incidents recorded in daily orders 11 were for absence without leave.[116] But here the lengths of time offenders were away from their units hint at men returning late to barracks after curfew having

---

110 TNA WO 166/1529 (War Diary, 117th Field Regiment, Royal Artillery), 4.7.40.

111 TNA WO 166/4454 (War Diary, 7th Manchester Regiment), 10.10.40.

112 *Ibid.*

113 TNA WO 166/4434 (War Diary, 2nd Liverpool Scottish), 21.10.40

114 TNA WO 86/97 (General Courts Martial Register of Charges).

115 TNA WO 166/8993 (War Diary, 6th South Wales Borderers), 25.3.42.

116 TNA WO166/12482 (War Diary, 5th Royal Berkshire Regiment), April 1943, *passim.*

missed buses or trains, rather than actual desertion. For such petty infractions a pragmatic approach was taken, one brigadier recommending that 'for minor offences, 2 days CB (confined to barracks) etc only irritated the men, and that it was much better to give the man a good telling off and really frightening him'.[117] There were probably countless minor incidents that went unmentioned and only a very few that escalated to such an extent that they found their way into the documentary record, such as the RSM of the 2nd Liverpool Scottish who was honourably acquitted over a charge of threatening to shoot a private and striking a soldier.[118]

Occasionally soldiers ended up in civilian courts for offences, and these cases conform to the pattern seen elsewhere in the army.[119] With so many houses in the Sandlings vacated by their owners, theft was a common offence and in 1940 units issued orders against looting.[120] In the majority of cases that came before civilian courts most instances of breaking and entering was caused by the lure of unoccupied but still partially furnished buildings, and in most cases were carried out by those with a criminal background. Cases such as the four privates who found themselves on charges of theft in 1940 and were bound over for a year were probably common; in this instance an officer stated that 'these men are distinctly unsavoury characters. They are no credit to any unit but a hindrance to all military discipline. They have been a continual source of trouble.'[121] A different, but probably equally telling, case was that of a Private Rawlins, who, wanting to return to his home town of Wrexham, stole a bicycle at Felixstowe but made only 30 miles and dumped the bike at Woolpit. With eight previous convictions and only a month out of a borstal, he was remanded for sentence but allowed to return to his regiment before receiving a three-month jail term.[122]

Conclusion

The 'experience' of military life in the Sandlings was thus defined by a range of factors that varied according to year, season, geography and rank. During 1940/41 coastal defence was characterised by hard labour, often in basic material conditions. In 1942/43, by contrast, it had become more akin to garrison duty, with greater physical comfort and a heavier emphasis on training. In this sense, it arguably became less distinctive and had more in common with the activities of other units in the Home Army. But there is a general agreement that it was characterised by hard physical work and long periods of time looking out to sea, and could be an isolating existence. But for the infantryman it was probably as close as you would get to the real operations while serving at home.

---

117 TNA WO 166/975 (War Diary, 125th Infantry Brigade), Points from Brigadier's Conference, 17.10.40.

118 TNA WO 166/4434 (War Diary, 2nd Liverpool Scottish), 29.5.40.

119 C. Emsley, *Soldier, Sailor, Beggarman, Thief: Crime and the British Armed Services since 1914* (Oxford, 2013).

120 TNA WO 166/4451 (War Diary, 5th Manchester Regiment), 5 Manch Operational Order No. 1, Amendment No. 1, November 1940.

121 *The Felixstowe Times*, 20.1.40.

122 *Ibid.*, 7.11.42.

Chapter 8

The civilian landscape

The previous chapter examined the wartime experience in the Sandlings through the eyes of the soldier; this discussion builds on some of these themes in order to assess how militarisation impacted upon the civilian landscape. While Britain's 'Home Front' is a subject in its own right, the effect of the conflict on non-combatants living in military zones has attracted little attention from the perspective of landscape history.[1] As has been seen, the militarisation of the Sandlings took a variety of forms: anti-invasion defences of considerable scale and longevity; large areas set aside for training; airspace actively defended from before the start of hostilities almost until their end; civilian buildings variously abandoned, occupied or given alternative uses. Yet, when placed in the longer view, the conflict was only a brief, albeit intense, period in a much longer and distinctive regional history. While the war shaped the landscape, the landscape also shaped perceptions of the war.

The wartime landscape

Almost from the start of the conflict, wartime governments enacted a series of measures that intruded on the peacetime civil liberties of their citizens, especially in regard to control of property, rights of entry and search, the detention of individuals appearing to contravene public safety or the defence of the realm and the production and dissemination of anti-war sentiment.[2] Although it hardly needs stating, the civilian population of the Sandlings ultimately had few legal rights when it came to military use of their land or property. While compensation could be claimed for loss of rent and income, when it came to deciding how best to deal with the defence of the realm the military had a legal framework at their disposal that ensured they could effectively do whatever they wished. The majority of military works were put in place under the

---

1   The classic study is A. Calder, *The People's War: Britain 1939–1945* (London, 1969), with a more recent general survey J. Gardiner, *Wartime Britain, 1939–1945* (London, 2004); of the more specialist literature perhaps the most relevant here is A. Marwick, *The Home Front: the British and the Second World War* (London, 1976); J. Harris, 'War and Social History: Britain and the Home Front during the Second World War', *Contemporary European History*, 1 (1992), pp. 17–35; H.L. Smith (ed.), *Britain in the Second World War: A Social History* (Manchester, 1996); M. Smith, *Britain and 1940: History, Myth and Popular Memory* (London, 2000); S. Rose, *Which People's War* (Oxford, 2003).

2   N. Stammers, *Civil Liberties in Britain during the Second World War* (Beckenham, 1983).

Figure 8.1. Late 1930s air-raid shelters in the grounds of St Felix School, Southwold.

authority of various regulations derived from the Emergency Powers (Defence) Act of 1939. Anti-invasion defences were chiefly enacted under the authority of Defence Regulation (DR) 50, which permitted the military to enter land and construct fieldworks (known as Temporary Defence Works) on the grounds of public safety or the prosecution of the war. In addition, DR 51, which gave the military full power of requisition and eviction of civilians, was occasionally used, but generally only where anti-invasions works had a more permanent character, such as ECDBs.[3] As was seen in Chapter 5, DR 51 was also used to take specific blocks of land for training, while other land was taken under the auspices of DR 52, which, while giving the military control, was less restrictive on civilians. That full powers of requisition were used only in particular circumstances is of interest in itself, as it stands in contrast to the use of coercive force to build fortifications elsewhere in Europe during the conflict. On the Atlantic Wall, for example, the use of forced labour and the arbitrary seizure of land were routine. While there is a critical distinction to be made between Britain's wartime landscape, which was created by a home army in defence of its sovereign territory, and that of occupied Europe, which was controlled by a totalitarian regime acting to protect its territorial conquests, the way in which the army used its legal powers indicates a certain subtlety both in how the military perceived its role and in the perception of militarisation by those whose lives were changed as a result.

---

3   Foot, *Beaches, Fields, Streets, and Hills*, p. 2.

The militarisation of the Sandlings took place slowly, with the tone set before the outbreak of war by the construction of air-raid shelters for the civilian population under fear of the bomber threat (Figure 8.1). As discussed in Chapters 2 and 4, thereafter the build-up was gradual, with modest forces deployed in November 1939 after the issue of the J.C. Plan, a flurry of activity on HAA sites and the initial deployment of searchlights. A more profound shift occurred in May 1940 with the onset of the invasion crisis, which changed the landscape out of all recognition and significantly intruded on the lives of the civilian population, as the coastal hinterland was declared a defence area and those living outside required a permit to gain entry. Within this zone the movement of civilians was curtailed and the use of private transport discouraged or banned; a curfew was imposed; beaches were closed to the public; residential and commercial properties were given over to or taken by the army; and road signs were removed. The iconic and historic buildings of the coastline underwent a transformation as seaside piers were immobilised, parish churches pressed into use as observation posts and landmarks camouflaged. There was also a large movement of people. From April 1940 the Sandlings witnessed a progressive influx of military personnel that were accommodated in towns, villages and new encampments; Ipswich was reported as 'swimming with troops enjoying a good city pavement' after 55th Division deployed to East Anglia that month.[4] The overcrowding at places such as Felixstowe and Lowestoft, which were becoming major naval establishments, is often a feature of post-war accounts; HMS *Europa*, in Lowestoft, was described as a 'poverty-stricken set up … [where] there were maltots [*sic*] in every room, and three or four to a bed if you could find a bed … table manners were unheard of, if you didn't grab it, ten others did'.[5] Somewhat ironically, given that the Suffolk coast had initially received evacuees from London, from the summer of 1940 civilians in the coastal defence zone were encouraged to leave and a significant drop in population took place as people fearful that their homes were about to become a battleground left to stay elsewhere. As one women from Woodbridge put it: 'I'm taking the kids and going to stay in Derby with my Dad for the duration, and I'm going to have a good binge here on Sunday night before I go.'[6] While the number of civilians who left at this time is difficult to gauge precisely, wartime estimates suggested a drop in population of approximately two-thirds in seaside towns.[7] Others chose to stay because their livelihoods depended on farming or fishing or simply because they decided not to leave or had no other place to go. Sufficient people remained to ensure that many local schools and businesses

---

4   TNA WO 166/4434 (War Diary, 2nd Liverpool Scottish), 20.4.40.

5   Foynes, *Battle of the East Coast*, p. 192.

6   Mass Observation Archive, File Report 170, Suffolk Village Report, 6.6.40.

7   TNA WO 166/957 (War Diary, 45th Infantry Brigade), Appendix CC Evacuation of Coastal Towns, 1.6.41; SRO (Ipswich) EE1/P12/2 (Aldeburgh Invasion Committee, Military Reps File), Aldeburgh Civil Defence Scheme, 30.6.42.

remained open, but one of the most vivid and enduring perceptions of the coastal landscape at this time was that the rural countryside was largely empty aside from the substantial military presence, with only military traffic on the roads.[8] The speed and nature of these changes provoked understandable tensions between the military and the civilian population that manifested itself in a variety of ways.

The arrival of thousands of soldiers provoked a certain amount of consternation from civilians, chiefly on account of behaviour that was usually the preserve of garrison towns. Exuberance on the part of troops drew much unfavourable comment. In June 1940 one report from the Mass Observation Survey noted that a young lady at a dance at Hollesley had remarked that 'I don't think much of these soldiers here tonight. They think so much of themselves. They're not real Scotsmen anyhow, even if they do wear a kilt' – a jibe clearly directed at the resident Liverpool Scottish – while an overheard conversation related how a group of soldiers had knocked at village doors one evening and threatened to enter and sleep with the female occupants. This particular incident had engendered the observation by one mother that 'They go up the pole, them young fellers, when they've had a drink or two. They don't do no harm though.'[9] By August of that year it was reported that in south Suffolk there was a 'distinct lack of friendliness towards the numerous soldiers in the area and there was some antagonistic talk about them'.[10] The following year a similar survey noted that around Alderton the main criticism was the 'destructive mass of soldiers' and the mess being created by the digging of defences.[11] Typical of such grievances was that by the owner of Hopton Beach Holiday Camp near Lowestoft, who complained in 1940 that

> When the 419 Battery RA left my camp, on the very day they left one of their Officers drove a vehicle into one of my Chalets … a washbasin in the lavatories was also broken by the men, and I understand these matters were reported to the responsible military authorities with a view to having them put right.[12]

Damages remained an issue throughout the war and while, as we have seen, there were incidents of looting, most losses were the result of constant low-level activity, such as taking building materials for firewood and day-to-day breakages, rather than pure vandalism, but their cumulative effect was considerable. On the Ogilvie estate around Thorpeness and Minsmere estate houses were found to be without floorboards, stairs, windows and doors when military control was relinquished, a situation that

---

8   Robertson, *Rose and the Arrow*, p. 49; I. Hamilton, *Alun Lewis. Selected Poetry and Prose* (London, 1966), p. 38.

9   Mass Observation Archive, File Report 170, Suffolk Village Report, 6.6.40.

10   Mass Observation Archive, File Report 372, Morale in Coastal Suffolk, 28.8.40.

11   Mass Observation Archive, File Report 703, East Suffolk Village, May 1941.

12   Jarvis, *Fortress Lowestoft*, p. 25.

was probably commonplace.[13] Tensions with civilian authorities also tended to surface when military activity led to the dislocation of normal routines or resulted in economic hardship. In Lowestoft as early as April 1940 the town clerk objected to the building of the battery on Gunton Cliff because the

'Esplanade is in a high class residential district and it would be a considerable inconvenience to the residents there to have a portion of this road closed' and to the closing of the North Sea wall because 'the military authorities will appreciate that while the civil population must be put to a certain amount of inconvenience in wartime, there should be as little interference with civil life as possible'.[14]

Restrictions on transport within the Defence Zone caused difficulties for many and were clearly resented: those used to taking summer trips to the coastline found they could no longer do so; the stopping up of roads and footpaths with barbed wire meant that even the most routine tasks were either difficult or impossible; fishermen complained that it was difficult to get their catches to market; and there was general annoyance at having to stop at roadblocks in order to show identity papers.[15] At Kessingland, in one of the few cases where the potential for direct conflict with civilians is recorded in a military war diary, local police reported to the army that there 'would likely be trouble' with local fisherman, as their slipways on the beach had been removed in order to create a field of fire.[16]

More contentious were the effects of the collapse of the tourist industry, which was particularly hard felt in holiday resorts. Even during the summer of 1940, when beaches were in the process of being closed and shoreline defences erected, town councils made attempts to keep the holiday season going for as long as possible. By the middle of June mines had still to be placed on the beaches at the main resorts, presumably because they were being saved until the last possible moment.[17] Even when minefields were laid, a clear tension existed between the military, who wanted to keep people away, and the desire on the part of residents to access parts of the coastline where possible; on occasion engineers were ordered to create the impression that whole beaches, rather than specific sections, were mined so that civilians would not intrude.[18] The loss of

---

13   H. Welch, *The Minsmere Scrapbook* (Westleton, 2000).

14   TNA WO 199/1167 (Fixed Defences, Lowestoft, 1940–42), Town Clerk to War Department Land Agent, 5.4.40.

15   Mass Observation Archive, File Report 372, Morale in Coastal Suffolk, 28.8.40; *The Felixstowe Times*, 3.8.40, 30.11.41; SRO (Ipswich) OHT 134.

16   TNA WO 166/4679 (War Diary, 1st/4th South Lancashire Regiment), 1.6.40.

17   SRO (Lowestoft) 491/12F/28 (Requisition of Land and Property), Instructions Regarding Safety Precautions, 13.6.40. When dates are given for the laying of minefields in 1940 from war diaries, it confirms that those beaches that received mines first were not those of holiday resorts, which, presumably, were still open.

18   TNA WO 166/3670 (War Diary, 200th Field Company, Royal Engineers), Orders, 4.11.40.

revenue from tourism was the source of protracted correspondence as town councils sought to offset the loss of earnings by obtaining compensation from the War Office. The corporation of Southwold claimed for loss of holiday lets, removal by the military of beach huts and other buildings, and lost revenue from bathing and chair plots.[19] A particular bone of contention was the extent to which the closing of beaches to the public could constitute a basis for loss of income. The War Department tended to take a dismissive approach to such grey areas, with one official summing up the position in relation to Southwold in simple terms: 'due to the fortunes of war many people may be debarred access from places which were apparently open to the public'; there was, the War Office felt, a limit to what could be claimed as a result.[20] This sense of dislocation caused to civilians by the rapid militarisation of the coastline was summarised by an observer from the Mass Observation Survey after a visit to Aldeburgh, where the depression of civilians, it was noted:

> would seem to a large extent to be directly due to economic facts, and therefore not to be comparable to true morale depression which is largely caused by fear and fantasies. The economic basis of Aldeburgh life is the summer holiday season, and this has been wiped out. Even the local golf club is shut down. No one is allowed near the beach, which is covered with obstructions, the cause of much unfavourable comment from the civilians who wonder whether it will ever be possible to make the beach look nice again.[21]

A closed landscape: settlement evacuation

The extreme end of requisitioning land and property was the compulsory evacuation of settlements, whole or in part. Such occurrences were rare in the Sandlings, as the military could usually meet their needs without enforced removals and occasions where they could not reflected very specific circumstances. One such case was the small fishing village of Shingle Street, the only place in the Sandlings where a whole community was displaced on account of anti-invasion works.

Here the spatial relationship between the defences and the settlement were unusual in that the village lay to the seaward side of the main defence line, marked by a wet anti-tank ditch a little inland. The single road from the village crossed this ditch at Dumb-boy Sluice, which formed the strongpoint for the local defence. The bridge was prepared for demolition and the road itself mined. Shingle Street therefore sat rather incongruously in the front line and would, in the event of an invasion, have been entirely cut off. A more immediate problem was the presence of the minefield, with the mines themselves initially relaid each night in order to permit civilian access during

19   SRO (Lowestoft) 491/12F/28 (Requisition of Land and Property), Southwold Borough Town Clerks World War Two Records, Town Clerk to W.D. Land Agent and Valuer, July–December 1941.

20   *Ibid.*, Harrison to Naunton, 23.12.41.

21   Mass Observation Archive, File Report 372, Morale in Coastal Suffolk, 28.8.40.

the day.[22] Such a situation became untenable as the invasion crisis developed, however, and 55th Division recommended that the village be compulsorily evacuated. Official notice on 23 properties was served on 22 June 1940, with the occupants having to depart by midnight three days later.[23] The inhabitants left without obvious protest and were assisted in so doing by the army, and a short time later almost all those affected had found alternative accommodation in neighbouring villages. But hardship had been caused. One widow related how she had had an income of ten shillings a week and lived in her own home prior to the evacuation, whereas 'now I am turned out and having to pay 6/- a week in rent'; and, to compound the situation, her empty house had been broken into and looted by soldiers.[24] An initial difficulty was that the official evacuation order had been served by civilian authorities, albeit on army advice, and this legal technicality clouded the issue over how compensation should be administered, as claims could be directed against the War Office only when property had been taken directly by the military themselves. Soon former residents and landlords began asking for clarity on the grounds on which they had been evicted and where to direct claims for loss of rent and income. It was only in 1941 that a resolution was agreed and a military requisition agreed upon and backdated, largely for the purposes of clarifying the situation with regards to compensation.

But, as a landscape devoid of civilians, in 1942 Shingle Street became the focus of interest from the Chemical Defence Research Department for use as an experimental bombing range. In a knowing breach of the initial undertaking that requisitioned properties would not be used as targets, the buildings were bombed by chemical ordnance in March 1943. Later that year the possibility of civilian reoccupation was mooted, but did not take place owing to the continued existence of mines and other anti-invasion defences and the fact that the bombing trials had rendered the majority of houses unfit for habitation and beyond repair. In 1945 one report commented that 'Shingle Street in short, cannot be looked at as a potential habitable hamlet, but as an extremely dangerous and awkward minefield' and the eventual clean-up was so protracted that residents started to return only from 1948.[25]

The events at Shingle Street were exceptional and did much to fuel the post-war myth that it was the scene of a failed German invasion. But the majority of dislocation to rural settlement during the conflict came not from the building of anti-invasion defences but rather from the establishment of training grounds, chiefly from 1942 onwards. The demands for land for training meant that the Sandlings was probably more heavily militarised during 1944 than it was at any other time in the conflict. When 79th Armoured and 49th Divisions were concurrently using the Orford and

---

22   TNA WO 166/1038 (War Diary, 165th Infantry Brigade), 18.6.40.
23   For what follows see, TNA HO 207/1175 (Compulsory Evacuation of Shingle Street).
24   *Ibid.*, Burwood to Defence Commissioner, 14.8.40.
25   TNA HO 207/1175 (Compulsory Evacuation of Shingle Street), F.W.C. to Philipson, 13.4.45.

Dunwich/Southwold areas respectively there were more troops stationed in the Sandlings than there had been guarding it in 1940–41. Military control was also more pervasive. The closer D-Day came the greater was the concern for secrecy, with the result that training areas became more than ever 'closed' landscapes, to the extent that Home Guard were to be excluded from coast-watching duties while exercises were ongoing.[26] The demands of training were also responsible for the displacement of civilians, which occurred on a large scale in two places: in June 1942 in the villages of Iken and Sudbourne, where over 400 civilians were compulsorily evacuated owing to the establishment of the Orford Battle Training Area, and the following year between Dunwich and Sizewell, where just over 100 people were removed in the expansion of the Dunwich Training Area.[27]

The arrangements for the removal of the civilian population are particular clear at Orford, where the civilian reaction to the notice to move was initially one of opposition but moved swiftly to one of compliant co-operation, in part because of the way in which the circumstances were handled. The short notice of the requisition orders caused a degree of shock bordering on outrage, especially given that farmers had been encouraged to plant crops the previous year. Antagonism also centred on the question of why occupants were required to leave their homes when there were other empty properties in the area, the nature of proposed rehousing and compensation, and how economic hardship would be offset. Letters of complaint were penned to government ministers and two residents visited Whitehall in an unsuccessful attempt to seek a personal meeting with Winston Churchill in order to voice their objections.[28] The tone of opposition is seen in one of the letters of protest, sent by a resident to the Minister of Security:

> why were we all allowed to plant every available piece of land, now, all the crops are coming on beautifully and we all asked to vacate our freehold houses leaving all behind … one does not expect to be forced from our homes when there are plenty of other vacant spaces about, is this what our men are fighting for? Only last evening a man who had a good deal of land under cultivation said it would have been better for us to have been bombed out by the germans [sic] as we would have received some consideration.[29]

These initial protests soon gave way to pragmatic fatalism as it became clear that the fate of the two villages was already sealed. The tipping point seems to have been

---

26 TNA WO 205/1092 (Assault Training Areas, Eastern Command 1943), 1.5.44.

27 TNA HO 207/1180 (Battle Training Areas, 1942–1945), File 1, Part 2, Women's Voluntary Services Report on the Evacuation of A Battle Area in East Suffolk, c.July 1942; TNA HO 207/1182 (Dunwich–Sizewell Battle Training Areas), Dunwich Battle Area, WVS to Cranbrook, 12.9.43.

28 TNA HO 207/1180 (Battle Training Areas, 1942–1945), File 1, Part 3, Chase to Minister of Security, 14.6.42; F. Waddell, 'The Evacuation of Sudbourne and Iken', *Orford and District Local History Bulletin*, 11 (2008), pp. 11–13.

29 TNA HO 207/1180 (Battle Training Areas, 1942–1945), File 1, Part 3, Chase to Minister of Security, 14.6.42.

public meetings in Sudbourne and Iken where the population were addressed both by an army general who explained the military rationale and also by the local MP, who made the point that he had already unsuccessfully lobbied on the villagers' behalf. The impression from government sources is one of stunned resignation on the part of those evacuated; most people, it was noted,

> have lived in the same parish for generations. The shock of eviction is therefore much greater than it would be for a more urban and sophisticated population, less tied by tradition to their homes and the surrounding country. Nevertheless, the majority showed very real self-sacrifice and patriotism in accepting the situation. It is interesting to note that the bitterness and most vocal opposition has come from a few 'intellectuals', newcomers to the area.[30]

In large part, therefore, those affected seem to have accepted that eviction was inevitable and instead sought to achieve the most beneficial settlement.

While carried out hurriedly, a number of government agencies worked collaboratively to ensure that the removal took place as smoothly as circumstances allowed, albeit with actions guided as much by sensitivity to adverse publicity as by altruism. Advice centres were established in both villages and it was at this very local level that the exact arrangements for relocation were worked out. The majority of householders found accommodation in neighbouring villages soon after the first notices of eviction were issued, but for those that could not properties were requisitioned as alternatives and a military building released so that it could provide a hostel for the elderly.[31] The Women's Voluntary Service (WVS) spent considerable time helping families to pack and move belongings, one report vividly describing how 'some families have been moved with their personal belongings, dogs, cats, canaries, baby chicks, old hens, clocks, wireless sets etc in WVS cars, …'.[32] For those whose livelihood was based on farming, the county War Agricultural Committee sought to minimise the economic impact. The requirements of the wartime economy meant that farm workers would easily find work elsewhere, with the greatest difficulty those farm hands who had lived in the area all their lives and did not want to work some distance away; here it was suggested that such individuals should be picked first by neighbouring farmers hiring new labourers.[33] The move was more disruptive for those with well-established farms. Of the 14 working farms in the new training area ten occupiers continued on reduced holdings elsewhere, three sold up completely and one

---

30   TNA HO 207/1180 (Battle Training Areas, 1942–1945), File 1, Part 2, June 1942.

31   *Ibid.*, File 1, Part 3, Battle Training Areas, 29.6.42.

32   *Ibid.*, File 1, Part 2, Women's Voluntary Services Report on the Evacuation of A Battle Area in East Suffolk, *c.*July 1942.

33   *Ibid.*, File 1, Part 3, War Agricultural Executive Committee County of East Suffolk to Cranbrook, 26.6.42.

Figure 8.2. Entrance to Orford Battle Training Area. Rare unofficial wartime photo c.1943 showing the rudimentary nature of one of the entrances. (Orford Museum)

sold up and relocated to a second, smaller farm. For those required to leave, the legal criteria for compensation were stretched to the limit. The evicted were to be treated in the same way as families who had lost homes and livelihoods as a result of bombing, specifically so that compensation and ex-gratia hardship payments could be issued.[34] But the way the evacuation was conducted should in no way deny the trauma of the events for those concerned. In the case of one elderly man who ran the local cobbling business, it was fatal. As a result of his concern over his livelihood considerable efforts were made to move his business and workshop to a new location near Woodbridge, but the man died before the move; his subsequent burial in Sudbourne church was one of only three occasions during the war when the training area was closed (Figure 8.2).

Perhaps because of the sensitivities involved, the War Office was subsequently at pains to ensure that the reasons for the evictions were seen to be bound up in the national war effort. The importance of the new training ground was stressed in the national and local media as journalists reported favourably and in great detail on the activities now taking place. Troop training was now more realistic and the area a proving ground for 'pluck and leadership', while at the same time civilian properties were being treated with respect; a visit of the king to view exercises gave royal sanction to the new arrangements.[35] On the area itself a series of concessions to the agricultural economy was enacted before the military had completely free rein. Training was suspended for two short windows to allow the harvesting of wheat and sugar beet and a series of standing orders was issued with the intention of militating against the worst excesses of military use: troops were forbidden to enter the two parish churches; buildings were not to be used as targets; woods, sea walls and sluices were not to be damaged.[36] While such efforts represented a well-meaning attempt to preserve the

---

34   *Ibid.*, File 1, Part 2, Memorandum dated 22.6.42.

35   *The Felixstowe Times*, 5.9.42; 19.9.42; *The Times*, 17.9.42.

36   TNA HO 207/1180 (Battle Training Areas, 1942–1945), File 1, Part 1, Instruction for the use of ORFORD Battle Training Area, October 1942.

interests of civilians, the reality fell far below the ideal. Army use of the area drew complaint, the most vocal of which came from the Ipswich MP and prominent military critic Richard Stokes, with the chief charge that the army had failed in their undertaking to keep property in good repair.[37] Here criticism was justified. By May 1943 a report on houses in the training area showed that some 90 per cent had either been forcibly entered, their boundary walls had been broken or they otherwise showed signs of damage. The windows at High House Farm were broken, with bullet holes in the internal doors and plaster, and the front door had been damaged by shrapnel; the three outbuildings at Valley Farm had been destroyed by fire, with the farmhouse itself having lost all its glass windows, with bullet and shrapnel holes internally and externally; the Chequers Inn at Sudbourne had been forced open and, despite the absence of a working flush, its toilets repeatedly used. A report by the Royal Engineers estimated that the area would need to be closed for two months to repair damage up to that date and thereafter for one week each month. This was evidently not possible, as it was in use seven days a week and only closed one day a month for maintenance, and, in the event, only 'first aid' repairs were carried out, with houses wind- and weather-proofed and points of entry secured against unauthorised access.[38]

In all these ways, the conflict impinged directly on the lives of the civilian population of the Sandlings. But the effects of militarisation were not confined to the physical dislocation caused by the building of defences and the establishment of training grounds. The changes brought about by the conflict also impacted upon perceptions of the landscape, not least because the appearance of the countryside after the changes was so much at odds with that of the pre-war period.

Imagining the wartime Sandlings

In many ways the Sandlings landscape is quintessential East Anglia. It is a place of long, gentle lines with a vast open sky. Much of its distinctive character derives from the juxtaposition of the coastline with heath and marsh, which in places blend almost seamlessly with the beaches to make, in extent if not always in detail, a landscape unique in the British Isles (Figure 8.3). The idiosyncrasies of the Sandlings first began to be appreciated in the late nineteenth century, with the growth of the tourist industry. It was at this time that the distinguishing characteristics that still draw visitors today began to attract favourable comment and the modern perception of the landscape took shape. The particular quality of the countryside was the inspiration for numerous cultural works. From the 1880s Walberswick became associated with the circle of Impressionists led by Philip Wilson Steer, with compositions such as 'The Beach at Walberswick' (c.1889) widely accepted as some of the most authentic

---

37 *Ibid.*, Part 4, Stokes to Cranbrook, 14.5.43.

38 *Ibid.*, Orford Battle Area, 7.5.43; Arrangement, Special Maintenance – Orford Battle Training Area. Period 24 May 43–June 1943, 25.5.43.

Figure 8.3. Typical Sandlings landscape at Benacre. The topography of the coastal landscape was crucial in defining the region's sense of place.

works of Impressionism in British art. Other notable figures from the arts whose work was influenced by the peculiarities of the Sandlings include Charles Rennie Mackintosh, Benjamin Britten, Alfred Lord Tennyson and George Orwell. During the 1930s numerous paintings depicted an idyllic landscape of villages, churches and wide open spaces, which represented a regional take on the inter-war sensibility that English national identity was bound up with notions of the rural landscape.[39] The imagined qualities of the Sandlings can also be seen in the artwork commissioned as part of the 'Recording Britain' programme, in which the nation's architectural heritage and historic environment was recorded by artists in a bid to keep a record of those places felt to be vulnerable to German bombing. Among the Suffolk material Orford, Sudbourne, Bawdsey and Woodbridge all feature prominently, with the dominant image one of a timeless, sleepy region largely untouched by modernity.[40]

Perceiving the military landscape

The extent and nature of the physical changes brought to this landscape by the war struck both residents and outsiders alike. The description of the area between Ipswich and Felixstowe by the American serviceman Robert Arbib, who wrote an account of his time in England almost immediately after the end of the war, stands for many:

39   D. Matless, *Landscape and Englishness* (London, 1988).
40   G. Cumberlege, *Recording Britain*, volume 2 (Oxford, 1947).

Figure 8.4. Photograph of a disguised pillbox at Yoxford taken by an American serviceman stationed at the nearby airfield, c.1944. Such images are valuable not only because they show the nature of local camouflage schemes – Yoxford was a nodal point on the 'Back Line' – but also for showing that even during the conflict such structures were worthy of recording in their own right. (Friends of Leiston Airfield)

the country was a fortress – and these coastal counties were a Siegfried Line. At every turn of the road were concrete pillboxes. The railway lines and aerodromes were lined and ringed with mountainous piles of rusting barbed wire; at every narrow intersection and in the village streets and at bends in the road were big cylinders of concrete, pyramidal blocks of concrete, V shaped stacks of iron rails ready to be formed into tank obstacles. Every flat field had its poles and wires strung out to snare and wreck gliders and airborne troop-carriers … . Everywhere scattered between the concrete pillboxes were the little dugouts in the hedges, lined with sandbags, concealed with bushes and vines and weeds.[41]

The numerous oddities of the defence landscape and the incongruence of the individual works with their surroundings are a consistent feature of wartime writing and often the photographic record (Figure 8.4). For the civilian inhabitants of the Sandlings, the visual transformation of familiar backdrops was so profound that some were moved to record their thoughts and experiences in writing and art. Here the theme of a landscape transformed underpins most works. In 'Walberswick, Then and

---

41   R.S. Arbib, *Here We Are Together: The Notebook of an American Soldier in Britain* (London, 1947), pp. 101–2.

Figure 8.5. Prunella Clough, *Closed Beach*, oil on canvas (1945). The coastal defences of the Sandlings formed the subject of a number of Clough's works as their austere appearance suited her abstract style. (Jonathan Clark Fine Art © Estate of Prunella Clough. All Rights Reserved, DACS 2018)

Now', written by two long-term village residents *c.*1944, it was the physical changes in the countryside that drew comment:

> The bridges have all disappeared
> The sluice is turned about
> To keep the water on the marsh
> Which always kept it out
> The beach is barricaded now
> The lanes are mud and mire
> The footpaths and the lovely walks
> Are strewn with barbed wire
> Big guns firing all around
> Shells burst with all their might
> And aeroplanes overhead are flying day and night
> O Walberswick, O don't despair good times will come again
> When war is done and peace declared prosperity will reign[42]

Similar sentiments can be seen in wartime works of art. While pre-war landscapes of the Suffolk coast tended to focus on subtle shorelines and pastoral scenes, wartime compositions were more avant-garde and neo-romantic in character; oils such as Prunella Clough's *Harbour Works* (1942), *Shoreline and War Defences* (1941–42) and *Closed Beach* (1945) exhibit more Cubist characteristics, with vivid depictions of scaffolding, concrete and wire. Here the surrealist concern with surprise and unusual juxtapositions were tailor-made for wartime defences, as their form contrasted so dramatically with the pre-war ideal (Figure 8.5).[43] Others set the changes down either in memoirs or in autobiography, most notably in the award-winning book *War Boy*, a bittersweet account of a wartime childhood in north Suffolk in a landscape that was variously dangerous and exhilarating and that conveyed, too, the nostalgic sadness at the passing of the wartime community and all the risk and excitement that went with it.[44] In subsequent decades recollections were increasingly recorded as oral history, as only later in life did it become apparent to participants that they were witnesses to events of wider historical importance.[45] But, whatever the means, such was the intensity of the conflict that a generation of East Anglians felt compelled to commit their experiences to posterity.

---

42   S. and C. Adams, 'Walberswick, Then and Now' (*c.*1944). A copy of the poem was exhibited in the village hall for several decades after the war.

43   I. Collins, *Making Waves: Artists in Southwold* (Norwich, 2005), pp. 123–31; P. Cannon-Brookes, *The British Neo-Romantics 1935–1950* (London, 1983).

44   M. Foreman, *War Boy. A Country Childhood* (London, 1989).

45   SRO (Lowestoft) 2250/1 (A Kessingland Boy at War).

The 'disruptive' narrative

For archaeologists interesting in interpreting landscapes with reference to the sensory experience of being within them – the field of phenomenology – there is much potential here.[46] The subject of civilian–military relations is also a subject of interest to those concerned with what is often called 'contestation': landscapes where there are conflicting interests at stake, both in the broadest sense of conflicts of ideology and in more local contexts that often involve questions of power, ownership and access to resources.[47] The military material culture discussed throughout this book could easily be 'read' in such a way as to support a narrative that highlights the disruptive changes brought by the conflict. Indeed, many accounts of militarised landscapes rightly tend to emphasise these kinds of elements and the impact on the farming landscape of military works during the Second World War is well known.[48] In the specific case here, superficially at least, there would appear to be a binary opposition between the pre- and post-war landscapes: the differences between peacetime and wartime, non-militarised and militarised, undefended and defended, rural idyll and modernity. Indeed, it could be argued that the very aspects of the Sandlings that were praised before the war represented complete anathema for the military. Its wide open spaces, long beaches, undulating terrain and broad expanses of heath constituted an almost perfect battlefield for a commander contemplating an amphibious landing. By contrast, those charged with *defending* it and the airspace above wanted the opposite of these pre-war ideals: they required a bounded landscape, one compartmented and broken up, where the enemy could be stopped, corralled and dispatched. As has been seen in Chapters 2–4, the close analysis of defences on the ground reveals the effort that went into creating such a 'closed' landscape, seen at the macro level in the successive divisional schemes of the formations that rotated through the Sandlings and at the micro level in the distribution and layout of pillboxes, barbed wire, anti-tank cubes and minefields. An archaeologically informed analysis would also accentuate the building materials and forms of the structures put into place to defend the coast. In a region characterised by, and often eulogised for, the landscape's softness, where the sea merged with the sand, the placing of rigid lines of anti-tank cubes, scaffolding and pillboxes represented the imposition of inflexible, unfamiliar geometric forms, often constructed from alien materials of concrete and steel, onto the existing countryside.

---

46   C. Tilley, *A Phenomenology of Landscape: Places, Paths and Monuments* (Oxford, 1994); C. Tilley, *The Materiality of Stone: Explorations in Landscape Phenomenology* (Oxford, 2004); J. Brück, 'Experiencing the Past? The Development of a Phenomenological Archaeology in British Prehistory', *Archaeological Dialogues*, 12 (2005), pp. 45–72; S. Hamilton and R. Whitehouse, 'Phenomenology in Practice: Towards a Methodology for a "Subjective" Approach', *European Journal of Archaeology*, 9 (2005), pp. 31–71.

47   B. Bender and M. Winer (ed.), *Contested Landscapes: Movement, Exile and Place* (London, 2000).

48   W. Foot, 'The Impact of the Military on the Agricultural Landscape of England and Wales in the Second World War', in B. Short, C. Watkins and J. Martin (eds) *The Front Line of Freedom. British Farming in the Second World War* (Exeter, 2007), pp. 132–42.

Such a narrative would undoubtedly have a great deal of validity and, as has just been seen, would be based upon a wealth of contemporary evidence – both historical and archaeological – that attests to the shock that militarisation was for the civilian population. It would also help to explain why such a short period of time left such an indelible mark in the region's cultural history.

While such a narrative is undeniably helpful and to a certain extent compelling, it does not tell the whole story. For all the evidence for 'dislocation' on the wartime coast, there is also what could be termed a 'negotiation' narrative that needs to be placed alongside the story of disruption. Such a narrative instead involves a more subtle consideration of how militarisation occurred and how military control actually showed itself on the ground. While, of course, the various schemes of defence and their physical manifestations were imposed by the agents of the state, they were also, at a very local level, 'negotiated'; that is, their placement in the landscape reflected a much wider set of concerns than simply military utility. These concerns revolved around addressing, implicitly or explicitly, the needs of the wartime economy and the civilian population. While the coastal landscape was characterised by dislocation, the evacuation of settlements for defences and training and restrictions on movement, it also saw civilian and military co-operation in the construction and manning of works, economic opportunity and various senses of fear, powerlessness and unity in the face of an external threat. It is significant that the Mass Observation Survey commentary on Aldeburgh in the summer of 1940 quoted above, which noted depression in the town, also went on to say that:

> Plenty of people have left the town, and some have returned again. Those who have never left express frequent contempt for the others, or show a feeling of superiority towards them. This gives a group strength which is helpful in maintaining people's spirits. Considering the town is now perhaps one of the quietest and dullest places in Britain, the degree of depression and irritation in Aldeburgh is not particularly high.[49]

Such comments blur the straightforward division between 'peacetime' and 'wartime' and instead draw attention to the complexity of civilian responses to the changes brought to the Sandlings by the conflict. While there were traumas, shortages and hardships there were also social and economic opportunities, and the landscape evidence – in its broadest sense – points to a particular *kind* of relationship (either real or imagined) between combatant and non-combatants and a certain set of experiences of wartime that were specific to the region. In many ways, it was the loss of this military–civilian relationship that was retrospectively mourned in post-war autobiography and oral history.

---

49   Mass Observation Archive, File Report 372, Morale in Coastal Suffolk, 28.8.40.

Figure 8.6. Rare civilian photograph of the pipe band of the 10th Cameronians on Walberswick Green, 1941. (Michael Stannard)

Figure 8.7. Tank demonstration at Sutton Common, 1941. Such displays were part of a programme of 'soft power', whereby the military attempted to give a softer edge to their activities on the coastline. (IWM H10266)

Civilian attitudes to the military

Military control of the landscape may have had a hard edge when it came to the taking of land and buildings, but such intrusion was carried out concurrently with a campaign of 'soft power' by the army that was intended to promote a particular public-facing image. This took the form of deliberate integration with aspects of civilian life, especially those that tended to reinforce existing hierarchies or power relationships, such as compulsory attendances of personnel at church services in villages closest to billets or camps and the taking of established sites of local importance, such as country houses, as headquarters.[50] The efforts of 15th Division in 1941 are particularly noteworthy in this regard, as the formation deliberately played on their Scottish identity by mounting ceremonial guards outside civic buildings and the shrewd use of regimental pipe bands and displays of highland dancing in public areas. In what is probably a distinct regional memory, the nine-month tenure of the Division seems to have left a lasting mark, appearing in both oral history and the photographic record (Figure 8.6).[51] Occasional larger-scale events also raised the profile of the military and emphasised the national war effort. A military tattoo on Sutton Common in August 1941 saw 4000 munition workers brought to the training area to see parades of tanks and massed pipe bands and be given rides on vehicles, one war diary noting that the occasion was 'Reminiscent of Brighton beach on pre-war Bank Holiday' (Figure 8.7).[52]

At the same time there is abundant evidence for civilian efforts to assist soldiers, usually in the form of recreational events such as concerts or other informal gatherings where individuals or communities showed their appreciation to local servicemen.[53] In January 1941, for example, Leiston arranged a week of evening entertainment for troops, the local press satisfactorily reporting that 'The atmosphere was well described by one man from a searchlight unit who said, mainly to himself, 'Cor this is lovely!'[54] The civilian attitude towards the military necessarily varied, but there is little evidence to suggest that relations were strained to the point where it became a serious issue. Typical of later recollections is that of a resident of Walberswick:

> The local women had a good time with the soldiers. The Cameronians were a wild lot and there were often fights on Saturday nights. There were dances at the pub on the pier in Southwold and the only way to be safe was to get hold of a good strong soldier and stick to

---

50 E.g. TNA WO 166/4434 (War Diary, 2nd Liverpool Scottish), 28.4.40, 1.9.40, 20.10.40; TNA WO 166/4346 (War Diary, 11th Highland Light Infantry), 23.3.41; TNA WO 166/3748 (War Diary, 279 Field Company, Royal Engineers), 27.7.41.

51 TNA WO 166/4592 (War Diary, 6th Royal Scots Fusiliers), 12.4.41, 26.4.41; SRO (Ipswich) OHT 149; Sharman and Whyte, *Further Suffolk Memories*, p. 193.

52 TNA WO 166/958 (War Diary, 46th Infantry Brigade), 31.8.41.

53 TNA WO 166/4134 (War Diary, 6th Beds and Herts Regiment), 20.1.40; TNA WO 166/4433 (War Diary, 1st Liverpool Scottish), 12.9.40; 17.9.40.

54 *The Leiston Observer*, 18.1.41.

him. The Cameronians used to go to dances and swim back across the river Blyth naked, holding their clothes over their heads, and the girls used to come out and watch them.[55]

Whatever petty tensions existed on the ground, the sum of anecdotal but cumulatively significant evidence is that the arrival of the military provoked small acts of kindness and co-operation that were at least as prevalent as those of contestation. Oral history again provides numerous examples of civilians providing beverages for soldiers on guard duty and of soldier–civilian relationships and marriages.[56] That not all such evidence simply represents post-war nostalgia is sometimes evidenced in war diaries: the 2nd/4th South Lancashires reported in the summer of 1940 that civilians had come forward to volunteer gifts of food and that in some cases soldiers had been allowed to help themselves to produce from orchards; references are made throughout the war to weekly dances for officers and other ranks organised by units to which civilians were invited, as well as various censures about the bringing of civilians, presumably women, into billets.[57] Although care needs to be taken with the recollections of individuals who were children at the time and who saw the war through child's eyes, the reminiscences encountered during the research for this book relate a litany of anecdotes ranging from joy rides on Bren Gun Carriers to amassing collections of cap badges from units stationed in the area. When viewed as a whole, a range of primary evidence is in agreement that the wartime use of the Sandlings was generally characterised by an absence of contestation, but this was never a given; rather, the lack of contestation was a reflection of the specific nature of the civilian–military relationship.

The landscape of negotiation: a closed landscape?

In the same way that the physical configuration of military defences often reflected very local concerns, so too did the social landscape of the wartime Sandlings. While arrangements such as delaying the flooding of marshes and the specific routing of anti-tank ditches reflected the needs of the agricultural landscape, as has already been seen, similar concerns for other civilian activities can also be discerned. This was particularly the case when it came to access to beaches, which, while officially out of bounds, were in fact neither wholly open nor closed. Those who had to use a beach for specific reasons, chiefly lifeboatmen and fishermen who required space to launch their boats and to return, were able to obtain passes to allow access. The importance of the inshore lifeboat arguably increased during the war, as this was the means of rescue for pilots who had ditched in the sea and those seamen whose vessels had struck mines or been

---

55   Shirreff and Sharman, *Suffolk Memories*, p. 17.

56   Sharman and Whyte, *Further Suffolk Memories*, pp. 71–2; *Rose and Arrow*, 48.

57   TNA WO 166/4680 (War Diary, 2nd/4th South Lancashire Regiment) October; TNA WO 166/4407 (War Diary, 1st/5th Lancashire Fusiliers), Battalion Orders, 24.12.40; TNA WO 166/4413 (War Diary, 9th Lancashire Fusiliers), 24.12.40.

crippled by air attack.[58] As a key part of the local economy, the inshore fishing industry had to be accommodated within defence schemes. The compromise was to leave deliberate gaps in the beach defences in order to permit access by small craft. There is evidence for such arrangements at Lowestoft, Kessingland, Southwold, Aldeburgh, Thorpeness and Sizewell; that at Southwold was known as 'Fisherman's Gap' and comprised some 220 metres (250 yards) of beach to the south of the pier.[59] The gaps at Aldeburgh and Thorpeness were smaller, but stand out in aerial photographs as clear breaks in the defences; at Aldeburgh the access point was close to the ECDB, while that at Thorpeness comprised a route straight through the beach defences to the sea. There is no doubt that this was a deliberate tactical compromise on the part of the army; as in the case of Aldeburgh, for example, it was simply assumed that the gap would be spotted from the air and exploited in the event of a raid, with the town's local defence scheme predicated on such an eventuality.[60]

Arrangements for the launching of fishing boats were heavily regulated. At Kessingland detailed instructions existed for what was permitted, with the orders making it plain that the privilege was at the local commander's whim.[61] Around Southwold night fishing seems to have been forbidden in a way that elsewhere it was allowed, while at Lowestoft a glimpse of how such agreements were arrived at comes from the anecdotal evidence that the military price for acquiescence was to receive part of the catch; a price possibly not unreasonable, given the evidence for their otherwise monotonous diet.[62] Such gaps, also the locations where soldiers held bathing parades during the summer, were, additionally, exploited by locals for recreation. For all the official directives stating that beaches were closed to the public and restrictions imposed, the reality was subtly different. While there were no seaside tourists or even those from a little further inland, those immediately on the coast in day-to-day contact with the troops on their doorstep retained some access to their beaches through a variety of small-scale negotiations with local troops. By the middle of the war, when the invasion threat had receded, some bathing had clearly returned to Southwold, where 'Fisherman's Gap' seems to have been habitually used by local swimmers.[63]

Examples of similar local negotiations can be found elsewhere, usually revealed only by oral history. One particularly clear case relates to the building of an encampment on

58   For the frequency of such events see Foynes, *Battle of the East Coast*.

59   SRO (Lowestoft) 491/12F/28 (Requisition of Land and Property), Clark to Naunton after 9.8.43; TNA WO 192/79 (Fort Record Book, Southwold Battery), Tides, Channels, Shoals and Landing Places; TNA WO 166/8726 (War Diary, 2nd Hertfordshire Regiment), Battalion Orders, 24.6.42; J.W. Holmes, 'The Spirit of Lowestoft, A Town at War' *Lowestoft Journal*, Supplementary Issue (1995), 1.

60   TNA WO 166/4413 (War Diary, 9th Lancashire Fusiliers), Revised Scheme for the Defence of Aldeburgh in the Event of a Smash and Grab Raid, 8.12.40.

61   TNA WO 192/72 (Fort Record Book, Kessingland Battery), Regulations for Fishing at Night, 19.9.41.

62   Foreman, *War Boy*, pp. 66–8. Southwold: SRO (Ipswich) OHT 148.

63   SRO (Ipswich) OHT 149; TNA WO 166/8726 (War Diary, 2nd Hertfordshire Regiment), 24.6.42.

Westleton Heath. In late 1943 a policeman and two officers appeared at the farmhouse of a young Roy Strowger with the news that his house was required by the military for an encampment and would be requisitioned. He later recounted how his father replied that 'the next time you come you can bring a gun'. The military subsequently appeared and duly constructed a barbed wire fence around the farmhouse and its driveway and then proceeded to build their camp around the cordoned-off area, leaving the farmhouse an island in the middle of their encampment. Relations between troops and farmer were friendly, with food from the canteen passed over the fence and the farm regularly taking in washing from the camp – albeit only that from the ranks, owing to the farmer's personal experience of the officer class during the First World War.[64] The boundaries of training areas were also not as impermeable as official directives suggested. Newspaper columns drew attention to the dangers of accessing training areas, a sure sign that breaches were routine. Oral history confirms that on occasion the military sanctioned the access of small groups of civilians so that the pre-war practice of taking rabbits and other game and probably also firewood and furze could continue; one resident from Orford noted the occasion a gunner 'played rough' by firing several training rounds at a party of six men taking game on the King's Marshes.[65] Such local agreements and petty negotiations were as much a characteristic feature of life in the wartime Sandlings as those cases where the military simply imposed their will.

Antecedent structures and pre-existing fortifications

Other, less easily described, factors also served to condition civilian attitudes to the military. Despite the increase in physical scale, wartime works were only the most recent manifestation of a much older military tradition. The major anchorages and landing places of the Sandlings at Felixstowe, Hollesley Bay, Sole Bay and Lowestoft Roads, had been defended for centuries and the anti-invasion defences of the Second World War need to be placed within a longer history of militarisation in the Sandlings that, conceptually, ameliorated their dislocating impact.

The rise of Germany in the late nineteenth century not only meant that the east coast ports faced the direction of strategic threat but also exposed the longer intervening stretches of coastline to potential attack.[66] During the First World War the fear of an invasion of Britain by Germany in order to break the deadlock of the Western Front led to the fortification of the east coast in a manner that, although moderate in scale compared with what came 20 years later, was nonetheless significant.[67] Trench systems existed at Leiston and Aldeburgh by late 1915 and the nature of the beach defences is indicated by reports written in the aftermath of the high tide of 13/14

64   Ron Strowger, 'War, Life and Nature on Westleton Common', unpublished typescript.
65   G. Kinsey, *Orfordness, Secret Site* (Lavenham, 1981), p. 71.
66   TNA WO 33/329 (Eastern Defence Scheme), 20.6.14.
67   Appleby *et al.*, *The Home Front in Britain*, pp. 45–9.

Coast Defences, Felixstowe

Figure 8.8. First World War defences at Felixstowe, *c.*1918. Such defences were an important antecedent structure for those built two decades later, both physically and conceptually.

January 1916, which washed away barbed wire and sandbagged emplacements from beaches at Southwold, Walberswick, Sizewell, Thorpeness and Aldeburgh.[68] In the later part of the war the coastal defences were augmented by concrete pillboxes, many of which stood in the same locations as those built two decades later. The extent and visual appearance of First World War defences is seen in a rare photograph of Felixstowe taken *c.*1917, showing barbed wire on the beach, a scene that would not have been altogether unfamiliar to a viewer of the 1940s (Figure 8.8).[69] In some cases this continuity of site took the form of the reuse of older structures. Landguard Fort again became an active military station, ECDBs at places such as Southwold stood close to gun sites of the eighteenth century, Martello towers were pressed into use as observation and machine-gun posts and, where not reused, in places such as East Lane, Bawdsey, the defences of the First World War and earlier conflicts stood cheek by jowl with those of the Second (Figure 8.9). Another portent of things to come was the invasion of airspace, as Suffolk found itself attacked by German bombers and Zeppelins; one of three Zeppelin crash sites in the country lay within the Sandlings, at Theberton.[70] Together with the placing of searchlights in and around Felixstowe and

68 TNA WO95/5455 (War Diary, 2nd/1st Welsh Horse), October 1915; WO 95/5458 (War Diary, 227th Mixed Brigade), 13–14.1.16.

69 SRO (Ipswich) K681/1/158/234 (Felixstowe, *c.*1917).

70 N. Faulkner and N. Durrani, *In Search of the Zeppelin War: The Archaeology of the First Blitz* (Stroud, 2008).

Figure 8.9. First World War pillbox alongside the observation post of the Second World War ECDB at East Lane, Bawdsey. Such places offer a reminder that the Second World War was only one, albeit extensive, period in a much longer history of militarisation.

Ipswich, mobile batteries of anti-aircraft guns were placed on the east coast alongside air stations for defending fighters.[71] The construction of anti-invasion works in the mid-twentieth century was not, therefore, a bolt from the blue; it followed on from a pattern established decades and, in some cases, centuries earlier. In a journal kept by the Southwold town clerk from 1914, the descriptions of German aerial raiders overhead, food shortages, the military presence in the town and the feeling of being in the front line of the war bear direct comparison with those of the subsequent conflict.[72] While the scale of works was greater and altogether more intrusive, large sections of the wartime community already had first-hand experience of what it was like to live in a military landscape. One military report on the morale of the civilian population commented that there was little trouble from East Anglians on account of the fact that 'they've seen it all before in the last war'.[73]

Localism in defence works

The second factor that militated against the excessive dislocating effects of the wartime works was the strong element of localism in their construction and manning. While some defence works were carried out by military personnel themselves much work was

71 C. Cole and E.F. Cheesman, *The Air Defence of Britain, 1914–1918* (London, 1984).
72 M. Moynihan (ed.) *People at War, 1914–1918* (Newton Abbot, 1973), pp. 187–214.
73 TNA WO 166/329 (War Diary, XI Corps), 12.11.39.

devolved to contractors. While some were national firms, such as the house-building firm Wimpey, who were active in north Suffolk in the summer of 1940, local contractors were well-placed to take advantage of the sudden demand. In the Sandlings the established building firm Reades, based in Aldeburgh, was the recipient of a number of significant contracts, including £4266 for the construction of the ECDB at Aldeburgh, £4133 for that at Sizewell and a further £2039 for that at Minsmere. A total of £4258 was paid for the construction of pillboxes, together with an additional £456 for pillbox camouflage and £2951 for anti-tank blocks. Ancillary contracts for war work were received throughout the war and could be of considerable value, such as the £958 recorded in 1941 for the construction of air-raid shelters and hutting.[74] The end of hostilities brought with it a surge of orders for repairs to bomb-damaged buildings; for Reades, the war was a highly profitable period. Such was the demand that much smaller contractors also received wartime contracts, with local firms benefiting from their proximity to the coastline. The aptly named Block Builders at Walberswick constructed the village's anti-tank cubes, with oral history relating how a small petrol-driven cement mixer was used for the task, with additional manpower supplied by the villagers themselves.[75] The longevity of the military presence also meant that, alongside valuable one-off contracts for works, there were recurrent piecemeal opportunities for local companies to supply a variety of items to camps, headquarters, canteens and officers' messes. W. Titlow and Son of Leiston, for example, supplied the military with items as diverse as rat traps, paint and ironmongery, and cork bathmats and brandy and gin for officers' messes.[76] Moreover, the construction of defence works involved not just building contractors but also a variety of other civil agencies, such as the Coastguard, the Water Catchment Board and the Ministry of Transport, all of which connected civilians directly to the anti-invasion landscape. The local element is also seen in the form of the defences themselves. The fabric of pillboxes indicates that, apart from pre-cast embrasures, the building materials were sourced locally. The use of pre-cast concrete blocks for shuttering was prevalent in the south of the county and in the area around Aldeburgh and Thorpeness, while further north, around Walberswick, such blocks were used only on the exterior, with brick shuttering on internal walls. Here the aggregate material was often poor, with the pebbles taken either from beaches or from the nearby Westleton Beds, whose characteristic stones can sometimes be positively identified in pillbox walls. From Southwold to Lowestoft in most cases wooden shuttering seems to have been used and the concrete is of an altogether more solid, less pebbly, aggregate, suggesting that it was made from the gravels around the Pakefield and Kessingland area, a place now known as 'the Denes' and where one extraction pit survives. For these reasons, the anti-invasion defences should, in part, be seen as local co-operative enterprises.

---

74   M.S. Oakes, Lowestoft Ltd, Reades Builders, uncatalogued ledgers, 1940–1945.

75   <http://www.walberswickww2.co.uk/wartime-memories/>, accessed 3.3.17.

76   Long Shop Museum, Leiston, W. Titlow & Son, Sales Ledger, 1940–1945.

Figure 8.10. Orford Defence Committee, 1941. Such committees were made up from a variety of local offices and had an important role in engaging communities in their own defence. (IWM D4847)

Together with civilians' role in the building of fortifications, a variety of civil bodies existed, all of which, at some level, either required liaison with the regular army or contributed to the war effort. The details of these organisations, such as Air Raid Precautions (ARP) or the Royal Observer Corps (ROC), are not important here, other than they all required civilian involvement. Of these, one of the most significant was the local invasion committees, whose purpose was to co-ordinate the civilian response to a military emergency in order to ensure that civil administration both remained in place for as long as possible and worked effectively alongside the military (Figure 8.10). While the extent of active co-operation with the army was necessarily dependant on the task at hand, it was through such agencies that the broader public was brought directly into the war effort.[77] Other collaborative activities included agricultural assistance provided by the army. Piecemeal work on harvesting had been ongoing since at least 1941, but during the winter of 1942/43 considerable manpower was directed at pulling potatoes and sugar beet, albeit that the chief effort took place outside of the Sandlings.[78] Some 1200 men from 54th Division took part in what the

---

77 See a broad discussion of how the Allies successfully harnessed their respective populations in a way the Axis powers did not in R. Overy, *Why the Allies Won* (London, 1995), chapter 9.

78 TNA WO 166/4346 (War Diary, 11th Highland Light Infantry), 25.8.41; TNA WO 199/2510 (Military Assistance to Civil Powers – Agriculture), Harvesting of Sugar Beet and Potatoes, 8.10.42.

Figure 8.11. The Home Guard at Leiston manning anti-tank guns, c.1942. Regardless of the state of training and military efficiency of the Home Guard, they represented an important link between civilian communities and the regular army. (Beyer Peacock & Co Ltd)

commander called a 'frightful infliction', but the task was successful, with the provision of direct payment for troops in cases where it had not been possible to supply working parties with alcohol, noted as a factor in increased efficiency.[79] Such activities drew criticism from commanders, who tended to see them as diverting time from training and downgrading the soldier to the status of a farm labourer, but they did serve to underline the national effort.

Perhaps the most important of civilian organisations was the Home Guard, which gradually assumed a greater significance in local defence schemes to the point that, by 1943, as has been seen, companies were fully deployed alongside regular troops. In some rear areas, especially along the Back Line and at Nodal Points, the majority of the static defence was devolved to Home Guard garrisons almost from the start of the conflict (Figure 8.11). While it was never a priority for regular troops, war diaries attest that co-operative training with the Home Guard was routine. Clearly this activity was believed to be beneficial: after one exercise it was noted that the Home Guard performed well and were capable of undertaking their role with a degree of initiative.[80] In other cases, the recipients of the training were themselves of dubious

79   TNA WO 166/10649 (War Diary, 54th Division, HQ), 3.1.43.
80   TNA WO 166/454 (War Diary, 15th Division, CRE), 10, 17, 24.8.41.

military value, conforming rather to the *Dad's Army* stereotype. In May 1941 the 11th Highland Light Infantry reported that during Exercise Kangaroo, which was designed to test Home Guard efficiency, 'the Home guard at least appeared to enjoy themselves, including 2 old warriors who lay behind a hedge, both over 60, and claimed to have put out of action one Coy, 2 tanks and Bn HQ. One of them was apparently used to a bottle of whiskey before breakfast.'[81] To judge from strength returns, recruitment to the Home Guard was never a problem; rather, across most of the county manning targets were met and sometimes exceeded, which to some extent indicates civilian attitudes to home defence. The social composition of the Home Guard also worked as a force of integration, containing as it did those below military age awaiting conscription, those of military age in reserved occupations and an older generation many of whom were veterans of the First World War. Whatever their military efficiency, as the inheritor of the British amateur military tradition the Home Guard was a crucial mechanism by which the gap between the regular army and the civilian population was blurred.[82]

In other ways, physical defence works did not represent an altogether 'alien' imposition. The idea that the Sandlings was a pre-war idyll may have existed in the mind, but the war was not the first time that state intervention had resulted in landscape change, as the recent Forestry Commission planting at Tunstall, Rendlesham and Dunwich reminded. Moreover, in one case the placing of geometric concrete structures along parts of the coast had been seen prior to the outbreak of war. At Thorpeness – a rare example of a deliberately planned seaside resort – the village was developed by the Ogilve family during the 1920s, when it became an exclusive retreat. The character of the village was set by timber-framed cottages and an element of the fantastic was provided by the creation of the mere and by idiosyncratic buildings such as the disguised water tower known as 'The House in the Clouds'. This facade of a fantasy playground hid an altogether more mundane fabric. Behind the timber framing the shells of the individual buildings were made of brick and concrete. The property boundaries and garden walls were also of concrete, but here they were left bare, with the blocks themselves arranged in decorative forms. Altogether more elaborate, however, were the golf course and the entrance to the tennis courts, the latter comprising a concrete archway reminiscent of a classical portal (Figure 8.12). The Ogilvie house at Sizewell Hall was made of the same material, albeit in this case covered over to give the impression of an antiquity. The fabric confirms that the aggregates are local – many of the pebbles were taken from the adjacent beach – with the blocks themselves manufactured at the nearby estate works. The clear similarities between the Ogilvie works at Thorpeness and the Suffolk Squares in the immediate hinterland of the village suggest that the estate brickworks were the source of the blocks for the pillboxes. It is therefore not quite the case that the creation of the wartime landscape represented the

---

81   TNA WO 166/4346 (War Diary, 11th Highland Light Infantry), 11.5.41.
82   I. Beckett, *The Amateur Military Tradition, 1558–1945* (Manchester, 1991).

Figure 8.12. Entrance to the tennis court at Thorpeness. The construction of pillboxes was not the first appearance of 'modernist' architecture in the Sandlings.

imposition of unfamiliar forms onto the region, as modernity had already, albeit in a small way, reached the Sandlings.

The threat

Underpinning all of the localism in the wartime Sandlings were wider international events. For civilians the war was not just a faraway conflict being played out in continental Europe, the Russian steppes, north Africa and the Pacific; rather, it was a daily reality, with the possibility of mortal danger ever-attendant. Here the concept of what is sometimes called the 'consciousness of war' – the extent to which those beyond the immediate military are aware of conflict – is relevant. As the war played out its course, from initial fear of invasion through to Operation Diver, in the Sandlings – unlike in some other parts of the country – the consciousness of war was high throughout the entire conflict.

The immediacy of the fighting manifested itself in a number of ways, but chiefly through bombing raids and strafing by aircraft. In such circumstances civilians could simply count themselves unlucky enough to be in the wrong place at the wrong time, especially during the 'Fringe' campaign of 1942–43. On other occasions civilians

Figure 8.13. The aftermath of a bombing raid in Lowestoft, 1941. (Suffolk Record Office, Lowestoft)

found themselves singled out for attack and, while there are so many stories it could legitimately be asked if some are apocryphal, oral history is full of accounts of cyclists and farm workers being machine-gunned by aircraft, which at least attests to a perception that such events were deemed likely (Figure 8.13).[83] Clear orders were issued by the military as to the correct procedure for dealing with shot-down enemy aircrew, in part to prevent random acts of retaliation by civilians. It was often during very personal events that the threat from and the attitudes to the enemy revealed themselves. On the rare occasions where the enemy was directly confronted the attitude of civilians was invariably a mixture of fear and hostility. One man recalled how, when he was out with his mother as a boy at Felixstowe,

> when sitting on a grassy bank near to the 'Spa' pavilion, a German fighter plane flew just across the sea-front, very low. The pilot was very clear and waved as he passed. Of course, we, particularly my mother, did not realise how unimportant we were and sat transfixed with fear.[84]

While such events were small beer compared to the campaigns then taking place across the globe, they nevertheless had an important local impact. It was in small-scale and personal encounters that the reality of the conflict was made real, such as the woman at Walberswick whose infant in a pram narrowly escaped death when a bomb landed in her garden and who recalled later that 'strangely I remember being not much frightened but angry about it all because the blast had killed the few chickens we has kept to supplement our rations'.[85]

The sense of vulnerability and powerlessness on the part of civilians fostered an understandable sense of dependency on the military. In 1940 the Mass Observation Survey noted that the feeling of being in the front line and vulnerable to bombing and parachute attack generated a sense of fear and 'underlying tension' among the civilian population that was in part ameliorated by the fortification of the coastline.[86] The vulnerability of civilians in the face of air attack was particularly acute and one resident of Lowestoft described how with the onset of raids in 1940 'we started to sense what real fear was like' and how people took to walking on the outskirts of the town to stay with friends in the hope of avoiding bombs.[87] When HAA batteries were first deployed to the Great Yarmouth/Lowestoft Gun Defended Area local dignitaries

---

83   SRO (Ipswich) OHT 149; BBC Peoples War, <http://www.bbc.co.uk/history/ww2peopleswar/stories/34/a2895834.shtml>, accessed 3.3.17.

84   <http://www.walberswickww2.co.uk/flying-enemy/>, accessed 3.3.17.

85   Sharman and Whyte, *Further Suffolk Memories*, p. 162.

86   Mass Observation Archive, File Report 170, Suffolk Village Report, 6.6.40; Mass Observation Archive, File Report 372, Morale in Coastal Suffolk, 28.8.40; P. Addison and J. Crang (eds), *Listening to Britain* (London, 2011), p. 107.

87   Holmes, *The Spirit of Lowestoft*, p. 20.

went so far as to personally visit the gun sites in order to express their appreciation.[88] Perhaps unsurprisingly, the blame for the hardship, privation and dislocation caused by the war was laid with little ambiguity at the door of the enemy. In so far as it is possible to tell, dislocation of normal life and damage to property caused by friendly forces, while not condoned, was seemingly grudgingly accepted as part and parcel of wartime conditions, whereas damage caused by German activity was interpreted differently. George Carter, who described returning to Aldeburgh while on leave from his position as a river pilot on the Thames, is worth quoting at length on this subject:

> I caught my breath, for Aldeburgh had had its share of the Luftwaffe's attentions. I had seen much bomb damage but this seemed different. My loathing for the Hun became suddenly a very personal thing. A hate too great for my will to contain burst up inside me like a volcano … people had died here, staunch-hearted Aldeburgh folk whom I had known intimately, who had known me as a child. Alf, the friendly postman, who was never too busy to stop for a yarn had been blinded. All the way up the street the little shops, against whose windows I had pressed my nose as a child, stood empty. Mere shells of brick remained, their walls pitted by cannon shell and machine-gun bullets. A jeweller's shop that had one exhibited gorgeous fragments of sea borne amber and cornelian was merely a charred framework.[89]

Such attitudes fed into the broader narrative concerning the civilian interpretation of the conflict. There was an enemy who was responsible for frequent and random violent events that often brought death and destruction to their doorstep. If the fact that the country was at war was obvious enough, then the rationale for the military presence did not need spelling out either. For all of these reasons, something of an unofficial bargain was struck between the military and the civilian population in the Sandlings. Where possible, the military respected the needs of the local population and gave a certain degree of latitude to ameliorate the worst excesses of their activities. In return, the civilian population were largely prepared to tolerate the existence of the military as long as it was felt that their presence was required.

Conclusion

Perhaps because of this, and despite all the physical changes, social dislocation and economic disruption they caused, wartime works became, albeit for a short space of time, an accepted part of the landscape. After 1945 artists returned to the places that had been denied to them during the war, and now, for a brief period, defences found their way into paintings and prints. The iconic places of the Sandlings coastline, such as Dunwich beach, again formed the subject for post-war art, but the anti-tank cubes, pillboxes and makeshift dumps of barbed wire were entirely acceptable parts of

---

88 TNA WO 166/2526 (War Diary, 245th Heavy Anti-Aircraft Battery), 18.10.41; 27.10.41.
89 G. Goldsmith Carter, *Looming Lights* (London, 1945), pp. 164–5.

Figure 8.14. Frederick Baldwin, *Walberswick and Southwold from Dunwich* (1953).

Figure 8.15. Photograph from Dunwich Beach. (By permission of Dunwich Museum)

compositions. Frederick Baldwin's *Walberswick and Southwold from Dunwich* (1953) shows anti-tank cubes and pillboxes seemingly without any attempt to render them as incongruous with otherwise idyllic scenery and holiday makers enjoying the beach (Figure 8.14). Works such as these retain the pre-war sense of landscape, but with the remains of the defences now part of the scene.

Dunwich beach also boasts a number of unusual photographs from the late 1940s or early 1950s in which the defences are the actual subject.[90] Two show the familiar artist's view, looking north from the beach towards Walberswick (that shown in Figure 8.15 seems to have been taken from almost the same spot where Baldwin painted his 1953 work), while another shows a line of anti-tank cubes running up the cliff. It is interesting that two have been colour tinted: that is, they are not simple records for posterity but rather artistic compositions in their own right. It would appear that an unknown photographer wished, on the one hand, to document the contrast between pre-war and post-war beach, and, on the other, record what was left for its own sake. In something of a paradox, the defences appear to have become in some way naturalised.

But such sentiments were ultimately short-lived. In post-war Britain the general mood was one of wanting to move on from the depredations and difficulties and consign the war to history. In such a climate little, if any, thought was given to preserving wartime works for posterity. Especially in the seaside towns, as soon as the perceived threat was gone and the need for coastal defences seen as non-existent the mood changed. Even before the war had finished thought had been given to the removal of defence works and the reopening of beaches for tourists and visitors. Such moves represent the start of the process of attrition and survival that has left the particular archaeological legacy that we can see today, and which forms the subject of the next chapter.

---

90   SRO (Ipswich), K463–127 (Dunwich Beach, *c.*1950).

Chapter 9

From eyesore to archaeology

As Chapters 2–6 have shown, the distribution of Second World War archaeological remains in the Sandlings is uneven. In part this is due to the original pattern of monuments – as we have seen, defences were not built uniformly everywhere – but selective patterns of removal have also left their mark. A number of 'agents of destruction' have served to remove military works: the action of the sea; programmes of deliberate clearance; post-war urban development; and agricultural intensification. At the same time 'agents of preservation' have left wartime remains intact: adaptation for new purposes; sympathetic land management by conservation bodies; and, latterly, the preservation of structures because of their value as historic monuments. These broad agencies do not impact evenly on the ground, however, and patterns of preservation and destruction both operate at a number of scales and often depend on the subtle interplay of a number of factors. At the level of the individual monument concrete structures tend to survive better than buildings that were only ever intended to meet a temporary purpose and an earthwork anti-tank ditch is more difficult to remove than a shallow slit trench. But, at a regional scale, survival and removal is bound up with broader changes in the landscape of the Sandlings after 1945. At the same time, Second World War remains are not just static archaeological reminders of a past conflict, but are subject to reinterpretation by succeeding generations, which in turn conditions our view of what we see in the landscape today. This chapter seeks to explain two separate, but closely connected, aspects of the 'afterlife' of the region's military archaeology: first, the process of deliberate removal at the end of the conflict and the wider forces of preservation and destruction that have shaped patterns of survival; and, second, post-war attitudes to the remains of the wartime landscape and their place in cultural memory.

While not anywhere near approaching the scale that was to characterise the period after 1945, it is worth noting that the abandonment and removal of military works took place during the war itself. As previous chapters have emphasised, defence schemes were reconfigured on numerous occasions and so structures of all kinds were prone to abandonment as strategies changed. Orders for the destruction of redundant pillboxes can be found as early as 1941 and small numbers of pillboxes were removed only a year after their initial construction; in September 1941 the 9th Cameronians casually noted the deliberate destruction of a pillbox in their battalion area by Royal

Engineers.[1] A similar fate awaited field positions that by the middle of the war were considered unnecessary; at the end of 1941 unoccupied trenches that could provide cover for the enemy were to be blocked or covered with rabbit wire, while in June 1942 two companies of the 2nd Hertfordshires were engaged in the 'dismantling of old positions and wire'.[2] Clearances such as these help explain why, even in otherwise remote areas, so many of the earthwork remains of trenches recorded as part of this study are backfilled, rather than retaining anything close to their original depth. As discussed in Chapter 6, a significant number of concrete defences were destroyed from 1943/44 as part of training and where redundant structures such as anti-landing ditches lay over potential arable land they began to be infilled from a similar time. Such cases offer a reminder that the lifespan of some military works was short.

We shall clear it off the beaches

When it became evident that the war was going to end government attention turned to how military remains were to be systematically removed. In 1944 it had been agreed that the Ministry of Works would be responsible for the derequisitioning of military property and the removal of the 'Temporary Defence Works', which included coastal defences and training infrastructure. The normal procedure was for the landowner to receive compensation for such works until they were cleared and the land 'restored' to its pre-war state, an arrangement that continued until 1960, when all claims were extinguished. Where the effort to clear defences was not felt to be in the public interest a one-off compensation payment was made to the landowner that could be used to cover the costs of removal. There was, however, no legal requirement on the part of the landowner to actually do so and so, especially in remote or unobtrusive locations, structures were often left untouched and became private property.[3]

In the case of seaside resorts in the south and east of England it was felt by government that it was in the national interest to expedite the process of clearance on municipal land and the War Office was prepared to meet bills for clearance directly.[4] To that end, in November 1944 local authorities were encouraged to draw up schedules for the removal of works and submit quotes that could then be assessed and authorised by the War Office's Lands Branch. Once the military has declared defence works redundant, a two-stage process followed: an initial phase of site clearance to make seafronts safe and accessible, then full 'reinstatement', which saw the full removal of defences and areas returned to their pre-war condition.[5]

---

1   TNA WO 166/4180 (War Diary, 9th Cameronians), 6.9.41.

2   TNA WO 166/4156 (War Diary, 6th Border Regiment), Commanding Officer's Instruction No. 10, 2.12.41; TNA WO 166/8726 (War Diary, 2nd Hertfordshire Regiment), June 1942.

3   Foot, *Beaches, Fields, Streets, and Hills*, pp. 3–4.

4   SRO (Ipswich) EE1/1/13/8a (Clearance of Coastal Defences), Coastal Resorts Distress Committee, Removal of Defence Works and Rehabilitation of Sea Fronts, 1.11.44.

5   Dobinson, *Anti-Invasion*, pp. 194–7; SRO (Ipswich) EE1/1/13/8a (Clearance of Coastal Defences).

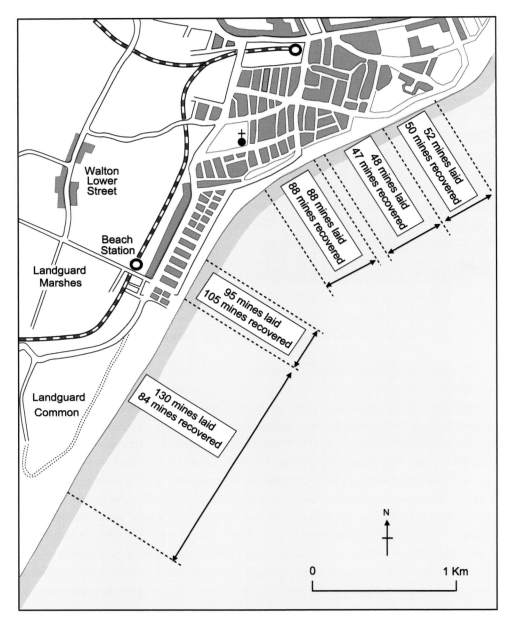

Figure 9.1. Mines removed at Felixstowe. As with other beach resorts, here the clean-up was ruthlessly thorough.

Figure 9.2. Young visitors to Dunwich Beach take to the water alongside dragon's teeth, c.1948. (W. Foreman)

On the ground some work was already in hand during 1944, with army engineer parties clearing sections of beach for civilian access at Felixstowe, Aldeburgh and Thorpeness.[6] The greatest impediment to the immediate opening of beaches for visitors was the presence of mines, and their clearance became the priority when the war was over. At Southwold sections of beach were declared clear throughout 1945, but parts remained mined into October the following year.[7] At Felixstowe clearance began in earnest in March 1945 and involved the stripping of sand and shingle on beaches down to low water mark and to a depth of several feet. The stretch of coast from Felixstowe Ferry to Landguard Point was systematically cleared from north to south, a process that went on until the autumn (Figure 9.1). While clearance was ongoing the whole beach was closed and public access restricted to the area of the pier pavilion and the promenade, barbed wire being deliberately left in order to prevent civilians from approaching the work area. In 1946 the reopening of the beach saw the army ordnance team responsible being suitably entertained on the pier pavilion.[8] When whole beaches or discrete sections were declared clear of mines visitors were free to return and in the immediate years after the war holidaymakers took to Suffolk's beaches surrounded by the relics of the wartime landscape (Figure 9.2).

6   TNA WO 166/14393 (War Diary, Essex and Suffolk District), August–September, 1944.
7   SRO (Lowestoft) 491/12F/45 (Removal of Mines and Coastal Defences), *passim*.
8   *The Felixstowe Times*, 26.6.46.

Figure 9.3. Aldeburgh, *c*.1948. This view probably shows the beach after initial site clearance. (Suffolk Record Office, Ipswich)

The wholesale removal of fixed obstacles was a more involved undertaking, and the process was often protracted. Detailed schedules of redundant defences give some sense of the scale of work involved. At Aldeburgh this included over 5000 metres of scaffolding, 4500 metres of barbed wire and 4000 anti-tank blocks, together with the removal of dragon's teeth and pillboxes: works that in total would cost an estimated £25,000 to clear.[9] In early 1945 the costs of the removal of defences on the town's land were submitted to the Lands Branch, who in turn requested a more detailed assessment of the work. There was then a delay until the summer of 1946 while this paperwork was complied, the town clerk later explaining that the Borough Surveyor was simply overworked and that they had instructed an outside firm of surveyors to act as consultants. By January 1947 the town clerk, his frustration with the Lands Branch evident, wrote that if the matter could be dealt with speedily the sea front could be cleared in time for Easter and that further delay would mean that 'the beach and promenade will be topsy turvy just at a time when our spring and summer visitors will be here'.[10] The work was put out to tender and the Lands Branch wished to award the contract to the lowest bidder, a company the council considered to have dubious merits, which caused further frustration and much alarm. In the end, a preferred bidder was persuaded to revise their initial costs and in May 1947 the contract, for £26,997 14s 6d,

9   SRO (Ipswich) EE1/1/13/8a (Clearance of Coastal Defences), 11.7.44.
10   *Ibid.*, Town Clerk to Lands Officer, 4.1.47.

was finally awarded and work undertaken that summer (Figure 9.3).[11] Matters were concluded only in December, when the contractors threatened legal action against the council for non-payment of the balance of the contract; it subsequently transpired that this was a policy on their part to receive prompt payment as in the past they had encountered delays when dealing with government agencies.[12]

The overriding concern of holiday resorts was the restoration of attractive seafronts, as tourism represented the principal means by which income could be brought into areas that had seen their economic fortunes collapse during the previous six years. While it was obligated to pay for the removal of military works in seaside towns, the War Office was clearly concerned that local authorities might make attempts to take advantage of the situation by carrying out otherwise unconnected improvements to facilities the costs of which would normally be met by councils themselves. This is most evident at Felixstowe, where extended negotiations took place over the costs of removal of defence works and, separately, over a claim for compensation for damage to the sea wall. Owing to the difficulty of accessing beaches during the war the three kilometres of coastline for which the council was responsible had deteriorated to such an extent that groynes had been washed away or damaged and parts of the sea wall had either collapsed or required maintenance. When physical access was permitted in 1946 council workers had effected repairs. The War Office eventually settled in 1950, but insisted that the costs of what would in other circumstances have been routine maintenance – £500 a year for the period June 1940–46 – be offset against the claim.[13]

The condition and restoration of the beach front was also a contentious matter, with the urban council complaining that the initial piecemeal repairs undertaken in order to make the area accessible for civilians meant that

> the surface of the promenade now resembles a patchwork quilt whereas immediately prior to the war it was in perfect and uniform condition throughout. It cannot remain like this indefinitely as it is a disgrace to a seaside resort and ultimately will have to be re-laid in its entirety.[14]

When it came to making payment for removal of works and making good, the Lands Branch was disinclined to replace 'new for old' and considerable squabbling took place to prevent money from being paid out unnecessarily. In the case of six seaside shelters

---

11   SRO (Ipswich) EE1/1/13/9 (Beach Clearance, Removal of Defences), Town Clerk to Leightons Contractors Ltd, 20.5.47.

12   *Ibid.*, Leightons Contractors to Town Clerk, 30.12.47.

13   SRO (Ipswich) EF12/1/8/3 (Felixstowe, Seafront Clearance of Defence Works), Claim against War Department in respect of the restoration of the sea front, etc. 12.4.50.

14   SRO (Ipswich) EF12/1/8/6 (Felixstowe Clearance of Defence Works), December 1944–September 1949), Borough Engineer to Sargent, Felixstowe, Claim under Section (4), 28.10.48.

Figure 9.4. Minsmere, c.1950, showing partially removed beach defences. (The Eric Hosking Charitable Trust)

on the front that had been substantially damaged it was agreed that repairs would be made but that only two, rather than three, coats of paint were permitted; and the claim for renewing the formal gardens, ruined by troops, was reduced by the Lands Branch until it represented a figure only slightly above what would have been necessary for routine maintenance. The figure for the final repaving of the promenade was reduced by 25 per cent on the assumption that such paving had a normal life of 100 years and the pre-war paving had already been 30 years old when taken by the military. The council was inclined to appeal, but was advised by its consultant surveyors that the Lands Officer they were dealing with had successfully settled on low figures with other councils and that taking the matter to a tribunal would open up the whole claim to reassessment. In the end, a sum of £30,838 was paid for the removal of defence works, considerably less than the £48,750 originally sought.[15] Away from coastal resorts important albeit less systematic programmes of clearance were ongoing. One such scheme in place on the Ogilvie estate by the summer of 1946 removed the majority of anti-invasion defences at Thorpeness and Sizewell, while a smaller-scale but equally thorough removal scheme was ongoing on the beaches at Walberswick. On those stretches of coastline away from the holiday resorts clearance was slower and, to judge from photographs c.1950 of Dunwich and Minsmere, while much had been done by this date the defences were still in the process of being removed (Figure 9.4).

---

15 *Ibid.*, March, 1941–December 1945; SRO (Ipswich) EF12/1/8/3 (Felixstowe Seafront Clearance of Defence Works), December 1944–September 1949.

Analysis of the tender documents drawn up at this time indicates why in some places there is almost no archaeological trace of works today: the details reveal that the clean-up was to be ruthlessly thorough. At Southwold, the ECDB at Gun Hill was to be completely demolished and the rubble removed. At the original battery site, just north of the Blyth, the concrete and brickwork was to be removed to a depth of 30 centimetres (12 inches) below ground level, with the rubble deposited in the underground rooms and then sealed with topsoil. Anti-tank cubes were to be broken up and the rubble placed at a minimum distance of some 1.8 metres (6 feet) away in an adjacent trench, which was then backfilled before the ground surface was returned to its original contours.[16] At Southwold Common the requirement was not only to remove four pillboxes but also to fill in trenches and craters representing successive infantry and artillery positions dug since 1940, to clear barbed wire and to remove surplus material from the site.[17]

Where possible, materials were salvaged, especially the metal from dragon's teeth and scaffolding, and in a small number of cases alternative uses were found for some works: at Aldeburgh anti-tank blocks were used as piling for the river wall at Slaughton and for raising the level of a new road, while at Dunwich cubes were used to shore up the shingle bank and provide bases for fishing huts.[18] The overall impression, however, is that much material was dumped, either on the grounds of expediency or because the waste was unfit for alternative purposes. It was found, for example, that the removed beach scaffolding at Aldeburgh was so corroded by sea-water and abraded by shingle that it was redundant and so it was placed in anti-tank ditches and covered over. The dumping of material in abandoned military positions was clearly commonplace and is attested in places right along the Sandlings coast where cliff erosion has exposed coils of barbed wire in backfilled trenches; it is probable that much of the hundreds of metres of barbed wire that covered the beaches during the war was disposed of in similar manner.[19] The details of contractual arrangements and the archaeological evidence of disposal help to underline that the removal of wartime works had a sense of finality about it in some respects archaeologically comparable to the dissolution of the monasteries or Beeching's removal of railway lines. The prevailing attitude is seen in the comments of the Aldeburgh Borough Surveyor to the government company charged with salvaging metal about the collection of scrap: 'my Town Council is against creating temporary dumps whenever this can be avoided for we want to rehabilitate

---

16 SRO (Lowestoft) 491/12F/45 (Removal of Mines and Coastal Defences), Removal of W.D. Defence Works etc.

17 *Ibid.*, REA Transport to Town Clerk, 10.5.46.

18 SRO (Ipswich) EE1/1/13/8a (Clearance of Coastal Defences), Notes for Committee, Beach and Crag Path Clearance; Borough Surveyor to River Catchment Board, 19.7.46.

19 For example, observed by author at Dunwich Cliff, 14.11.05.

Figure 9.5. Lone pillbox at Stratford St Mary on the A12, the sole survivor of the defences that linked this Nodal Point with the Back Line. The visible damage is a sign of an unsuccessful attempt at removal.

the Town and its environs by clearing up this "mess" once and for all.'[20] This attitude explains why the beaches that were defended so heavily from 1940 now retain almost nothing in the way of upstanding wartime archaeology. A measure of how thorough the clearance was comes from a run of aerial photographs of Felixstowe, Aldeburgh and Southwold taken from 1949 to 1951, which shows beaches devoid of defences.[21] In the same amount of time that the defences had been built and used, in places all trace of their existence had gone completely.

In the towns and villages of the Sandlings a similar level of attrition to that seen in holiday resorts took place, albeit for slightly different reasons. Here urban expansion was chiefly responsible for the removal of wartime works. The defences originally placed on what had been the perimeter of settlements were now in locations that were often the first to be developed for post-war housing or industrial estates. At Leiston buildings soon encroached on the sites of the town's Nodal Point defences, while at Felixstowe the development of the container port involved the sweeping away of nearly all the structures associated with the wartime naval station. Even in small conurbations defences intended to constrict movement by vehicles could not have been more at odds with post-war development that assumed widespread use of the motor car. Numerous

20 SRO (Ipswich) EE1/1/13/8a (Clearance of Coastal Defences), 'Borough Surveyor to Iron and Steel Disposables', 23.1.47.

21 *Britain from Above*: Felixstowe, EAW024307 (4.7.49); Aldeburgh, EAW037847 (17.7.51); Southwold, EAW024298 (4.7.49).

accidents occurred as car drivers crashed into obstructions or snagged their vehicles on barbed wire placed adjacent to roadsides or spigot mortar pedestals. The removal of roadblocks had been ongoing since the middle of the war but accelerated at the end of hostilities. Road-widening schemes also had a strong hand in the removal of former defences, in the wider countryside as well as in the towns; the almost complete absence of Second World War remains along the course of the 'Back Line' is in large part due to the widening of the modern A12 (Figure 9.5).

Defences in urban areas also drew complaint for other reasons. A 'blockhouse' in Birkfield Lane, Ipswich, was singled out in a letter from a resident to the council on 5 July 1948 that described how during the week it was 'used by tradesmen visiting this locality as a public convenience' and 'at the weekends and holidays by children from the town who picnic and play there' and that blocking the entrance would safeguard the health of the children of Ipswich.[22] In such cases a council would usually respond by saying that responsibility lay with the government and the landowner but, in practice, where public safety or health were deemed to be at stake, the Ministry of Health would pay for the removal of works. By the 1950s there is a sense from complaints that the public were alive to the idea that relic structures that were deemed dangerous were more likely to be speedily removed. One complainant wrote, similarly, about a pillbox on the corner of Digby and Rushmere Roads in Ipswich, saying that

> very unpleasant smells come out of this place and … these are to the detriment of the young children on this neighbourhood who seem to enjoying playing around this unpleasant reminder of the past … . I consider that the Public Health Department should take steps to inspect this place and board up the entrance as soon as possible.[23]

Such comments indicate that, for some, doing away with the defences was a positive move towards an improved post-war environment.

Agents of destruction: arable, marshland and forestry

Away from seaside resorts and urban areas the survival of wartime monuments is connected with the broader development of the post-war landscape of the Sandlings. While the beaches of the chief holiday resorts were cleared relatively rapidly, military works in the hinterland – such as anti-tank and anti-landing ditches, infantry and artillery positions and the remains of training – were subject to slightly different patterns of attrition.

Arguably the most dramatic change to the landscape of the Sandlings since 1945 has been the conversion of heath and wetland environments to arable cultivation. The

---

22   SRO (Ipswich) DC10/1/6/8 (Ipswich Borough: Demolition of Defence Works, 1948–1951), 'Holland to Public Health Dept', 5.7.48.

23   *Ibid.*, 'Jessup to Town Clerk', 13.9.51.

Figure 9.6. Iken Heath in 1943, showing anti-landing ditches and training works, now all removed by post-war agricultural expansion. (Reproduced by permission of Historic England Archive (USAAF Photography))

national requirement for food security and the post-war availability of government subsidies for improvement schemes led to the widespread renewal of cultivation on arable land that had reverted to pasture during military use as well as the extensive ploughing up of untilled land for the first time.[24] A noticeable pattern exists in that those places used by the military *and* shown as arable by the late 1930s Land Utilisation Survey tend to retain no wartime archaeology; here the conflict represented only a temporary interruption to cultivation. The evidence from aerial photographs shows that these places were often reverting back to farmland before the end of the conflict. At Blythburgh Lodge near Walberswick, for example, some of the westward defences of 1941 were already back under the plough in 1945 and those positions that survive as

---

24   For summary see Williamson, *Sandlands*. P. Armstrong, 'Changes in the Suffolk Sandlings', *Geography*, 58 (1973), pp. 1–8.

earthworks today were in places that were permanent pasture or heath before the start of the war.

Of equal significance is the estimation that in the period between 1949 and 1970 just under 1416 hectares (3500 acres) was given over to the plough for the first time in the Sandlings, chiefly at the expense of heathland south of the Alde.[25] Here ploughing was sufficient to remove those military works that were sited back from the beaches, such as anti-landing and anti-tank ditches, almost wholesale. At Sutton Common, which was covered with anti-landing ditches by 1941, the scale of post-war arable expansion was such that the sole survivors today are within the grounds of the National Trust estate at Sutton Hoo. Around Iken Heath, where aerial photographs show heathland littered with anti-landing ditches in 1945, none now remain (Figure 9.6).[26] Agricultural intensification at this time was also responsible for the removal of lengths of anti-tank ditch. Where ditches ran adjacent to field edges the excavated soil that formed the accompanying bank could simply be bulldozed back – a moment captured by an aerial photograph of 1949 at Mount Pleasant Farm near Dunwich, which shows a ditch in the process of being backfilled.[27] During field amalgamation or hedge removal it is probable that the infantry positions that often favoured such locations for the purposes of camouflage were lost; anecdotally this is known from at least one example at Walberswick, where the broken remains of a Suffolk Square were moved to their present location by machinery during field clearance.

In wetland areas similar patterns are apparent. The 1953 floods were a key moment as, subsequently, in those areas that had been inundated drainage ditches were recut, sea walls were raised and pumps replaced gravity sluices, all of which lowered the water table sufficiently to permit ploughing. Once the saline content of flooded land had sufficiently reduced former wetlands could also be underdrained; in this way by 1970 some 3439 hectares (8500) acres of pre-war wetland were converted to arable.[28]

To a lesser extent, the activities of the Forestry Commission also tended to remove wartime remains. Post-war opposition to the widespread planting of the Suffolk heaths was significant enough to limit the number of new conifer plantations after 1945, but, while new creations were generally small in scale, they were sufficient to remove significant quantities of wartime remains. At Goose Hill, north of Sizewell, the site of a firing range for the Aldeburgh Battle School, where the digging of training trenches is documented, contains no wartime archaeology as a result of wholesale replanting. The removal of what were undoubtedly significant earthworks also occurred at the southern tip of Dunwich Forest, to the east of Cuttens Hill, which is shown on maps of

---

25 P.J.O. Trist, *A Survey of the Agriculture of Suffolk* (London, 1971), p. 121; Williamson, *Sandlands*, pp. 72–3.

26 HE (NMR) RAF Photography, 106G/UK/832/RP/3180, 23.9.45.

27 *Britain from Above*, EAW024304, 4.7.49.

28 Trist, *Survey*, pp. 130–32; Williamson, *Sandlands*, p. 49.

Exercise Teller II as the site of enemy positions that the training troops were expected to take and consolidate.

Zones of erosion

The final agent of destruction was, and continues to be, the sea. The classic images of pillboxes being submerged beneath shingle or perched hazardously on a retreating cliff face, while often undeniably dramatic, are more applicable to some places than others. The coastline itself can be divided into zones of erosion, areas where the coastline is prone to being washed away; and zones of deposition, where actions such as longshore drift result in spits and bars or banks.[29] In a very straightforward way, this aspect of the natural geography has impacted directly on the survival of Second World War defences. In those places prone to deposition beach defences were being subsumed by sand and shingle during the war itself and today remnants are periodically exposed by the action of the sea. Coastal erosion is most heavily pronounced in the areas between Benacre and Southwold, around Dunwich and to the south of Shingle Street around East Lane, Bawdsey. Regardless of the extent of immediate post-war clearance, in these places the coastline upon which the coastal crust was built has been removed wholesale, taking wartime works with it; at Covehithe, for example, the coastline has retreated some 250 metres since the end of the war.[30] At East Lane, Bawdsey, the majority of the concrete beach defences have been washed away and were it not for the construction of modern sea defences the site of the Emergency Coastal Defence Battery, the best preserved in the Sandlings, would have been lost.[31] It is probable that many relic defences disappeared during significant inundation 'events', the most important of which were the 1953 floods. At Walberswick pillboxes close to the Blyth were moved some distance from their original position by the action of the floodwater and it is probable that many otherwise ephemeral earthwork positions disappeared at this time; with the exception of a small number of earthworks at Sizewell, sandwiched between the dunes and arable fields, no actual beach positions appear to survive at all in the Divisional Sector. The widespread construction of sea defences in the aftermath of the 1953 floods may also have destroyed a good deal of what would now be classified as archaeology, with numerous structures potentially buried beneath shingle or earthwork banks. At Walberswick, the otherwise well-preserved line of 1940 defences lacks remains of the posts in the village itself, as they underlie the modern sea wall. Elsewhere in zones of erosion the loss of Second World War sites has been piecemeal but cumulatively significant, with an unrecorded number of structures being lost to the sea, a process often facilitated by demolition where they constituted a hazard to coast walkers (Figure 9.7).

---

29 Williamson, *Sandlands*, pp. 128–32.
30 Hegarty and Newsome, *The Archaeology of the Suffolk Coast*, p. 7, fig. 76 at p. 137.
31 Kent, *Fortifications of East Anglia*, shows extant remains prior to erosion, p. 139.

Figure 9.7. Army personnel preparing a wartime building for demolition at Benacre in 1987. (Suffolk Record Office, Lowestoft).

The fieldwork for this study has brought some quantitative information to questions of survival. Of the estimated 50 concrete pillboxes in the 2nd/4th South Lancashire's area noted to have existed in July 1940, 13 survive either fully intact or as pieces of broken concrete – a figure that is the highest for the Sector and in one of the areas in which conditions for survival were best. A more typical case is that of the 2nd/4th Essex Regiment, who listed 26 pillboxes in a return of July 1942, of which now only four remain. In the case of anti-tank ditches, of the 31 kilometres of deliberately excavated ditch in the Divisional Sector just under three kilometres survives on the ground today, the majority on heathland now in the care of Natural England or the RSPB. A point made elsewhere about the survival of wartime monuments needs to be underscored here: it should not be thought that because these remains belong to the recent past they are plentiful. Some are not.

Agents of preservation: nature reserves

Working alongside these agents of attrition were equally significant changes that acted, albeit mostly unwittingly, as forces of preservation of wartime remains. Within the broad 'zones of destruction' there are, of course, individual examples of preservation. At Lowestoft Grand Hotel ECDB the observation post and fire control post were converted to a scientific laboratory and one gun house was reused as a seafront shelter – classic examples of 'survival by adaptation'. In the countryside Nissen huts were regularly bought up by farmers and used for agricultural buildings, and their presence today is a good indicator of a former wartime site in close proximity. In other cases significant survivals are simply serendipitous; at Wrentham the wood that had served as an artillery troop position established in 1940 and abandoned in 1942 escaped being grubbed out and was simply left for pheasant cover, leaving an archaeological survival almost without comparison anywhere in the Sandlings.

Aside from chance survivals, two main structuring forces have served to preserve wartime remains. The first is continued military use. As has been seen, the draw-down at the end of the conflict saw the dismantling of the majority of the Sandling's radar stations, but RAF Bawdsey continued in military use until 1992, rather unusually in the region, and this had the effect of preserving many of the Second World War structures, some of which survive in the grounds of a private school and others through use as a museum. But by far the most important factor in preservation was the establishment of nature reserves and the passing of significant areas of the Sandlings into environmental stewardship. Arguably the most important scheme was at Minsmere, where the wartime inundation had unintentionally created an ideal habitat for wetland birds of some 160 hectares (400 acres). In 1947 the RSPB leased 600 hectares (1500 acres) of the newly created marsh along with adjacent woodland and heath from the Ogilvie estate and, following full release by the War Office two years later, the area became a nationally important bird reserve with a place in the history of conservation as the first habitat recolonised by the avocet after the war.[32] The establishment of Minsmere should be seen in the context of two other RSPB acquisitions at North Warren near Aldeburgh, immediately before the war, and at Havergate Island on the Alde in 1947, as together they set the tone for much of the post-war conservation agenda.[33] The establishment of North Warren and Minsmere were heavily influenced by the role of Colonel Ogilivie, a keen ornithologist who did much to broker the initial agreements with the RSPB and who drove through the project in the face of opposition from tenant farmers intent on reclaiming the wetlands for agriculture. In the late 1970s Minsmere was bought outright and subsequent acquisitions for the reserve consolidated the concentrated holdings around the Minsmere levels and on Westleton Walks, taking the area to just under 1000 hectares.[34]

Minsmere is simply the best-known nature reserve on the Suffolk coast. During the 1970s large parts of the Sandlings were designated an Area of Outstanding

32   H. Axell and E. Hosking, *Minsmere: Portrait of a Bird Reserve* (London, 1977), p. 181.
33   Axell and Hosking, *Minsmere*, pp. 21–2, 176.
34   RSPB, *Minsmere Reserve Plan* (2003–08).

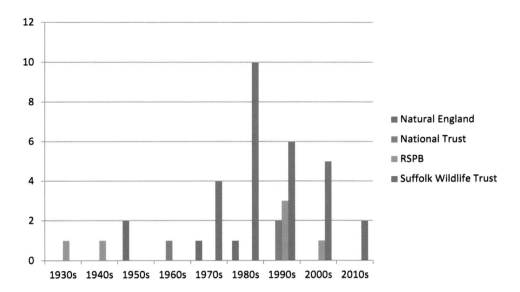

Table 1. Bar chart showing the number of sites in the study area in the ownership of, or managed by, conservation bodies. This chart shows the date of first acquisitions, rather than additions to existing reserves (for example, RSPB Minsmere, was progressively expanded from the 1970s), but nonetheless shows the rise of conservation areas in the Sandlings in the post-war period. Not all such areas retain Second World War remains, but the majority of the region's military archaeology is concentrated in the principal nature reserves.

Natural Beauty (Suffolk Coast and Heaths, 1970) and Suffolk Heritage Coast (1973), which in turn facilitated an increase in the area directly under the management of conservation bodies.[35] Areas now important for their military remains include the substantial Natural England nature reserves of Suffolk Coast (first declared 1972) around Walberswick and that at Benacre (first declared 1985); the large RSPB reserves at Boyton Marshes (1990) and Hollesley Marshes (2006); The National Trust sites at Dunwich Heath (1968), Orford Ness (1993) and Sutton Hoo (1998); and, chiefly since the 1980s, holdings of the Suffolk Wildlife Trust, especially at Simpson's Saltings (1991) and Gunton Warren (2013) (Table 9.1).[36]

The cumulative effect of the increase in the area held by conservation bodies can be seen in the fact that almost all of the archaeological sites discussed in Chapters 2–6 either form part of nature reserves or lie on land under close environmental stewardship, and so lie in 'zones of preservation': as at Boyton, Hollesley, Walberswick, Gunton, Minsmere, North Warren and Westleton Walks. Mapping datasets of monuments as they exist today against the boundaries of these areas shows the extent to which, outside the bounds of protected areas, Second World War monuments are rare (Figure 9.8). Additionally, by their very nature the *kinds*

---

35   *National Character Area Profile, 82: Suffolk Coasts and Heaths* (Natural England, 2013), p. 15.
36   English Nature, National Trust, Royal Society for the Protection of Birds, Suffolk Wildlife Trust, pers comm.

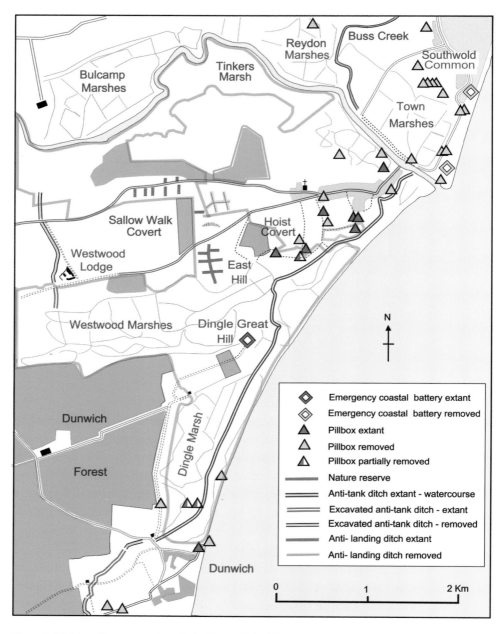

Figure 9.8. Nature Reserves and survival of Second World War monuments. The majority of wartime works survive within the bounds of land under stewardship.

Figure 9.9. Clean-up party of Eastern Europeans at Dunwich Heath, late 1960s. (National Trust)

of landscapes that became protected habitats have tended to define the nature of archaeological survivals. It is no accident that training archaeology is unusually well-preserved, as the remote heaths and wetlands that were favoured as practice grounds and gunnery ranges are also those that have been judged as valuable for their distinctive biodiversity and so brought into stewardship or passed into the hands of conservation bodies.

But it does not necessarily follow that just because an area is under stewardship or otherwise protected all kinds of monument will survive well, or that monuments do not survive in places that are not under protection. Orford Ness and Dunwich Heath both lie within broad 'zones of preservation', but their military remains are far from a straightforward and unproblematic archaeological record of all that originally existed. At Orford Ness the post-war use of the site has largely removed remains dating to the Second World War, but paradoxically the Ness is rich in First World War and Cold War remains. At Dunwich Heath most of the Second World War concrete structures were removed under National Trust stewardship. The heath was donated to the National Trust in 1968 as part of the National Trust's programme of coastline acquisition Project Neptune, but a subsequent heathland fire exploded such large quantities of ordnance that a nine-month period of clearance followed

Figure 9.10. Former 'German' pillbox at Dunwich Heath now used as bat hibernaculum.

in which the concrete remains were broken up and sold for hardcore (Figure 9.9).[37] The upstanding remains of concrete wartime structures today therefore comprise a small number of chance survivals, whereas earthwork remains are more numerous. This is in contrast to neighbouring Westleton Walks, large areas of which escaped post-war ploughing owing to their inclusion within the Minsmere reserve, and so in parts preservation is exceptionally high, the remains ranging from defence works to training trenches and what is probably close to a complete run of concrete works built for Exercise Kruschen.

What remains in the landscape today, then, is the result of the influence – sometimes dramatic, sometimes more subtle – of a range of factors. But at the regional level of the Sandlings, by the mid-1980s these influences had largely worked themselves out on the ground, leaving the pattern of archaeological remains that we see today.

From eyesore to archaeology

It is important to appreciate, however, that until the late 1980s the survival of Second World War archaeological remains on nature reserves and in other protected areas

---

37   J.R. Hunn and K. Semmelmann, *Historic Landscape Survey: Dunwich Estate, Suffolk* (Milton Keynes, 2009).

was a by-product of the desire to preserve particular habitats and their biodiversity. It was another decade before wartime military archaeology started to be valued for its historical importance and only very recently that an interest in such remains could be considered mainstream, rather than niche or 'nerdy'. The rise of Second World War archaeology to academic respectability was both a cause and an effect of the English Heritage-sponsored research projects discussed in Chapter 1, themselves reflecting societal interest sparked by the 50-year anniversaries of the conflict. As well as undertaking the widespread recording of sites, the Defence of Britain project raised awareness of the historical importance of the subject. Landguard Fort at Felixstowe illustrates this broader change in perception: the fort's military use ceased with the abolition of coast artillery in 1956 and the site was subsequently left derelict until public interest in the late 1980s eventually led to its restoration in the following decade.[38] At a local level there is also evidence of a general shift towards preservation for posterity, rather than destruction, at this time; in the early 1990s at Barking Tye near Ipswich, for example, the parish council repeatedly voted against the demolition of two pillboxes on the grounds of their historic importance.[39]

At the time of writing, but still very recently, some wartime remains have found alternative uses which will in all probability guarantee survival some way into the future. Owing to their specific interior atmospheric conditions, structures such as pillboxes and subterranean buildings now have an important role as bat hibernacula (Figure 9.10). Increasingly, the wartime use of land now occupied by nature reserves is of interest in its own right and is seen as a way of attracting visitors that are otherwise not interested in wildlife. At sites already valued for their historic importance the Second World War is now more likely to be treated as 'history' rather than simply the remembered or recent past; at the National Trust's Sutton Hoo the anti-landing ditches are now part of the site's story, albeit justifiably in the shadow of the Anglo-Saxon burial mounds.

What cannot be stressed enough is the future role of heritage and conservation bodies in preserving Second World War archaeology in the Sandlings, for the simple reason that the vast majority of remains exist on land in their care. Such agencies are now effectively the sole guardians of what is now a much diminished material legacy. But, as naturalists are rarely trained as historians or archaeologists, the identification of remains, let alone of their significance, often falls outside the expertise of those regularly working in these environments and responsible for management. Over the course of researching and writing this book the authors have observed instances of damage to unrecorded monuments and, in a small number of cases, their total destruction. This applies in particular to earthworks, many of which can be unwittingly damaged or obliterated by the planting or removal of trees or by the

---

38   D. Rayner, *An Update on Landguard Fort, Felixstowe in Suffolk* (privately published, 1995).

39   SRO (Ipswich) HD1654/1–2 (Notes on Pillboxes).

current practice of ploughing up sections of heath to act as firebreaks or to encourage biodiversity. In other cases, root damage to earthworks caused by tree growth means that some monuments are in an appreciably worse state now than was the case even a few years ago. This, of course, stems from unawareness of the existence or significance of an archaeological feature, rather than any wish to do damage. But at the same time there is abundant evidence of good practice, especially by the RSPB at Minsmere, where management takes place in full knowledge of the archaeological remains and is a model of its kind.

Remembered memory, landscape and folklore

At the same time as physical remains of the Second World War in the Sandlings were variously being removed, adapted and abandoned, the events of which they formed a small material legacy were far from forgotten. The impact of the conflict on post-war British society was enormous, but in popular memory the events that were collectively remembered, and why, varied considerably.[40] In a somewhat curious aspect of cultural amnesia, the exact extent and purposes of Britain's anti-invasion landscapes were, following 1945, largely forgotten.[41] In contrast to the situation in occupied nations in continental Europe, where the physical remains of wartime defences often became resented monuments of oppression, in Britain pillboxes and the circumstances of their construction became something to laugh at, typified by the BBC's *Dad's Army*, which presented a view of the wartime experience that scholars have sought to challenge ever since.

The 'loss' of collective memory is arguably the result of a number of factors. There were fewer people resident in the Sandlings during the conflict, many restrictions on movement existed and a bewildering number of military units came to and departed the area, so exactly what had occurred and why remained to a large extent either unknown or preserved in memories that were often very localised in their scope. In addition, those present on the ground (soldier and civilian) were not, of course, privy to the finer details of the military agenda, which was for the most part secret and discussion of which was a criminal offence. In oral history today it is the incidental and anecdotal that is recalled, and it is noticeable that the 'bigger picture' of what occurred in the region and why remains largely unknown. The lack of detailed knowledge of the recent past is also connected to that fact that obtaining information relating to the wartime history of the area in the decades after 1945 was difficult. Collier's official history of national defence strategy (1957) confined itself to higher order planning and spent no time on the fabric of coastal defences or on activities such as training.[42] The Divisional and Regimental histories of units that had rotated

---

40 M. Connelly, *We Can Take It! Britain and the Memory of the Second World War* (London, 2004).

41 Foot, *Beaches, Fields, Streets, and Hills*, p. 5.

42 Collier, *Defence of the United Kingdom*.

through the Sandlings usually passed quickly over their time spent there and accounts with any meaningful detail are rare.[43] While of course numerous publications dealing with foreign campaigns or personal memories appeared in the post-war period, local history tended to treat the conflict as a recent event rather than a subject for scholarly reflection and so rarely touched on the subject.[44] Moreover, until the mid-1970s it was essentially impossible for any researcher to write a detailed regional military history, as the majority of the relevant War Office files remained classified. For this reason, in the East Anglian volume of the popular Regional Military Histories series, published in 1974, discussions of the region's medieval castles and post-medieval forts were followed by chapters on the Second World War focusing on the foreign campaigns in which local regiments took part rather than the twentieth-century defences erected on home soil.[45] It was only in the 1980s that what could be called 'regional histories' that included the matter of fortification began to appear, but in the majority of cases only sporadic use was made of official records.[46]

In the absence of detailed information or a narrative framework in which to place visible remains, the local dimensions of the Second World War were interpreted variously through the lenses of individual memory, shared stories, oral history, newspapers and magazines and the numerous films and books that charted the nation's war effort. Moreover, given that the function and purpose of many wartime structures is not always immediately obvious, and as monuments are often extremely difficult to interpret without technical or historical knowledge, exactly what the archaeological remains in the region represented was probably not always straightforward to gauge; it is easy to recognise a castle, less so to positively identify a concrete bunker as an artillery observation post. Without detailed information or any kind of 'official history' it is not altogether surprising that knowledge of the history and purpose of archaeological remains has slipped from collective memory or was woven into other narratives. What is of interest, but perhaps equally unsurprising, are the ways in which the wartime monuments were subsumed within a more deep-seated sense of place and perception of the past.

How the landscape changes brought by the conflict impacted upon perceptions of the Sandlings was discussed in the previous chapter, but other, more intangible qualities also underpin the region's sense of place. One is the sense of a landscape remote and

---

43   Martin, *History of the Fifteenth Scottish Division*; an exception is that of the 79th Armoured Division, which contains photographs of training on the Orford area, but this is a preamble to the account of their active campaigning. Anon., *The Story of 79th Armoured Division*.

44   F. Jenkins, *Story of Southwold* (Southwold, 1948).

45   M. Bates, *East Anglia. Regional Military Histories* (London, 1974).

46   R. Douglas Brown, *East Anglia, 1939–1945*, 7 volumes (Lavenham, 1980–94); Kinsey, *Orfordness*; Kinsey, *Bawdsey*. The notable exception is Kent, *Fortifications of East Anglia*, which made considerable use of material held at the then Public Record Office, chiefly for fixed batteries. See also P. Kent, 'East Anglian Fortifications in the Twentieth Century', *Fortress*, 3 (1989), pp. 4–57.

Figure 9.11. Covehithe church. The ruined hulks of this and other churches in the Sandlings help convey the impression of a rural backwater now faded from a once more glorious past.

set apart from surrounding places that gives the visitor an impression of being alone and isolated. The muted relief often gives a sensation of a limitless continuum; this is a place that lacks clear and firm boundaries, where the land merges effortlessly with sea and sky. Perhaps this helps to explain why the atmosphere is somewhat melancholic, something given added resonance by the sense of a landscape that has faded from a once greater past. This idea of decayed splendour is given expression by the hulks of semi-ruined medieval churches such as those at Covehithe and Walberswick, which are now only shells of their former magnificence (Figure 9.11). The legacy of the past is most clearly felt at Dunwich, where the remains of the once thriving medieval port, lost to the sea through coastal erosion, are captured in the backdrop to Turner's famous c.1830 painting of the cliffs. The sense of an isolated landscape shrouded in a distant and often mysterious past informs much of the region's early historiography and folklore. Bulcamp marshes near Blythburgh is the putative site of the battle in c.654 in which King Anna of East Anglia was killed before his burial in the grounds of the nearby minster church. Traditionally, this stretch of coast was a haunt of the East Anglian supernatural hound 'Black Shuck' and is where, in one of his most famous appearances, again at Blythburgh, he appeared during a thunderstorm, walked down the nave of the parish church, killed two parishioners and left fiery claw marks in the north door. A more direct connection between an eerie sense of place and the supernatural can be found in M.R. James' famous works 'Oh, Whistle and I'll Come to You, My Lad' (1904) and 'A Warning to the Curious' (1925), both of which rely heavily on the backdrop of the historic coastline for their sense of loneliness and jeopardy.[47] The landscape is also at the centre of Sebald's 1995 novel *The Rings of Saturn*, a powerful physiological account of a walking tour along the Sandlings coast.[48] For whatever reason, the Sandlings is a landscape that has the power to make people see ghosts: in 1931 George Orwell related in a letter to a friend how he witnessed an apparition in the grounds of Walberswick churchyard.[49] In what is now part of the modern mythology of the Sandlings, it was the sight of ghostly figures and a white horse on the burial mounds at Sutton Hoo that in part prompted the late 1930s excavations of the pagan Anglo-Saxon cemetery.[50] More recent folklore saw Rendlesham Forest achieve notoriety as the supposed scene of a UFO landing in 1980 dubbed as Britain's 'Roswell', while the region can also boast a lesser-known case of a UFO sighting in 1956 known as the 'Lakenheath–Bentwaters Incident'.[51]

The myth of Shingle Street

It is against this background that the folk memories of the Second World War should be considered, the most significant of which is the idea that in 1940 a failed German invasion attempt took place at Shingle Street (Figure 9.12). Numerous variations on the story exist, but most involve hundreds of burnt bodies of German servicemen being washed ashore and a subsequent cover-up by the British authorities, who feared the effect that the news would have on civilian morale. The burning of the bodies was apparently due to the British use of petroleum weapons that had set the sea on fire. Alternatives included the idea that the events in question were a 'friendly fire' incident in which British troops taking part in a training exercise were fired upon, either by comrades who mistook them for invading Germans or by British bombers practising with secret weapons under the direction of the scientist Barnes Wallis.

The historical basis of the story has been comprehensively analysed by James Hayward and the idea of an invasion attempt utterly debunked; rather, the myth has been shown to lie in a series of otherwise unconnected incidents.[52] In the autumn of 1940 a naval engagement in the North Sea was misinterpreted as a prelude to an invasion; the issue of codeword 'Cromwell' in September was misconstrued as

---

47 J. Simpson, '"The Rules of Folklore" in the Ghost Stories of M.R. James', *Folklore*, 108 (1997), pp. 9–18.

48 W.G. Sebald, *The Rings of Saturn* (London, 1998).

49 P. Davison, *The Complete Works of George Orwell. Vol. 10 A Kind of Compulsion, 1903–1936* (London, 1998), pp. 211–12.

50 M. Carver, *Sutton Hoo: Burial Ground of Kings?* (London, 1998), pp. 3–4.

51 P. Heazell, *Most Secret: The Hidden History of Orford Ness* (Stroud, 2010).

52 Hayward, *The Bodies on the Beach*, reiterated in J. Hayward, *Burn the Sea* (Stroud, 2016).

Figure 9.12. The isolated hamlet of Shingle Street, the setting for a post-war myth of a failed German invasion. This modern folklore represents a continuation of much older perceptions of place.

signalling that an actual invasion was underway; foreign newspapers fed the story of a failed invasion and were probably encouraged to do so as part of a wider British black propaganda campaign; and, while the army did develop a 'flaming barrage' weapon and its placement at four points on the Sandlings coast was mooted, it was never deployed. There is no contemporary evidence of any German landing, a burning sea or an abundance of bodies. The only German bodies washed up on the Suffolk shore were those of deceased aircrew or sailors and even then not in great number. Evidence from the Mass Observation Survey does indeed show that in 1940 stories were in circulation that invasion attempts had been made and enemy ships beaten back, and it was this tense atmosphere that was the ultimate genesis of the myth.[53]

As was discussed in the previous chapter, the wartime history of Shingle Street was unusual and this in itself was probably a cause of speculation, especially as few individuals were in a position to know what had actually occurred. In the 1970s journalistic interest was aroused by the fact that the official file concerning the civilian evacuation in 1940 remained classified in what was then the Public Record Office, while thousands of others were being released to the public. In the 1990s journalists

---

53   Addison and Crang, *Listening to Britain* (London, 2011), pp. 428–9.

spuriously conflating the loss of life in Exercise Tiger, a pre-D-Day American exercise at Slapton Sands in Devon, with supposed events in Suffolk produced a veritable explosion of stories and 'evidence' relating to what had supposedly happened.[54] Something of a media scramble ensued, with lurid tales of hundreds of coffins being sent to the coast during the war, the existence of mass graves and bodies burnt beyond recognition washed up. Eventually the relevant government file was declassified and the information therein found to be so prosaic (its contents can be gauged in the discussion in Chapter 8) that conspiracy theorists claimed a cover-up. In all of this there is no reason to see the myth of Shingle Street as anything other than an example of the well-documented phenomenon whereby when an outside agency give credence to hearsay, witnesses to, and evidence of, events that simply never happened suddenly abound.[55] None of this diminishes the potency of the story, however, or the vibrancy of the myth in the Sandlings today, which during the course of research for this book has been found to be alive and well. In the way that the battlefields of the twentieth century and East Anglia's Second World War airfields have almost become places of pilgrimage and remembrance in post-war decades, so too Shingle Street now has a cultural significance in its own right, with the story of the evacuation finding expression in contemporary fiction and poetry.[56]

Shingle Street is, however, simply the most famous example of a folk myth concerning the wartime Sandlings. Others, either in print or heard during the research for this book, include stories of groups of soldiers vanishing while on beach patrol; of servicemen snatched by the enemy in commando-style raids and subsequently found in POW camps in Germany; that the one remaining (and hidden) crown of the Anglo-Saxon kingdom of East Anglia was what prevented a German invasion in 1940; and of apparitions at Blythburgh connected with the death of Joseph Kennedy in 1944, when the experimental aircraft he was piloting exploded high over the village. These stories are interesting in themselves but also significant is what is *not* finding its way into folk memory. No phantom wartime aircraft roam the skies (as they do in other parts of Britain); no spectral ships can be seen at sea; the ghosts of those who lost their lives in minefields or in training accidents are not said to wander the beaches and heaths. The essence of the folklore of the Second World War instead revolves around subjects closely connected to the regional character of place: mysterious events taking place in otherwise remote and lonely places, the sinister or unexpected brought to the land by the sea, and events connected with military confrontation.

The pedigree of some of these themes of wartime mythology can be traced as far back as the thirteenth century and accounts of military expeditions along the east coast being shipwrecked, resulting in hundreds of bodies being washed up on the shoreline.

---

54   Hayward, *Bodies on the Beach*, chapter 7, *passim*.

55   D. Clarke, *The Angels of Mons: Phantom Soldiers and Ghostly Guardians* (Chichester, 2004), p. 69.

56   B. Morrison, *Shingle Street* (London, 2015).

During the civil war of King John's reign the mercenary captain Hugh de Boves and his army were shipwrecked off the Sandlings during an attempt, so the chronicler Roger of Wendover related, to unjustly claim Norfolk and Suffolk for the king. Roger described how, as a result of the storm that scattered the fleet and claimed the life of Hugh and most of his followers,

> at each of the ports on that part of the sea cost there was found such a multitude of bodies of men and women that the very air was tainted by their stench; a great number of bodies of children were also found, who being drowned in their cradles were thus washed ashore, and afforded a dreadful spectacle to the multitude. They were all, however, given up to be devoured by the beasts of the sea and the birds of the air, so that not one out of forty thousand men escaped alive. All these people had come to England with their wives and children, with the intention of expelling and totally exterminating the natives, and of possessing the land themselves by perpetual right... [57]

In what is a remarkable parallel, here is the same story of hundreds of disfigured and stinking bodies of invaders hell-bent on invasion, but thirteenth-century style.

The theme of the sea bringing the unwanted or unexpected to the shoreline also finds expression in other folk tales, such as the 'Dark Heart of Dunwich', in which the heart of a jilted woman of the town is washed up on the shore and brings bad luck to anyone who finds it. It might not be too fanciful even to suggest that the idea of the sea bringing the unheralded to the land rather echoes the story related by the medieval chronicler Ralph of Coggeshall, in what is one of the earliest accounts of its kind, of how, around 1167, a merman was caught by fishermen and imprisoned in the castle at Orford.[58] What is more interesting from a landscape point of view is that the wartime myths map almost directly onto those places with established folkloric traditions. The Hollesley marshes around Shingle Street have long been associated with will-o'-the-wisps, while the place-name Toby's Walks at Blythburgh relates to the ghost of Tobias Gill, a drummer in a dragoon regiment who was hanged on the common after being found guilty of murder in the mid-eighteenth century.[59] When seen from the perspective of cultural geography, this suggests that the myths of the Second World War represent the continuation of much older perceptions. The additional layer provided by the twentieth century to these existing traditions is that of the secret and scientific. The remote Suffolk coastline may have fed into a particular perception of place, but it also served a more utilitarian purpose in that, throughout the twentieth century, it was a favoured location for military science and weapon testing. At Orford Ness clandestine scientific work for government agencies defined the area's use for

57   Rogeri de Wendover, ed. H.O. Coxe, *Chronica sive Flores Historiarum* (London, 1841–44), vol. 4, pp. 332–3.
58   R. Allen Brown, *Orford Castle* (London, 1988), p. 20.
59   E. Porter, *Folklore of East Anglia* (London, 1974).

much of the twentieth century and, together with Bawdsey Manor, ensured that the history of the coastal landscape was for a similar span of time defined by secrecy. Bawdsey acquired a reputation as a place where 'hush hush' work was carried on, with speculation that the site was being used to develop death rays and was responsible for the mysterious phenomena of car engines failing when in close proximity to the station.[60] At the time of writing the events of the Second World War are actively becoming part of East Anglia folklore, but they are arguably a continuation of a much longer tradition of superstition borne out of a particular sense of place.

---

60   *The Felixstowe Times*, 18.8.45; Kinsey, *Bawdsey*, pp. 44–5.

Conclusion

There are no memorials in the Sandlings to the soldiers who served there during the Second World War. Those monuments that do exist commemorate Lowestoft seamen, civilians killed during air raids and servicemen drawn from its towns and villages who lost their lives elsewhere. The absence of any formal marker to those who passed through the region is unsurprising; the expected invasion never happened and training was a means to an end that was played out on foreign shores. The graves of those who served on the Suffolk coast but who did not outlive the conflict are spread across the globe from Burma to North Africa and throughout Europe, and they offer a reminder that, for the majority, their time in the region was a transient episode in a longer period of wartime service. Many of the units discussed in this book went on to take their place in the order of battle in the Italian campaign, the battle for Normandy, at Arnhem, at the Rhine Crossing and at countless other actions, and so months or weeks on the Suffolk coast were soon surpassed by subsequent events. But it is easy to forget that manning the coastal defences and undertaking training were real enough experiences at the time. And, as has been seen throughout this book, six years of military use had a considerable effect on the physical and social landscape of the Sandlings.

At the core of this study has been the relationship between the physical landscape and militarisation at this particular point in the twentieth century. There are doubtless some who would see much of this book as relating what is obvious: that the structure of military landscapes are influenced by geography, topography and land use. But, as has hopefully been made clear here, the subtle variations in regional landscapes are often *not* in themselves immediately apparent – or too often are glibly or uncritically accepted – and their relationship with military monuments is in fact complex. Even in a region such as the Sandlings, which possesses a geographic coherence and identity, military planning did not operate across an undifferentiated environment and it is thus important to understand one in order to fully understand the other. We have seen how in the northern Sandlings the existence of 'spurs' between low-lying river valleys determined the character of the anti-invasion defences, the nature of the Diver strip and the location of training grounds. In the southern Sandlings the same principles held true, but the subtle difference in soils and topography led to equally subtle differences in the distribution and character of monuments. Even for the recent past, we would therefore emphasise the benefits to be gained by taking a 'landscape approach'.

Much of this book has also been concerned with the minutia of how this military landscape was enacted, changed and perceived. In so doing it has, again deliberately, emphasised the role of men on the ground, which the abundance of war diary evidence at brigade and battalion level allows us to see in great clarity. The history of anti-invasion landscapes in particular is often told largely with reference to officers at the highest level of command, and there are, of course, good reasons for this, but we have argued here that, in some periods, key components of the defences as they came to exist were enacted as much from below. But this is not to posit some kind of binary opposition between 'top down' or 'bottom up'; rather, it is to emphasise that the military landscapes of the Sandlings were *created* through processes, and here the physical environment was a major structuring influence.

To say this is in no way to deny, however, the importance of human agency or military doctrine. Military men prepared battlefields to meet invasion and planned training to suit particular demands. A detailed study such as this helps to illuminate at what point in the organisational hierarchy decisions were made that resulted in the regional forms of monument and their distribution that we can see today. In the case of built structures, the level of Division and Brigade was critical, be it in the design of concrete pillboxes or the morphology of Diver domestic sites. Here, in fact, we would go further, and argue that when it comes to understanding spatial patterns on the ground the key place in the chain of command is that of Brigade and to a lesser extent the Battalion, commanded by Brigadiers and Lieutenant Colonel respectively. These were the senior field officers who transformed orders from the General staff to a physical reality. As individuals, these men tend not be those who leave archives or papers for academic study and, to some extent, appear in war diaries only as faceless men in uniform. But it is in the archaeology that we see their decisions – the ways in which they interpreted their orders from above and how they, crucially, mediated those commands through the physical landscape over which they had control. The processes are encoded in the written evidence of defence schemes and occasionally in war diary entries that record these officers physically siting positions and ordering their own arrangements, but are most clearly visible in the siting of pillboxes, the course of anti-tank ditches and the arrangement of beach defences. A consequence of this is that in anti-invasion landscapes it is the Sub-Sector that might be termed the 'unit' of regional variation, meaning that it is with each Sub-Sector – and with the Brigade – that we see the manifestation of subtly different archaeological arrangements. This conclusion emerges most forcibly from the study of the Sandlings through time: while parent Divisions had their own schemes, it was their constituent Brigades who varied the principles to suit local environments.

A second conclusion to emerge from this study concerns the chronology of the anti-invasion landscape. The overriding observation to emerge from the study of one Sector through time is that of the importance of continual alterations at a local level that together made change a *defining characteristic* in itself. Unpicking these detailed chronologies elsewhere in the country would be a worthwhile undertaking. How applicable the chronology detailed here is to those elsewhere is at present unclear; however, it is reasonable to suppose that as a place seen to be particularly vulnerable throughout the war it would be mirrored in Kent and Sussex. The chronology seen in Suffolk was certainly not the same in other areas. In neighbouring 18th Division in Norfolk, for example, during 1941, and at the same time as they were being abandoned in the Sandlings, a major campaign of pillbox construction was ongoing.[1]

In taking a landscape biographical approach this study has tried to give equal weight to the range of military activities undertaken in the Sandlings. In so doing, it has highlighted the role of the coastline as a training landscape not just in the well-known run up to the D-Day landings but also in the first half of the conflict. The different circumstances of training engendered different kinds of landscape, but here, too, the particular choices made by commanders were all shaped, either directly or indirectly, by the nature of local conditions. The pattern of structures created in one period survived into, and often helped to configure the details of, the next. So it was that the training landscapes of the Sandlings tended to be located in particular areas and eschew others; the absence of defences at Orford Ness, for example, was a factor in giving over the hinterland to training. So, too, why those places abandoned in 1941 as part of Brooke's reforms tended to be reused for training purposes from 1943 onwards. Even within such a short time frame as the six years of the war, the particular military landscape described in this book was the result of successive changes brought about by different circumstances.

The wartime experience of the Sandlings also needs to be set against a longer view. The invasion crisis of the mid-twentieth century was in many ways the last of its kind. The state first built fortifications in the region in the sixteenth century, when Landguard Point formed part of Henry VIII's chain of coastal forts intended to resist French and Spanish invasion.[2] But it was during the Napoleonic Wars that serious consideration began to be given to the overall scheme with which coastal landscapes – rather than just ports and anchorages – were to be defended, and here it is revealing to see how the arrangements conceived at this time mirror those discussed in this book. Over two centuries before Ironside and others wrestled with them, an earlier generation of commanders faced the familiar problems of not enough men to hold the coastline, where exactly to place batteries, what parts of the hinterland could be inundated and the exact role of mobile reserves. In Sir John Moore's proposition of an inland defence line, which in the Sandlings would run from Beccles to Woodbridge, and from where reserves would advance to push back against a landing, we see the ultimate precursor to Brooke's strategy and the Second World War 'Back Line'.[3] Even the revolutionary

---

1   TNA WO 166/3709 (War Diary, 240th Field Company, Royal Engineers), Progress Report, 13.4.41.
2   Saunders, *Fortress Britain*, pp. 34–52.
3   J.P. Foynes, *East Anglia Against the Tricolor, 1789–1815* (Cromer, 2016), pp. 74–82.

changes in warfare during the nineteenth century did little to alter appreciations of how the Sandlings should be defended, with cavalry and artillery placed on the 'spurs' to hold back those advancing from the beaches.[4] While it remains frustratingly opaque, the defence of the coast during the First World War also appears to have been conceived along these earlier lines. To nineteenth- and early twentieth-century eyes the principles behind the schemes of 1939, 1941 and 1942 would have looked familiar, even if the concrete obstacles and fieldworks were of a different character. The oddity is the scheme of 1940 – with its long thin line and little by way of reserve – which can be characterised as a short-lived aberration in the longer-term military history of the region. Here the unusual circumstances of its origin, outlined in Chapter 2, are underscored. And, when placed against this longer background, the archaeology of the Second World War can be said to mark the end of a period when the physical coastline was defended by guns and men. Since 1800 military strategy, regardless of technology, was intimately linked to topography. This direct link was broken soon after 1945, when the landscape of national defence during the Cold War became one of missiles and underground monitoring posts. This marked a fundamental change in the archaeological character of home defence and it is one that is clearly apparent in the Sandlings. Even though it faced the strategic direction of threat, military confrontation would not be occasioned by foreign troops splashing ashore on the beaches, but by obliteration by atomic weapons delivered from over the horizon. In the atomic age, the Sandlings became a landscape of early warning, rather than one of active defence. At the time of writing, a further shift seems to be taking place, with home defence now more associated with counter-terrorism and cyber- and biosecurity, rather than confrontation of a traditional kind, although talk of a new Cold War has resurrected some older themes.

Finally, if topography tended to influence the distribution of military works, what we see preserved in the landscape today is also largely a reflection of the subsequent perception of the particular environments in which they are situated as worthy of stewardship. The wartime remains in these areas are not necessarily representative of what was originally built, of course, but they do represent a diminished archaeological resource and as such deserve sensitive management. To end on a more personal note. One of the most memorable aspects of researching this volume has been working on a period that lies on the cusp of human memory. To talk to men and women who experienced the Second World War at first hand while at the same time undertaking archival work and field survey on its material remains (which, historically and archaeologically speaking, belong to a period that seems utterly remote) we have found to be, for whatever reason, an experience both exhilarating and disconcerting. From the perspective of the early twenty-first century the Second World War seems a very foreign country; albeit, thanks to this book, it is one in which we have been privileged enough to travel.

---

4   SRO (Lowestoft) 741/HA12/A6/3 *Memoir on the Defence of East Suffolk* (1854).

Bibliography

Primary sources

Bovington Tank Museum
E2009.142 (79th Armoured Division Training Instruction)
E2009, 1964 (L.A. Wells, *Projectors to Petards. A Sapper's Tale, 12 September 1940–10 May 1946*)
Neave, J.A.S., *The War Diary of Julius Neave, Winter 1942/3–May 1945*, unpublished typescript (n.d.)

Historic England
National Monuments Record, RAF Photography
RAF 2/BR11/14 Frm.34 (8.7.40)
RAF E2/BR260 PO6988 (7.7.41)
RAF S349/H.51.1416 (23.7.41)
RAF 106G/UK/832/RP.3180 (23.9.45)
RAF 106G/UK/832/RS/4167 (23.9.45)
National Monuments Record, USAAF Collection
7PH/GP/LOC 288, F24 (19.4.44)

Imperial War Museum
ART LD2890 (Edward Bawden, Exercise Kruschen, 1943)
Oral History
14252 (interview with George Perkins, 5th Royal Berkshire Regiment)
20007 (interview with James Kelly, 10th Battalion the Cameronians)
14129 (interview with Sidney East, 1st Battalion Liverpool Scottish)
19768 (interview with Tom Barlow, 2nd/4th South Lancashire Regiment)
18254 (L.C.H. Dodd, 2nd/7th Royal West Surrey Regiment)
Photographic Archive
D 4846–4878 (Invasion Village: Everyday Life in Orford, Suffolk, 1941), 1.9.41.
H2240–2245 (Inland Defence), 16.7.40
H2669–2706 (Assault on Pillbox), 2.8.40

H11451–11480 (Camouflage, Eastern Command), 8.8.41
H20990–21011 (Eastern Command Divisional Exercise), 27.6.42
H23550–23556 (The Army's Handicraft), 2.9.42
H25860–25869 (Young Soldiers Training Under Modern Warfare Conditions, Orford Battle Area, Eastern Command), 3.12.42
H28386–28398 (MPs Visit to an AA Battery near Harwich), 27.3.43
H27328–27355 (Battle School Training), 15–17.2.43
H29035–29069 (Eastern Command Exercise), 14.4.43
H34455–34472 (79th Armoured Division, Development Unit, Home Forces), 18.11.43
H365920–36602 (Special Assignment for 79th Armoured Division), 11.3.44
H37029–37042 (Special Assignment for 79th Armoured Division), 29.3.44
H37465–37469 (Special Assignment for 79th Armoured Division) 31.3.44–6.4.44
H40430–40438 (Guns Switch Over), 9.10.44
Film Archive
AYY 41 (Troop Exercises), 27.9.40
AYY 340/3 (54th Division Battle School Infantry Training in Assault Tactics), 15.2.43
AYY387 (Exercise Kruschen), 14.4.43

Long Shop Museum, Leiston
W. Titlow & Son, Sales Ledgers, 1940–1945

Low Parks Museum, Hamilton, South Lanarkshire
The Covenantor, 1941

Mass Observation Archive, University of Sussex
File Report 170, Suffolk Village Report, 6.6.40
File Report 372, Morale in Coastal Suffolk, 28.8.40
File Report 703, East Suffolk Village, May 1941

M.S. Oakes, Lowestoft Ltd
Reades Builders, uncatalogued ledgers, 1940–1945

Newspapers
The Felixstowe Times
The Glasgow Herald
The Leiston Observer
The Times

Norfolk County Council
Historical Environment Record

Suffolk County Council
Historical Environment Record

Suffolk Record Office, Ipswich
DC10/1/6/8 (Ipswich Borough: Demolition of Defence
  Works, 1948–1951)
EE1/1/13/8a (Clearance of Coastal Defences)
EE1/1/13/9 (Beach Clearance, Removal of Defences)
EE1/P12/2 (Aldeburgh Invasion Committee, Military
  Reps File)
EF12/1/8/3 (Felixstowe, Seafront Clearance of Defence
  Works)
EF12/1/8/6 (Felixstowe Clearance of Defence Works)
HD1654/1–2 (Notes on Pillboxes)
K463–127 (Dunwich Beach, *c*.1950)
K463–131 (Dunwich Beach)
K681/1/3/12/8 (Aldeburgh, *c*.1948)
K681/1/158/234 (Felixstowe, *c*.1917)
OHT 134 (Oral History, Anon.)
OHT 148 (Oral History, Anon.)
OHT 149 (Oral History, Anon.)

Suffolk Record Office, Lowestoft
491/12F/28 (Requisition of Land and Property)
491/12F/45 (Removal of Mines and Coastal Defences)
741/HA12/A6/3 *Memoir on the Defence of East Suffolk*
  (1854)
2250/1 (A Kessingland Boy at War)
1300/72/48/37 (Pillbox being Blown up at Benacre,
  c.1987)
1300/72/48/50 (Lowestoft Second World War Barrage
  Balloons)

The National Archives, Kew
ADM 199/66 (AA Defence of Ports and Naval
  Establishments)
ADM 1/13117 (AA Defence of Gt Yarmouth and
  Lowestoft)
AIR 16/149 (Defence of Harwich)
WO 33/329 (Eastern Defence Scheme)

WO 86/97 (General Courts Martial Register of
  Charges)
WO 95/5455 (War Diary, 2nd/1st Welsh Horse)
WO 95/5458 (War Diary, 227 Mixed Brigade)
WO 99/2528 (Home Defence, Pillboxes)
WO 166/1 (War Diary, GHQ Home Forces)
WO 166/11 (War Diary, GHQ Home Forces, Coast
  Artillery)
WO 166/329 (War Diary, XI Corps)
WO 166/499 (War Diary, 49th Division)
WO 166/450 (War Diary, 15th Division, GS)
WO 166/451 (War Diary, 15th Division, GS)
WO 166/453 (War Diary, 15th Division, CRA)
WO 166/454 (War Diary, 15th Division, CRE)
WO 166/464 (War Diary, 18th Division, GS)
WO 166/494 (War Diary, 42nd Division, GS)
WO 166/495 (War Diary, 42nd Division, GS)
WO 166/498 (War Diary, 42nd Division, CRE)
WO 166/673 (War Diary, 54th Division, GS)
WO 166/688 (War Diary, 55th Division, GS)
WO 166/693 (War Diary, 55th Division, CRE)
WO 166/957 (War Diary, 45th Infantry Brigade)
WO 166/958 (War Diary, 46th Infantry Brigade)
WO 166/975 (War Diary, 125th Infantry Brigade)
WO 166/976 (War Diary, 126th Infantry Brigade)
WO 166/977 (War Diary, 127th Infantry Brigade)
WO 166/1036 (War Diary, 163rd Infantry Brigade)
WO 166/1037 (War Diary, 164th Infantry Brigade)
WO 166/1038 (War Diary, 165th Infantry Brigade)
WO 166/1051 (War Diary, 198th Infantry Brigade)
WO 166/1052 (War Diary, 199th Infantry Brigade)
WO 166/1441 (War Diary, No. 1 Armoured Train
  Group)
WO 166/1529 (War Diary, 117th Field Regiment,
  Royal Artillery)
WO 166/1835 (War Diary, 355th Coast Battery)
WO 166/1885 (War Diary, 58th Heavy Regiment,
  Royal Artillery)
WO 166/1935 (War Diary, 72nd Medium Regiment,
  Royal Artillery)
WO 166/2168 (War Diary, 6th Anti-Aircraft Division, G)
WO 166/2229 (War Diary, 6th Anti-Aircraft Brigade)
WO 166/2278 (War Diary, 41st Anti-Aircraft Brigade)
WO 166/2525 (War Diary, 244th Heavy Anti-Aircraft
  Battery)
WO 166/2526 (War Diary, 245th Heavy Anti-Aircraft
  Battery)
WO 166/2529 (War Diary, 248th Heavy Anti-Aircraft
  Battery)
WO 166/2581 (War Diary, 309th Heavy Anti-Aircraft
  Battery)

WO 166/2662 (War Diary, 409th Heavy Anti-Aircraft Battery)

WO 166/3088 (War Diary, 69th Searchlight Battery)

WO 166/3094 (War Diary, 74th Searchlight Regiment)

WO 166/3095 (War Diary, 32th Searchlight Regiment)

WO 166/3317 (War Diary, 469th Searchlight Battery)

WO 166/3670 (War Diary, 200th Field Company, Royal Engineers)

WO 166/3698 (War Diary, 229th Field Company, Royal Engineers)

WO 166/3709 (War Diary, 240th Field Company, Royal Engineers)

WO 166/3719 (War Diary, 250th Field Company, Royal Engineers)

WO 166/3748 (War Diary, 279th Field Company, Royal Engineers)

WO 166/4134 (War Diary, 6th Beds and Herts Regiment)

WO 166/4153 (War Diary, 1st Border Regiment)

WO 166/4156 (War Diary, 6th Border Regiment)

WO 166/4180 (War Diary, 9th Cameronians)

WO 166/4181 (War Diary, 10th Cameronians)

WO 166/4249 (War Diary, 4th East Lancashire Regiment)

WO 166/4271 (War Diary, 2nd/4th Essex Regiment)

WO 166/4339 (War Diary, 1st Hertfordshire Regiment)

WO 166/4340 (War Diary, 1st Hertfordshire Regiment)

WO 166/4341 (War Diary, 2nd Hertfordshire Regiment)

WO 166/4346 (War Diary, 11th Highland Light Infantry)

WO 166/4351 (War Diary, 2nd Kensington Regiment)

WO 166/4357 (War Diary, 13th King's (Liverpool) Regiment)

WO 166/4367 (War Diary, 6th King's Own Scottish Borderers)

WO 166/4393 (War Diary, 5th King's Own Royal Regiment)

WO 166/4407 (War Diary, 1st/5th Lancashire Fusiliers)

WO 166/4409 (War Diary, 1st/6th Lancashire Fusiliers)

WO 166/4412 (War Diary, 2nd/8th Lancashire Fusiliers)

WO 166/4413 (War Diary, 9th Lancashire Fusiliers)

WO 166/4433 (War Diary, 1st Liverpool Scottish)

WO 166/4434 (War Diary, 2nd Liverpool Scottish)

WO 166/4451 (War Diary, 5th Manchester Regiment)

WO 166/4452 (War Diary, 6th Manchester Regiment)

WO 166/4454 (War Diary, 7th Manchester Regiment)

WO 166/4462 (War Diary, 1st/7th Middlesex (Machine Gun) Regiment)

WO 166/4516 (War Diary, 6th Border Regiment)

WO 166/4524 (War Diary, 5th Royal Berkshire Regiment)

WO 166/4537 (War Diary, 22nd Royal Fusiliers)

WO 166/4547 (War Diary, 22nd Royal Fusiliers)

WO 166/4592 (War Diary, 6th Royal Scots Fusiliers)

WO 166/4679 (War Diary, 1st/4th South Lancashire Regiment)

WO 166/4680 (War Diary, 2nd/4th South Lancashire Regiment)

WO 166/4707 (War Diary, 4th Suffolk Regiment)

WO 166/4709 (War Diary, 6th Suffolk Regiment)

WO 166/6020 (War Diary, Eastern Command Royal Artillery Branch)

WO 166/6380 (War Diary, 54th Division, HQ)

WO 166/6138 (War Diary, XI Corps)

WO 166/6623 (War Diary, 162nd Infantry Brigade)

WO 166/6645 (War Diary, 212th Infantry Brigade)

WO 166/7199 (War Diary, 232nd Coast Battery, Royal Artillery)

WO 166/7210 (War Diary, 232nd Coast Battery, Royal Artillery)

WO 166/7247 (War Diary, 75th Medium Regiment, Royal Artillery)

WO 166/7376 (War Diary, 6th Anti-Aircraft Brigade)

WO 166/7711 (War Diary, 125th Light Anti-Aircraft Regiment)

WO 166/8159 (War Diary, 249th Field Company, Royal Engineers)

WO 166/8608 (War Diary, 7th Border Regiment)

WO 166/8671 (War Diary, 2nd/4th Essex Regiment)

WO 166/8696 (War Diary, 10th Gloucestershire Regiment)

WO 166/8725 (War Diary, 2nd Hertfordshire Regiment)

WO 166/8726 (War Diary, 2nd Hertfordshire Regiment)

WO 166/8739 (War Diary, 8th King's Regiment)

WO 166/8851 (War Diary, 5th Royal Berkshire Regiment)

WO 166/8853 (War Diary, 7th Royal Berkshire Regiment)

WO 166/8993 (War Diary, 6th South Wales Borderers)

WO 166/10649 (War Diary, 54th Division, HQ)

WO 166/10710 (War Diary, 79th Armoured Division, G)

WO 166/10782 (War Diary, 146th Infantry Brigade)

WO 166/10795 (War Diary, 163rd Infantry Brigade)

WO 166/10805 (War Diary, 198th Infantry Brigade)

WO 166/10975 (War Diary, 163rd Infantry Brigade)
WO 166/11096 (War Diary, 43rd Royal Tank Regiment)
WO 166/11642 (War Diary, 161st Heavy Anti-Aircraft Regiment)
WO 166/11995 (War Diary, 5th Assault Regiment, Royal Engineers)
WO 166/11996 (War Diary, 6th Engineer Assault Regiment)
WO 166/12029 (War Diary, 77th Assault Squadron, Royal Engineers)
WO 166/12031 (War Diary, 79th Assault Squadron, Royal Engineers)
WO 166/12033 (War Diary, 81st Assault Squadron, Royal Engineers)
WO 166/12482 (War Diary, 5th Royal Berkshire Regiment)
WO 166/12494 (War Diary, 6th Border Regiment)
WO 166/12496 (War Diary, 1st Bucks Battalion, Ox and Bucks Light Infantry)
WO 166/12537 (War Diary, 2nd/4th Essex Regiment)
WO 166/12589 (War Diary, 8th King's Regiment)
WO 166/14393 (War Diary, Essex and Suffolk District)
WO 166/14537 (Area War Diary, East Suffolk Sub-District)
WO 166/14617 (War Diary, 1st Anti-Aircraft Group)
WO 166/14640 (War Diary, 5th Anti-Aircraft Brigade)
WO 166/14666 (War Diary, 57th Anti-Aircraft Brigade)
WO 166/14671 (War Diary, 632nd Anti-Aircraft Brigade)
WO 166/14679 (War Diary, 102st Anti-Aircraft Brigade)
WO 166/14728 (War Diary, 83rd Light Anti-Aircraft Regiment)
WO 166/14784 (War Diary, 122nd Heavy Anti-Aircraft Regiment)
WO 166/14798 (War Diary, 140th Heavy Anti-Aircraft Regiment)
WO 166/14841 (War Diary, 189th Heavy Anti-Aircraft Regiment)
WO 166/16693 (War Diary, 57th Anti-Aircraft Brigade)
WO 166/16695 (War Diary, 63rd Anti-Aircraft Brigade)
WO 177/412 (ADMS, 54th Division)
WO 171/499 (War Diary, 49th Infantry Division)
WO 171/506 (War Diary, 49th Division Reconnaissance Regiment)
WO 171/653 (War Diary, 70th Infantry Brigade)
WO 171/664 (War Diary, 146th Infantry Brigade)
WO 171/841 (War Diary, 22nd Dragoons)
WO 171/1165 (War Diary, 139th Heavy Anti-Aircraft Regiment)
WO 171/1291 (War Diary, 9th Durham Light Infantry)
WO 171/1292 (War Diary, 10th Durham Light Infantry)
WO 171/1293 (War Diary, 11th Durham Light Infantry)
WO 171/1314 (War Diary, 2nd Princess Louise Kensingtons)
WO 171/1383 (War Diary, 1st Tyneside Scottish)
WO 171/1398 (War Diary, 5th Battalion East Yorkshire Regiment)
WO 171/1797 (War Diary, 1st Assault Brigade, Royal Engineers)
WO 171/1804 (War Diary, 26th Assault Squadron, Royal Engineers)
WO 171/1805 (War Diary, 42nd Assault Regiment, Royal Engineers)
WO 171/1806 (War Diary, 77th Assault Squadron, Royal Engineers)
WO 171/1808 (War Diary, 80th Assault Squadron, Royal Engineers)
WO 171/1811 (War Diary, 87th Assault Squadron, Royal Engineers)
WO 171/1816 (War Diary, 617th Assault Squadron, Royal Engineers)
WO 192/56 (Fort Record Book, Easton Wood Battery)
WO 192/72 (Fort Record Book, Kessingland Battery)
WO 192/79 (Fort Record Book, Southwold Battery)
WO 192/215 (Fort Record Book, Pakefield Battery)
WO 195/4617 (Ministry of Supply, Advisory Council on Scientific Research and Technical Development)
WO 195/4618 (Ministry of Supply, Advisory Council on Scientific Research and Technical Development)
WO 199/44 (Concrete Defences Policy)
WO 199/1167 (Fixed Defences, Lowestoft, 1940–42)
WO 199/85 (HQ Home Forces)
WO 199/805 (Assault Training Areas)
WO 199/808 (Land for Training – Formation Battle Training Areas General)
WO 199/811 (Assault Training Area, Southwold)
WO 199/940 (Tours and Visits to Coast Defences)
WO 199/2510 (Military Assistance to Civil Powers – Agriculture)
WO 199/2623 (Army's Commander's Personal Memorandum No. 2)
WO 199/3078 (Coast Watching, Overlord)
WO 205/1C (General Paget's Conferences as Commander in Chief Home Forces)

WO 205/417 (79th Armoured Division Training Areas, General)

WO 205/419 (79th Armoured Division Training Areas)

WO 205/624 (79th Armoured Division Organisation, Equipment, Training Part I)

WO 205/1088 (Reports on Assault Training Areas)

WO 205/1092 (Assault Training Areas, Eastern Command)

WO 205/1159 (79th Armoured Division. Final Report, 1945)

WO 277/36 (Training in the British Army, 1939–1945)

WO 277/37 (Defence Plans for the United Kingdom, 1939–45), Cabinet Historical Section (1948)

HO 207/1175 (Compulsory Evacuation of Shingle Street)

HO 207/1180 (Battle Training Areas, 1942–1945)

HO 207/1182 (Dunwich–Sizewell Battle Training Areas)

TNA 231/282 (The Co-Operation of Tanks and Infantry, 1943)

War Office Publications

Field Service Pocket Book, Pamphlet No. 4, Field Engineering, 1939

Field Service Regulations, volume 1: Organisation & Administration, 1930

Home Guard Manual, 1941

Infantry Training Part VIII Fieldcraft, Battle Drill, Section and Platoon Tactics, 1944

Manual of Field Engineering Vol. 1 (All Arms), 1936

Manual of Field Works (All Arms), 1925

Military Training Pamphlet No. 2 – The Offensive, 1943

Military Training Pamphlet No. 23: Operations. Part II: The Infantry Division in the Defence, 1942

Military Training Pamphlet No. 30 Part III, Field Engineering All Arms, Obstacles, 1940; 1941

The Co-Operation of Tanks and Infantry, 1943

Websites

http://www.walberswickww2.co.uk/flying-enemy/

http://www.walberswickww2.co.uk/wartime-memories/

http://www.britainfromabove.org.uk/

http://www.bbc.co.uk/history/ww2peopleswar/

Secondary sources

Addison, P. and Crang, J. (eds), *Listening to Britain* (London, 2011).

Alexander, C., *Ironside's Line* (Storrington, 1998).

Allen Brown, R., *Orford Castle* (London, 1988).

Allport, A., *Browned Off and Bloody Minded. The British Soldier Goes to War 1939–1945* (New Haven, CT, 2015).

Anderson, R.C., *Cracking Hitler's Atlantic Wall. The 1st Assault Brigade Royal Engineers on D-Day* (Mechanicsburg, PA, 2010).

Anon., 'Battle School', *New Statesman*, 24/595 (1942).

Anon., *The Story of 79th Armoured Division* (Hamburg, 1945).

Anon., *The 6th Battalion Royal Scots Fusiliers, 1939–1946* (Ayr, 1946).

Anon., *Bildheft Neuzeitlicher Stellungsbau* (1942); reprinted as *German Fieldworks of World War II* (Bracknall, 1969).

Appleby, C., Cocroft, W. and Schofield, J. (eds), *The Home Front in Britain, 1914–1918. An Archaeological Handbook* (York, 2015).

Arbib, R.S., *Here We Are Together: The Notebook of an American Soldier in Britain* (London, 1947).

Armstrong, P., 'Changes in the Suffolk Sandlings', *Geography*, 58 (1973), pp. 1–8.

Axell, H. and Hosking, E., *Minsmere: Portrait of a Bird Reserve* (London, 1977).

Bailey, J.B.A., *Field Artillery and Firepower*, 2nd edn (Annapolis, MD, 2004).

Barclay, G., *If Hitler Comes. Preparing For Invasion: Scotland 1940* (Edinburgh, 2013).

Bates, M., *East Anglia. Regional Military Histories* (London, 1974).

Beaverstock, K., *Breaking the Panzers* (Stroud, 2002).

Becker, J.M., *Story of Southwold* (Southwold, 1948).

Beckett, I., *The Amateur Military Tradition, 1558–1945* (Manchester, 1991).

Bellis, M., *Divisions of the British Army, 1939–1945* (Crewe, 1986).

Bender, B. and Winer, M. (eds), *Contested Landscapes: Movement, Exile and Place* (London, 2000).

Bidwell, S. and Graham, D., *Fire Power: The British Army – Weapons and Theories of War, 1904–1945* (Barnsley, 2004).

Bond, B., 'Ironside', in J. Keegan (ed.), *Churchill's Generals* (London, 1992), pp. 17–33.

Bond, B., 'The British Field Force in France and Belgium, 1939–40', in P. Addison and A. Calder (eds), *Time to Kill: The Soldier's Experience of War in the West* (London, 1997), pp. 40–49.

Bourke, J., *An Intimate History of Killing: Face to Face Killing in Twentieth-Century Warfare* (London, 1999).

Bowyer, M., *Air Raid! The Enemy Air Offensive against East Anglia, 1939–45* (Wellingborough, 1986).

Brown, M. and Patterson, P., *Beacon Hill Fort, Essex* (English Heritage, Archaeological Field Survey Report. Requested Survey, 1997).

Brown, M., Barrett, N., and Patterson, P., *Landguard Fort Report No. 3: Right Battery, Felixstowe, Suffolk* (English Heritage, Archaeological Investigation Report Series AI/34/2004).

Brück, J., 'Experiencing the Past? The Development of a Phenomenological Archaeology in British Prehistory', *Archaeological Dialogues*, 12 (2005), pp. 45–72.

Buckley, J., *British Armour in the Normandy Campaign 1944* (London, 2004).

Buckley, J. (ed.), *The Normandy Campaign 1944. Sixty Years On* (London, 2006).

Buckley, J., *Monty's Men. The British Army and the Liberation of Europe* (New Haven, CT, and London, 2013).

Butcher, R.W., *The Land of Britain. The Report of the Land Utilisation Survey of Britain. Parts 72–73 Suffolk (East and West)* (London, 1941).

Calder, A., *The People's War: Britain 1939–1945* (London, 1969).

Cannon-Brookes, P., *The British Neo-Romantics 1935–1950* (London, 1983).

Carmen, J., *Archaeologies of Conflict* (London, 2013).

Carver, M., *Sutton Hoo: Burial Ground of Kings?* (London, 1998).

Chamberlin, P. and Gander, T., *Anti-Aircraft Guns* (London, 1975).

Clarke, B., *Britain's Cold War* (Stroud, 2009).

Clarke, D., *The Angels of Mons: Phantom Soldiers and Ghostly Guardians* (Chichester, 2004).

Clay, E.W., *The Path of the 50th* (Aldershot, 1950).

Cocroft, W. and Alexander, M., *Atomic Weapons Research Establishment, Orford Ness, Suffolk. Cold War Research & Development Site. Survey Report* (English Heritage Research Department Report Series, No. 10, 2009).

Cole, C. and Cheesman, E.F., *The Air Defence of Britain, 1914–1918* (London, 1984).

Collier, B., *The Defence of the United Kingdom* (London, 1957).

Collins, I., *Making Waves: Artists in Southwold* (Norwich, 2005).

Connelly, M., *We Can Take It! Britain and the Memory of the Second World War* (London, 2004).

Cooper, A.J., *Anti-Aircraft Command, 1939–1955, The Other Forgotten Army* (Fleet Hargate, 1994).

Crang, J.A., 'The British Soldier on the Home Front: Army Morale Reports', in P. Addison and A. Calder (eds), *Time to Kill: The Soldier's Experience of the War in the West, 1939–1945* (London, 1997), pp. 60–74.

Crang, J.A., *The British Army and the People's War, 1939–1945* (Manchester, 2000).

Cumberlege, G., *Recording Britain* (Oxford, 1947).

Davison, P., *The Complete Works of George Orwell. Vol. 10 A Kind of Compulsion, 1903–1936* (London, 1998).

Delaforce, P., *The Polar Bears* (Stroud, 1995).

Delaforce, P., *Churchill's Secret Weapons. The Story of Hobart's Funnies* (London, 1998).

D'Este, C., *Decision in Normandy* (London, 1983).

Dewing, G., *Aldeburgh, 1939–45* (Aldeburgh, 1995).

Dobinson, C.S., *Twentieth-Century Fortifications in England, vol.1 Anti-aircraft Artillery: England's Air Defence Gunsites, 1914–46* (York, 1996).

Dobinson, C.S., *Twentieth-Century Fortifications in England, vol. 2 Anti-Invasion Defences of World War II* (York, 1996).

Dobinson, C.S., *Twentieth-Century Fortifications in England, vol. 4. Operation Diver* (York, 1996).

Dobinson, C.S., *Twentieth-Century Fortifications in England, vol. 5 Operation Overlord* (York, 1996).

Dobinson, C.S., 'Twentieth-Century Fortifications in England: the MPP Approach', in J. Scofield (ed.), *Monuments of War. The Evaluation, Recording and Management of Twentieth-Century Military Sites* (English Heritage, 1998), pp. 2–5.

Dobinson, C.S., *Fields of Deceptions: Bombing Decoys of World War Two* (London, 2000).

Dobinson, C.S., *Twentieth-Century Fortifications in England, vols 6.1–2 Coast Artillery: England's Fixed Defences Against the Warship* (York, 2000).

Dobinson, C.S., *Twentieth-Century Fortifications in England. Supplementary Study. Experimental and Training Sites: An Annotated Handlist* (York, 2000).

Dobinson, C.S., *AA Command: Britain's Anti-Aircraft Defences of the Second World War* (London, 2001).

Dobinson, C.S., *Building Radar: Forging Britain's Early-Warning Chain, 1935–1945* (London, 2010).

Dobinson, C., Lake, J. and Schofield J., 'Monuments of War: Defining England's Twentieth-Century Defence Heritage', *Antiquity*, 71 (1997), pp. 288–99.

Doherty, R., *Hobart's 79th Armoured Division at War* (Barnsley, 2011).

Douglas Brown, R., *East Anglia, 1939–1945*, 7 volumes (Lavenham, 1980–94).

Doyle, P. and Bennett, M.R. (eds), *Fields of Battle. Terrain in Military History* (London, 2002).

Duncan, N., *79th Armoured Division: Hobo's Funnies* (Windsor, 1972).

Dymond, D. and Martin, E. (eds), *An Historical Atlas of Suffolk* (Ipswich, 1999).

Ellis, J., *The Sharp End: The Fighting Man in World War II* (London, 1980).

Ellis, J., *Brute Force: Allied Strategy and Tactics in the Second World War* (London, 1990).

Emsley, C., *Soldier, Sailor, Beggarman, Thief: Crime and the British Armed Services since 1914* (Oxford, 2013).

English, J.A., *The Canadian Army and the Normandy Campaign* (Mechanicsburg, PA, 1991).

Faulkner, N. and Durrani, N., *In Search of the Zeppelin War: The Archaeology of the First Blitz* (Stroud, 2008).

Flavius Josephus, *Wars of the Jews* (Pantianos, n.d.).

Fleming, P., *Invasion 1940* (London, 1957).

Fletcher, D., *Vanguard of Victory. The 79th Armoured Division* (London, 1984).

Foot, W., *Beaches, Fields, Streets, and Hills: The Anti-Invasion Landscapes of England, 1940* (York, 2006).

Foot, W., 'The Impact of the Military on the Agricultural Landscape of England and Wales in the Second World War', in B. Short, C. Watkins and J. Martin (eds) *The Front Line of Freedom. British Farming in the Second World War* (Exeter, 2007), pp. 132–42.

Ford, E., Horlock, S. and Tremlett, S., *National Mapping Programme Project for Lothingland, Greater Lowestoft and North Suffolk Coasts and Heaths*, National Heritage Protection Project Commissions Programme Project No. 6642 (Norfolk Museums Service, English Heritage, 2015).

Foreman, M., *War Boy. A Country Childhood* (London, 1989).

Forty, G., *Handbook of the British Army* (Stroud, 1998).

Foynes, J.P., *The Battle of the East Coast 1939–1945* (privately published, 1994).

Foynes, J.P., *East Anglia Against the Tricolor, 1789–1815* (Cromer, 2016).

French, D., '"Tommy is No Soldier": The Morale of the Second British Army in Normandy, June–August 1944', in B. Holden-Reid (ed.), *Military Power. Land Warfare in Theory and Practice* (London, 1997), pp. 154–78.

French, D., *Raising Churchill's Army* (Oxford, 2000).

French, D., 'Invading Europe: The British Army and its Preparations for the Normandy Campaign, 1942–44', *Diplomacy and Statecraft*, 14/2 (2003), pp. 271–94.

French, D., *Military Identities: The Regimental System, the British Army and the British People, c.1870–2000* (Oxford, 2005).

Gardiner, J., *Wartime Britain, 1939–1945* (London, 2004).

Goldsmith Carter, G., *Looming Lights* (London, 1945).

Hamilton, I., *Alun Lewis. Selected Poetry and Prose* (London, 1966).

Hamilton, S. and Whitehouse, R., 'Phenomenology in Practice: Towards a Methodology for a "Subjective" Approach', *European Journal of Archaeology*, 9 (2005), pp. 31–71.

Hammerton, I., *Achtung! Minen! The Making of a Flail Tank Troop Commander* (Lewes, 1991).

Harris, J., 'War and Social History: Britain and the Home Front during the Second World War', *Contemporary European History*, 1 (1992), pp. 17–35.

Harrison, R. and Schofield, J., *After Modernity: Archaeological Approaches to the Contemporary Past* (Oxford, 2010).

Harrison Place, T., 'Lionel Wigram, Battle Drill and the British Army in the Second World War', *War in History*, 7 (2000), pp. 442–62.

Harrison Place, T., *Military Training in the British Army, 1940–1944, From Dunkirk to D-Day* (Oxford, 2000).

Harsgor, M., 'Total History: The Annales School', *Journal of Contemporary History*, 13 (1978), pp. 1-13.

Hart, S., *Colossal Cracks. Montgomery's 21st Army Group in Northwest Europe, 1944–45* (Mechanicsburg, PA, 2007).

Hayward, J., *The Bodies on the Beach. Sealion, Shingle Street and the Burning Sea Myth of 1940* (Dereham, 2001).

Hayward, J., *Burn the Sea* (Stroud, 2016).

Heazell, P., *Most Secret: The Hidden History of Orford Ness* (Stroud, 2010).

Hegarty, C. and Newsome, S., *The Archaeology of the Suffolk Coast and Inter-tidal Zone. A Report for the National Mapping Programme* (2912) (Suffolk County Council, English Heritage, 2005).

Hegarty, C. and Newsome, S., *Suffolk's Defended Shore, Coastal Fortifications from the Air* (Swindon, 2007).

Hodge, C., Burton, R., Corbett, W., Evans, R., and Searle, R.S., *Soils and Their Use in Eastern England* (Harpenden, 1984).

Hogg, I.V., *Allied Artillery of World War Two* (Marlborough, 1998).

Holding, J.A., *Fit for Service: Training of the British Army, 1715–1795* (Oxford, 1981).

Holmes, J.W. (ed.), 'The Spirit of Lowestoft, A Town at War', *Lowestoft Journal*, Supplementary Issue (1995).

Hunn, J.R. and Semmelmann, K., *Historic Landscape Survey: Dunwich Estate, Suffolk* (Milton Keynes, 2009).

Jarvis, R., *Fortress Lowestoft* (Lowestoft, 2002).

Jenkins, F., *Story of Southwold* (Southwold, 1948).

Jenkins, F., *Port War: Lowestoft at War* (Lowestoft, 1984).

Joslen, H.F., *Orders of Battle of the Second World War* (London, 1960).

Keegan, J., *The Face of Battle* (London, 1976).

Kennedy, K., *Engineers of Victory: The Problem Solvers Who Turned the Tide of the Second World War* (London, 2013).

Kent, P., *Fortifications of East Anglia* (Lavenham, 1988).

Kent, P., 'East Anglian Fortifications in the Twentieth Century', *Fortress*, 3 (1989), pp. 4–57.

Kinsey, G., *Orfordness, Secret Site* (Lavenham, 1981).

Kinsey, G., *Bawdsey. Birth of the Beam* (Lavenham, 1983).

Lewis, A., 'A Sheaf of Letters from Alun Lewis, 1941–1943', *Wales*, 28 (1948), pp. 410–31.

Lewis, A., 'Dawn on the East Coast', in I. Hamilton (ed.), *Alun Lewis, Selected Poetry and Prose* (London, 1966).

Lewis, P.J. and English, I.R., *Into Battle With the Durhams. 8th DLI in World War II* (London, 1949).

Liddiard, R. and Sims, D., 'A Hedgehog on the Heath: The Second World War Landscape of Exercise "Kruschen", Dunwich, Suffolk', *Archaeological Journal*, 169 (2012), pp. 519–49.

Liddiard, R. and Sims, D., 'A Piece of Coastal Crust: The Origins of a Second World War Defence Landscape at Walberswick, Suffolk', *History*, 97 (2012), pp. 402–30.

Lowry, B. (ed.), *20th Century Defences in Britain: An Introductory Guide* (York, 1996).

Lowry, B., *British Home Defences 1940–45* (Oxford, 2003).

Lowry, B., *Pillboxes and Tank Traps* (Oxford, 2014).

Macksey, K., *Armoured Crusader* (London, 1967).

Martin, H.G., *The History of the Fifteenth Scottish Division 1939–1945* (Edinburgh and London, 1948).

Martin, T.A., *The Essex Regiment, 1929–50* (London, 1952).

Marwick, A., *The Home Front: the British and the Second World War* (London, 1976).

Matless, D., *Landscape and Englishness* (London, 1988).

May, D.Y. and May, K., *From Flint Knappers to Atom Splitters. A History of Leiston cum Sizewell* (Leiston, 2001).

Morrison, B., *Shingle Street* (London, 2015).

Mowat, F., *And No Birds Sang* (Vancouver, 2012).

Moynihan, M. (ed.), *People at War, 1914–1918* (Newton Abbot, 1973).

Muldowney, M., *World War II Defences on The Swale, Brightwell Heath, Ipswich* (Ipswich, 2009).

Murray, W., 'British Military Effectiveness in the Second World War', in Williamson Murray and A.R. Millet, *Military Effectiveness*, Vol. 3 (Boston, MA, 1988).

National Character Area Profile, 82: Suffolk Coasts and Heaths (Natural England, 2013).

Neillands, R., *The Battle for Normandy, 1944* (London, 2002).

Newbold, D., 'British Planning and Preparations to Resist Invasion on Land, September 1939– September 1940', PhD thesis (King's College London, 1988).

Newsome, S., 'The Coastal Landscape of Suffolk During the Second World War', *Landscapes*, 4 (2003), pp. 42–59.

Nicholson, W.N., *The Suffolk Regiment, 1928–1946* (reprinted from *East Anglian Magazine*, 1960).

Osborne, M., *Defending Britain: Twentieth-Century Military Structures in the Landscape* (Stroud, 2004).

Osborne, M., 'Review of J. Wells, *The Anti-Invasion Defences at Bognor Regis in World War Two*', *Casemate*, 109 (2017), pp. 44–5.

Osborne, M. and Graham-Kerr, A., *Twentieth-Century Defences in Britain: Suffolk* (Market Deeping, 2008).

Overy, R., *Why the Allies Won* (London, 1995).

Partridge, C., *Hitler's Atlantic Wall* (St Peter Port, 1976).

Patterson, P., Williams, A., Barker, L., *Landguard Fort Report No. 4: Darrell's Battery, Felixstowe, Suffolk* (English Heritage, Archaeological Investigation Report Series AI/8/2005).

Phillips, T.R. (ed.), *Roots of Strategy* (Harrisburg, 1985).

Picot, G., *Accidental Warrior. In the Front Line from Normandy Till Victory* (London, 1993).

Pikoulis, J., *Alun Lewis: A Life* (Bridgend, 1984).

Pollard, T. and Banks, I., 'Why a Journal of Conflict Archaeology and Why Now?', *Journal of Conflict Archaeology*, 1 (2005), pp. iii–vi.

Porter, E., *Folklore of East Anglia* (London, 1974).

Powers, S.T., 'The Battle of Normandy: The Lingering Controversy', *Journal of Military History*, 56 (1992), pp. 455–72.

Rayner, D., *An Update on Landguard Fort, Felixstowe in Suffolk* (privately published, 1995).

Robertson, G.W., *The Rose and the Arrow. A Life Story of 136th (1st West Lancashire) Field Regiment Royal Artillery, 1939–1946* (Dorchester, 1986).

Robertson, T., *Dieppe, the Shame and the Glory* (London, 1965).

Rogeri de Wendover, ed. H.O. Coxe, *Chronica sive Flores Historiarum* (London, 1841–44).

Rolf, R., *Atlantic Wall Typology* (Middlelburg, 2008).

Rose, S., *Which People's War* (Oxford, 2003).

Rottman, G., *German Field Fortifications, 1939–1945* (Oxford, 2004).

Routledge, N.W., *Anti-Aircraft Artillery, 1914–55* (London, 1994).

RSPB, *Minsmere Reserve Plan* (2003–08).

Saunders, A., *Fortress Britain* (Liphook, 1989).

Saunders, A., *Hitler's Atlantic Wall* (Stroud, 2001).

Scarfe, N., *Assault Division* (London, 1947).

Schofield, J., 'D-Day Sites in England: An Assessment', *Antiquity*, 75/287 (2001), pp. 77–83.

Schofield, J., *Modern Military Matters. Studying and Managing the Twentieth-Century Defence Heritage in Britain: A Discussion Document* (York, 2004).

Schofield, J., *Combat Archaeology* (London, 2005).

Sebald, W.G., *The Rings of Saturn* (London, 1998).

Sharman, A. and Whyte, P. (eds), *Further Suffolk Memories* (Sudbury, 2001).

Sheffield, G., 'The Shadow of the Somme: The Influence of the First World War on British Soldiers' Perception and Behaviour in the Second World War', in A. Calder and J. Crang (eds), *A Time to Kill: The Soldier's Experience of War in the West, 1939–1945* (London, 1997), pp. 29–39.

Shirreff, D. and Sharman, A., *Suffolk Memories* (Sudbury, 1998).

Simpson, J., '"The Rules of Folklore" in the Ghost Stories of M.R. James', *Folklore*, 108 (1997), pp. 9–18.

Smith, H.L. (ed.), *Britain in the Second World War: A Social History* (Manchester, 1996).

Smith, M., *Britain and 1940: History, Myth and Popular Memory* (London, 2000).

Stammers, N., *Civil Liberties in Britain during the Second World War* (Beckenham, 1983).

Thompson, P., *Voice of the Past: Oral History*, 3rd edition (Oxford, 2000).

Tilley, C., *A Phenomenology of Landscape: Places, Paths and Monuments* (Oxford, 1994).

Tilley, C., *The Materiality of Stone: Explorations in Landscape Phenomenology* (Oxford, 2004).

Trist, P.J.O., *A Survey of the Agriculture of Suffolk* (London, 1971).

Waddell, F., 'The Evacuation of Sudbourne and Iken', *Orford and District Local History Bulletin*, 11 (2008), pp. 11–13.

Wade-Martins, S. and Williamson, T., *The Countryside of East Anglia: Changing Landscapes, 1870–1950* (Woodbridge, 2008).

Wales, O.H., 'Exercise Kruschen', in *Conference on Landings Assaults, 24 May–23 June 1943* (US Assault Training Centre, 1943).

Waugh, E., *Put Out More Flags* (London, 1942).

Welch, H., *The Minsmere Scrapbook* (Westleton, 2000).

Wilks, M., *The Defence of Worcestershire and the Southern Approaches to Birmingham in World War II* (Logaston, 2007).

Williamson, T., *Sandlands* (Macclesfield, 2005).

Williamson, T., *Sutton Hoo and its Landscape. The Context of Monuments* (Macclesfield, 2008).

Wills, H., *Pillboxes: A Study of UK Defences* (Trowbridge, 1985).

Wymer, J., 'Surface Geology', in D. Dymond and E. Martin (eds), *An Historical Atlas of Suffolk* (Ipswich, 1999), pp. 18–19.

Unpublished material

King, Trooper Alan, 1st East Riding Yeomanry, interview with authors, January 2015.

Strowger, R., 'War, Life and Nature on Westleton Common', unpublished typescript.

Thompson, Major Christopher, 558 Field Company, Royal Engineers, interview with authors, November 2009.

Index